Children's Spirituality

Children's Spirituality

Christian Perspectives, Research, and Applications

Second Edition

Editors

KEVIN E. LAWSON,
Ed.D., Talbot School of Theology, Biola University

SCOTTIE MAY,
Ph.D., Wheaton College

Senior Associate Editor

MARCIA McQUITTY,
Ph.D., Southwestern Baptist Theological Seminary

Associate Editors

HOLLY CATTERTON ALLEN,
Ph.D., John Brown University

CHRIS J. BOYATZIS,
Ph.D., Bucknell University

SHIRLEY MORGENTHALER,
Ph.D., Concordia University

BETH POSTERSKI,
Ph.D., Tyndale College and Seminary

CATHERINE STONEHOUSE,
Ph.D., Asbury Theological Seminary

CASCADE *Books* · Eugene, Oregon

CHILDREN'S SPIRITUALITY
Christian Perspectives, Research, and Applications
Second Edition

Cascade Books
An Imprint of Wipf and Stock Publishers
199 W. 8th Ave., Suite 3
Eugene, OR 97401

www.wipfandstock.com

PAPERBACK ISBN: 978-1-5326-7249-1
HARDCOVER ISBN: 978-1-5326-7250-7
EBOOK ISBN: 978-1-5326-7251-4

Cataloguing-in-Publication data:

Names: Lawson, Kevin E. (Kevin Ethan), 1956–, editor. | May, Scottie, editor.

Title: Children's spirituality : Christian perspectives, research, and applications ; second edition / edited by Kevin E. Lawson and Scottie May.

Description: Eugene, OR: Cascade Books, 2019. | Includes bibliographical references and index.

Identifiers: ISBN 978-1-5326-7249-1 (paperback). | ISBN 978-1-5326-7250-7 (hardcover). | ISBN 978-1-5326-7251-4 (ebook).

Subjects: LCSH: Children—Religious life. | Christian education of children | Church work with children.

Classification: BV1474 C480 2019 (print). | BV1474 (ebook).

Manufactured in the U.S.A.   05/23/19

Contents

II. Encouraging Children's Spirituality in the Home

III. Encouraging Children's Spirituality in the Church

IV. Encouraging Children's Spirituality in the School and Other Contexts

Introduction to the Revised Edition

KEVIN E. LAWSON[1]

So when they had finished breakfast, Jesus said to Simon Peter, "Simon, son of John, do you love Me more than these?" He said to Him, "Yes, Lord, You know that I love You." He said to him, "Tend My lambs." (John 21:15, New American Standard Bible)

Beginnings

In October 2000, a handful of people in Toronto, attending the North American Professors of Christian Education conference (now the Society of Professors in Christian Education), met early one morning to talk about the possibility of a North American conference on the spiritual life and nurture of children from a Christian confessional perspective. We met for coffee and donuts and discussed the experiences of several who attended an international conference in England a few months earlier that addressed children's spirituality in a fairly generic manner. Since that conference, several North American professors had sensed the need for a gathering that explored issues of children's faith and spiritual life from a Christian faith commitment. We enjoyed our breakfast and talked about what we would like to do. After an hour or so it was decided that we would seek funding for the proposed conference and see if the doors opened for us to pursue it. We also prayed together and encouraged each other to continue to seek God's leadership in all areas of conference planning. That winter I applied for funding at one agency and was turned down. Another opportunity came and I applied to The Louisville Institute for a $20,000 conference-planning grant. By March of 2001 I received word that the grant was approved and we now had the funds needed to make and carry out our plans.

1. Kevin E. Lawson earned his Ed.D. in Educational Administration from the University of Maine after receiving his MA in Christian Education from Trinity Evangelical Divinity School (IL). He serves as Professor of Educational Studies, teaching in the PhD and EdD programs at Talbot School of Theology, Biola University and is currently editor of the *Christian Education Journal: Research on Educational Ministry*. He served as editor for *Understanding Children's Spirituality: Theology, Research, and Practive* (2012, Cascade Books) and as co-editor for *Infants and Children in the Church: Five Views on Theology and Ministry* (2017, Broadman & Holman). He has also published articles in academic journals on the history and theology of ministry with children. He and his wife Patty have three grown children.

Our goal for the conference was three-fold: (1) to network Christians who are doing research and writing on children's spiritual development and formation, (2) to provide a forum for integration of biblical, theological, and social science perspectives on children's spiritual experiences, development, and formation, and (3) to explore innovative approaches in children's ministry and provide encouragement to those in this important area. As a team, we took an intentionally broad perspective on this gathering, seeking to bring together people from different traditions within the Christian faith to see what might be learned from one other. We recognized there would be many differences between participants and presenters, but also realized there would be a common concern for the spiritual life of children and commitment to the historic Christian faith. A key goal was to stir up a generation of church leaders to consider more carefully the spiritual nurture of children and to invest significantly in equipping the church to more faithfully carry out its ministry with them.

The conference date was set for June 8–11, 2003. Over the subsequent two years the planning team met several times to develop the conference plan and work out the details of the conference. Shirley Morgenthaler, from Concordia University, River Forest, kindly proposed having the conference at her school, with their education department sponsoring the event and providing a site team for conference logistics and support. Others on the planning team contacted plenary speakers, recruited seminar leaders and children's choirs, and developed and distributed promotional materials. It was exciting to see it all taking shape, but the nagging question was, "Would many people come?" This was a first-of-its-kind conference and we were not sure how people would respond with so many other conference options to choose from. We knew about 200 people would need to attend to make the conference work and felt that 300 was the most that could be handled. The question was, "How many would come?"

It was a pleasant surprise when slightly more than 300 people attended the conference. Almost half of the attendees were church ministry leaders eager to think more deeply and carefully about their ministry with children, while the other half were professors, graduate students, researchers, and writers in the area of the spiritual life of children and the church's ministry with them. This was a great mix of people! The conference provided a rich time together of discussion and presentations. Children's choirs from the area came and led us in worship each evening and during the closing session Wednesday morning. Jerome Berryman, Walter Wangerin, Klaus Issler, Marcia Bunge, Rebecca Nye, and Brenda Salter McNeil shared their insights in the plenary sessions, along with panels on theological perspectives on children and ethnic perspectives on nurturing the spiritual lives of children. One morning was devoted to presentations of newer models of ministry with children, providing a potpourri of ideas and approaches to consider. The presenters challenged everyone present to think biblically, theologically, historically, psychologically, sociologically, culturally, and practically about the spiritual life of children and the church's ministry with them. It was an amazing four days.

Coming out of that conference the conference planning team considered ways we might share the results of the conference with a broader population. This book, which consists of chapters from papers and research presented at the conference, is our major effort to make this material available. We hope that it will stimulate additional thought and efforts to invest in the spiritual lives of children for the sake of Jesus Christ.

As I look back at the conference, I see it as the start of new efforts in North America to better understand how God works in the lives of children to call them to Himself and how all involved might be helpful in that process. This ties in with a number of initiatives across the continent and around the world that are lifting up the importance of the church's ministry with children. Here are a few examples around the time of the conference and in the first few years after it was over:

The Child Theology Consultations. At the turn of the twenty-first century, the "Child Theology" movement became active on most of the continents of the world, bringing together church leaders and theologians to consider what it means to do theological work with an eye on the child. It takes seriously Jesus' actions of placing a child in the midst of the disciples as a model of those who inherit the kingdom of heaven (Matthew 18).

The 4–14 Window Initiative. In early 2004, several evangelical children's ministry organizations came together to examine and promote effective ministry with children during a critical time of their lives, ages 4 to 14. This movement recognizes the formative power of early experiences and teaching for the spiritual nurture of children, and encourages their response of faith to the gospel. This effort elevates the importance of ministry with children and challenges the church to invest its resources in ministry with them.

The Viva Network and the Lausanne Forum. Internationally there is a growing movement highlighting the importance of the needs and lives of children, including their spiritual nurture. The Viva Network connects Christian organizations that minister with "children at risk." They sponsor days of prayer for the needs of children, provide resources for ministry with children, and are an advocate for church leaders and ministry organizations to keep the needs of children central in their work. It was through their influence that the Lausanne Forum for World Evangelization, held September and October 2004 in Thailand, included representatives with a concern for the needs of children on each of the more than 30 issue groups.

New books on ministry with children. As of the printing of the first edition of this book in 2004, the editors were aware of a half-dozen new volumes that are in various stages of being written or published on ministry with children and the spiritual life of children. Publishers were responding to the needs of the church and the growing interest in the spiritual experiences of children and how the church can nurture their growing faith. George Barna's book, *Transforming Children into Spiritual Champions* (Regal, 2003), is one example of this new wave of publications that challenges the church in its ministry with children. In the 15 years since this first conference, this trend has continued.

Following this initial conference, the decision was made to hold similar conferences every three years. In 2006, 2009, and 2012, children's spirituality conferences were again held at Concordia University Chicago, in River Forest, IL. Each of these conferences followed a similar format to the original one and led to the publication of another collection of conference presentations and papers in a book.[2] This has been a rich season of learning from one another regarding important issues and helpful practices for nurturing the spiritual formation of children from a range of Christian perspectives.

This has also been a great time to be working with the church for the sake of children. I hope that this revised publication of adapted presentations from the first conference, and the similar books published from the subsequent conferences, will help stimulate others to value and invest in research, writing, and ministry efforts with children.

Organizational Renewal and Future "Summits"[3]

With a change of leadership and the opportunity to meet at another venue, on June 12–14, 2016, the fifth Children's Spirituality Conference: Christian Perspectives convened for the first time in Nashville, Tennessee, at Lipscomb University. Approximately 150 academics and thoughtful practitioners gathered around the children's spirituality table and discussed child theology, best practices, sociological research, and ministry implications for nurturing children's spiritual growth and development.

Men and women from Canada, Nigeria, Albania, Australia and the United States shared their current research, their innovative ministry models, and their stimulating workshops with spiritual formation leaders, children's ministers, developmental psychologists, Christian educators, sociologists, youth ministers, and theologians from a wide spectrum of Christian faith traditions.

The plenary speakers, Robbie Castleman, Dave Csinos, Pamela Ebstyne King, and Almeda Wright, opened our eyes to new ways to welcome children, bless children, nurture children, and join children on their spiritual journeys. These speakers,

---

2. For the books published from the conferences in 2006, 2009, and 2012, see the following:

Allen, H. C. (Ed.). (2008). *Nurturing children's spirituality: Christian perspectives and best practices.* Eugene, OR: Cascade Books.

Lawson, K. E. (Ed.). (2012). *Understanding children's spirituality: Theology, research, and practice.* Eugene, OR: Cascade Books.

Tolbert, L. (Ed.). (2014). *Exploring and engaging spirituality for today's children.* Eugene, OR: Wipf & Stock.

3. Information on the 2016 and 2018 conferences was provided by Dr. Holly Catterton Allen, the chair of the Children's Spirituality Summit Board.

as well as our panelists, Kathie Amidei, Dana Pemberton, and Dave Scott, challenged us to *see* the children in our midst and beyond who need all the spiritual resources available to them to survive their daily circumstances. The book from the fifth conference, *Story, Formation, and Culture: From Theory to Practice in Ministry with Children,* was edited by Benjamin Espinoza, James Estep, and Shirley Morgenthaler (Eugene, OR: Pickwick Publications, 2018).

The 2018 Children's Spirituality Conference convened with a new name. The sixth gathering, now known as the Children's Spirituality *Summit,* met June 27–29, 2018, once again at Lipscomb University in Nashville, Tennessee. Following the 2016 gathering, the conference board had made the decision to convene the conference biennially rather than triennially for several reasons: (1) high interest from participants, (2) the frequency of fresh and innovative research in the field, and (3) the increased ability to build on momentum from conference to conference. Approximately 130 academics and thoughtful practitioners gathered around the children's spirituality table and discussed child theology, best practices, sociological research, and ministry implications for nurturing children's spiritual growth and development.

Men and women from Australia, Canada, Hong Kong, the Philippines, and Papua New Guinea, and from twenty-three states shared their current research, their innovative ministry models, and their stimulating workshops with children's ministers, professors, youth ministers, graduate and doctoral students, medical professionals, curriculum writers, Christian education directors, and other church and family leaders.

Our plenary speakers, Dr. Steve Kang, Dr. Robert Keeley, and Dr. Scottie May, provided insightful historical and theological context for children's spiritual formation in the world today and challenged us to think more intentionally and creatively as we move forward. The two traditional aspects of our conference consisted of twelve rich and well-delivered paper presentations and nineteen amazing workshops.

A new feature of the Summit was the Pecha Kucha session. Six presenters showed twenty slides narrating each one for twenty seconds, addressing such fascinating topics as spiritual direction with children, the "Pray-Ground," and welcoming children with developmental disabilities. Another new feature was the Taste and See event: on Thursday evening, all participants chose three of six prepared experiences to enter as a child. These moments participating in child-sized worship, entering a Godly Play story, learning to listen to the voice of God, and leaning in to imaginative prayer will linger with the participants as they return to bless the children in their care.

It was a successful gathering, and we are busily planning the 2020 gathering to be held once again at Lipscomb University in Nashville, Tennessee, and every two years following that. To learn more about the Children's Spirituality Summit, future events, and publications, visit the organization website: http://societyforchildrensspirituality.org.

In this revised edition, other than for the editors (May and Lawson), we have retained the original information provided about each of the authors in the first edition.

In many cases these authors may have changed their roles or employment in the years since the first edition came out in 2004.

References

Allen, H. C. (Ed.). (2008). *Nurturing children's spirituality: Christian perspectives and best practices.* Eugene, OR: Cascade Books.

Barna, G. (2003). *Transforming children into spiritual champions.* Ventura, CA: Regal.

Espinoza, B., Estep, J., & Morgenthaler, S. (Eds.). (2018). *Story, formation, and culture: From theory to practice in ministry with children.* Eugene, OR: Pickwick Publications.

Lawson, K. E. (Ed.). (2012). *Understanding children's spirituality: Theology, research, and practice.* Eugene, OR: Cascade Books.

Tolbert, L. (Ed.). (2014). *Exploring and engaging spirituality for today's children.* Eugene, OR: Wipf & Stock.

PART I

Definitions, Theologies, Theories and Methods of Research

Identifying Children's Spirituality, Walter Wangerin's Perspectives, and an Overview of This Book

SCOTTIE MAY[1]

There is a spiritual essence that all humans share. It is a craving deep within for transcendence and meaning. It surfaces from time to time as awe and wonder, perhaps in response to a red, purple, and orange sunset that fills the evening sky, leaving adults and children amazed at the progression of colors and shades, wondering about the source of sky and sun, or possible meanings to such an incredibly beautiful event. People may approach a spiritual state during a movie that profoundly touches the emotions and leaves the viewer longing to stay in the world seen so vividly on the big screen. They may begin to wonder why a story resonates deeply, drawing the individual beyond self to something bigger, perhaps even something that provides ultimate meaning in one's life.

Children are just as much spiritual beings as are the adults in their lives. From the very beginning of life, infants seem to live a life of awe and wonder, often transfixed in the moment. Watch a baby who gazes at the face of her mother in wonder at this mysterious other, that is so close and warm, nourishing and caring, yet also somehow separate and different from the self. Perhaps the infant thinks none of these things, but just is caught up in the wonder of a face that is so much more familiar than others.

1. Scottie May obtained a Ph.D. in Education with emphasis on children's faith experiences, at Trinity Evangelical Divinity School (IL) after receiving a MA in Educational Ministries from Wheaton College (IL) with a focus on ministry to families. Presently, she is Associate Professor Emerita in the Department of Christian Formation and Ministry at Wheaton College. Along with Cathy Stonehouse, Beth Posterski, and Linda Cannell, she co-authored *Children Matter*, a textbook on children's ministry published in 2005 by Eerdmans, and co-authored *Listening to Children on the Spiritual Journey* (Baker) with Cathy Stonehouse in 2008. Scottie has also written articles published in academic and popular journals on children's ministry. She has three children, eight grandchildren and one great grandchild.

Special thanks go to Chris Boyatzis for many helpful comments on early drafts of this chapter.

Regardless of the child's thoughts, the fascination with the mother's face may mark an highly affect-filled germination of thought that will eventually become an understanding of a transcendent Other.

When just a little older, youngsters can lose track of time and space as they watch ants doing their work. The child's wonder of the moment may reflect a transcendent impression of an ultimate order to life, or the single-minded focus on a goal larger than that of any one member of the colony. Or it may be that children are awed by the ability of the ant to carry a crumb several times his weight. Perhaps it is just the busy-ness of the ants, going in so many directions at once, yet accomplishing so much in the process. Spiritual aliveness knows no age barriers.

In June, 2003, researchers and scholars, teachers and leaders, and even a few parents and children, met in an inner suburb of Chicago to talk about the spirituality of children. There were also moments in which those present moved beyond talk to experience the spirituality that both adults and children share. The planning team summarized the general goal of the conference as being the examination of the research and theory of children's characteristics, growth, and experiences of a spiritual nature within a Christian framework, as understood from a wide variety of theological and denominational backgrounds. The objective was stated on the web page that described the conference (located at www.childrensspirit.org).

The general goal of the conference helped frame this book, most of which is adapted from conference presentations. Not every presentation at the conference is represented here; only 22 of the more than 50 were selected (this chapter and the last were written subsequent to the conference). Sessions that became chapters were among the most popular and of the highest quality that were delivered during the proceedings; there has been much demand to see them in print.

Defining Spirituality

While the conference team began with clear-cut goals, the definition of spirituality was left open-ended. What is meant by "spirituality" in relation to the child? Sometimes the term spirituality implies the idea of being self-directed and exuberant—as in "That child has plenty of spirit." Sometimes spiritual refers to a mystical "otherness" of the child that may be immaterial yet ill-defined. Rebecca Nye (1998; Hay & Nye, 1998), a leading scholar on children's spirituality, has coined the term "relational consciousness" to describe spirituality. Based on her interviews with many children, Nye states that the child's spirituality is "an unusual level of consciousness or perceptiveness relative to other passages for that child" that is also inherently relational, as "this was often in the context of how the child *related* to things, especially people including themselves and God" (Nye, 1998, p. 237). Relational consciousness is built upon three fundamental categories that outline some parameters of children's spiritual experiences: (1) *Awareness Sensing* which includes an emphasis upon here and now experience, "tuning" such as the sense of feeling one with nature, Csikszentmihalyi's (1975) concept of "flow," and "focusing" which involves insight that is a "natural knowing," (2) *Mystery Sensing* that highlights experiences of wonder and awe, as well as use of the imagination, and (3) *Value Sensing* which includes experiences of delight and despair, a sense of the ultimate goodness of life, and "meaning-making and sensing" (pp. 129–40).

Yet the term "spirituality" is also a theological term, reflecting historic Christianity's affirmation of a spirit world that coexists with a material world, a world generally unseen yet which is thought to pervade the experience of the child as well as the adult. While the idea of a parallel reality, coexisting with and regularly intersecting with the material world, fell into disfavor during the Enlightenment era and its intellectual offspring, modernism, the possibility of a spiritual realm is more resonant with some aspects of postmodern thought. Since postmodernity has helped demonstrate that ample portions of reality surpass the measurements by objective scientific methods, perhaps more individuals are open to the idea that the material world is not the sum total of all of life, even though most individuals are more acutely aware of this tangible world than the spiritual realm.

From a Christian perspective, the emphasis on the whole child—affirmed by most children's spirituality writers, whether or not they affirm a transcendent spirit realm—is crucial. From the beginning, Jesus "placed a child in the midst" (Matt 18:2) as an example of what His kingdom was all about. Adult concern should be for the material well-being of the child (Jas 1:27), but also a sensitivity to the personhood of the child is crucial (Col 3:21). Every child has two immediate functions: to be and to become. The "to be" aspect is the value of children as they are, not just for what they will become—Jesus said we adults are to become like children, not that children are to become like us. But adults also have a responsibility to nurture and guide children—a pervasive theme in scripture as Deut 6:7 and many other passages reveal—as well as learn from them. While the child is to be "in the midst," that does not mean that parents, teachers, and other adults should abdicate their roles as guides, mentors, and friends. Ultimately, children have incredibly high value because they are products of a creative God.

While there is much to be valued in the various forms of Christian spirituality, perhaps there is also value in having a multiplicity of definitions for spirituality, as reflected in Rebecca Nye's chapter to follow. It may be, as she argues, that this area of study is too new to define adequately, and any given definition will necessarily restrict what is considered. If children's spirituality is to be considered as involving the whole person, every area of the child, perhaps there is benefit in deferring the development of an ultimate definition and entertaining a multiplicity of definitions. With time, this area of study will either become self-defined by what is studied under the rubric "spirituality," or—like the topic of "learning" in psychology—will come to have multiple definitions reflecting a variety of perspectives on the topic. Regardless, it is important that any given analysis or study of children's spirituality identify the definition being used in that work, whether the definition is assumed prior to the study or emergent from it. It is important to know what is being studied or discussed.

Spirituality and Religion

In the 1990s, children's spirituality flourished as the previous interest in children's religious development declined. Children's understanding of religion dominated much of the research in religious education, particularly in the United Kingdom and Europe, during the Twentieth Century. This research, summarized in Kenneth Hyde's (1990) massive *Religion in Childhood and Adolescence*, tended to emphasize how children thought about religion, but rarely did the research cited consider their experiences of faith and spirituality. Often dominated by the theory of Jean Piaget, research perspectives tended to emphasize an invariant sequence of stages of *thinking about* religion rather than the *experience of* religion—the latter being an area of common ground between spirituality and religion (see Boyatzis on the hegemony of cognitive-developmentalism).

As noted above, spirituality and religion share a common ground—they both relate to ultimate meanings in life and the quest for transcendence—yet they are also distinctive in many ways. They can be envisioned as overlapping circles, with the doctrines and creeds of religion distinctive to the circle of religion, while experiences of awe and wonder apart from an explicit reference to God are distinctive to the circle of spirituality. There are many other distinctive elements in each circle. But what is important for the present book is that there is overlap; religion and spirituality share much in common.

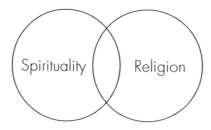

At the conference, there were some sessions that were primarily religious in content—such as the theological perspectives panel. There were others where spirituality was the stronger emphasis. But most of the conference, like most of this book, highlighted those issues in the overlapping area, an aspect of spirituality—and also an aspect of the Christian religion—that has too rarely been explored in the past.

Walter Wangerin's Perspective of Spiritual Development and Stories

Wangerin, writer in residence at Valparaiso University, was a plenary speaker at the conference who helped illuminate the area of overlap between religion and spirituality in his unique, creative manner. Author of best-selling and award-winning volumes such as *The Book of God, The Orphean Passages, The Book of the Dun Cow,* and many others, Wangerin spoke at length about the importance of children moving into stories with their whole being and selfhood, and how adults can help encourage children's active involvement in stories. The best stories are often religious, but the experience of a good story is always profoundly spiritual, because it helps children connect with deeper truths and ultimate meanings in life, as well as move them into a different realm that transcends everyday life and the world as youngsters usually see it.

A context for Wangerin's comments on stories is provided by quoting from an earlier work (Wangerin, 1986) where he summarized the child's spiritual development. His ideas shed further light on what is meant by the phrase "Christian perspectives" in the title of this book. This is the theory of a literary artist, more poetry than research, yet the truth value may be as strong as that found in a formal study of children. Wangerin's view of spiritual development serves as a vivid and useful reference point for the rest of the book.

> Who can say when, in a child, the dance with God begins? No one. Not even the child can later look back and remember the beginning of it, because it is as natural an experience . . . as the child's relationship with the sun or with his bedroom. And the beginning, specifically, cannot be remembered because in the beginning there are no words for it. The language to name, contain, and to explain the experience comes afterward. The dance, then, the relationship with God, faithing, begins in a mist.
>
> At first, the child has no name for this Someone so significant, this Other, the Dear, or else the Terrible Almighty (El-Shaddai!), yet the holiness and glory, the power and even the righteousness of the Other are very real to him—and the love, though kindness and the expression of that love may wax and wane, depending upon the child's own sense of goodness and his health. It is the common lot of all children to encounter and to experience the Deity. And so faithing begins. And because it begins in children, regardless of their cultures, regardless of what languages shall later contain, explain, and edit reality for them—because it begins, in fact, apart from the interpretive function of language . . . It is a universal human experience. We all have danced one round with God. But we danced it in the mists. (Wangerin, 1986, pp. 20–21)

In his usual artful way, Wangerin goes on to describe the stages of the dance with God through stories of childhood. The naming of the dance begins when the child hears names for God and also the language of faith. Containing the dance follows later as the child grasps language in richer ways that help her contain the stories of

God's actions and character. Then explaining the dance can happen. This occurs as the child hears explanations of faith so that she can explain her faith for herself. As her understanding and use of language matures, she is able to confirm, preserve, and, yes, confess her faith. The claiming of the dance naturally follows, and must. At a certain point, often in early adolescence, she may declare by "truly, truly confessing and confirming a relationship: *He is my Lord!*" (Wangerin, 1986, p. 52).

Woven throughout the explanation of the dance are warnings, warnings that the dance can die. It is as if the music for the dance is conducted primarily by the parents, but also by the church. "Silent parents, parents impoverished of the language of faith . . . parents whose apparatus for explaining experience discounts God as myth . . . parents who choose to 'let my child choose for himself'" (p. 48) may tragically, unknowingly, stifle the music. And the church may put the dance into a rigid box with fixed doctrine that may kill the dance. But it does not have to be that way. "As long as there is mystery, there may be change and growth and the freedom for the dance" (Wangerin, 1986, pp. 23–24).

The Role of Story in Spiritual Formation

At the conference Walter Wangerin (2003) spoke on the use of story in the spiritual formation of the child. He emphasized that it matters little how well individuals know the craft of telling a story, but it is far more important that they genuinely love the story—it must be vitally important to storytellers and they must be wrapped up in the story—and that storytellers love the ones to whom they are telling the story. The communication will flow as a result. These two components reflect the two great commandments—loving God (the story) and others (the children). Method follows motive, Wangerin suggested. He acknowledged the important influence of Bruner's work in his ideas about stories (see Bruner, 1986, for example).

Wangerin suggested that while a story can be used as an illustration of a principle, it should be more than that: "A story, when it is told, is first and foremost a world, a little cosmos, a place in which the listening child may dwell." If stories are only illustrations, then only parts of the child are invited into the story. But if the child sees the story as an invitation into a world, then it invites the whole child, and the child begins to identify not only with the cognitive content, but also the emotions, the suspense, the totality of the story, and all of the senses as well as reason and imagination are involved. The child is "into" the story.

Stories not only communicate, they also form the soul and personality. Stories that are told well shape those who hear them; the listeners are inundated. Stories influence children—and adults—powerfully. The storyteller crafts in the imagination the people being described in the story, as well as the story line itself, but the storyteller also shapes those who hear the story because of the shaping of characters and plot.

Walter Wangerin commented that as a story gets told over and over, it draws children into the cosmos of the story. If the story cosmos accords with the child's experience of life to some extent, then when the child leaves the story it becomes a framework by which the child interprets the rest of the world. Everyday experiences for a child are often chaotic and lack the structure of a good story. Thus, stories have the potential to make daily experiences more comprehensible by offering that needed structure by which the child interprets life.

In a well-told story, the child enters a different world and dwells there for a while. It is a *cosmos*, as all time and space collapse into the story's time and space while the story is told. Children need to dwell within the story, so the story will affect behavior, and not just their intellectual thinking. Those in the West tend to think through things and then prescribe actions, but in many tribal cultures people live the story without analyzing it. Similarly, there can be religion without theology, indeed that is often the case with many religions of the world, but there cannot be religion without stories.

When a story is told well, and the listeners enter the story frame, it is as if they are actually at the location and time of the story. Certain things must be present before the child can enter into a story. The context must grant the child personhood—one can only invite the child, one cannot demand or force a child into the story, and it is the child's spirit that lets the child know that the story is really heard.

The story needs a good teller, someone the child appreciates. A story is always an act of community. In other words, the child is a companion with the storyteller in the story. "I am here too," the storyteller is saying indirectly. The joys and guilt in the story are those of both the adult and the child. People tend to fear ambiguity, thus there needs to be an effective beginning and ending to the story. This communicates to children that there is a moral order in the chaos of everyday life, an idea communicated through a satisfying conclusion.

Wangerin continues, when the child is ready, perhaps with the seventh or eighth telling of the story, the child often begins to dwell in the story and begins to see the events as like her own experiences. The major character—or supporting character—may become a surrogate for the child's own real life. During the storytelling, the feelings expressed are being felt by the child. This may be why children want stories told and retold many times. The child's motivation for the retelling is not to arrive at the ending, but to embrace the mood of the story. It becomes "a soul event." If the child is not ready for the story, then the spirit of the child says, "not yet."

To be allowed to touch a child requires that the adult learn the language of the child, and thus earn the right to tell stories. The adult must read the child's body language; to communicate effectively with a child one must learn that language. Watch for signals that reveal who children really are and use the language that they use to signal to them. For example, one can speak with the eyebrows or with a hand gesture. Once the language is learned, the child will often allow a touch, and then one can tell stories most effectively. Stories are a means of the child discovering the self in relationship. There is a ritual to telling stories, and that ritual invites dialogue. "You weave a story to the child." Wangerin's final words were, "Stories work."

Overview of This Book

The present volume is divided into five major sections. It opens with the longest section—11 chapters—that relates to defining and setting parameters on the topic, examining the history of children's spirituality as expressed in church theology and the Bible, exploring relevant theories and research related to children's spirituality, and summarizing current and anticipated methods of research. The second section—chapters 12 through 14—highlights children's spirituality as expressed and fostered in the Christian home, both at the present time and in history. A third section—chapters 15 through 18—considers the spirituality of children in the church. This is followed by chapters 19 through 23 where schools and other contexts of life are considered in relation to the child's spirituality. The final chapter provides a more personal reflection of the conference from which this book was taken and anticipates a future conference scheduled for 2006.

The following chapter is authored by the founder of Godly Play and author of the book by the same name (1991). Jerome Berryman suggests that two crucial questions confront the church regarding children: "What is the basic nature of children?" and "What is the basic nature of the adults who teach children?" The relationship between adult spirituality and that of children needs to be considered carefully, as even a brief overview of church history reflects a deep ambivalence regarding the nature of children, in contrast with the high view of children held by Christ.

Through a critical retrieval of insights from the Bible and the Christian tradition, Marcia Bunge in chapter 3 guides readers in forming a rich, complex view of children. Such a biblically informed theological understanding of children has several positive implications for strengthening religious education and spiritual formation programs, deepening theological and ethical reflection on children, and renewing the church's commitment to serving and protecting all children.

In the fourth chapter, theologian/Christian educator Klaus Issler considers the question, "What does the Bible say about a child's status before God and the child's relationship with God?" Key biblical passages indicate that children are a special class before God; they are regarded as within some kind of "safe" zone until they arrive at the age of discernment. Yet children are similar to adults in that they are persons created in the image of God and thus are to be welcomed into a genuine relationship with God appropriate to their developmental abilities.

In chapter 5 Shelley Campagnola highlights several other key biblical passages, particularly some of the Old Testament texts and themes that speak to the theological and biblical value of the child in the biblical community. These texts form an important background to understanding Jesus' profound statement recorded in Matt 18:3: "I tell you to the truth, unless you change and become like little children, you will never enter the kingdom of heaven." What Jesus said here was not new theology but rather a profound and climatic summary of what God revealed throughout the Old Testament era.

Well-known researcher and theorist Rebecca Nye, in chapter 6, considers the research of children's religion, faith, and spirituality, which has an extensive history. However, she points out that the spiritual nature of the child has often been overlooked for most of this history. Nye's research of children and key constructs that help develop an adequate definition of children's spirituality are highlighted, as well as the difficulty of helping children articulate their spiritual experiences.

In chapter 7 Wendy Haight emphasizes that spiritual development is embedded within a social and historical context, as children actively observe and increasingly participate with others in the routine, everyday practices through which culture is maintained and elaborated. The author's own study of children's socialization within an African American church focuses on the ways adults and children co-construct spiritual stories during Sunday School. This illustrates the importance of an expanded perspective on diverse cultural groups to disentangle universal from culturally variable aspects of spiritual development, as well as bring to the fore questions that have not yet been adequately addressed in a developmental literature focused on the European-American middle-class.

Eugene Roehlkepartain of Search Institute explores scientific and theological perspectives on children's spirituality in chapter 8. He asks questions such as, "What is known about spiritual development from both scientific and theological perspectives?" and "What are critical questions and issues for strengthening this field of inquiry?" Search Institute has launched a major initiative—which is interfaith and international in scope—to address these questions, advance interdisciplinary understanding, and improve spirit-nurturing practices in families, congregations, and other settings.

Chapter 9 highlights the attention given to children by early Methodists and examines Wesleyan theological perspectives on the child's spirituality and potential for relationship with God. Understandings of spirituality during childhood are also drawn from the broader Wesleyan theology by author Catherine Stonehouse. Wesley's views on the nurture and education of children are explored for insights applicable in the nurture of 21st century children.

In chapter 10, Scottie May considers how brain development and function relate to children's spiritual experience. She asks, "Why do children in settings that appear to evoke wonder and awe become slow-paced and calm, producing a reflective mood?" and "What, if any, might be the role of the limbic system of the brain in children's responses to these types of settings?" Children's awe-filled experiences with God is an important topic for future study and research.

Chris Boyatizis and Babette Newman argue in chapter 11 that a comprehensive and valid understanding of children's spirituality requires a multi-method approach that will provide insight on the multifaceted essence of spirituality. Definitions of children's spirituality are explored, as well as a wide variety of research methods that can be adapted for use with children. The chapter concludes with a call for researchers to ensure high levels of methodological rigor, increasing the visibility and acceptance of research on children's spirituality by a scholarly audience and providing maximum applied value for families, congregations, schools, and communities.

Chris Boyatzis returns in chapter 12 to consider the research literature on family socialization processes that has characterized the child as a rather passive recipient of parental "transmission" of religion and spirituality. Boyatzis challenges that venerable view of children with data from at-home conversations between parents and children about religious and spiritual issues. The content and structure of parent-child conversations were analyzed, leading to the conclusion that children are active participants in family exploration of religion.

Relevant psychoanalytic and developmental psychologies are reviewed in chapter 13 to draw implications for the development of the child's concept of God and sense of relatedness to God. This chapter by authors Bellous, Summey, and de Roos, is an exercise in practical theology, a key intersection of academic, church, and public life. While Ana-Maria Rizzuto's work is of central concern, additional understandings from the work of Bowlby, Stern, Erikson, Kohut, Cohler, Galatzer-Levy and Orthodox theology are addressed, as well as a recent research study by one of the authors.

In Chapter 14 Timothy Sisemore examines the development of the doctrine of original sin, with emphasis upon how it was expressed in Puritan writings. He considers how this doctrine worked out in the practice of these believers, and the implications for modern ministry to children and parents.

Chapter 15 portrays six children seeking God and highlights the context of spiritual development. While child development theories have been very influential in the study of religious and faith development, they tend to emphasize universal stages that may obscure the importance of family, religious, and social contexts. Author Dana Hood studied six kindergarten children, their families, and their Sunday school teachers, emphasizing the interactive, multifaceted nature of children's spiritual development.

Chapter 16 explores congregational practices that nurture the faith of children, reporting on preliminary analysis from the Children in Congregations Project. The research team for this project—including authors Mercer, Matthews, and Walz—was involved in a year-long ethnographic study of three Protestant congregations and their practices with children. Common features across the three congregations' practices that nurture the faith lives of children are summarized.

Holly Catterton Allen examines intergenerational Christian experiences empirically, theoretically, practically, educationally, and theologically in chapter 17. Specific intergenerational Christian experiences that can promote children's spirituality are surveyed. Biblical and theological evidence and empirical support for the benefits of this approach are provided.

Chapter 18 summarizes the spirituality of African American and Latino children and cultures, presented by authors Crozier and Conde-Frazier, with attention to the role narrative inquiry can play in doing research on children's spirituality and Christian education. The study of a three and a half year old African American female is discussed which focuses on several key themes: 1. spiritual gifts, 2. the role of prayer, 3. the position and presence of Jesus, and 4. the power of Jesus and God. The spiritual characteristics of Latino children are also considered in this chapter.

Narrative education is an effective process by which the moral formation of children can be advanced, chapter 19 by Ford and Wong claims. Narrative education involves the integration of traditional methods of teaching with the shared experiences of students and promotes sharing their experiences. The value of the narrative approach to Christian education in facilitating the spiritual development of children is also considered.

James Estep and Lillian Breckenridge, in chapter 20, state that while the social contexts of spiritual formation in childhood have often been emphasized by Christian educators, there is much to be gained by adding the often overlooked insights of Urie Bronfenbrenner and Lev Vygotsky. Spiritual direction during the childhood years should be primarily based upon life span development and the social-cultural environment.

In chapter 21 the stages of faith development in children are considered by Joyce Ruppell, with an exploration of the ways teachers and caregivers can implement appropriate practices in their work with children in relation to spiritual and moral growth. Faith should be integrated into the total curriculum, with an emphasis upon faith, hope and love within a healthy environment that nurtures faith.

Chapter 22 considers spiritual influences in helping children cope with life stressors. A summary of existing theory and research is presented by authors Pendleton, Benore, Jonas, Norwood, and Herrmann, who then summarize their own three original research studies representing their own perspectives as psychologists, medical doctors, and a missionary studying missionary children. Throughout the chapter the story of little Sarah and her struggle with cancer exemplifies the common means children use to cope with the tragedies and hardships of life.

In chapter 23, Gary Newton examines the components of effective programs for unchurched, at-risk children in urban contexts, components that contribute to the goals of long-term spiritual growth and the establishment of stable families, churches, and communities. Leaders from 14 highly effective inner-city children's programs in the United States and Canada were interviewed in the United States and Canada, who provided valuable insights in helping urban children, families, and communities.

Chapter 24 completes the book. Kevin Lawson—the director of the conference planning team and coordinator of the entire effort—reflects on the conference and anticipates the next conference currently scheduled for 2006. He summarizes how the "Children's Spirituality Conference: Christian Perspectives" came to be, what came out of the conference, some signs of children's ministry renewal in the church, and plans for the future conference.

Special Thanks to the Associate Editors and Planning Team

Special thanks go to our Senior Associate Editor, Marcia McQuitty, for all her assistance in reviewing submissions and helping prepare the document for publication, and to our associate editors (in alphabetical order): Holly Catterton Allen, Chris J. Boyatzis, Scottie May, Shirley Morgenthaler, Beth Posterski, and Catherine Stonehouse, each of whom did the initial editing and revising of the first draft of the chapters, often "going the extra mile" by engaging in dialogue directly with authors. Every editor worked on at least two chapters. Each was involved in the conference in a significant manner, and most of these special people were on the conference planning team. This book would not be near the quality it is without the careful attention to detail of these amazing people who served without compensation for their work.

Thanks also goes to those individuals who served on the planning team for the conference and also provided wonderful input that helped make the conference a success. They helped perform a "first cut" in determining who would and would not be speaking at the conference. In addition to most of the people mentioned in the above paragraph, thanks goes to Jerome Berryman, Ronald Cram, and Marcia Bunge for their tireless efforts as part of that team.

Thanks also go to Concordia University and the Concordia students, staff, and faculty that helped make the conference functional. There are literally thousands of details to holding a conference of this nature, and this was another team that worked well together. Special thanks go to Beth Becker who coordinated so many details during the conference, student volunteers from Wheaton College and Biola University, and Shirley Morgenthaler who connected the conference team with Concordia.

Gratitude goes to the Louisville Institute for providing a grant that funded the planning of the conference. Finally, we thank God, who guided it all. Thank You for loving children and loving those of us who are adult children. *Deo Solo Gloria.*

References

Berryman, J. W. (1991). *Godly play: A way of religious education.* San Francisco: HarperCollins.

Boyatzis, C. J. (2005). Religious and spiritual development in childhood. In R. F. Paloutzian & C. L. Park (Eds.), *The handbook for the psychology of religion and spirituality* (pp. 123–143). New York: Guilford.

Bruner, J. (1986). *Actual minds, possible worlds.* Cambridge: Harvard University Press.

Csikszentmihalyi, I. (1975). *Beyond boredom and anxiety.* San Francisco: Jossey-Bass.

Hay, D., & Nye, R. (1998). *The spirit of the child.* London: Fount.

Hyde, K. (1990). *Religion in childhood and adolescence.* Birmingham, AL: Religious Education Press.

Nye, R. (1998). *Psychological perspectives on children's spirituality.* Doctoral dissertation, University of Nottingham, UK.

Ratcliff, D., & Nye, R. (2005). Childhood spirituality: Strengthening the research foundation. In E. C. Roehlkepartain, P. E. King, L. Wagener, & P. L. Benson (Eds.), *The handbook of spiritual development in childhood and adolescence* (pp. 473–483). Thousand Oaks, CA: Sage.

Wangerin, W. (1986). *The Orphean passages.* Grand Rapids: Zondervan.

Wangerin, W. (2003, June). *The use of story for spiritual formation.* Session at the meeting of the Children's Spirituality Conference: Christian Perspectives, River Forest, IL.

Chapter Two

Children and Mature Spirituality

JEROME W. BERRYMAN[1]

Jesus stimulated thought about spiritual maturity by both spoken and unspoken parables. He showed and said that adults need to become like children to enter God's domain. This leap of the imagination was as great for his disciples in the past as it is for people today.

Erik Erikson (1902–1994) was less parabolic when he made a similar claim. He spoke the language of developmental psychology and argued on the basis of his clinical experience that adults stagnate in self-absorption unless they take an interest in the next generation. If they do take such an interest they are likely to become "generative." Being generative moves one towards a wise and satisfying old age. The self-absorbed, however, move toward despair. They become "elderlies," distinguished only by old age, instead of "elders," who quietly live up to their role as bearers of wisdom and dignity for the next generation (Erikson, 1997).

---

1. Jerome Berryman is Executive Director of the Center for the Theology of Childhood, but is best known for developing "Godly Play," an approach to children's spiritual education and experience that encourages quiet reflection on stories adapted from the Bible. Berryman has served as an adjunct professor for The Houston Graduate School of Theology as well as Baylor College of Medicine in relation to pediatric pastoral care. His degrees include a J.D. from the University of Tulsa Law School, as well as a D.Min. and M.Div. from Princeton Theological Seminary, and additional work at Oxford University and the Center for Advanced Montessori Studies in Italy. An Episcopalian priest, Jerome served as Canon Educator at Christ Church Cathedral in Houston for ten years, and also as a hospital chaplain with seriously ill and dying children. He has authored several books including *Godly Play*, *Teaching Godly Play*, and a series of curriculum guides for Godly Play. He also wrote some 30 journal articles and more than 10 chapters of edited books. In 1997 he received the Kilgore Creative Ministry Award from Claremont School of Theology and in 2003 he was presented with the Episcopal Communications Polly Bond Award of Excellence for the best Theological Reflection. He presently serves on the national board of The Association of Professors and Researchers in Religious Education.

An earlier version of this chapter appeared as Chapter Seven: "Toward a Theology of Childhood" in *The Complete Guide to Godly Play, Volume 1: How to Lead Godly Play Lessons* by Jerome W. Berryman (Denver, CO: Living the Good News, 2002). Used with permission of the publisher.

The church has overlooked the child's key role in the development of spiritual maturity because of three conflicted views. First, ambivalent feelings about children are deeply held, both a high and a low value. Second, adult communication with them is conflicted by mixing spoken and unspoken messages. Third, what adults require them to do is inconsistent. Sometimes we make them obey and other times we invite them to be creative.

The problem that ambivalent feelings, mixed messages, and inconsistent guidance creates is often unconscious, so it paralyzes the ability to think clearly, responsibly, and creatively about children without realizing it. The tragedy that results from this paralysis is that the profound but parabolic clue is missed that Jesus left about spiritual maturity.

To become aware of this paralysis one needs to realize that both the high and low views of children are correct. They are valued at times and at other times they "drive us crazy." Both spoken and unspoken messages are important and need to be consistent. Both requiring children to obey and to be creative are necessary for growth.

My hope is that this small theology of childhood will provide a fresh look at adult spiritual maturity with children in mind. This will involve seven steps. First, Jesus' parabolic view of children will be touched on. Second, the translation from parabolic narrative to eight concepts will be outlined. Third, the logical move from the eight concepts to three propositions will be made. Steps four through six will develop the three propositions of this theology and then I will conclude with the seventh and final step.

Jesus' Parabolic View of Children

Jesus did not define the child he told adults to be like. To discover what is spiritual maturity one must consult Jesus' parabolic sayings and actions in scripture, take a deeper look at the children around us, and inquire into one's own childhood. Jesus' parabolic method forces people to discover what adult maturity is for ourselves. He only states where to look. It is the experience of that discovery, which prepares the individual to enter God's domain.

Like all parables, the ones about children are brief and few. Only about eight clusters of sayings and narratives are in the gospels to stimulate thinking. Still, this provides more than enough raw material from which to conceive a book, as Hans-Reudi Weber's *Jesus and the Children* shows (Weber 1994).

Jesus' parabolic method has also and more recently stimulated whole issues of theological journals about the meaning of children. Note especially *Theology Today* which includes Judith Gundry-Volf's (2000) "To Such as These Belongs the Reign of God: Jesus and Children," which was expanded into a chapter in *The Child in Christian Thought* (Gundry-Volf 2001). *Interpretation: A Journal of Bible and Theology* also devoted an issue to children in April of 2001 and *The Sewanee Theological Review* has an issue on the same topic scheduled for December of 2004.

My interpretation of this material assumes that Jesus took a high view of children, which gives the events and sayings their best coherence (Berryman, 2002). This is not to suggest that Jesus was unrealistic about children, but he was challenging the prevailing view of children in his and our time to make a point. My interpretation of this material has yielded eight concepts.

From Narrative and Sayings to Concepts

The following eight concepts are generalized from eight instances of stories and sayings concerning Jesus and children in the gospels:

1. Sometimes a game should not make, as with the children in the market place. This is because children are being invited to play the wrong game (Matt 11:16–19; Luke 7:31–35).

2. A silent child is placed among the talking disciples for ontological appreciation. It is the silent child who teaches (Matt 18:1–5; Mark 9:33–37; Luke 9:46–48).

3. Do not hinder children. Let them come to Jesus for a blessing, which they nonverbally realize they need and know where this need can be satisfied (Matt 19:13–15; Mark 10:13–16; Luke 18:15–17).

4. Causing children to stumble (not be blessed?) is a matter of life and death (Matt 18:6; Mark 9:42; Luke 17:2).

5. To enter the Kingdom one needs to become like a child (Matt 18:3; Mark 10:15; Luke 18:17).

6. Nicodemus discovers the need for a complete transformation, a second naiveté, to enter God's domain as an adult (John 3:3–8).

7. Children can intuit Jesus' presence and express their discovery, like the children in the temple (Matt 21:15–16).

8. Children can intuit Jesus' power in a way many over-confident adults cannot (Matt 11:25–26; Luke 10:21).

From Concepts To Propositions

The concepts from the above list will now be grouped logically and, by drawing on a general knowledge of children, used to create three propositions for this theology of childhood. Together the three propositions form a single urgent statement about the child's role in the formation of mature spirituality, so this is thematic theology, such as for example liberation theology, and must be read together with more systematic statements to give a rounded view of Christian thought.

Proposition One is constructed by combining concepts 1 and 6 to suggest that playing hide-and-seek is fundamental to human nature. This has been dignified in theology by the Latin phrase *Deus Absconditus atque Praesens* (God is hidden yet also present.). People play this game to continue playing rather than to win, which would end the game and break the relationship with God and each other.

Proposition Two is the result of combining concepts 2, 5, 7, and 8. Infants and young children reveal the importance of nonverbal communication. Adults tend to forget this because they rely primarily on words to communicate. Despite this distraction even adult spirituality remains fundamentally unspoken and provides the connotations for language whether we notice the unsaid in what is said or not. Speaking sometimes even hides what presence reveals.

The third proposition is the result of clustering concepts 3 and 4. Adults know that infants will die without nourishing relationships. This proposition emphasizes the importance of mutual blessing as such a nutriment. Blessing affirms the person as he or she actually is, and yet calls forth the best one can offer, since the blessing is asked for in God's name. This ultimate speech act stimulates change in both the one who is blessed and the one who blesses. It is in such mutual blessing between children and adults that mature spirituality is primarily revealed.

These three propositions have seldom been emphasized in the history of theology. Jesus' parabolic sayings and actions concerning children need to be set again in the midst of distracted and talking disciples, which is the goal of this theology of childhood.

Unusual theological language will be used to do this, but the terms—hide-and-seek, showing, and blessing—are closer to childhood interests and more open in reference than normal theological language. God-talk is usually impersonal, abstract, and closed by the effort to make precise, denotative descriptions and explanations. All of that is good, but the language of this proposed approach invites the whole person to respond in a wondering, active, and creative way, following Jesus' parabolic method to some degree.

Usually a theology is large, but this one will remain small, like a child. As Jorge Luis Borges, a modern master of parable, said in the Prologue to his *Ficciones* (1962), "To go on for five hundred pages developing an idea whose perfect oral exposition is possible in a few minutes! A better course of procedure is to pretend that these books already exist, and then to offer a resume, a commentary" (p. 15). The task then is to develop these three propositions in the spirit of parabolic children without going on for five hundred pages!

Proposition One: Children Reveal How To Play Hide-and-Seek with God

The game of hide-and-seek begins at birth. Touching an infant near the mouth causes the child to turn towards the touch to seek life by sucking. This act is neither reasoned nor willed. It takes nothing or no one else into consideration. Among the fundamental aspects of human nature, then, is this urge to establish nourishing relationships. Infants are the silent bearers of this revelation.

Many mothers are so in tune with their infants that they can anticipate their needs. When this happens the infant is not aware that there is anything "out there" or an "other," because desire and satisfaction merge. Seeking and finding appear to be unified.

The game of hide-and-seek enters the child's awareness when the mother regains her interest in the world around her and no longer anticipates her child's every need. Donald W. Winnicott, an English psychiatrist, called this compromise "good enough mothering" (Winnicott, 1971). An intimate "space" appears between what is "me" and "not me." Winnicott called this a "transitional space" and suggested that this is where play, religion, and culture originate. A baby blanket, a stuffed animal, or some other object can be a "transitional object," existing in that in-between place, that is not self but is not entirely separate either.

The game of hide-and-seek needs an in-between, safe place for its playing. Laughter signals that play has been established as the basis for the relationship. When framed by play both presence and absence can be engaged at levels unavailable in any other way. If one hides too long, moves too quickly or roughly, or shouts "peek-a-boo" too loudly the transitional space is shattered and the play is over. The game disintegrates and all lose!

As infants mature their play begins to incorporate language. As they grow into adulthood this language proliferates into a variety of "worlds" such as poetry, physics, religion and other linguistic domains. The language games in which individuals participate shape the way they relate to each other, to nature, to the deep self, and to God. This is why it is so important to take great care when introducing religious language to children. I have, therefore, proposed a way of teaching religious language called Godly Play™. It shows the art of how "to speak Christian" in a way that invites children to create meaning about the absence and presence of God while it is being learned in the safety and intimacy of play (Berryman, 1991, 1994, 2002, 2003).

As the young child develops, the words of the game change. Instead of "peek-a-boo" the question "Where are you?" can be heard. The little one, who is supposedly hiding, cannot help but call back, "Here I am." The game remains as much about being found as about hiding.

"Now you hide," the child laughs and gestures with his or her play face showing what kind of relationship is needed to continue. The adult's hiding, of course, needs to be in plain sight. Perhaps, the child will cover up the adult, because this keeps him or her in control of the hiding and being found and keeps the game located in the transitional space. The alternative is for the relationship to collapse into loss and terror.

About the time children go to school and begin to interact with other children on a regular basis, the game changes again. Now children are running and not merely crawling. They have a greater range and hide better. Sometimes competition is added to the complexity of the game by running to a base to avoid being "it." The game is more scary now, but in the end all the children gather to confirm that being found is still part of the game and that the fundamental relationship is that of play.

More variations of this game appear during the teenage years. Adolescents play hide-and-seek with their parents, their teachers, and with each other. Courtship includes hide-and-seek in its rituals, even today when custom dictates a virtual non-courtship. Adolescents are also at play with their own deep selves, as they attempt to discover who they are amidst the many changes taking place. The necessity of working out how to perceive one's view of God, how to be creative, and to obey one's parents and God becomes uncomfortably apparent to all. This is true even without the theological overtones of the two divergent creation stories from Genesis clanging in their ears!

A little later the game of hide-and-seek becomes more overtly theological. The poets seem to be the best and most articulate players of this game. Perhaps their love for and artful use of metaphor is a kind of compressed game of hide-and-seek in itself, which makes them more comfortable with such play. The poets also make it quite clear that this game is not trivial.

Francis Thompson (1859–1907) had not been allowed to enter the Anglican priesthood as he hoped. He failed at his medical studies. Finally, all he could do was wander the streets of London, addicted to opium. Still the game of hide-and-seek with God went on, as his "The Hound of Heaven" cries out:

> I fled Him, down the nights and down the days;
> I fled Him, down the arches of the years;
> I fled Him, down the labyrinthine ways
> Of my own mind; and in the mist of tears
> I hid from Him and under running laughter.
> Fear wist not to evade as Love wist to pursue.
> Still with unhurrying chase,
> And unperturbed pace,
> Deliberate speed, majestic instancy,
> Came on the following Feet,
> And a Voice above their beat—
> "Nought shelters thee, who wilt not shelter Me." (Abrams, 1962, p. 1053)

A more contemporary example of playing with absence and presence is exemplified by the poetry of the Welsh Anglican Priest R. S. Thomas (1913–2000). By my own conservative count about 50 out of 190 poems in *Poems of R. S. Thomas*

(Thomas, 1985) reverberate with hide-and-seek. Perhaps, this is the "one furrow" he returned to again and again after the "learning's gate" had "swung wide." His "In Church" is an example:

> Often I try
> To analyse the quality
> Of its silences. Is this where God hides
> From my searching? I have stopped to listen,
> After the few people have gone,
> To the air recomposing itself
> For vigil. It has waited like this
> Since the stones grouped themselves about it.
> These are the hard ribs
> Of a body that our prayers have failed
> To animate. Shadows advance
> From their corners to take possession
> Of places the light held
> For an hour. The bats resume
> Their business. The uneasiness of the pews
> Ceases. There is no other sound
> In the darkness but the sound of a man
> Breathing, testing his faith
> On emptiness, nailing his questions
> One by one to an untenanted cross. (p. 54)

L. William Countryman (1999) wrote in *The Poetic Imagination* that "The dynamic created by the alternation of absence and presence is simply a defining fact of human existence." At least in Anglican spirituality, which he was studying, there appears to be a "dialectic of absence and presence." It is where "the life force that gives energy and movement to the rest resides" (p. 92).

Understanding this primal rhythm preserves the freedom with which humans were created so we can continue to be creators in God's image and yet never be left absolutely alone. As people obey God about being creative they still paradoxically need God's guidance. It is in this hiding and seeking that self identity and what is possible with genuine maturity is revealed.

The game of hide-and-seek is not the excusive province of poets and mystics, however. It is also found in scripture. Samuel Terrien's *The Elusive Presence* (Terrien, 1978) describes what is being termed "hide-and-seek" as the single thread that unifies the Hebrew and Christian Scriptures. It is the *experience* of God's elusive presence, which weaves the sweeping narrative and other genres together. Of course, abstractions, such as "covenant relationship" arise, but they are grounded in and refer to the experience of absence and presence or else they become only words about words.

Finally, each individual meets hide-and-seek again at his or her own death. The play then is with the absence and presence of all that is known. The deep self, others, nature, and God may still be there but in a very different and silent, non-linguistic way. It is then that God is completely found and finds the seeker. The individual returns to the unity the journey began with, when "me" and "not me" were merged before the distinction the game requires became conscious.

In Eden God was always present. Adam and Eve hid, but God found them. God then sent them away, but God was still there, playing hide-and-seek, so the relationship could continue. That original game continues today, recapitulated in each child's life as the little one develops into adulthood and beyond.

Proposition Two: Children Reveal the Importance of Silence for Knowing God

Play is signaled by nonverbal actions. One can play with words but words cannot constitute play. There is nothing that a person can do that cannot be done in a playful way, so play is not a class of actions. I have already called attention to the importance of play for coping with presence and absence in life and death. It is now time to examine what is communicated in the silence of being at play with God.

Children are better than adults at tracking relationships without language, because they are not yet as dependent on language as adults. This "relational consciousness" is a profound part of their spirituality as has been shown by David Hay and Rebecca Nye (1998). This study was based on careful listening to and the classification of children's language about spirituality during interviews conducted primarily by Nye. The verbal points to the nonverbal.

Adults also intuit that there is more sometimes more meaning in talk than the words can carry. Still, human beings are language creatures and must try to put silence into language to assess its importance. In fact, the distinction I am making between verbal and nonverbal communication cannot be made without language.

To better understand the relationship between talking and silence it is helpful to emphasize the related brain functioning. Three different models will be used to do this. First, verbal and nonverbal communication will be differentiated. Second, the knowing of the limbic system will be contrasted with that of the cerebral cortex. Finally, the functioning of the left versus the right hemispheres of the cerebral cortex will be considered.

Silence as Communication: The Verbal and Non-Verbal Communication Systems

Silence communicates as powerfully as words. Perhaps this is why Jesus placed the silent child in the midst of the talking disciples. There are three communication problems in religion that this model may shed light on. First, words are suspect when they are severed from experience. Second, when verbal and nonverbal communication are at odds, something goes wrong with relationships. Third, religious education is sometimes framed so that the unintentional teaching of the misuse of Christian communication results.

Terrance Deacon's *Symbolic Species: The Co-Evolution of Language and the Brain* (1997) will be primarily followed to explicate this. He wrote, "Language evolved in a parallel, alongside calls and gestures, and dependent on them—indeed, language and many human nonlinguistic forms of communication probably co-evolved" (p. 54).

In the nonverbal communication system "iconic" and "indexical" referencing exist, according to Deacon (1997). Iconic referencing is limited to signaling what is like and unlike. Indexical referencing develops from the iconic experience and establishes connections such as the one between smoke and fire. These two kinds of referencing provide the ground from which "a leap" in the complexity of relationships is made, which results in symbolic communication. Referencing with symbols is different from but is built up from iconic and indexical referencing. Since symbols are only tokens of meaning, they cannot function without social agreement. This is because they are not connected to their referent in any other way. If one does not incorporate iconic and indexical referencing all that is left is words about words.

Some adults retain a special sensitivity to their iconic and indexical referencing, even after symbolic-referencing is well developed. Artists who play with words, dance, stone, colors, music, and other media are especially gifted at this. Children, on the other hand, have no choice but to be in tune with their iconic and indexical referencing, since their symbolic referencing is still developing.

Words, however, need more than mere social agreement to make meaning with any depth. They need to be rooted in iconic and indexical referencing. A sad and dramatic example of what happens when this is not the case is called Williams Syndrome. People with this disorder cannot help but talk about things they have not experienced. Everyone does this at one time or another, but people with Williams Syndrome have no alternative. Their symbolic referencing is not grounded in iconic and indexical referencing.

The tragedy of Williams Syndrome, however, is not limited to using words about words. It also includes the disability of not being able to reason from one's words to any new or related knowledge. Williams Syndrome raises a worrisome question about God-talk: Is it reliable?

John Wesley (1703–1791) illustrates both the problem and its complexity. Wesley did not suffer from Williams Syndrome. He was instead a "reasonable enthusiast," as Henry Rack (2002) called him in the title of his biography. His analytical powers coupled with his respect for emotion made him chronically suspicious of his own nonverbal knowing. This tendency may have disrupted the connection between his iconic and indexical knowing and his symbolic referencing.

John Wesley wrote to his brother Charles in June of 1766:

> In one of my last I was saying that I do not feel the wrath of God abiding on me; nor can I believe it does. And yet (this is the mystery) I do not love God. I never did. Therefore I never believed, in the Christian sense of the word. Therefore I am only an honest heathen. And yet, to be so employed of God! And so hedged in that I can neither get forward nor backward! Surely there was never such an instance before, from the beginning of the world! If I ever have had *that faith,* it would not be so strange. But I never had any other evidence of the eternal or invisible world than I have now: and that is none at all, unless such as faintly shines from reason's glimmering ray. I have no direct witness (I do not say, that I am a child of God, but) of anything invisible or eternal.
>
> And yet I dare not preach otherwise than I do, either concerning faith, or love, or justification, or perfection. And yet I find rather an increase than a decrease of zeal for the whole work of God and every part of it. I am borne along. I know not how, that I can't stand still. I want all the world to come to what I do not know. (Quoted in Tomkins, 2003, p. 168)

Wesley was trying to be honest with his brother and himself. Still, for whatever reason, he seems to be speaking of what he did not know or was in doubt about knowing physically. He also thought that he might come to know what he spoke of if he spoke of it often enough. Still, using only words about words to create meaning can sometimes lead to a lack of flexibility and openness in one's thinking as well as a proclivity to plagiarize, since the richness of experience is not there to ground the words with personal authenticity. These were characteristics of Wesley that may have been caused by using language that was not rooted in experience.

Wesley's doubt about being a Christian was chronic. His reviews of the experience when his "heart was strangely warmed" wavered back and forth, as reviewed by Heitzenrater in *The Elusive Mr. Wesley* (2003, p. 35). Finally, Heitzenrater wrote that "to see Wesley whole" there is only one way: "His main significance, then or now, rests not in his private meanderings, but in his thoughts and actions that touch upon the concerns of other persons" (p. 393). Still, did he know non-verbally what he talked about or not? If he did not know from experience what he spoke about how can his reasoning based on those ungrounded words be trusted?

T. S. Eliot observed that the reason so much Christian poetry is of poor quality is that the authors wrote what they thought they ought to write instead of what they actually experienced. Deacon's work suggests why this may be so. It also cautions us about all God-talk.

The second problem this model of brain functioning underscores is the need to keep our verbal and nonverbal communication systems in harmony. Keeping them in tune is important for authentic relationships to develop with other people, with God, with nature, and with our own deep self. Discord between the spoken and the unspoken is especially tragic for children. This is because discord is sometimes learned as normal communication, since that is the only kind of communication they experience with significant others. It is difficult to overcome such a distorting start, because when the child responds correctly in one system he or she responds incorrectly in the other one.

Young children have no way to cope with such unrelenting error, because they cannot take the perspective of a third person to see what is happening in the relationship. The pain of discord can finally outweigh the fundamental need for relationship and they will withdraw from trying to form any relationships, since their only experience of communication is toxic.

The third problem upon which this model sheds light is related to religious education. Christian language is sometimes taught to children in a way that does not promote deep connections between symbolic referencing and the nonverbal iconic and indexical referencing. An example of this is when religious education is restricted to the memorization of scripture or a catechism limited to adult questions and answers about doctrine. Such teaching promotes the unspoken lesson that Christian language, ungrounded in experience, is the norm for religious knowing. Teaching that can lead to its irrelevance, despite the importance of memorization in religious education.

Teaching religion needs to keep symbolic referencing connected to iconic and indexical referencing in general, but it is also important to do so because spirituality may be located in the nonverbal system (Berryman, 2001). If that is true the result could be a kind of religious education, which severs religious language from human spirituality.

Fortunately, children usually have more sense than to take part in much of what is of concern above. They walk away from such religious education as soon as they can and reject such "religion" as irrelevant to their need for meaning.

Silence as Connection: The Limbic System and the Neocortex

A sensitivity to silence can disclose the disconnection between what is said and not said in communication, as described above. A second model will now be described that shows the importance of silence for how human beings establish relationships.

The worlds of infants and young children prior to language are less differentiated than those of adults. Nonverbal communication is relied upon for knowing and it remains somewhat idiosyncratic. It could be, however, that in this unique mix God is experienced as a significant part of all the relationships in which the child lives. This is possible, because love does not depend on reason to identify it or will it into place. To explore this it is again necessary to return to brain theory.

Paul MacLean (1990) argued that the human brain is comprised of three distinct sub-brains. Each is considered the product of a separate age in evolutionary history with the oldest and inner area identified as "the reptilian brain." The limbic brain developed next and is the middle layer. The last to develop is the neocortex, which covers the whole brain like bark or a shell, as the Latin term *cortex* implies.

The neocortex is the site for speaking, writing, planning, and reasoning, while the so-called "limbic brain" is the location of non-verbal communication such as distress cries, play, nurturing, and social signals such as smiling or frowning. The limbic system moves the human being in ways that the neocortex can only imprecisely translate into language.

The joint operation of the limbic brain and the neocortex is at the center of the argument presented in *A General Theory of Love* (Lewis, Amini, & Lannon 2000). The authors searched for a kind of language to bridge the translation gap between the neocortex and the limbic system. Their solution was poetry. For example, Robert Frost wrote that a poem "begins as a lump in the throat, a sense of wrong, a homesickness, a love sickness. It is never a thought to begin with" (p. 34).

The Christian language system is a complex repository of such "poetry." There are sacred stories, parables, and liturgical gestures combined with words in addition to silence in this linguistic domain. Most of this language functions more like poetry than the propositions, explanations, and descriptions, which dominate most professional discourse. Christian language, then, is most appropriate for connecting the limbic system and the neocortex. It works in an indirect way, which surprises one from time to time with the grace of discoveries. The use of reason, logic, and tradition are needed to guard this language system against misuse, but they do not have this poetic power to evoke what is silent in human relationships.

It appears that love's attachment is made in the limbic system. This is not a decision. It is, instead, a matching. A "decision" implies the logic of language, which only resides in the neocortex. It appears, according to Lewis, Amini, and Lannon (2000) that the cerebral cortex "makes up" reasons for the connections that have already been established in the limbic system.

When it is proposed that a child cannot "know" God's will because the child's will and reason are defective, care needs to be taken to compare such a statement with what twentieth century science has shown about how the brain works. If love does not depend on either reason or will, then it can occur in young children, as is evident especially to parents and grandparents, who know them best. If that is true, then, children can show us this connection with God by their very being and can truly guide us toward mature spirituality by their knowing silence.

Silence as Existential Orientation: The Left and Right Hemispheres of the Cerebral Cortex

The final model to be discussed to emphasize the importance of silence in Christian knowing involves the two hemispheres of the brain. It may be true that the three models presented here might overlap in their functioning or be redundant, but such a synthesis would move beyond the scope of this presentation. What is important to notice here is that there are at least three ways to explain how silence is related to the maturing of human spirituality.

For most individuals—and nearly all right-handed persons—the left hemisphere is considered dominant. It controls the activity of the right side of the body and it is crucial for all language and language-related activities as well as for many other cognitive capacities.

Research about "split brains" began in the early 1950s when Ronald E. Myers and R. W. Sperry, then at the University of Chicago, noticed that when the corpus callosum, which connects the two hemispheres, is cut the unique function of each hemisphere can be demonstrated. This is because the hemispheres can no longer communicate.

Sperry and his associates carried this research forward at The California Institute of Technology, as described for a general audience by Michael S. Gazzaniga (1967) who was part of this research team. The implications of this research for religious topics, such as meditation, were discussed early in this process by Robert E. Ornstein (1972).

People who have major injuries to the right hemisphere usually find the movement of the left side of their body impaired, but their language ability remains essentially normal. On the other hand, most people with even a minor injury to certain portions of the left hemisphere, especially Wernicke's area for understanding as well as Broca's area for speech, suffer impaired linguistic functioning. A major injury makes them unable to use or understand words. This is why the left hemisphere is associated with language.

The right hemisphere is not usually associated with language, but it is where the emotional meaning of speech is processed. People who suffer injury to the right hemisphere lose their ability to understand and produce delicately nuanced emotional meanings in their communication. This is especially true when the locations of the damage in the right hemisphere are the mirror images of Wernicke's and Broca's areas in the left hemisphere.

What is most relevant for children's spirituality is that some researchers consider the silent, right hemisphere to be the site of human orientation in space and time. That would make the fundamental existential orientation unable to be articulated. Perhaps, this explains what theologians are talking about when they say that there are limits to language and knowing. All three models of brain functioning, especially as they are integrated, inform this intuition and make sense of what mystics report about experiencing a presence that cannot be put into words.

The two hemispheres model also helps provide insight into the silence aspect of conflicted knowing. When people who have had their corpus callosum severed are asked questions they sometimes begin to speak and at the same time shake their heads to affirm or deny what is being said. Perhaps the reader has felt such agreement or disagreement within his or her own experience. This subtle evidence of silent knowing, then, from the right hemisphere is important to remind us to continuously monitor nonverbal intuitions. This is especially true, since the play with God, as in any kind of play, is signaled in a nonverbal manner.

Three models of brain functioning have been discussed, which show the importance of nonverbal and verbal communication working together for the development of mature spirituality. Children are living revelations of how to play with the presence and absence of God and how nonverbal communication is used to track this. Children also can illuminate an ethic of blessing, the third proposition of this theology of childhood, to guide all Christians toward spiritual maturity.

Proposition Three: Children Reveal How To Bless and Be Blessed

To begin this discussion of ethics a fundamental question must be asked. Why was Jesus "indignant" when the disciples prevented the children from coming to him to be blessed? Why did he use such violent language in his millstone comments about not hindering children? Perhaps, the extreme language was used because of the absolute necessity for human children to be reared in nourishing relationships to survive and because the quality of such child rearing is deeply connected to the spiritual maturity of adults.

The ethic of blessing rests on the blunt fact that the human species will die out by its own misuse of creativity unless it begins to live by an ethic of blessing. The church has everything it needs to make known a new awareness of the relationship between children and spiritual maturity. However, the message is primarily nonverbal, so it must be modeled and not merely discussed.

Jesus showed us this by the action of touching. When Jesus blessed he also touched and that touching also healed. There is a massive transfer of affirmation in the nonverbal communication of touching that accepts people where they are. This is the beginning of the blessing process. The fact that the blessing is in God's name then challenges those being blessed to be the best kind of human being imaginable, but because of the limits to the imagination only God may know what that unique quality is for each person. The verbal simplicity of the act, a performative utterance, should not distract us from the complex nonverbal transaction that is taking place. Both words and gestures communicate that this is not a power play to put down people who are blessed. It is a sign of affirmation and aspiration to lift them up.

Blessing is at the beginning of scripture when God blessed the whole creation as good (Gen 1:1—2:3). It was present when Abraham was blessed into being a blessing to others (Gen 12:1–2). It was there when Jesus laid hands on the children and blessed them. It is also there at the end of the Bible. John heard a voice from heaven telling him to write, "Blessed are the dead who die in the Lord henceforth." He then wrote, "Blessed indeed, that they may rest from their labors, for their deeds follow them" (Rev 14:13). Blessing is fundamental to the wholeness of creation.

Still, this is not primarily a matter of scriptural authority or an appeal to Jesus' life as an ethical model. These considerations are important, but what needs to be emphasized here is that *if* one wants to reach spiritual maturity, *then* living by an ethic of blessing is necessary.

The ethic of blessing is more synthesis rather than analysis. It does not intend to be completely impartial nor is it a mechanical application of decision-making principles. It does not distinguish what people do from who they are, but takes motive, action, and consequences into account.

The first part of the ethical situation that requires examination is the whole person. It is motive that moves one to act in the first place and to act in a certain way. Sometimes the motive is so strong that people will do things for others that cause them pain or even death. Motive must be taken into consideration to understand the whole context for blessing.

The focus on the good person as the source of good deeds is an ancient tradition, usually associated with Aristotle (384–322 BCE). He promoted the idea that a moral agent will experience happiness or flourishing (*eudaimonia*) when motivated by living a golden mean. He developed a theory of various moral values to guide such a happy life. They included courage, self-control, wisdom, and justice, which were virtues common to his culture's tradition.

Christian theologians such as Paul, Augustine (CE 354–430) and Aquinas (CE 1225–1274) added the theological virtues of faith, hope, and love to Aristotle's list, which was also subsequently revised as the history of theology progressed. Aquinas identified justice, fortitude, temperance, and prudence as the cardinal (Latin: *cardo* meaning hinge) virtues. The rich complex of the theological virtues—loving regard for others, faith in the present, and hope for the future—provide the generative power for an authentic blessing, but it can also take courage, self-control, wisdom, humility, and a thirst for justice to accomplish the task.

To say that what one ought to do is what a virtuous person is motivated to do, is helpful to define an ethic of blessing, but by itself stands only as a circular argument. It is, therefore, necessary to move on to the act itself and then finally the results of the act to work out a complete ethic of blessing.

The second part of the ethical situation is the act itself. Here the focus is on the action. This is especially true when the action involved is so important that it commands one's attention and a sense of duty to accomplish it. The classical origin of this emphasis is Immanuel Kant (1724–1804) and is called "deontology" after the Greek word for "duty," which is *deon*.

"Importance" may be assigned to an act because it is of its ultimate, final implications. An obvious example is killing while a more subtle one is any act that if not done would make moral conduct impossible. Examples are keeping promises or telling the truth. A blessing is an ultimate act, because it can stimulate mutual blessing, which in turn can generate spiritual maturity across the generations. To be fully authentic as a blessing, however, the action still involves motive and results.

The third part of the ethical situation focuses on the results of the motive and action. The classical term for this interest in consequences is "utilitarianism." Its origins are usually associated with the English philosophers Jeremy Bentham (1748–1832) and John Stuart Mill (1806–1873). The focus on results requires one to engage in a risk/benefit analysis to predict the outcome of an act with a particular motive. Blessing encourages a utilitarian, risk/benefit analysis, but it also acknowledges that despite all best efforts to determine the future, human beings will never be able to know with certainty what the future holds. There are simply too many variables to arrive at such a conclusion. An example of this is the blessing of a child or grandchild who will probably outlive the person who does the blessing.

Sometimes there are no good options for actions. The alternatives are only shaded, complex alternatives. To bless, then, is to be aware of all three viewpoints about the ethical situation and to integrate them as well as possible. The final step is to move forward imperfectly into the unknown, asking for forgiveness for the limited ability to know and control the future. Having done this, responsibility is still accepted for what has been done.

As noted earlier, such blessing stimulates blessing in return. The two blessings are mutual logically and emotionally. The one who blesses recognizes that the one who is blessed is not being manipulated to act in a certain way. The one who blesses, then, releases control and in so doing is open to being blessed in return through the quality of the relationship established. Acceptance and aspiration flow back to the one who first performs the blessing. This is structural and is not related to the attitude of the one who is blessed or how things turn out. Blessing approached in this way avoids the danger of dominance and control so that blessing can be mutual.

Mutual blessing opens up a spiritual "place" of safety and intimacy analogous to Winnicott's transitional space. It also invites God to come and play, for it is done in God's name. Sometimes even sacred objects invested with God's presence are used to bless. They are like transitional objects and contribute to the safety and intimacy of the play.

It is difficult to bless when one is powerful. It tends to dominate the one who is blessed and suggests he or she should be only submissive in the relationship. To manage this Jesus blessed children as those who could bless, but also included others who could easily bless. They are the poor in spirit, those who mourn, the meek, those who desire what is fair, the merciful, the pure in heart, the peacemakers, those persecuted for righteousness' sake, and those who are spoken of falsely. Such people can bless easily for they are not powerful.

The Sermon on the Mount, especially in Matthew 5–7, provides a list of those who can bless, because they have nothing to offer except a blessing. The powerless know they cannot control the future. They cannot coerce the present. The powerful, on the other hand, have difficulty blessing, because their power always implies control. This is as structural and impersonal as is the blessing received by the one who blesses.

This complicates the normal view of church development. For example in Norwich, England, Samuel Wells found that the Anglican parish of St. Elizabeth's of which he was vicar, needed a new approach to its relationship with the community. Misunderstanding and mistrust blocked communication at every turn until Sam discovered the importance of thinking of the church as a powerless child rather than as a powerful parent.

When a new building was built in 1991, there was terrible vandalism for the first five years. In conversation with a girl who had thrown rocks at the previous vicar's house, Wells (2000) discovered something about the position of the church from a child's perspective.

> Gently the church has come to see that the young person who threw the stone is in fact more representative of a widespread view, and thus more like a parent, whereas the church, being small and not taken seriously, is in fact more like a child. The power of the church is not that of a parent—greater resources, more experience, greater physical strength; instead, the church's power is that of the child—stubbornness and doggedness, and the tendency to ask awkward or embarrassing questions. So when the time comes to sit down with the other groups in the community, the church sits down as a child, still learning, potentially disruptive, rather than as a parent, saying "come to where we already are. (p.123)

This leap of imagination is remarkable. Usually church development does not take children into consideration unless it is to *use* them to draw in their parents or to be politically correct. Children are assumed not to be able to make any kind of contribution on their own except, perhaps, in a deferred way as "the church of the future." Here the church is seen as a child.

The contribution of children, however, is so fundamental that it is very hard to see, especially when an unconscious ambivalence about them is also involved. Churches work hard to maintain the institution and to draw people in to develop the congregation. The question not always asked is why the institution should be maintained or to what the invited strangers are invited. If the goal of church development is to provide a way to help people enter the domain of God, then children are at the very center of what it takes for the church's mission to be accomplished. Building a child-like church, however, sounds weak and powerless, but that is just the point. It acknowledges the difficulty of the powerful being able to bless in a way that elicits mutual blessing. Such "weakness" is very strong (2 Cor. 12:9) because it makes the church into a doorway into God's realm.

Nietzsche (1956) argued that statements about valuing such weakness are nothing but a rationalization, which discloses an ethic of necessity he called "slave morality." It makes a virtue of being powerless, when the reality is that what human beings really want and need is power. In his *The genealogy of morals* he wrote that this is a "conspiracy of the sufferers against (the) happy and successful" (p. 259). He also exclaimed that it is "the ascetic priest, that virtuoso of guilt" (p. 277) who reduces the "vital energy" of human beings to its lowest point (p. 268) by preaching such an ethic.

On the contrary I propose that mutual blessing generates "vital energy" across the generations. When people forget that they are creatures and not God, they become too inflated to enter the small doorway into God's domain. It is for children and the child-like, rather than for the powerful who must expand their power to find their worth. There is nothing generative about that. It absorbs rather than generates energy.

Nietzsche at times confused the God-Man and the Man-God in his urgency, pain, loneliness, and desperate attempts at honesty and self-awareness. Nevertheless, his use of the images of blessing, "second innocence," the child, the personal quality of morality, and his critique of Christianity all contribute to a better understanding of what is meant by an ethic of mutual blessing.

Perhaps Nietzsche understood nonverbally what he needed and could not find it in the ambivalent feelings, the mixed messages, and the inconsistent actions of the Christians around him in the Nineteenth Century. There are many good medical reasons for his well-documented insanity, but the Christianity he knew did not contribute to his health. Still, at the end of his sanity his nonverbal communication was clear. He threw his arms around a horse being mistreated near the Via Po in Turin, Italy about January 3, 1989. He then collapsed.

Before being taken to Basel, as a mad man, he begged his Italian landlord, "Dear Signor Fino, will you let me have your *papalina*?" He wanted Fino's triangular popish nightcap with a tassel on it for the journey. He wanted people to know him as a popish clown. As Lesley Chamberlain concluded in her book *Nietzsche in Turin* (1996) this was the visual image of himself he bequeathed to posterity. "His message had to be certain beyond words" (p. 217).

Nietzsche risked madness to critique Christianity. Christianity risks madness not to listen. It is the power of spiritual maturity through hide-and-seek, attending to the nonverbal quality of relationships, and living an ethic of mutual blessing that is needed and not the kind of power that Nietzsche and much of contemporary society think will make one spiritually mature.

Conclusion

It is hoped that the three conflicts distorting the church's view of children—ambivalent feelings, mixed messages, and inconsistent actions—will lose their power as they are discussed in these pages and elsewhere. It is further hoped that the three propositions of this theology will be useful to help find the doorway into God's domain through child-like churches.

Children are not adults. Adults are not children. Adults, however, can become like children and over time such adults can nourish children to become even more like children as they mature. This is not madness. It is the pathway of infinite progress into the domain of God. All else is an infinite regress.

References

Abrams, M. H. (Ed.). (1962). *The Norton anthology of English literature* (Vol. 2). New York: Norton.

Berryman, J. W. (1991). *Godly play: A way of religious education*. San Francisco: HarperSan Francisco.

Berryman, J. W. (1994). *Teaching Godly Play: The Sunday morning handbook*. Nashville: Abingdon.

Berryman, J. W. (2001). The nonverbal nature of spirituality & religious language. In J. Erricker, C. Ota, & C. Erricker (Eds.), *Spiritual education: Cultural, religious & social differences* (pp. 9–21). Brighton, UK: Sussex Academic.

Berryman, J. W. (2002). Toward a theology of childhood. In *The complete guide to Godly play* (Vol. 1) (pp. 108–142). Denver: Living the Good News.

Berryman, J. W. (2002). *The complete guide to Godly Play* (Vols. 1–3). Denver: Living the Good News.

Berryman, J. W. (2003). *The complete guide to Godly Play* (Vol. 4). Denver: Living the Good News.

Borges, J. L. (1962). *Ficciones*. New York: Grove.

Chamberlain, L. (1996). *Nietzsche in Turin: An intimate biography*. New York: Picador.

Countryman, L. (1999). *The poetic imagination: An Anglican spiritual tradition*. Maryknoll, NY: Orbis.

Deacon, T. (1997). *The symbolic species: The co-evolution of language and the brain*. New York: Norton.

Erikson, E. H. (1997). *The life cycle completed: Extended version with new chapters on the ninth stage of development by Joan M. Erikson*. New York: Norton.

Gazzaniga, M. (August, 1967). The split brain in man. *Scientific American*, 24–29.

Gundry-Volf, J. (2000). To such as these belongs the reign of God: Jesus and the children. *Theology Today*, 56, 469–480.

Gundry-Volf, J. (2001). The least and the greatest: Children in the New Testament. In M. J. Bunge (Ed.), *The child in Christian thought* (pp. 29–60). Grand Rapids: Eerdmans.

Hay, D. & Nye, R. 1998. *The spirit of the child*. London: HarperCollins.

Heitzenrater, R. P. (2003). *The elusive Mr. Wesley* (2nd rev. ed.). Nashville: Abingdon.

Lewis, T., Amini, F. & Lannon, R. (2000). *A general theory of love*. New York: Random House.

MacLean, P. D. (1990). *The triune brain in evolution*. New York: Plenum.

Nietzsche, F. (1956). *The birth of tragedy and the genealogy of morals* (G. Francis, Trans.). Garden City, NY: Doubleday Anchor Book.

Ornstein, R. E. (1972). *The psychology of consciousness*. San Francisco: Freeman.

Rack, H. (2002). *Reasonable enthusiast: John Wesley and the rise of Methodism* (Rev. ed.). Nashville: Abingdon.

Terrien, S. (1978). *The elusive presence*. New York: Harper & Row. Reprint, Eugene, OR: Wipf & Stock, 2000.

Thomas, R. S. (1983). *Poems of R. S. Thomas*. Fayetteville: University of Arkansas Press.

Tomkins, S. (2003). *John Wesley: A biography*. Grand Rapids: Eerdmans.

Weber, H. (1994). *Jesus and the children*. Loveland, OH: Treehaus Communications.

Wells, S. (2000). In an urban estate. In M. Thiessen. & S. Wells (Eds.), *Faithfulness and fortitude: In conversation with the theological ethics of Stanley Hauerwas*. Edinburgh: T. & T. Clark.

Winnicott, D. W. (1971). *Playing and reality*. New York: Basic Books.

Chapter Three

Historical Perspectives on Children in the Church: Resources for Spiritual Formation and a Theology of Childhood Today

MARCIA J. BUNGE[1]

Many people today are concerned about children nearby and in the wider culture, and wonder: Are they being raised with love and affection? Are they receiving a good education? Are they safe in their homes and schools? Are they being exposed to good role models? Will they have a sense of meaning and purpose in their lives? Will they contribute in positive ways to society? Those in the church also ask: Will our children have faith? Will they live out that faith in service and compassion toward others?

Although these concerns are expressed, many countries fail to meet even the basic needs of children, and children around the world suffer hunger, poverty, abuse and neglect, and depression. In the United States, for example, 16% of children live in poverty and approximately nine million children have no health insurance. Many children attend inadequate and dangerous schools, and solid pre-school programs, such as Head Start, lack full funding. Children are one of the last priorities in decisions about budget cuts on the state and federal level; road maintenance and military budgets take precedence over our children, even though politicians pledge to "leave no child behind" in terms of health care or education.

1. Marcia Bunge is Professor of Theology and Humanities, Christ College, Valparaiso University; editor of *The Child in Christian Thought* (Eerdmans, 2001); co-chair of the "Childhood Studies and Religion Consultation" of the American Academy of Religion; and director of the Childhood Studies, Religion and Ethics Project. She is currently working on a book on the vocation of parenting. Sections of this article appear in her essay, "A more vibrant theology of children" in *Christian Reflection: A Series in Faith and Ethics* (July, 2003). She has spoken widely on the theological understanding of children and has written several articles on the subject.

This chapter includes material previously published in Marcia Bunge, "A More Vibrant Theology of Children," Children, issue 8 of *Christian Reflection: A Series in Faith and Ethics* (Waco, TX: The Center for Christian Ethics at Baylor University, 2003), 11–19, and available online at www.ChristianEthics. ws. I thank the publisher for permission to reprint that material.

Although many in the church care for children and have created beneficial programs for them, the church often lacks a strong commitment to children and treats them as "the least of these." This was witnessed, for example, in the child sexual abuse cases within the Roman Catholic Church. The abuse of children involved is shocking, as well as the ways in which financial concerns, careers of priests, and reputations of bishops or particular congregations came before the safety and needs of children. Yet the church as a whole exhibits a lack of commitment to children in other, more subtle ways. Here are just four examples.

Many congregations offer weak religious education programs and fail to emphasize the importance of parents in faith development. The curricula and lessons of many religious education programs are theologically weak and uninteresting to children, and qualified teachers are not recruited and retained. Furthermore, there is little coordinated effort between the church and the home in terms of a child's spiritual formation. Many parents do not even know what their children are learning in Sunday School, and parents are not given the sense that they are primarily responsible for the faith formation for children.

As a result, many parents within the church are neglecting to speak with their children about moral and spiritual matters, and neglecting to integrate practices that nurture faith into their everyday lives. This claim is confirmed by many of my college students. I have taught primarily at church-related colleges, and although my students are bright and articulate, and while most of them come from Lutheran or Catholic backgrounds, have attended church, and are confessing Christians, they know little about the Bible and their own faith traditions. They also have difficulty speaking about relationships between their beliefs and their everyday lives and concerns. These students also tell me that they rarely, if ever, speak to their parents about any issues of faith, and they regret that they did not even pray together at home.

The experience of my students is confirmed by several recent studies of the Search Institute and Youth and Family Institute. For example, according to one study of 8,000 adolescents whose parents were members of congregations in eleven different Protestant and Catholic denominations, only 10% of these families discussed faith with any degree of regularity, and in 43% of the families, faith was never discussed (Strommen & Hardel, 2000).

In addition, many churches consider reflection on the moral and spiritual formation of children as "beneath" the work of their theologians and as a fitting area of inquiry only for pastoral counselors and religious educators. Consequently, systematic theologians and Christian ethicists say little about children and offer few well-developed teachings on the nature of children or adult obligations to them. Although churches have highly developed teachings on related issues such as abortion, human sexuality, gender relations, and contraception, they do not offer sustained reflection on children or parental and communal obligations toward them. Children also do not play a role in the way that systematic theologians think about central theological themes, such as the nature of faith, language about God, and the task of the church.

A fourth example of a lack of commitment to children is that national churches have not been consistent public advocates for children. Mainline Protestant churches support legislation to protect children's health and safety, yet they hesitate to contribute significantly to public debates about strengthening families. Protestant evangelical and conservative churches, on the other hand, are more vocal in nationwide debates about marriage, divorce, and the family. However, these churches sometimes focus so narrowly on the rights of parents to raise and educate their own children without governmental intrusion that they inadequately address the responsibilities of parents, church, and state to protect, educate, and support all children.

Related to inadequate commitment to children in the church and the wider culture are several simplistic views of children and the ethical obligations to them. Scholars have argued, for example, that in a consumer culture a "market mentality" influences attitudes toward children (Whitmore, 1997). Thus, instead of seeing children as having inherent worth, they are viewed as being commodities, consumers, or even economic burdens. The language of children as commodities is most blatant in discussions of reproductive technology, in which "high quality" donor eggs from an Ivy League female cost more than "regular" eggs. But children are considered commodities in more subtle ways when parents say that they "belong" to them or view them more as expressions of themselves than beings with intrinsic worth. In American culture, children are also certainly understood as major consumers, and corporations market countless goods to children in TV shows, videos, and fast-food restaurants. Adults also treat many children, especially the poor, as burdens and do not supply the resources they need to thrive.

Other scholars note that children tend to be viewed as either all good or all bad. For example, popular magazines or newspapers tend to depict infants and young children as pure and innocent beings to be adored and teenagers as hidden and dark creatures to be feared.

In the Christian tradition, the focus is often on children merely as sinful or as creatures who are "not yet fully human." These kinds of simplistic views diminish children's complexity and intrinsic value, and thereby undermine a commitment and sense of obligation to them. These are just a few examples, but they reflect the regular one-dimensional perspective of children often portrayed.

Encouraging a Broad and Complex View of Children

Much can be done to overcome these simplistic views of children and thereby strengthen the church's commitment to them by retrieving a broader, richer, and more complex picture of children from the Bible and the Christian tradition. Although theologians within the Christian tradition have often expressed narrow and even destructive depictions of children and childhood, there are six central ways of speaking about the nature of children within the Christian tradition that—when critically retrieved and held in tension—can broaden the conception of children and strengthen our commitment to them.

Gifts of God and Sources of Joy

First, the Bible and the Christian tradition often depict children as gifts of God, who ultimately come from God and belong to God, and are sources of joy and pleasure. Many passages in the Bible speak of children as gifts of God or signs of God's blessing. For example, Leah, Jacob's first wife, speaks of her sixth son as a dowry, or wedding gift, presented by God (Gen 30:20). Several biblical passages indicate that parents who receive these precious gifts are being "remembered" by God (Gen 30:22; 1 Sam 1:11, 19) and given "good fortune" (Gen 30:11). To be "fruitful"—have many children—is to receive God's blessing. The Psalmist says children are a "heritage" from the Lord and a "reward" (Ps 127:3).

All children, whether biological or adopted, are "gifts." They are not mere "reproductions;" they will develop in ways that cannot be imagined or controlled. Scientists are still exploring the mysteries surrounding conception; even with great advances in reproductive technology, it is impossible to understand or control all of the factors that allow for conception and a full-term pregnancy. There is wonder and mystery, too, in the process of adoption. Adoptive parents often relate stories of the spiritual journey they underwent to adopt, and they cannot understand or explain the miraculous "fit" they sense between themselves and the new member of their family.

Children are God's gifts not only to their parents, but also to the community. They are members of a community from the start, and they play various and complex roles within it. In addition, they will grow up to be not only sons and daughters but also husbands, wives, friends, neighbors, and citizens. Viewing children as gifts of God to the whole community radically challenges common assumptions of them as "property" of parents or "economic burdens" to the community.

Related to this notion that children are gifts and signs of God's blessing, the Bible and Christian tradition speak of them as sources of joy and pleasure. Here, too, there are many examples. Abraham and Sarah rejoice at the birth of their son, Isaac. Even in his terror and anguish, Jeremiah recalls the story that news of his own birth once made his father, Hilkiah, "very glad" (Jer 20:15). An angel promises Zechariah and Elizabeth that their child will bring them "joy and gladness" (Luke 1:14). In the gospel of John, Jesus says, "When a woman is in labor, she has pain, because her hour has come. But when her child is born, she no longer remembers the anguish because of the joy of having brought a human being into the world" (John 16:20–21).

Some parents in the past wanted children for reasons that are not always emphasized today, such as to perpetuate the nation or to ensure someone would care for them in their old age. Nevertheless, there is a sense today and in the past that one of the great blessings of interactions with children is simply the joy and pleasure they provide.

Sinful Creatures and Moral Agents

Second, the Christian tradition often describes children as sinful creatures and moral agents. "The whole nature" of children, John Calvin (1536/1975) says, is a "seed of sin; thus it cannot be but hateful and abominable to God" (p. 97).[2] Johann Arndt (1979) claims that within children lies hidden "an evil root" of a poisonous tree and "an evil seed of the serpent" (pp. 34–35). Jonathan Edwards (1742/1972) writes that as innocent as even infants appear to be, "if they are out of Christ, they are not so in God's sight, but are young vipers, and are infinitely more hateful than vipers."[3]

This view is based on several biblical texts. For example, Genesis states that every inclination of the human heart is "evil from youth" (Gen 8:21) and, in Proverbs, that folly is "bound up in the heart" of children (Prov 22:15). The Psalms declare that humans are sinful at birth and that "the wicked go astray from the womb; they err from their birth" (Pss 51:5; 58:3). All people are "under the power of sin," the Apostle Paul writes, so "there is no one who is righteous, not even one" (Rom 3:9–10).

On the surface, this way of thinking about children can seem negative and destructive. What good does it do to speak about children, especially infants, as sinful? Is not this view of children hopelessly out of touch with contemporary psychological conceptions of children that emphasize their potential for development and need for loving nurture? Does not this emphasis on sin lead automatically to the harsh and even brutal treatment of children?

Certainly, in some cases, viewing children as sinful has led to mistreatment and even abuse. Recent studies of the religious roots of child abuse (Capps, 1995) show how the view of children as sinful or depraved, particularly in some strains of European and American Protestantism, has led Christians to emphasize that parents need to "break their wills" at a very early age with harsh physical punishment. This kind of emphasis on the depravity of children has led, in some cases, to the physical abuse and even death of children, including infants.

Although this abuse and even milder forms of physical punishment must be rejected, and although viewing children exclusively as sinful often has warped Christian approaches to children, the notion that children are sinful is worth revisiting and

2. Quoted by Pitkin (2001).

3. Quoted by Brekus (2001).

critically retrieving. There are four helpful aspects of the notion that children are sinful that should be considered to avoid narrow and destructive views of children.

First, when stating that children are sinful, this implies that they are born into a "state of sin," into a world that is not what it ought to be. Their parents are not perfectly loving and just; social institutions that support them, such as schools and governments, are not free from corruption; and communities in which they live, no matter how safe, have elements of injustice and violence. All levels of human relationships are corrupted. Furthermore, in addition to the brokenness of relationships and institutions in which they are born, human beings find a certain kind of brokenness within themselves. As humans grow, develop, and become more conscious of their actions, it is easy for them either to be self-centered or to place inordinate importance on the approval of others.

Second, to say children are sinful, also means they carry out "actual sins;" that they are moral agents who sometimes act in ways that are self-centered and harmful to themselves and others. A child has the capacity to accept some degree of responsibility for harmful actions. These "actual sins"—against others or oneself—have their root in the "state of sin" and a failure to center lives on the divine. Instead of being firmly grounded in the "infinite" that is greater than self, life becomes centered on "finite" goals and achievements, such as career success, material gain, physical appearance, or the approval of others. When this happens, it is easy to become excessively focused on self; thus losing the ability to love neighbors as self and to act justly and fairly. This view of "actual sins" of children becomes distorted when theologians mistakenly equate a child's physical and emotional needs or early developmental stages with sin. However, when used cautiously and with attention to psychological insights into child development, it can also strengthen the awareness of a child's growing moral capacities and levels of accountability.

Although it is important to recognize that children are born in a state of sin and are moral beings capable of actual sins against God and others, a third important aspect of the notion that children are sinful—emphasized by many theologians in the tradition—is that infants and young children are not as sinful as adults and therefore need to be treated tenderly. They do not need as much help to love God and neighbor. They have not gotten into bad habits or developed negative thoughts and feelings that reinforce destructive behaviors. The positive way of expressing the same idea is that young people are more easily formed than adults, and it is easier to nurture them and set them on a straight path. This is one reason that most theologians who have emphasized that children are sinful have never concluded that children should be physically punished or treated inhumanely. Rather, they view them as "tender plants" that need gentle and loving guidance and care instead of harsh treatment. For example, A. H. Francke (1702/1885), an Eighteenth Century German Lutheran Pietist, claimed that treating children with "gentleness and sweetness" instead of "strictness and harshness" is the best way "to present to them the love of God in Jesus Christ" and thus "to plant within their hearts a longing for and love of the Word of God," "to awaken faith in them," and "to bend their hearts toward the good" (pp. 162–163).

A fourth and final dimension of viewing children as sinful is that some theologians who have viewed children as sinful also view them as equals, and have thereby shattered barriers of gender, race, and class. For example, Francke responded to the needs of poor children in his community in Halle, Germany, by building an extensive complex of charitable and educational institutions to address their needs. He even allowed gifted poor students and orphans to prepare for a university education alongside children of the upper and middle classes—something unheard of in his time. His notion of original sin provided a kind of positive, egalitarian framework of thought that opened a door to responding to the needs of poor children, seeing them as individuals with gifts and talents to be cultivated, and positively influencing educational reforms in Germany (Bunge, 2001).

Developing Beings Who Need Instruction and Guidance

A third central perspective within church tradition is that children are developing beings who need instruction and guidance. Because children are "on their way" to becoming adults, they need nurture and guidance from adults to help them develop intellectually, morally, and spiritually. They need to learn the basic skills of reading, writing, and thinking critically. They also need to be taught what is right and just and to develop particular virtues and habits that enable them to behave properly, to develop friendships, and to contribute to the common good.

The Bible encourages adults to guide and nurture children. In Genesis, Proverbs, Deuteronomy, and Ephesians, there are many passages about the responsibilities of adults to nurture children. Adults are to "train children in the right way" (Prov 22:6) and bring up children "in the discipline and instruction of the Lord" (Eph 6:4). Parents and caring adults should tell children about God's faithfulness (Isa 38:19) and "the glorious deeds of the Lord" (Ps 78:4b). They are to teach children the words of the law (Deut 11:18–19; 31:12–13), the love of God with the whole heart (Deut 6:5), and doing what is right, just, and fair (Gen 18:19; Prov 2:9).

There are also many examples of theologians who took seriously the education and formation of children. John Chrysostom, in the Fourth Century, wrote sermons on parenting and the duties of parents to nurture the faith of their children (see Guroian, 2001). He viewed the home itself as "a little church" and ranked parental neglect of children's needs and their spiritual formation among the gravest injustices. Luther and Calvin also wrote catechisms and religious education materials for parents to use in the home, and they emphasized the responsibility of parents to guide and to instruct their children in the faith (see Strohl, 2001; Pitkin, 2001). In his popular book,

Christian Nurture, Horace Bushnell (1861/1994), the Nineteenth Century Congregational pastor and scholar, emphasized that parents are the primary agents of a child's spiritual formation, claiming that "Religion never penetrates life until it becomes domestic" (p. 63, also see Bendroth, 2001).

Adults are to attend to the "whole being" of children and provide them with emotional, intellectual, moral, and spiritual guidance. Thus, in addition to providing children with a good education and teaching them skills that are necessary to earn a living and raise a family, adults are to instruct children about the faith and help them develop moral sensibilities, character, and virtue so that they can love God and neighbor with justice and compassion.

Fully Human and Made in the Image of God

Fourth, although children are developing, they are, at the same time, whole and complete human beings made in the image of God. Thus, they are worthy of dignity and respect. The basis of this claim is Gen 1:27, which states that God made humankind in the image of God. Thus, all children, regardless of race, gender, or class, are fully human and worthy of respect. Although children are developing, they are, at the same time, whole and complete human beings.

This theme has often been neglected in the Christian tradition, and church tradition uses language regarding children as "almost human" or "beasts" or "on their way to becoming human." But there also are some theologians who have emphasized the full humanity of children, such as the Twentieth Century Catholic theologian, Karl Rahner. In contrast to those who claim that children are not quite fully human or are beings "on the way" toward humanity, Rahner (1971) asserts that children have value and dignity in their own right and are fully human from the beginning. Thus, he believes that children are to be respected from the beginning of life. They are a "sacred trust" to be nurtured and protected at every stage of their existence (see Hinsdale, 2001).

Models of Faith and Sources of Revelation

Fifth, the New Testament depicts children in striking and even radical ways as moral witnesses, models of faith for adults, sources or vehicles of revelation, and representatives of Jesus. In the gospels Jesus blesses children, embraces them, rebukes those who turn them away, heals them, and even lifts them up as models of faith. He identifies himself with children and equates welcoming a little child in his name to welcoming himself and the One who sent him. "Unless you change and become like children, you will never enter the kingdom of heaven," Jesus warns. "Whoever becomes humble like this child is the greatest in the kingdom of heaven. Whoever welcomes one such child in my name welcomes me" (Matt 18:2–5). He adds, "Let the little children come to me, and do not stop them; for it is to such as these that the kingdom of heaven belongs" (Matt 19:14).[4]

The perspectives on children found in the gospels continue to be as striking today as they were in Jesus' time. In the first century, children occupied a low position in society, abandonment was not a crime, and children were not put forward as models for adults. Even today, adults learning from children is rarely emphasized.

One of the theologians who did emphasize what adults can learn from children was Friederich Schleiermacher, the Nineteenth Century Protestant theologian. He emphasized that adults who want to enter the kingdom of God need to recover a childlike spirit. For him, this childlike spirit has many components that can be learned from children, such as "living fully in the present moment" or being able to forgive others and to be flexible (see DeVries, 2001).

Orphans, Neighbors, and Strangers in Need of Justice and Compassion

Finally, in the sixth place, there are many biblical passages and examples in the tradition that remind us that children are also orphans, neighbors, and strangers who need to be treated with justice and compassion. There are numerous biblical passages that explicitly command us to help widows and orphans—the most vulnerable in society.[5] These and other passages clearly show us that caring for children is part of seeking justice and loving the neighbor.

There are many examples within the Christian tradition of leaders who have taken seriously the situation of poor children. Martin Luther and Phillip Melancthon influenced positive policies and reforms in Germany for universal education that included girls and the poor. Francke, the Eighteenth Century Pietist, attended to poor children in his community and built hospitals, schools, and orphanages to serve them and their families. Like Luther and Melancthon, he also influenced positive educational policies and reforms in Germany so that all children could receive a good education. John Wesley, the founder of Methodism, is another strong example of a theologian who attended to the poor in concrete ways, and he inspired Methodists from his time until today to care for the poor and to establish a number of institutions and initiatives to serve them.

4. Some of the most significant passages in the gospels are Mark 9:33–37; Luke 9:46–48; Matt 18:1–5; Mark 10:13–16; Matt 19:13–15; Luke 18:15–17; Matt 11:25 and 21:14–16. For a discussion of these and other passages in the New Testament, see Gundry-Volf (2001).

5. See, for example, Exod 22:22–24; Deut 10:17–18; and 14:28–29.

Dangers in Retreating from the Broad and Complex Views of Children Found in the Bible and Christian Tradition

Whenever people retreat from this rich, complex, and almost paradoxical view of children found in the Bible and Christian tradition, and focus instead on only one or two aspects of what children are, there is the risk of falling into deficient understandings of children and adult obligations to them, and adults risk treating them in inadequate and harmful ways.

On the one hand, if children are viewed primarily as gifts of God and as models of faith, then they will be enjoyed and adults will be open to learning from them. However, their moral responsibilities may be neglected and the role that parents and other caring adults should play in a child's moral development may be minimized. In the end, adopting a "hands off" approach to parenting or religious education underestimates the responsibilities of both adults and children. The weaknesses of this approach to children are reflected in the past and also today. For example, contemporary Christians who emphasize the innocence or spiritual wisdom of children often fail to articulate the full range of adult responsibilities to children, as well as a child's own growing moral capacities. They also neglect building strong educational programs for children or emphasizing the responsibilities of parents.

On the other hand, if children are perceived primarily as sinful and in need of instruction, the emphasis will be on the role of parents and other caring adults in guiding and instructing children, with recognition of a child's own moral responsibilities. However, one may neglect to learn from children, delight in them, and be open to what God reveals through them. Furthermore, the understanding of parenting and religious education may be restricted to instruction, discipline, and punishment. Focusing on children solely as sinful and in need of instruction also has real dangers, since it has often been easier for Christians who regard children solely as sinful to brutally punish them or "beat the devil" out of them. Even when Christian parenting manuals today emphasize that children are to be treated kindly but continue to speak of children primarily as sinful, they neglect other important lessons of the Bible and church tradition of enjoying children, treating them as fully human, listening to their questions, and learning from them.

In order to avoid these and other dangers, a solid and biblically informed approach to children must take into account all six perspectives on children outlined here. It must incorporate a complex view of the child that holds together the inherent tensions of being a child: being fully human and made in the image of God yet still developing and in need of instruction and guidance; gifts of God and sources of joy yet also capable of selfish and sinful actions; metaphors for immature faith and childish behavior and yet models of faith and sources of revelation.

Implications

If these kinds of inadequate approaches to children in the culture and the church, can be avoided, and if all six biblical perspectives of children can be appropriated and held in tension, commitment to children can be strengthened in several ways.

For example, these six ways of speaking about children could strengthen spiritual formation and religious education programs. If children are seen as gifts of God and sources of joy, then they will be included in worship services as true participants and welcomed as full members of the church. As a result, more joy and laughter will be incorporated into religious education at home and at church. Furthermore, when children are perceived as sinful and in need of instruction, then more substantial religious educational materials and programs for children will be developed in the church. Christian education programs that emphasize the importance of the family in spiritual formation and faith development are more likely to be created. The growing moral capacities and responsibilities of children will be more readily cultivated in many other ways, such as by introducing them to good examples, mentors, and stories of service and compassion; by including children in service projects and teaching them financial responsibility; and helping them discern their vocations and explore how they can best use their gifts and talents to contribute to the common good. Finally, if one truly believes, as Jesus did, that children can teach adults and be moral witnesses, models of faith, and sources of revelation, then one will listen more attentively to children and learn from them; structure religious education programs in ways that honor their questions and insights; and recognize the importance of children in the faith journey and spiritual maturation of parents and other adults.

The six ways of speaking about children could also deepen theological and ethical reflection on children and inform a strong theology of childhood. For example, if children are viewed as gifts of God and developing beings in need of instruction, then children will no longer be seen as "belonging" to their parents, but rather as gifts to them and the whole community. Obligations to all children will be taken more seriously, and theological and ethical reflection on the role of church and state in protecting children and on the responsibilities of parents will be strengthened. Adults will also begin to understand spiritual formation as a serious area of inquiry in all areas of theological and biblical studies—not just pastoral care or religious education. In these and other ways, the church could develop a strong theology of childhood.

The six ways of speaking about children could help renew the church's commitment to serving and protecting all children. If children are viewed as having been made in the image of God, as fully human, and as orphans, neighbors, and strangers in need of compassion and justice, then all children, regardless of age, race, class, or gender, will be treated with more dignity and respect. Abuse or harsh treatment of children will no longer be tolerated. Leaders will warn against equating "discipline" with physical punishment. Furthermore, local and federal legislation will be supported that addresses the needs of all children and families, such as fighting for adequate working wages, parental leave policies, and strong educational programs for all children. Resources will be provided that youngsters need to thrive, including proper nutrition and adequate health care. The needs of poor children will be given attention in the local community and around the world, as people work more diligently to protect and serve all children in need, and as they become stronger and more creative advocates for children.

There are many other implications of a complex and biblically-informed understanding of children. A more vibrant view of children can combat simplistic and destructive conceptions of them and thereby strengthen commitment to them in a number of areas. By appropriating a view of children that incorporates these six central perspectives on children found in the Bible and church tradition, everyone within the church can strengthen their efforts in spiritual formation and religious education. A stronger theology of childhood in the church also will be facilitated, and adults will take up more wholeheartedly and responsibly the Christian call to love and care for all children.

References

Arndt, J. (1979). *True Christianity* (P. Erb, Trans.). New York: Paulist.

Bendroth, M. (2001). Horace Bushnell's *Christian Nurture*. In M. J. Bunge (Ed.), *The child in Christian thought* (pp. 350–364). Grand Rapids: Eerdmans.

Brekus, K. (2001). Children of wrath, children of grace: Jonathan Edwards and the Puritan culture of child rearing. In M. J. Bunge (Ed.), *The child in Christian thought* (pp. 300–328). Grand Rapids: Eerdmans.

Bunge, M. (2001). Education and the child in Eighteenth-Century German Pietism: Perspectives from the work of A. H. Francke. In M. J. Bunge (Ed.), *The child in Christian thought* (pp. 247–278). Grand Rapids: Eerdmans.

Bushnell, H. (1861/1994). *Christian nurture*. Cleveland: Pilgrim.

Capps, D. (1995). *The child's song: The religious abuse of children.* Louisville: Westminster John Knox.

DeVries, D. (2001). "Be converted and become as little children": Friedrich Schleiermacher on the religious significance of childhood. In M. J. Bunge (Ed.), *The child in Christian thought* (pp. 300–328), Grand Rapids: Eerdmans.

Edwards, J. (1742/1972). *Some thoughts concerning the present revival* (C. C. Goen, Ed.). *The Great Awakening*. New Haven: Yale University Press.

Francke, A. H. (1702/1885). *Ordnung und Lehrart, wie selbige in denen zum Waisenhause geh rigen Schulen eingef, hret ist.* In G. Kramer (Ed.), *Pädagogische Schriften* (pp. 162–163). Langensalza: Beyer, 1885.

Gundry-Volf, J. (2001). The least and the greatest: Children in the New Testament. In M. J. Bunge (Ed.), *The child in Christian thought* (pp. 29–60). Grand Rapids: Eerdmans.

Guroian, V. (2001). The ecclesial family: John Chrysostom on parenthood and children. In M. J. Bunge (Ed.), *The child in Christian thought* (pp. 61–77). Grand Rapids: Eerdmans.

Hinsdale, M. A. (2001). "Infinite openness to the Infinite": Karl Rahner's contribution to modern Catholic thought on the child. In M. J. Bunge (Ed.), *The child in Christian thought* (pp. 406–445). Grand Rapids: Eerdmans.

Pitkin, B. (2001). "The Heritage of the Lord": Children In the Theology of John Calvin. In M. J. Bunge (Ed.), *The child in Christian thought* (pp. 160–193). Grand Rapids: Eerdmans.

Rahner, K. (1966/1971). *Gedanken zu einer theologie der Kindheit.* D. Bourke (Trans.). *Schriften zur Theologie, 8,* 313–329. Subsequently released as *Ideas for a Theology of Childhood* (D. Bourke, Trans.). *Theological Investigations, 8,* 33–50.

Strohl, J. (2001). The child in Luther's theology: "For What Purpose Do We Older Folks Exist, Other Than to Care for . . . The Young?" In M. J. Bunge (Ed.), *The child in Christian thought* (pp. 134–159). Grand Rapids: Eerdmans.

Strommen, M. P., & Hardel, R. (2000). *Passing on the faith: A radical new model for youth and family ministry.* Winona, MN: St. Mary's.

Chapter Four

Biblical Perspectives on Developmental Grace for Nurturing Children's Spirituality[1]

KLAUS ISSLER, PH.D.[2]

What does the Bible say about a child's status before God and the child's relationship with God? Borrowing a phrase from the study of future things in theology, might we depict children as "already here, but not yet fully here"? Consider the following prayer from Marcy, aged eight. "Dear friendly God: I think you are like a regular person. I do not believe those people who say you are dead or far away. You probably live on the next street" (Heller, 1987, p. 32). Although very concrete and incomplete, her theological understandings are certainly perceptive. In the first segment of this chapter I present an argument from Scripture, summarized in the following two foundational claims, that clarifies a Christian understanding of this "in between" status of children, summarized in the following two foundational claims.[3]

(a) Children are different from adults and form a special class before God. Regarding matters of salvation and the Kingdom of God, children under the age of moral discernment/accountability are a unique class. Due to God's design for human development, children prior to becoming fully adults are given a measure of divine

---

1. Klaus Issler is Professor of Christian Education and Theology, at Talbot School of Theology, Biola University, primarily teaching in the Ph.D. in Educational Studies program. He earned a B.A. in Philosophy at California State University, Long Beach; an M.A. in Education at the University of California, Riverside; a Th.M. at Dallas Theological Seminary, Dallas, Texas; and a Ph.D. in Education at Michigan State University. Dr. Issler authored *Wasting Time with God: A Christian Spirituality of Friendship with God,* and co-authored *Teaching for Reconciliation: Foundations and Practice of Christian Educational Ministry* and *How We Learn: A Christian Teacher's Guide to Educational Psychology.* He also has published a handful of journal articles and book chapters. In 2004 he received the faculty Award of Excellence in Scholarship at Biola University.

2. Appreciation is expressed to Cathy Stonehouse and Holly Allen for helpful comments on an earlier version of this chapter.

3. See Gundry-Volf (2001) for a thorough study of New Testament passages on children, with various citations of previous work in the field of biblical studies on the topic of children.

grace and blessing, and are regarded as being within some kind of "safe" zone until they arrive at the age of discernment. (b) Children are similar to adults in that they are persons created in the image of God and thus welcomed into experiencing a genuine relationship with God appropriate to their developmental abilities. These two important foundational parameters can offer church leaders, teachers and parents a balanced perspective for ministry with children.

In approaching the practice of children's ministry, two extreme positions must be avoided. On the one hand, it is certainly problematic to avoid *any* sensitivity to children's developmental processes and simply treat young children as little adults who already have fully developed adult capabilities. Here extreme urgency is the tone with teachers and parents, as they are in a hurry to get the child "saved," either by arranging infant baptism the day of birth or by urging the young child to make a profession of faith at the earliest age possible. On the other hand, to assume that genuine faith and discipleship are not possible during childhood is also problematic. Some churches, based on their understanding of the demands of adult discipleship posed by Jesus—such as self-denial, "hating" father and mother—would then deny *any* public and official welcoming of children prior to becoming morally accountable, until reaching their young adult years (e.g., 18 years of age).

After discussing the biblical data related to these issues, I will draw implications for the practice of Christian ministry with children in one important arena, nurturing the faith of children through corporate practices offered both *before* and *after* children reach an age of discernment. I come at this task not only as a seminary professor of Christian education and theology, but also as a parent, now of two young adults and as a former associate pastor who directed children's ministries and taught children of various ages. From infancy I have been nurtured through the teaching and mentoring of various children's ministries along with important post-childhood influences, experiences, and encounters with God. My earliest memory of serving God is as a sixth grader, running the slide projector for Mr. Woodhouse, who led Friday evening children's rallies. I continued active participation in church through my teen and adult years.

Children Are a Special Class in the Kingdom of God

In a world of adult privilege and responsibility, God has set a temporary and gracious "hedge" or boundary around children as a distinct class regarding eternal destiny. Ultimately, two cosmic kingdoms vie for allegiance, the Kingdom of God and the kingdom of Satan (e.g., Matt 12:26, 28; Col 1:13). Accordingly, Scripture contrasts two basic classes of people in various ways (e.g., Ps 1:1–6; Matt 7:13–27; Rom 2:6–11; 1 Cor 2:14–15; Eph 2:1–10; 1 John 3:4–10; Rev 21:6–8): (a) believers or Christians—those within God's Kingdom, who have responded to God's gracious gift of salvation accomplished by the atoning work of our Lord Jesus Christ—and (b) non-believers or not-yet Christians—those still outside of the Kingdom of God. In a previous day, some would have used the popular labels "saved" and "unsaved."

Yet God has also set up a special third category for children who have not yet reached the developmental milestone of an age of moral, adult discernment.[4] This class would also include those who probably may never reach that milestone due to some mental disability. The primary basis for this claim of special status is the concept of a developmental age of moral discernment/ accountability. Despite the centrality of this concept for a theology of children's spirituality, extensive Biblical exposition and grounding of the concept have not always been undertaken. Perhaps the following survey of the key passages will stimulate more in-depth analyses by Bible scholars and theologians to provide the needed grounding to guide a Christian approach in ministering with children.

Theologian Millard Erickson (1996) offers one succinct formulation for how to connect some of the theological dots relevant to the spiritual status of children.

> Until the first conscious or responsible moral action or decision by a person, there is no imputation of the Adamic sin, just as there is no imputation of Christ's righteousness until there is a conscious acceptance of that work. In the case of the [Adamic] sin, there is a period at the beginning of life when one is not really capable of distinguishing between good and evil. This is because there is, in effect, actually no awareness of the concept of rightness and wrongness or of responsibility. This is prior to what we term the "age of accountability." (p. 250)

Thus from God's perspective regarding the plan of salvation, Erickson infers children are in a "safe" zone until they arrive at an age of discernment. Of course, more dots—other theological issues—will need to be connected; a brief discussion of these issues is offered later.

First, some general verses from the New Testament indicating some kind of developmental distinctions between children and adults will be considered (1 Cor 13:9–11 and John 9:20–21). The major grounding for the age of discernment concept will come from two passages in the Hebrew Scriptures. Deuteronomy 1:39 and Isa 7:15–16 (and 8:4) make a clear reference to a child's time in life when there is not yet any knowledge of good or evil (cf. Gen 2:9; 3:22). Furthermore, to complete the biblical study, three additional passages support some kind of distinctive developmental class of children will be examined: Jer 19:4–5; Jonah 4:11; and Neh 8:2. Finally, evidence for the special class of children will be drawn from theological formulations regarding the eternal destiny of infants who die.

---

4. For sake of brevity, I will generally use the term "children" to signify those who have not yet reached the age of discernment.

New Testament Passages

1 Corinthians 13:9–11

In this passage, Paul's general affirmation of developmental differentiation can be discerned:

> For we know in part and we prophesy in part, but when perfection comes, the imperfect disappears. When I was a child, I spoke like a child, I thought like a child, I reasoned like a child; when I became an adult, I put an end to childish ways. (1 Cor 13:9–11, New International Version)

The Apostle Paul draws on the commonplace developmental distinctions between childhood and adulthood as a metaphorical analogy. Paul wishes to highlight the difference between current adult capacity for knowing as compared to the more complete kind of knowing believers will have when Christ returns. Although not a literal reference to child development, Paul's analogy only works if it is accepted that childhood and adulthood are different classes with differing capacities.

John 9:20–21

When Jesus healed a man who had been blind from birth, his parents responded with hesitation to the judgmental questioning of the religious leaders.

> We know that this is our son, and that he was born blind; but we do not know how it is that now he sees, nor do we know who opened his eyes. Ask him; he is *of age*. He will speak for himself. (John 9:20–21, New Revised Standard Version, as in subsequent citations unless otherwise noted, emphasis added)

George Beasley-Murray (1987) explains, "'He is of age' signifies that he has passed his thirteenth birthday, and so attained the age of legal responsibility" (p. 157).

Passages from the Hebrew Scriptures

Deuteronomy 1:39

The book of Deuteronomy is largely made up of Moses' exhortation to the Israelites while camped in Moab. Following forty years of wandering in the Sinai wilderness, they were about to cross over the Jordan River into the Promised Land (what would become Israel). In chapters 1–4, Moses provides an historical review of God's faithfulness to them as well as reminding them of God's judgment on their parents for their disobedience. Chapter 1:26–40 summarizes Israel's critical moment of rebellion at Kadesh Barnea, where they refused to trust God's promise and enter the Land. God confirmed their wish: all of the adults 20 years old and up—with the exception of Joshua and

Caleb—would not enter the Land (Num 14:28–31).[5] They would all die in the desert and then their children, the next generation, would enter the land:

> And as for your little ones, who you thought would become booty, *your children, who today do not yet know right from wrong*, they shall enter there; to them I will give it, and they shall take possession of it. (Deut 1:39, emphasis added; cf. Num 14:31).

J. G. McConville (2002) explains what is of primary concern in this verse: "The next generation is now characterized as not knowing the difference between right and wrong. That is, at this moment ('today'), they are not morally responsible (cf. Is. 7:15) . . . They are, indeed, guiltless with respect to the failure to enter the land at the first command" (p. 72).

Isaiah 7:14–15 and 8:4

In the book of Isaiah, the prophet addresses the southern tribes of Israel, known as "Judah,"[6] around the period of 740 to 700 B.C., in a time when Assyria was the dominant political and military world power in the Ancient Near East (about 900–650 B.C.). One of the key themes in the first half of the book—chapters 1–39—is whether Israel will trust God or Assyria. In chapters 7–8, God challenges King Ahaz to trust in him, and invites Ahaz to ask God for a sign of His trustworthiness (Isa 7:10–11). The king need not fear an attack from the Arameans (or Syrians; capital in Damascus) or the ten tribes of Israel (or Ephraim; capital in Samaria; Isa 7:1–9); nor should he rely on a politicial alliance with Assyria. But Ahaz declines, claiming he does not want to "test the Lord" (Isa 7:12), something forbidden in the Law (Num 14:22; Deut 6:16). Yet, as John Oswalt (2003) explains, "the testing referred to in the Torah is *not* believing God's promises!" (p.139, emphasis added). In spite of Ahaz's unbelief, God will give a sign; a child to be born to Isaiah.

> He [the predicted son, child of Isaiah] shall eat curds and honey by the time he *knows how to refuse the evil and choose the good*. For before the child *knows how to refuse the evil and choose the good*, the land before whose two kings you are in dread will be deserted. (Isa 7:15–16, emphasis added)

To understand the passage, first, a clarification of the historical context is offered and then an explanation of the particular phrases relevant to the concept of an age of discernment. John Oswalt (2003) pieces together the disparate details in the following manner. Isaiah the prophet, already had a son Shear-jashub—whose name meant "a remnant shall return," as mentioned in Isa 7:3—by his first wife. Apparently she has

---

5. This age marker, 20 years old, would set a very generous upper limit for arriving at the age of adult moral discernment and responsibility.

6. "Judah" represented the two southern tribes of Israel, Judah and Benjamin. The remaining ten tribes of the north were called "Israel," "Ephraim," or sometimes "Jacob."

since died, making the prophet a single parent. As a widower, Isaiah now predicts that he, Isaiah, will father another child with an unmarried woman—"the prophetess" in 8:3—whom he will be marrying in the near future. In Isa 8:1–3 that prophecy is fulfilled. Following their marriage and conception of the child, this boy was finally born and given the name, Maher-shalal-hash-baz (Isa 8:1, 3).

Regarding the meaning of the words "good and evil" in Isa 7:15–16, Oswalt (2003) offers this commentary.

> Before this child who is shortly to be conceived is able to "reject the wrong and choose the right" (7:15–16), Syria and Israel will be destroyed. This phrase most likely refers to the age of accountability, the time when, in later parlance, a boy became a 'son of the commandment' [cf. Gen 2:17]. Although this is now considered to occur at age twelve, there is no precise statement of the age in the Bible. (p. 111)

Oswalt (1986) also provides more detail about the timing of the conquest for both neighboring nations. If the prophecy was given in 735 BC, and the child was born in 734 BC, before the child could clearly speak (cf. 8:4), destruction and plunder would occur. Damascus was destroyed in 732 BC, and both Rezin, king of Aram (Syria), and Pekah king of Israel died about that time. Furthermore, much of Israel's territory was reduced to that of the tribes of Ephraim and Manasseh. Yet Israel's own destruction took place later, as Oswalt explains.

> But it is also true that it was not until some *twelve or thirteen years* later that Samaria [i.e., Israel] was destroyed and Israel ceased to exist. On balance, given the evident connection of the phrase with [the age of] moral discernment at several points, and given the lack of clear evidence to the contrary, the best interpretation seems to be that by the time the child has reached *an age of official accountability*, both of the threatening powers will have ceased to exist. (p. 214, emphasis added)

Jeremiah 19:4–5

As the prophet denounces the sins of the people, Jeremiah connects the word "the innocent" (verse 4) with "children" (verse 5):

> Because the people have forsaken me, and have profaned this place by making offerings in it to other gods whom neither they nor their ancestors nor the kings of Judah have known; and because they have filled this place with the blood of *the innocent,* and gone on building the high places of Baal to burn their *children* in the fire as burnt offerings to Baal, which I did not command or decree, nor did it enter my mind. (Jer 19:4–5, emphasis added)[7]

---

7. Also see Thompson (1980), p. 449; F. Huey (1993), p. 187; and Lundbom (1999), p. 839.

Douglas R. Jones (1992) explains,

> The shedding of innocent blood, in the Old Testament, refers usually to the miscarriage of justice, and particularly to the wrongful application of the law of vengeance . . . But here the use of the plural shows that the familiar language is applied to the innocents who were victims of the child sacrifice practiced in Hinnom (see 7:31); 'this place' is therefore Hinnom. (p. 266)

Jonah 4:11

In the last verse of the book of Jonah, God highlights his mercy to the Gentile people of the Assyrian capital in Nineveh, particularly their children who did not yet know "their right hand from their left."

> And should I not be concerned about Nineveh, that great city, in which there are more than a hundred and twenty thousand persons who do not know their right hand from their left, and also many animals? (Jonah 4:11)

Jewish commentator Uriel Simon (1999) explains that "their right hand from their left" refers "specifically to children, that is, to those Ninevites who lack understanding on the ethico-religious plane" (p. 47).[8]

Nehemiah 8:2

When the postexilic Israelite community had finishing building the wall, they requested Ezra the priest and scribe to read the Law in a public worship time. On the first day of the seventh month, accordingly, the priest Ezra brought the law before the assembly, both men and women and *all* who *could* hear with understanding (Neh 4:2, emphasis added). Children who could understand also participated, as Charles Fensham (1982) clarifies: "We take it, however, in the sequence men, women, and all who could understand, as referring to children who have reached the stage of understanding."

In summary, Deut 1:39 and Isa 7:15–16, with corroboration from Jer 14:9–10; Jonah 4:11; and Neh 8:2, provide clear guidance from the Bible that children prior to a certain age of discernment do not yet have a fully conscious knowledge of the difference between good and evil. Based on Isa 7:15–16, it is possible that this age of discernment comes around 12 or 13 years of age.

---

8. Simon (1999) explains, "'their right hand from their left.' That is, between good and evil . . . Normally, in biblical Hebrew, the collective noun *'adam* (rendered above as 'persons') refers to an entire human population—especially when paired with the word 'beast' (e. g., Josh 11:14; Jer 32:43). In the present case, however, context demands that the word refers only to a part of the whole population. Here we must evidently gloss [explain, interpret] it—following Rashi, Samuel ben Meir (on Num 23:9), Ibn Ezra, David Kimhi, and others—as referring specifically to children, that is, to those Ninevites who lack understanding on the ethico-religious plane" (pp. 46–47). Simon then makes a reference to the other passages discussed earlier, Deut 1:39 and Isa 7:15–16.

Theological Affirmations of Developmental Distinctions

Beyond the biblical data, various theologians throughout church history have recognized developmental distinctions as Barbara Pitkin (2001) explains, "Like many of [Calvin's] contemporaries [e.g., Luther] and classical and medieval predecessors [e.g., Aquinas], Calvin divides childhood into three stages, each lasting approximately seven years [i.e., to age seven, to age fourteen, and to age twenty-one]" (p. 164).

Furthermore, almost all Christian theologians who have considered the issue of the eternal destiny of infants who have died have recognized the distinctive class of children by a making special case for children going to heaven *without* having made a conscious response to God's offer of salvation in Christ. Factors to be considered in developing a theological statement on the matter include the following:

1. All humans have been created in the image of God (e.g., Gen 1:26–27; Ps 8; Jas 3:9).

2. Since the Fall, all humans come into this world under God's judgment and wrath as being in sin, (i.e., "original sin;" e.g., Rom 3:23; 5:12; 6:23; Eph 2:1–3) and all are in need of God's gracious salvation (e.g., John 3:3–8).

3. Only Jesus Christ's substitutionary atoning death propitiates God's wrath against all sin and makes reconciliation with God possible (e.g., Rom 3:22–26; 5:6–11; Acts 4:12; Col 2:13–4).

4. As a part of receiving God's gracious offer of salvation, one must consciously and responsibly believe, placing one's faith and reliance—involving repentance—in Jesus Christ (e.g., Luke 24:46–47; John 1:12; 3:16; Rom 10:9–10). For the final issue, the term "responsibly" implies some measure of moral awareness and competence to recognize one's own sinful condition, need for God's grace and conscious reception of God's gracious offer.

5. Each one must give an account to God of their life on earth (Rom 14:12).

The task, then, is to synthesize and integrate these foundational theological teachings with the biblical teaching of a child's special status before God. Will a dying infant spend eternity with God in heaven? Three *logical* options are possible: (a) All children who die go to heaven, (b) some children who die, go to heaven, and (c) no children who die go to heaven. Table 4.1 surveys the diverse views offered within Christianity—including Protestant and Roman Catholic, liberal and conservative—culled primarily from helpful summaries by R. A. Webb (1907), John Sanders (1992), Millard Erickson (1996), and Timothy Sisemore (2000), and organized according to the first two categories of "a" and "b" (I know of no published claim for option "c"). Notice that each view, except for the simplest view of physical baptism (view 5a), in some way recognizes that children are a unique case, distinct from adults, by stipulating some special condition in the matter of dying infants.

In summary, there is biblical support for the claim that children are a class distinct from adults in relation to moral discernment, a concept also recognized by theologians in their treatment of the status of infants who die. Both church and society have affirmed certain boundaries between childhood and adulthood, as Marlin Jeschke (1983) clarifies,

> Pedobaptist churches recognize [the age of discernment] in the practice of confirmation. Judaism has its 'bar mitzvah,' or 'bas mitzvah,' when a child becomes a 'son' or 'daughter' of the law [at age 13]. Secular society makes a definite distinction between juveniles and adults in courts of law. It establishes a minimum age for marriage. It protects children through labor laws. (p. 112)[9]

Table 4.1: Theological Evidence: Views of Dying Infants Going to Heaven

Option A: *All* Children Who Die Go to Heaven.

1. *Universalism*: The fatherhood of God brings universal salvation regardless of moral condition of all infants. [Liberal]

2. *Innocence*: All infants are innocent. Variations on this theme: (a) Infants have no original sin, thus no need for personal salvation. [Pelagius] (b) God's intervening (prevenient) grace applies the benefits of Christ's atonement to all, including infants, thus nullifying the guilt of infants' original sin. [John Wesley] (c) God's intervening grace applies the benefits of Christ's atonement to all infants, thus nullifying the guilt of infants' original sin [Charles Hodge]

3. *Election*: (a) All dying infants have been elected by God for salvation. Other elect infants and all non-elect infants will grow up beyond the age of accountability and will consciously sin affirming their sinful nature. [C. H. Spurgeon] (b) (Combining Views #2c and #3a) All dying elect infants are "innocent" since they have not ratified their Adamic nature, not having reached the age of accountability. [M. Erickson, many Arminians]

Option B: *Some* Children Who Die Will Go to Heaven.

4. *Covenantal/Believing Parent*: (a) All dying infants from families with at least one believing parent (1 Cor 7:14) have been elected by God for salvation (whereas other elect infants will grow to maturity). [Richard Baxter, Synod of Dordt] (b) Primarily all dying infants from families with at least one believing parent have been elected, but God may elect others outside the covenant. [Westminster Confession]

---

9. It appears that the classic framework of periods of seven years continues to under gird the American criminal justice system, as noted by Bob Pugsley, Professor of Southwestern Law School. "Children under 7 are not responsible for their actions under the law. Children 7–14 are usually not responsible. If prosecutors can prove the young offender knew what he or she was doing, they can charge the child with a crime. Children over 14 should know what they are doing. They will be charged unless they are found to be insane" (Pepper, Rams & Walker, 2004, p. A25).

5. *Sacramental*: (a) Only dying infants who have been physically baptized will go to heaven. The Church's baptism of infants is the necessary means of regeneration to be in right standing with God. [Augustine; Roman Catholic: Council of Trent; Lutheran Augsburg Confession] (b) If parents had wanted their dying child to be baptized (labeled as a "baptism of desire or intention"), this would be counted as a baptism and thus the child would go to heaven. [Martin Luther, many Lutherans, many Roman Catholics] (c) The eternal destiny of dying unbaptized infants is neither heaven nor hell but *limbus infantum* (children's limbo), a special place of neither joy nor punishment. [former medieval Catholic view]

6. *Responsible Consent*: (a) God will assign the appropriate place of destiny for the dying infant in light of God's knowledge of what the infant would have decided had the infant grown to maturity. [Middle Knowledge view] (b) After death—during the intermediate state—infants will grow to their age of accountability and will then be capable of receiving or rejecting God's gracious offer of salvation. [John Sanders, Greg Boyd]

7. *Cautious/Agnostic*: One really does not know how or why; the matter is solely in God's hands. God will assign the appropriate place of destiny for the dying infant in light of his bountiful love, just wisdom, and gracious mercy.

Of course the exact timing of the arrival of the age of discernment will vary among children due to differing individual and environmental factors—such as family life, degree of psychological health, educational opportunities—yet a very general or average demarcation around age 13 might be affirmed, occurring about the same time as the onset of puberty with its evident physical manifestations. Prior to this milestone event, whenever it is reached by each individual, a child does not yet have sufficient moral cognitive, emotional, and social development to make responsible decisions in matters of good and evil, particularly in relation to the child's accountability before God. There is a measure of developmental grace. Yet on the human plane, children are increasingly morally accountable for their words and actions.

Children Are Blessed by God and Can Relate with God

Although children do not have full adult capabilities, nonetheless Scripture supplies sufficient evidence that children are blessed by God's favor and that children have the capacity to have a relationship with God. The Hebrew Scriptures support the idea that God has a special place in His heart for orphans (Deut 10:18; Ps 10:14; Hos 14:3; also Jas 1:27). From cases of children, both Jewish and non-Jewish, a child can (a) be consecrated by God from the womb (e.g., Samson, Judg 13:5; Isaiah, Isa 49:1; Jeremiah, Jer 1:5; John the Baptist, Luke 1:15); (b) hear God speaking (e.g., Samuel, 1 Sam 3:1–14), (c) receive God's intervention by healing (daughter of a Gentile woman, Matt 15:21–28) and being raised from the dead (son of a Gentile widow, 1 Kgs 17:8–14; cf.

Luke 4:26), and (d) become a king in God's theocratic economy for Israel (e.g., Joash at age seven, 2 Chr 24:1–2). Also 2 Sam 12:23 is a classic passage on the status of a dying infant. When the child resulting from King David's adulterous union with Bathsheba died, David stopped fasting and praying for the child. He offered this reason, "But now he has died; why should I fast? Can I bring him back again? *I will go to him*, but he will not return to me" (2 Sam 2:23, emphasis added). The implication is that David, in the after life, will see his child again.

In the Gospels, the classic passage indicating children's status within the Kingdom of God and God's blessing on children is when Jesus permitted the children to come to him (Mark 10:14, 16; parallel Matt 19:13–15; Luke 18:15–17):

> But when Jesus saw this, He was indignant and said to them [his disciples], "Permit the children to come to Me; do not hinder them; *for the kingdom of God belongs to such as these . . .*" And He took them in His arms and began *blessing* them, laying His hands upon them. (Mark 10:14, New American Standard Version, emphasis added)

New Testament scholars offer the following comment on the phrase, "the kingdom of God belongs to such as these."

1. "This text cannot simply refer to those adults who are childlike to the exclusion of actual young children being brought to Jesus. It can refer to both" (Witherington, 2001, p. 279; on Mark 10:14.

2. "Jesus replies by stating that the kingdom belongs to children and people like them" (Marshall, 1978, p. 681; on Luke 18:16).

3. "Even little children find their place in [the kingdom]. Little children indeed intrinsically have an affinity for the kingdom. They too in their way are members of the community of faith" (Hagner, 1995, p. 553 on Matt 19:13–15).

4. "A more emphatic statement of children's reception into the reign of God by Jesus could hardly be made" (Gundry-Volf, 2001, p. 38).[10]

Finally, a reference to Jesus' own childhood must be included as an indication for the child's capability to relate with God and be blessed by God. Although Jesus Christ is fully God, due to the incarnation, he also became and is fully human, being born as child, and experiencing all the phases of childhood development according to God's design, as recorded in two verses that introduce and conclude Jesus' twelve-year old visit to the temple:

---

10. Gundry-Volf (2001) understands Jesus' statement within Paul's more restrictive stance from 1 Cor 7:14: "Children *qua children* in this sense [their vulnerability and powerlessness]–referring presumably to children within the covenant community—are the *intended* recipients of the reign of God" (p. 38).

1. "The child grew and became strong, filled with wisdom; and the favor of God was upon him" (Luke 2:40, New Revised Standard Version).

2. "And Jesus increased in wisdom and in years, and in divine and human favor" (Luke 2:52).

Furthermore, Jesus walked in the power of the Holy Spirit as an adult (e.g., Luke 4:1, 16; Acts 10:38). Was this solely an adult lifestyle and pattern? In his comment on Luke 2:47, when the child Jesus amazed the religious teachers in the temple, Earle Ellis (1974) explains that the use of the term "amazed" was

> intended not just as a tribute to Jesus' intelligence but as a witness to his relationship to God. Luke often uses the word to express the reaction to the present working of the divine power of the coming age. The same 'Holy Spirit' power, later to be manifested in Jesus' ministry, *even now is at work*. Jesus interprets the Scripture not from the knowledge gained in rabbinic training but from the 'wisdom' given by God. (p. 86. emphasis added)

Following the example of Jesus is not only an ideal for adults, but also for children. Jesus' own childhood demonstrates the possibility and capability for children to be blessed by God and to be guided by the Spirit.[11]

From birth on—and perhaps in the womb as well—children are receptive to God's overtures and interventions in their lives. Teachers and leaders can help *all* children seek God and enter into a growing relationship with him.

Practical Implications

The main purpose of this chapter has been to develop a biblical argument for two main points: (a) the special case of the child in God's program, in light of developmental factors, and (b) that a child is blessed by God and capable of relating with God. But these truths do not in themselves offer complete guidance. In the remaining section, implications are offered to illustrate the process of transferring these biblical claims into practical means for nurturing the faith of children. If, as most theologians hold, *dying* infants are welcomed by God, would it not be wise, then, to offer the *living* children in the midst of the church, a similar special welcome during their days prior to the age of discernment?

The church that welcomes children will offer opportunities for instruction and commitment-making *before* and *after* children reach the age of discernment/ accountability. With a continuing ministry emphasis on both sides of this

11. In a previous article I claimed, "If Jesus as a child could walk so closely with the Spirit, it opens up new possibilities for children, if parents and teachers can show them how to walk with the Spirit." Issler (2000, p. 12, footnote 21). For further exploration of Jesus and the Holy Spirit in childhood, see Hawthorne (1991) and Issler (2003); on the topic of Christian spirituality, see Issler (2001).

developmental milestone, these children-turned-adults can continue to affirm their relationship with God—or not affirm it, if that is their choice. Influencing children's spirituality and character formation cannot wait until they are older. They are learning creatures from day one of life. Yet the appropriate time to discern whether the child will *continue in discipleship* is in adulthood, not in childhood. Thus, until the arrival of adulthood, the appropriate posture for the church is to follow the example of Jesus by *welcoming* children as members of the Kingdom of God and nurturing their faith in God as much as possible.[12]

Furthermore, both children and adults will experience degrees of these twin tensions: (a) love from God and (b) estrangement from God. There is no need to emphasize one to the neglect of the other. Adult believers, although within the family of God, are both saint and sinner this side of heaven, as Luther claimed. One can affirm this tension in teaching ministry with children as well, as appropriate to their developmental capacities, that God loves them and desires to relate with them, and that as well, they are estranged from God. Teachers and parents can share from their own journey this continuing tension in their lives.

The following practical suggestions are offered to stimulate further discussion. Proposals address the path of children from birth until they reach the young adult age of 21, with a sensitivity to distinctive church traditions regarding timing of baptism—infant baptism, adult or believer's baptism, or child baptism.

Ceremonies and Practices that Can Nurture Children's Faith

When children's ministry leaders focus *solely* on one age-level—infant, toddler, pre-school, early or later elementary—the spiritual nurture of children is limited. Children are best served when leaders chart an integrated path for the "developmental career" in all related ministry programs of the child from birth through entering the young adult years. Rather than leave these independent age-level units of instruction detached as a handful of pearls, why not string the pearls together for a more holistic approach? Table 4.2 proposes one framework, to serve as an illustration for church leaders to construct and develop a contextualized model fitting their respective tradition.[13]

12. Offering comfort to grieving parents is one prod to arrive at some theological view on this difficult issue. Yet one must also be cautious regarding the logical implications of a particular view, if taken to an extreme, as represented in the "infanticide problem." This particular issue was brought to national prominence in the case of mother Andrea Yates who drowned her five children in the bathtub. Why? "She told a jail psychiatrist that her bad mothering had made the kids 'not righteous,' and, as a result, they would 'perish in the fires of hell.' If she killed them while they were young, God would show mercy on their soul." (Gesalman, 2002, p. 8). Both pastoral sensitivity and thoughtful theological deliberation are required on this complex and very personal issue.

13. The idea of developing these corporate practices originally came from Sparkman (1983) and a previous version appeared in Issler and Habermas (1994, p. 150).

Table 4.2: Nurturing Children's Faith Through Corporate 'Family' Classes and Ceremonies			
A. Rites of Passage for Child/Teen	B. Public Ceremony: Progressively Welcoming Child into God's Household of Faith	C. Individual Readiness & Suggested Age Ranges	D. Educational Preparation *Prior to* Public Ceremony
1. Church Family **Reception**	*[1] Infant Baptism or [2,3] Parent-Child Dedication (as child grows, participates in main worship meeting as appropriate)	Part 1: Following birth, during child's first year	Orientation class for parents, grandparent, sponsors, godparents
	[1,2,3] White carnation placed at front of auditorium, symbolizing growing sense of new birth (children's sermons in main worship as one way to welcome children)	Part 2: Ages 5–13 years; as acquiring moral accountability: making a personal profession of faith; determined on an individual basis	Pastoral interview with child and parent(s) to assess personal commitment to Jesus Christ
2. Church Family **Presentation**	[1,2] First Communion or [3] Child Baptism & Communion (now eligible to use gifts to serve)	Ages 5–13 years; as acquiring moral accountability; during elementary school period; determined on an individual basis	Orientation class for child and parent(s) (4–8 sessions; weekend retreat)
3. Church Family **Re-Affirmation**	[1,3] Public Affirmation of Faith or [2] Adult Baptism (increasing use of gifts to serve)	Ages 13–18 years, with full onset of moral accountability; determined on an individual basis	Mentoring and doctrine catechism classes for teen (1–2 years prior to ceremony; [see Osmer])
4. Church Family **Vocational Commissioning**	[1,2,3] Vocational Commissioning with laying on of hands (now eligible to serve in a church leadership capacity)	Age 18 years, with full-time employment, at start of career; determined on an individual basis (perhaps another at age 30 years)	Orientation class on vocation

*Numbers identify specific church traditions that practice [1] infant baptism, [2] adult baptism, or [3] child baptism

As a minimum, four factors should be considered in developing such a model: (a) working out an appropriate scheme of age ranges fitting knowledge of child development and church history (column "C") by designating respective "phases" or rites of passage that can serve as milestones and indicators of movement for children/teens through their "developmental career" (column "A"), (b) integrating and welcoming children's ministry into the adult ministry through distinctive public ceremonies that take place during the main worship meeting, appropriate to each church tradition (numbers in square brackets in column "B" indicate the three main traditions for baptism), (c) providing or requiring supportive educational sessions/classes to orient and prepare participants for this particular milestone in the child's/teen's development (column "D"), and (d) progressively welcoming children, by increasing the child's/teen's participation in the main church ministry over the years (suggestions in parentheses in Column "B").

Participation in Holy Communion is a powerful symbol of welcome for children as well as adults. In traditions that practice adult baptism, how might children be welcomed at the Lord's Table? Consideration might be given to permit the child's participation in Communion once an initial profession of faith has been made and assessed. Smith (2001) also suggests,

> In the traditions that baptize adult believers, an open approach to the Table would acknowledge that children are members of the covenant community even though they cannot yet assume adult responsibility for their lives, evidenced in baptism. For now they come to the Table under the spiritual authority and identity of their parents. And they are welcome. (p. 217)

In summary, church leaders should design appropriate official and contextual means to welcome children as Jesus did. In this way, as argued earlier, they honor the example and teaching of Jesus, and welcome and bless children because "the kingdom of God belongs to such *as these* [i.e., includes]" (Mark 10:14), as argued earlier. Otherwise, adults emulate the disciples and marginalize children, keeping them invisible until they become adults. By this exclusionary practice, children are treated as second-class citizens of the Kingdom, or, worse, as "outsiders" altogether and as a result the church risks losing them to the world. Children belong to a distinctive class in God's program; they are not little adults, but they are blessed by God and able to relate with God.

A Practice for Teens to Re-Affirm Their Faith

The practice of Confirmation has a long history in liturgical traditions that hold to infant baptism. In his book-length treatment of the history of the practice, Richard Osmer (1996), Professor of Christian Education at Princeton Seminary, proposes a few modifications to re-invigorate this important developmental milestone in which a teen, now with increasing adult capacities of reasoning and understanding, can re-affirm his or her faith. One critical component is emphasizing the individual developmental readiness of a young teen to make a public re-affirmation of his or her faith, rather than just making it a routine group phenomenon that occurs for all at the same age.

> If the church is to grant a more important place to personal appropriation of faith for theological reasons, then it must be willing to allow the element of personal choice to be real. . . . The church cannot claim to support a genuinely free and personal profession of faith as long as it continues a programmatic approach to confirmation in which young people automatically enter this program when they reach a certain age. . . . The church would do well to become clear about its theological commitments and then shape its practice accordingly. (Osmer, 1996, p. 196)

Although this historic practice has *not* been a part of my own faith tradition, as a Christian educator I see the value of developing this rite of passage of "Reaffirmation" as an important means for all Christian churches to help sustain and nurture the faith of teens who have passed to the age of discernment.

Conclusion

Nurturing the faith of children and teens is a complex theological and practical endeavor, however, only a few theological and practical issues could be addressed here.[14] The biblical instructions are clear. Welcome and bless children as Jesus did, since they are a unique developmental class in God's Kingdom program, distinct from adults. God has provided children a measure of developmental grace, before they become adults, to grow in their faith and experience God. Leaders, teachers, and parents will need to learn how to be sensitive to and respect this divine design and come alongside these little ones with love and grace, and without hurrying them or making judgments. Adults must avoid marginalization of youngsters. Childhood is a special season to nurture faith in ways appropriate to developmental capacities.[15] Frankie's prayer represents an ideal for children, an outcome that those working with children would love to see deeply acquired by these special ones.

14. Many theological issues remain to be addressed, such as how the atonement of Christ is applied to an infant who dies and has no conscious faith at that time; why God permits the demonization of innocent children (e.g., Mark 9:14); why innocent children have died for the sins of their parents (e.g., Jewish: Korah's rebellion, Num 16:27–33; Gentile nations: Deut 2:33–34); discerning the indwelling and filling of the Spirit in young children; as well as further historical study of the concept of an age of accountability.

15. Work on this project was initially begun in the late 1980s. Resources on biblical theological discussions related to children that I have found helpful include Erickson (1996), Jeschke (1983), Osmer (1996), Smith (2001, ch. 9), Cragoe (1987), Ingle (1970), Nash (1999), Sisemore (2000), Sparkman (1983), Strange (1996), Volf-Gundry (2001), Waggoner (1999), Webb (1907), Warfield (1897), and Zuck (1996).

Jesus, I feel very near to you. I feel like you are beside me all the time. Please be with me on Thursday. I am running in a 3-mile race then. I will need all the speed in the world. If you are not busy with other things, maybe you could be at the starting line, the finish line, and everywhere in between. Frankie [age 11] (Heller, 1987, p. 22).

References

Beasley-Murray, G. R. (1987). *John*. Word Biblical Commentary 36. Waco, TX: Word.

Cragoe, T. H. (1987). An examination of the issue of infant salvation. *Dissertation Abstracts International, 48*(10), 2656. (UMI No. 8729700).

Ellis, E. E. (1974). *The Gospel of Luke*. Greenwood, SC: Attic.

Erickson, M. (1996). *How shall they be saved?* Grand Rapids: Baker.

Fensham, F. C. (1982). *The Books of Ezra and Nehemiah*. Grand Rapids: Eerdmans.

Gesalman, A. B. (2002, March 18). Examining a spiritual leader's influence. *Newsweek 139*, 8.

Gundry-Volf, J. (2001). "The least and the greatest: Children in the New Testament." In M. J. Bunge (Ed.), *The child in Christian thought* (pp. 29–60). Grand Rapids: Eerdmans.

Hagner, D. A. (1995). *Matthew 14–28*. Word Biblical Commentary 33B. Dallas: Word.

Hawthorne, G. F. (1991). *The presence and the power: The significance of the Holy Spirit in the life and ministry of Jesus*. Dallas: Word.

Heller, D. (1987). *Dear God: Children's letters to God*. New York: Doubleday.

Ingle, C. (Ed.). (1970). *Children and conversion*. Nashville: Broadman.

Issler, K. (2000). The spiritual formation of Jesus: The significance of the Holy Spirit in the life of Jesus. *Christian Education Journal, 4*(2), 5–24.

Issler, K. (2001). *Wasting time with God: A Christian spirituality of friendship with God*. Downers Grove, IL: InterVarsity.

Issler, K. (2003). *An exemplar incarnation model: A basis for Jesus as our genuine example*. Paper presented at the Evangelical Theological Society annual meeting, Atlanta.

Issler, K., & Habermas, R. (1994). *How we learn: A Christian teacher's guide to educational psychology*. Reprint, Eugene, OR: Wipf & Stock, 2002.

Jeschke, M. (1983). *Believer's baptism for children of the church*. Scottdale, PA: Herald.

Jones, D. R. (1992). *Jeremiah*. Grand Rapids: Eerdmans.

Lundbom, J. R. (1999). *Jeremiah 1–20*. Anchor Bible 21A. New York: Doubleday.

Marshall, I. H. (1978). *Commentary on Luke*. New International Greek Testament Commenty. Grand Rapids: Eerdmans.

McConville, J. G. (2002). *Deuteronomy*. Apollos Old Testament Commentary. Dowers Grove, IL: InterVarsity.

Nash, R. H. (1999). *When a baby dies: Answers to comfort grieving parents*. Grand Rapids: Zondervan.

Osmer, R. (1996). *Confirmation: Presbyterian practices in ecumenical perspective*. Louisville: Geneva.

Oswalt, J. (1986). *The book of Isaiah chapters 1–39*. Grand Rapids: Eerdmans.

Oswalt, J. (2003). *Isaiah*. Grand Rapids: Zondervan.

Pepper, A., Rams, B. & Walker, T. (2004, February 15). Truth and consequences. *The Orange County Register*, A25.

Pitkin, B. (2001). "The heritage of the Lord": Children in the theology of John Calvin. In M. J. Bunge (Ed.), *The child in Christian thought* (pp. 160–193). Grand Rapids: Eerdmans.

Sanders, J. (1992). *No other name: An investigation into the density of the unevangelized*. Grand Rapids: Eerdmans.

Simon, U. (1999). *Jonah*. JPS Bible Commentary. Philadelphia: Jewish Publication Society.

Sisemore, T. (2000). *Of such is the kingdom of God: Nurturing children in light of Scripture*. Ross-shire, UK: Christian Focus.

Smith, G. T. (2001). *Beginning well: Christian conversion and authentic transformation*. Downers Grove, IL: InterVarsity.

Sparkman, G. T. (1983). *The salvation and nurture of the child: The story of Emma*. Valley Forge, PA: Judson.

Thompson, J. A. (1980). *The book of Jeremiah*. New International Commentary on the Old Testament. Grand Rapids: Eerdmans.

Waggoner, E. (1999). Baptist approaches to the question of infant salvation. *Dissertation Abstracts International, 61*(01), 656 (UMI No. 9961391).

Warfield, B. B. (1897). *Two studies in the history of doctrine*. New York: Christian Literature.

Webb, R. A. (1907). *The theology of infant salvation*. Richmond, VA: Presbyterian Committee of Publishers.

Witherington, B., III. (2001). *The Gosepl of Mark*. Grand Rapids: Eerdmans.

Zuck, R. (1996). *Precious in his sight: Childhood and children in the Bible*. Grand Rapids: Baker.

Chapter Five

Unless You Become as One of These:
Biblical Perspectives on Children's Spirituality

SHELLEY CAMPAGNOLA[1]

A seven-year-old boy had finished painting his walking stick earlier that day. At the time, he didn't seem to give any thought to the colors he had used—black, red, green, and deep maroon—which he called purple; it was just a fun activity. But as he sat at the picnic table to eat his lunch with his mom, he piped up, "Mom, do you know what the colors on my walking stick mean?" Humoring her son, not expecting the answer that was about to come, the mom answered "No, tell me what they mean." The little boy, with a gentle but decisive manner, said, "Black is for sin that makes our hearts dark, red is for Jesus' blood shed on the cross to clean our hearts, green is for the new life he gives us, and purple is for the wine to remember him at communion." In both surprise and admiration the mom asked, "Who taught you that son?" "No one," he replied. "I just figured that's what the colors should mean."

I tell you the truth, unless you change and become like little children, you will never enter the kingdom of heaven. (Matt 18:3, New International Version)

The scene opens with the disciples coming to Jesus and asking, "Who is the greatest in the kingdom of heaven?" The other gospel writers provide greater insight into the discussion. What the disciples really wanted to know was *who among them* would be the greatest in heaven? In response, Jesus called a little child, a *paidion*, to come and stand in their midst. "I tell you the truth, unless you change and become like little children, you will never enter the kingdom of heaven." The contemporary church has

---

1. Shelley Campagnola has a business degree from the University of Guelph and an M.T.S. degree from Heritage Theological Seminary. She is an adjunct professor at Heritage Bible College in Cambridge, Ontario, teaching courses in Children's Ministries; a pastor with the Mennonite Brethren Conference, and she is also Chair of the Children's Ministry Forum with the Evangelical Fellowship of Canada. This contribution is preliminary work toward a doctoral thesis.

often understood this verse to teach what great kingdom citizen character looks like—a child-like faith, humble and meek and ever ready to believe in Jesus. But Jesus took the disciples beyond the questions of character and greatness and challenged their theology of salvation and kingdom life. He made the child the reference point for:

- conversion—*change* and become like little children if you want to enter the kingdom

- community—*become* like little children in order to exemplify kingdom life

- calamity—*unless* you change . . . *you will never* enter the kingdom of heaven.

He unfolds this in the subsequent verses with parallel language: *change* is evident when you humble yourself like this child; *become* is evident when you *welcome* a little child like this in my name; *calamity* awaits you if you cause one of these little ones to sin. This teaching should not have been a surprise to the disciples. This was not new theology. The Old Testament continually pointed with increasing intensity to the theological realities that Jesus so beautifully and succinctly summarized here.

But it *was* a surprise for the disciples, and it *was* difficult for them to understand. One might wonder how that could be, but in the contemporary church there are still many disciples who also do not fully understand Jesus' words here. This is particularly evident in the increasing movement in our churches to separate the children from the adults for their own worship and teaching, and to protect the so-called "intimacy" of the worship and teaching of adults. Children are seen as a distraction, and indeed they can be distracting as they respond to what is happening in worship and teaching that does not reflect their presence. If what Jesus said is true (a rhetorical "if"), and kingdom entrance and living depends upon becoming like children, then separating them from adults is the last thing that should be done. Change is needed in churches to realize fully what God has revealed in children in order to help everyone on the faith journey. The human standards that have been used to define spirituality and maturity need to be challenged, and the view of the child and his/her spirituality needs to be rethought, and the value that spirituality brings to the faith community.

I submit that what Jesus said was much more profound than most people realize. To understand both the meaning and the impact of Jesus' words in Matthew 18, there needs to be an understanding of the theological and ethical value of the child according to the Old Testament text and the culture in which that value was expressed. Using a redemptive hermeneutic, which will be defined, this paper will seek to address this value by highlighting four key redemptive themes in the Old Testament in reference to children: children brought into the midst, children as models of kingdom life, children as mirrors of kingdom hearts, and children as martyrs of kingdom rejection.

This paper will not be exhaustive. Rather, it is a preliminary paper, using wide brush strokes, as a precursor to a full thesis on *The Theological and Ethical Value of the*

Child in the Bible. The intent is to develop from such a study practical applications for the contemporary faith community.

Defining a Redemptive Hermeneutic

How one approaches the biblical record has significant impact on the conclusions and applications reached. A redemptive hermeneutic seeks to address the influence of culture on a given biblical text with the understanding that "many aspects of the biblical text were *not* written to establish a utopian society with complete justice and equity" (Webb, 2001, p. 41).[2] This hermeneutical approach seeks to provide a framework within which one decides what is cultural and is therefore limited to that culture's application, and what is transcultural and therefore may be applied today. It also asks whether the application is to be by principle or by direct application. An example reflective of this paper's topic is found in Lev 27:1–8,

> The Lord said to Moses, "Speak to the Israelites and say to them: 'If anyone makes a special vow to dedicate persons to the Lord by giving equivalent values, set the value of a male between the ages of twenty and sixty at fifty shekels of silver, according to the sanctuary shekel, and if it is a female, set her value at thirty shekels. If it is a person between the ages of five and twenty, set the value of a male at twenty shekels and of a female at ten shekels. If it is a person between one month and five years, set the value of a male at five shekels of silver and that of a female at three shekels of silver. If it is a person sixty years old or more, set the value of a male at fifteen shekels and of a female at ten shekels. If anyone making the vow is too poor to pay the specified amount, he is to present the person to the priest, who will set the value for him according to what the man making the vow can afford.

Is this text relevant to the contemporary covenant community? How can one be certain? What theological conclusions and what principles of application give a probable reflection of God's intent? Are boys/men more valuable than girls/women? Are people in the prime of life more valuable than those who are young or old? Is this passage the final word on the value of a person in the covenant community?

A redemptive hermeneutic states that one must look at biblical context, the Israelite culture, the surrounding culture from which Israel is made distinct, and the

---

2. In his book, Webb spends considerable time and care explaining the redemptive hermeneutic and how it addresses the fact that some passages in scripture seem redemptive to the biblical culture but appear regressive to the present culture. The concept of redemptive movement or spirit in the text is not to be confused with the hidden message approach of allegory or mysticism. The words of the text are taken at face value; however, there is also the understanding that those same words, if left in isolation, can lead the reader to miss the spirit of the text that pulls the culture away from one ideal and toward another, without necessarily taking that culture to the final ideal *at that time*. The slavery texts of the Bible are perhaps the easiest ones to illustrate this, and it is well worth the biblical student's time to read Webb's book in order to gain a better understanding of this hermeneutic.

present culture seeking to apply the text, to determine both immediate theological truth and practical application. With this, most would agree. But a redemptive hermeneutic also seeks to determine if there is continued movement toward an ethical ideal. It suggests that the biblical passage in question may not be the final word, but that it *points towards* a final ethic. It is at this point that some will struggle. This approach seems to suggest that the Bible is not the final word. What, in fact, is being said by this hermeneutical approach, is that a particular *passage* may not be the final word, and one must examine the whole of scripture for continued movement of the biblical culture, determined by using criteria that the text itself provides, toward an ultimate ethic that may or may not be clearly defined but is definitely envisioned. This study will seek to show that there is, indeed, an ethical ideal connected to the value of the child that the scriptures begin to unfold in the Old Testament, and that Jesus himself clearly points to when He identifies the child as the model for a citizen of the kingdom of heaven.

Israel among the Nations

The establishment of Israel was the fulfillment of a promise by God made to one man that He would make him into a great nation through his descendants, and that nation in turn would be a blessing to all the other nations of the earth. Superceding that promise was another more significant promise—the promise of a Savior who would rescue humans from sin. That Savior would come through a line of promise, and Israel would provide that line. As Israel journeyed through history, the promise of a Savior and the promise of land become the twin foci of the nation. But by the time of Jesus, Israel was in her land but did not control it, and the expectations of a Savior from sin had become a watching for a Savior from the oppression of Rome. By the time Jesus placed a child in the midst of his disciples and called them to a new understanding of kingdom life, Israel had forgotten her own childhood and the promises of her Father, and she now struggled just to survive as a nation among the nations. What happened along the way is key to understanding Jesus' statement, "I tell you the truth, unless you change and become like little children, you will never enter the kingdom of heaven."

Canaan

A recent archaeological dig in the ancient Canaanite city of Askelon has provided significant insight into the Canaanite culture during the time of the Israelites' return from Egypt. A Baal calf unearthed by the archaeological team is just one of many finds that point to a culture and religion vastly different from that of the Israelites who would come and take over the land. In a location nearby, one thousand dogs are buried, "carefully laid on their sides in a shallow pit with the tails wrapped around their hind legs" (Gore, 2001, p. 83) indicating some aspect of reverence either for the canines themselves or for a god they may have represented.[3]

Then, there are the children. In one grid, the skeletal remains of small children are found wearing sacred jewelry perhaps communicating their great value or indicating that these children were a "sacred" offering. In another grid, an infant is found carefully buried in what is either the cornerstone or the courtyard of a home, suggesting an offering made in thanksgiving for being able to establish a home. In a third grid, a "grave" of one hundred infants is uncovered, many of them boys, seemingly tossed on a pile into the gutter of the sewer system, along with other garbage.[4] It is into this land that used children for its own purposes that Moses prepared the Israelites to enter with the instructions: "Make no treaty with them, and show them no mercy" (Deut 7:2).

Egypt

The Israelites were only one generation removed from another culture, whose practices were no better. Egypt had significant and prolonged influence upon the Israelite community. What began as a triumph through the life of Joseph, who was raised up by God through the schemes of men to rescue Israelites and Egyptians, became a life of treachery at the hands of the Egyptians and a life of mere survival in the hearts of the Israelites. As the generations passed, Joseph was forgotten, and Egypt's Pharaoh no longer saw the Israelites as an asset and friends, but rather as a threat to Egypt's—and his own—political survival. Israel was brought under bondage, and when they continued to multiply and spread, Pharaoh sought the death of their children through the Israelites midwives. "The king of Egypt said to the Hebrew midwives, whose names were Shiphrah and Puah, 'When you help the Hebrew women in childbirth and observe them on the delivery stool, if it is a boy, kill him; but if it is a girl, let her live'" (Exod 1:15–16). When the midwives failed to do Pharaoh's dirty work, he commissioned all his people, "Every boy that is born you must throw into the Nile, but let every girl live" (Exod 1:22). Boys would grow up to become potential soldiers and therefore were to be eliminated. Girls, however, were "breeders," used by the Egyptians to produce

---

3. This dig, led by seasoned Harvard University archaeologist Lawrence Stager has provided significant insight into the Canaanite culture second perhaps only to the biblical record. Since its inception, the work at the site of Ashkelon has not only revealed considerable evidence corroborating biblical records concerning Canaan, it has also provided a greater understanding of what the Israelites were being called away from by absolute imperative.

4. DNA testing was used to distinguish between male and female. That many were boys was a surprise given that the practice of infanticide in the Ancient Near Eastern cultures, as well as the Greek and Roman cultures that succeeded them, usually targeted female infants because they were seen as an economic liability as opposed to an asset. It is speculated that the boys were the offspring of either temple or "red-light district" prostitutes. Female infants could be raised to perpetuate the system but there would be significantly less demand for boys and so they would be discarded.

more slaves in order to maintain the building programs and economy of Egypt, so the Hebrew girls were allowed to live (McKenna, 1994, p. 41).[5]

Perpetuating the Blessing

With this history behind them, and Canaan before them, Israel came to their promised land. Their stay there would depend on them keeping the commands, decrees and laws the Lord gave them through Moses. They were to be different from the nations that surrounded them, and they were to teach each succeeding generation the nature of that difference. The familiar *Shema* passage in Deuteronomy provides a perpetual call of faith that was to be passed on:

> Hear, O Israel: The Lord our God, the Lord is one. Love the Lord your God with all your heart and with all your soul and with all your strength. These commandments that I give you today are to be upon your hearts. Impress them on your children. Talk about them when you sit at home and when you walk along the road, when you lie down and when you get up. (Deut 6:4–7)

In addition to the daily living of the word of God, the Israelites were provided with feasts and festivals that were special reminders of all God had done for them in fulfilling the promise to give them their own land. Sons and daughters, male and female servants, Levites, aliens, the fatherless and widows were all to participate in these special days.[6]

Centuries later, because God's people had not kept his commands, decrees and laws, the Psalmist Asaph called again for the faith community to teach the next generation about the Lord so that they would not fall into the same traps their forefathers had:

> We will not hide them from their children; we will tell the next generation the praiseworthy deeds of the Lord, his power, and the wonders He has done. He decreed statutes for Jacob and established the law in Israel, which He commanded our forefathers to teach their children, so the next generation would know them, even the children yet to be born, and they in turn would tell their children. Then they would put their trust in God and would not forget his deeds but would keep his commands. (Ps. 78:4–7)

---

5. McKenna has some unique insight into the scriptures concerning the attitude and handling of women and children. She does an excellent job capturing the culture of the day and identifying some transferable principles, particularly as they relate to children. But some of her conclusions also inadvertently highlight why a redemptive hermeneutic is needed. She fails to capture the movement of scripture and ends up bound to theological conclusions that are the result of limiting her study to the isolated text and the contemporary grid which sees those texts as regressive and fails to see the movement toward an ethical ideal.

6. Deut 16 specifically identifies these groups of people in verses 11 and 14, but all of the festivals were community events in which everyone was expected to participate.

Nations Beyond

While Israel wrestled to be what God intended her to be, other Ancient Near Eastern nations grew. Syria, Assyria, Babylon, and Persia, by turn became world powers. Even Rome had its beginnings as one small town while Israel occupied the land of promise. Like Egypt and Canaan, these nations worshiped many gods, saw children as a means to an end, and viewed Israel as a nation to be dominated. Often the leaders of these countries considered themselves not only to be divine representatives of their gods, but in fact believed themselves to be divine. Israel was an attraction to them not so much because they had a problem with the worship and practices of Israel, but because Israel had land that was strategic to their own expansion politically and economically; such expansion was evidence of the might of their gods over the gods of other nations. From their records it is clear that their barbaric[7] advances were not personal, but served as effective warnings and deterrents against resistance by any nation that was in their way (Saggs, 1984).[8]

Not Like the Nations

Israel's journey, from her exodus out of Egypt to her exile in Persia, was one of slipping into conformity with other nations and repeatedly being called by God to be different from them. And while God's intentions went far beyond the care of Israel, and He repeatedly reminded her of His more global mission, yet it appears that Israel could never do more than try to affirm God's codes for her own sake. Even in that, Israel missed the point. While it did not start out that way, the ones to suffer the most in the end were the children.

7. Hazael, king of Syria, fulfilled the prophecy of Elisha recorded in 2 Kgs 8:12, "I know the harm you will do to the Israelites," he answered. "You will set fire to their fortified places, kill their young men with the sword, dash their little children to the ground, and rip open their pregnant women." Also, in the records of Ashurnasirpal II, the King of Assyria from 883–859 BC, we find "While I stayed in Aribua, I conquered the (other) towns of Luhuti, defeating their (inhabitants) in many bloody battles . . . I destroyed (them), tore down (the walls) and burned (the town) with fire; I caught the survivors and impaled (them) on stakes in front of their towns" (Pritchard, 1969, p. 8).

8. Saggs brings the Ancient Near East to life as he traces Assyria's beginnings to its end, including its consolidating of all the Near East from Egypt to what is now Iran into a single power structure. Insight into these other nations from Assyria's perspective is invaluable as it both corroborates and adds perspective to the biblical records concerning all the nations Israel dealt with. Assyria's practice of assimilation that broke down ethnic and national borders explains the disappearance of the ten northern tribes of Israel after Assyria conquered them in 722 B.C. It also paved the way for the future spread of Hellenism, Judaism, Christianity and Islam.

Children Brought Into the Midst

Return to Leviticus 27 and observe the shekel values placed on various people in the Israelite community. For the purposes of this paper, the values set on the children are those in question. The contemporary reader looks at this passage and automatically thinks, "Irrelevant. We do not do this today. This is regressive. It violates all kinds of equality codes. Let's move on." But is it irrelevant? Consider the context Israel had emerged from and the context she was about to enter. For centuries, Israelites had been told they had no value except as a means to an end for the Egyptians. Their children were free labor and were used and abused in order to protect the political and economic stability of Egypt. Israel looked for a deliverer but did not recognize him when He came—He was just an infant who had been rescued when many others were slain in order to prevent such a deliverer from emerging. It was no better in Canaan for children, as shown earlier.

Thus, for Israel, having any value at all placed on any person was a significant move away from the practices of the surrounding cultures. A value being placed on their children was a major shift. That there were differences between boys and girls almost pales in comparison to previous practices. In the context of the Ancient Near Eastern world, the shekel allotment was a step in the right direction. That the measure of that value was done in monetary terms, and that there were gender differences, should be evaluated in light of the greater context. Survival anywhere was dependent on the ability to produce. Age and gender were significant factors for an agricultural community when it came to who could produce what, and how much. In one stroke, God bridged culture and commission. He validates gender differences in an agricultural economic community while at the same time declaring worth for everyone in a nation that had believed for too long that its only value was based on the whims and ambitions of cruel and insecure leaders.

Is there a contemporary application? An Ecuadorian pastor with whom I am acquainted said he could always tell when a man had converted to Christ because of the change in the way he treated his children. Did the children become valuable through the man's conversion, or did the man's conversion help him to see his children's value? Had God proclaimed a new value on the Israelite children, or did He instead begin to open the eyes of the adults to a value already there? With these questions, it becomes apparent that perhaps Leviticus 27 is not so irrelevant after all and has significant transcultural application. This act of God brought children into the midst of a covenant people who had received the promise, and who now needed to think beyond themselves to the broader and earlier mission given to their forefather Abraham. The role of the children would give evidence of Israel's understanding of kingdom life and purpose, in the same way that the role provided children today in faith communities gives evidence to believers' understanding of Jesus' words.

Children as Models of Kingdom Life

Numerous lessons and sermons have been taught declaring the possibility of God using even children to accomplish His plans. The record of Samuel moves this idea out of the realm of possibility into the realm of actuality. Israel was completing a period of four hundred years of judges, during which time, "everyone did what was right in their own eyes" (Judg 17:6). The sons of the high priest Eli were corrupt and wicked, grieving the heart of God and many of his people. The situation was so bad, that "in those days, the word of the Lord was rare; there were not many visions" (1 Sam 3:1). In the midst of this there was a child—a child who was a gift from the Lord, a reward, a blessing, an answer to prayer, and all the other things that people thought of when they had a child, particularly a son. But he was also more.

God broke the rules with this child named Samuel. "But Samuel was ministering before the Lord—a boy wearing a linen ephod" (1 Sam 2:18). Men between the ages of thirty and fifty years old were set apart for service in the work at the Tent of Meeting (Num 4). For the first time in the history of Israel, a child was placed in the position of service, and in fact, more than service—the linen ephod was a priestly garment connected with the word of God and indicated a special relationship with God. "And the boy Samuel continued to grow in stature and in favor with the Lord and men" (1 Sam 2:26).

Samuel would also be the first child to take on the role of prophet, his first prophecy being a call of judgment on Eli and his sons; no small task for anyone, but particularly a young boy. "The Lord was with Samuel as he grew up, and he let none of his words fall to the ground. And all Israel from Dan to Beersheba recognized that Samuel was attested as a prophet of the Lord. The Lord continued to appear at Shiloh, and there He revealed himself to Samuel through his word. And Samuel's word came to all Israel" (1 Sam 3:19—4:1). Aside from being priest and prophet, Samuel would grow up to be the last judge and the first king-maker of Israel. He was the bridge between the period of the judges and the period of the monarchy. Why was Samuel called to the task? Surely there must have been a man in the priestly line who could have stepped into the role! Perhaps there was . . . but God chose a boy, just weaned from his mother. With this choice, God moved his people toward a different ideal; He planted a seed idea, He broke out of the norm, probably in the face of other options, and left his people—then and now—with a strong theological truth. A young child, brought forth from a barren place—his mother Hannah suffered the shame of barrenness before Samuel was born—was brought into the midst of God's people to do his will, speak his truth, and lead in the center of worship, and bring God's people to revival. That child was (and is) the walking essence of what God's kingdom is all about.

Children as Mirrors of Kingdom Hearts

Jesus said that becoming like a child would be evidenced by welcoming the child in his name. Nowhere is this tested more than when the Bible speaks of orphans and the fatherless. In Israel, no good Jewish father—or mother—would reject his own child. But in the world around Israel, as highlighted by John Dominic Crossan in *The Essential Jesus* (1994, p. 20), "a newborn child could easily be abandoned (to slavery at best, death at worst) if the father did not lift it into his arms and declare it was to live as his child." David J. Williams in *Paul's Metaphors* (1999, p. 60) speaks further to this with respect to the time of Jesus: "A Roman did not 'have' a child; he 'took' a child, literally 'raised him up' from where he had been placed at the father's feet *if* the father decided to keep him" (emphasis added).

There were no laws in the ancient Near East or in the Roman era that protected the fatherless or the orphan. The only remote option was adoption which, unlike the contemporary understanding of the practice, often was rooted in a business transaction from which both the adopter and the adoptee—who was often an adult—gained; adoption was not often due to a lack of parents or an act of compassion toward the one abandoned.[9] If a father did not want the child, no one else was likely to desire the child except as a slave.

How different it was to be in the house of Israel. There were no adoption laws because there was no need for them. At one level, there was economic reasoning for this. Each family in Israel had an inheritance, and no one could take it from the family. If a father died, his children had the rights to his land, and they were to be protected. In fact, so important was the protection of this land, that if a man died before having children, then the rule of the kinsmen redeemer applied, where the closest available male relative was called to take the widow as his wife and rear children in the name of the first husband, thus maintaining the family line and inheritance. The story of Ruth is a beautiful picture of this rule being fulfilled.

Beyond the economics of inheritance laws, there was the redemptive covenant relationship between the orphan Israel, and her adoptive Father, the Lord, that the community of Israel was expected to live out in practical ways toward others:

> . . . your father was an Amorite and your mother a Hittite. On the day you were born your cord was not cut, nor were you washed with water to make you clean, nor were you rubbed with salt or washed in cloths. No one looked on you with pity or compassion enough to do any of these things for you. Rather, you were thrown out into the open field, for on the day you were born you were despised. (Ezek 16:3b-5)

---

9. The most famous code, that of Hammurabi provides details of adoption where the adoptee is taken into sonship, which could be anything from being an apprentice to being the heir of a household. Each of the details is in the context of a business transaction (Pritchard, 1969, pp. 185–193).

Israel's beginning was pictured as being the same as that of the abandoned children of the nations.

> Then I passed by and saw you kicking about in your blood, and as you lay there in your blood I said to you, "Live!" I made you grow like a plant of the field. You grew up and developed and became the most beautiful of jewels. Later I passed by and saw that you were old enough for love, I spread the corner of my garment over you . . . I gave you my solemn oath and entered into a covenant with you, declares the Sovereign Lord, and you became mine . . . And your fame spread among the nations on account of your beauty, because the splendor I had given you made your beauty perfect. (Ezek 16:6–14).

God rescued the orphan Israel, an alien, from certain death, not to be God's slave, but to experience all the best the Lord had to offer in covenant relationship. He expected this same attitude and action from his people toward the orphan and the fatherless, whether that child was an Israelite or not. Israel was to be like her adoptive father—"He defends the cause of the fatherless and the widow, and loves the alien, giving him food and clothing. And you are to love those who are aliens, for you yourselves were aliens in Egypt" (Deut 10:18–19). To act on behalf of the orphan and the fatherless was to demonstrate a love for the Lord "with all your heart and all your soul" (Deut 11:13).

The command did not change through the centuries and it remained consistently in opposition to the cultures around Israel throughout her history. This welcoming of the child, any child, into the community by caring for him or her was a reflection of God's heart that continued to be redemptive in Jesus' day and remains redemptive today. Its lack of fulfillment during the Old Testament became a "sore point" with God; He looked at the state of the orphan and the fatherless in Israel and saw a mirror reflection of the heart of Israel (see the Old Testament book of Amos, for example). After being warned repeatedly through his prophets to repent, Israel experienced judgment from God—"We have become orphans and fatherless, our mothers like widows" (Lam 5:3). The nation regressed to the low state where she had started and had—herself the orphan—come to despise the orphan. Jesus' words of judgment in Matthew suddenly have new meaning in light of this reality.

Children as Martyrs of Kingdom Rejection

One does not need to go very far back into history to find children dying at the hands of cruel and ruthless people. Whether it is one child who is the victim of an abuser, or many children who are caught in war and genocide, believer's hearts are wrenched in grief, confusion and a sense of helplessness. Colin Tatz in his book, *With Intent to Destroy* (2003, p. 20), writes, "Genocide has always been a part of human history—in each [instance] we detect some vaguely rational purpose; whether economic, nationalistic, punitive, linguistic or political." One of the great tragedies is that children are always among the victims in genocide. In reference to the Jewish Holocaust at the hands of Nazi Germany, Tatz writes, "[They] delivered children to the Nazis on the rationale that adults could bear children later (if they survived) (p. 32)." There is a cold callousness reflected here that makes one shudder.

A thirteen year old, blue collar, Canadian girl named Shar, expresses through her poem, *My Last Breath*[10] the pain-filled voice of millions of children who suffer around the world:

I lay on the ground gasping for air,
Blood pours from my body, this isn't fair.
What did I do to deserve this pain
You don't know anything about me, not even my name.
I heard someone call for help as they were walking by,
"No, No", I tried to say, "Just leave me here to die."
I don't want more torture or any more pain.
If I have to go through this again, I'll go insane.
Minutes passed and sirens filled the sky
I lay in the rain and let out a sigh
Before I knew it, I was in a hospital bed
I had tubes through my body and bright lights above my head.
I closed my eyes and waited for death.
Moments later, I took my last breath.

The effort to respond to the death of children is troubled by biblical text which records the slaughter of whole nations, including the children, in obedience to God's own commands. The records concerning Heshbon (Deut 2:34), Bashan (Deut 3:6), Jericho (Josh 6:21), Makkedah (Josh 10:28), and the Amalekites (1 Sam 15:3) are just a sample. Were it just one segment in time, it would be easier to capture what is happening, but this kind of activity spans Old Testament history so that when speaking of Babylon centuries later, Isaiah prophesies, "Their infants will be dashed to pieces before their eyes" (13:16). Perhaps the most shocking of all is that this prophecy finds its way into the worship book of the Israelites as they sit in exile in Babylon, "Happy is he who repays you for what you have done to us—he who seizes your infants and dashes them against the rocks" (Ps 137:8–9).

Have the Israelites fallen to the depths of the Canaanites practices, which included discarding infants into the sewer gutters? Psalm 137:8–9 is a statement that the one who rips infants out of their parents' arms and throws them against the rocks will be blessed and happy. The language here indicates the idea of experiencing great

---

10. Shar is a young girl I have met recently whose life has been indicative of what happens when God is ignored. This poem was part of a private collection which she agreed to share as a help to this text, and as finding hope in what has been for her, a very hopeless situation.

joy in the stomping to death of infants as a repayment for what Babylon has done to the Israelites.

This is utterly regressive and repulsive viewed through the grid of contemporary culture. No one would dream of treating children in this manner, even if they were from the cruelest of the nations. Take down their leader and their fighting men, yes, but this kind of behavior—never! So what is to be done with texts like this? What kind of God is the Christian God? Where is the redemption in this?

Texts such as these, that seem to espouse the cruel and vicious slaughter of children, challenge readers at many points. They challenge the prevailing view of children. People today are horrified that children die at all, even apart from atrocity, largely because of their presumed innocence. Yet it must be asked if this is a correct view of the child who cries, "Innocent!" If answered affirmatively, this naturally leads to the challenge of one's view of God—how can He slay innocent children? What does that say about his character? Stirred into this controversy are the challenges to existing doctrines of sin, accountability and election that—no matter how well they are explained—leave sensitive adults broken-hearted because they inevitably proclaim death to those "outside" of a relationship with our God.

To attempt to resolve this, particularly in a chapter, is impossible. But there is room to take a step toward resolution and it is here that perhaps the redemptive hermeneutic can help the most. There are some criteria[11] that are specifically helpful in leading to a better understanding of the biblical text. The first echoes loudly a well-rehearsed response of the church to horror—what is happening here finds its basis in the Fall and Curse. Rather than see this as a pat answer—or as an avoidance of a tough issue—it would be wise to examine these truths carefully again. The entrance of sin into the world put humanity into a downward spiral that could lead only to death. The subsequent suffering of children is a natural, albeit grievous, consequence included in this spiral. The whole point of redemptive history is to reveal this truth and provide the way back to life.

If, for example, the favorite children's story of Noah is considered carefully, agreeing that God was right in bringing the flood to deal with the extreme evil of the times there must also be agreement that He was right in judging wickedness in a way that included destroying all the children who lived at that time. Through an act of horrific judgment God brought the possibility of life. This pattern is repeated over and over through the Bible until Calvary, where again, a horrific act of judgment serves to bring life. This is redemptive movement.

The second criterion looks at specific instructions versus general principles. God told his people to wipe out entire groups of people including children. God used other nations to horrifically judge his own people, including children who were slaughtered. Does that give people in subsequent generations the permission

---

11. There are several other criteria that fit here as well, but the ones addressed are the strongest for fulfilling the current objectives.

to do the same? The Crusaders thought so, but the answer is no. What God did and what the ancient Near Eastern cultures did are two very different things. God is God; the leaders of the different nations were not gods, though they chose to believe they were. God struck down many people in response to sin. The leaders killed innocent people to expand their territory. God pronounced death only after many warnings were ignored. The leaders killed innocent children and struck without warning. God had rightful claim to the judgment seat—He after all, was (and is) the Creator of mankind. The leaders' claim to be gods was rooted in pride and a show of power. God judged in order to promote the life of his creation. The leaders judged to promote their own lives, even if it meant destroying others around them and everything else around them. (This latter truth remains today, so that innocent people of all ages die for the advance of the cause of evil.)

And thus, while the specific details are horrific, the general principle of God's rightful claim to act without being accused of being like the evil nations is clear. The fact that He ultimately spoke in the "language" of the nations because that was the only thing that got the attention of his people is tragic, but apparently was necessary.[12]

Add to this the voice of Genesis through to Revelation which describes both the relationship that man has to God and the holiness of God against the sinfulness of man. This voice is a call from a holy and truly innocent God who cries for justice in the face of a rebellious creation which is so distorted that even the "innocent" get swept up in the destruction. The tragedy of justice is that it eludes understanding, and so when it happens, it may appear unjust. It is often a struggle to reconcile the sometimes perceived as competing characteristics of God—love and holiness—as He metes out justice.

A third criterion that is being developed is in the area of genre.[13] Concerning the specific verses in question, this means going beyond the recognition that Psalm 137 is a poetic communal lament psalm, to the literary patterns within the poetry, particularly in the context of the literature of the ancient Near East. The Bible is the result of God breathing his word through human authors using a variety of literary forms and genres typical to their day. The editors of *The Bible as Literature* (Gabel, Wheeler & York, 2000) have very sensitively and effectively developed this truth, which is affirmed by conservative as well as more liberal biblical scholars (see Ryken & Longman, 1993).

Of particular interest are: the literary uses of hyperbole and metaphor common to the day; the literary context of exilic trauma[14]; and the use of literary stereo-

12. William J. Webb, the author referred to earlier in the text concerning the redemptive hermeneutic, is presently engaged in significant study around the biblical authors' use of ancient Near Eastern genre and the implications that usage has for our interpretation of the text.

13. In the words of Daniel L. Smith-Christopher, "To read these texts without some sense of the trauma of exile is tantamount to blaming the victims at the very least, and perhaps grossly misunderstanding much of the power of the text in its social context" (2002, 104).

14. The exile in Babylon put an end once and for all idolatry and child sacrifice, the two greatest

types also typical to ancient Near Eastern literature. John A. Wood notes that, "The writings of the Bible were, to some degree, historically and culturally conditioned" (1998, p. 4) and concerning exilic material, Daniel L. Smith-Christopher writes, "Biblical literature arises from the experience of these [exile] events, as well as being deeply influenced by social, economic and political contexts" (2002, p. 73). Smith-Christopher goes on to address the issue of stereotypes in his analysis of Deuteronomic bless-curse formula as it is played out in Ezekiel and Lamentations. What he develops is relevant to all of the difficult war and suffering passages of the bible including Psalm 137, "the descriptions of suffering are among the 'curses' with which Israel is threatened if they choose to disobey the laws . . . and that these curses take the expected form of traditional curses that follow the literary pattern of an international treaty in the ancient Near East" (p. 97).

Thus, while much of the language of war in the Bible is harsh and even grotesque, and it certainly communicates the horror and inevitable grief and rage of war, there may be more to the language than just a description of actual events or desires. The use of the accepted literary forms of the day leaves the reader confronted with a text that in turn confronts presumed concept of what it means to be the people of God in a world full of injustice (McEntire, 1999, pp. 122–126). The Twentieth Century experienced more war, genocide and injustice than any other century in history, and this 21st century has not started out much better. If the "offense" of a literary text like Psalm 137 can be received as a challenge for people to consider more realistically the injustices of the present day, leading to a cry for and pursuit of justice, then the redemptive aspect of verses 8 and 9 will be discovered, as these verses declare the hope that those who cruelly mete out injustice will be punished.

What does a cry for justice mean for today? Consider the injustice that is perpetuated against children that are nearby, never mind in other countries—poverty, child prostitution, racism, abuse, murder; or the more subtle injustice found in rejection, abandonment, separation, commercial branding,[15] ignoring, and patronizing. The ethical ideal also needs to be revealed for contemporary society. There are huge injustices in the current day and in every society. Children die as a result because children are the martyrs of kingdom rejection—they are the ones who suffer the most when the people forsake the holy God who made them. It will always hurt and it will never make sense that children die, because deep within the human psyche there is an awareness that there is something inherently wrong with a world where such evil takes place. Jesus' words about the treatment of little ones needs to be read in the light of Old Testament perspectives of children.

---

abominations Israel committed against God. It was the exile and the destruction of their children that finally "won" them over. It is tragic it took such extreme measures for God's people to reject the low value placed on children by the Canaanites.

15. The practice of commercials teaching the supposed superiority of one brand over another, so that the child comes to prefer that brand in general throughout life.

To Rome and Jesus

Six hundred years after Psalm 137 was written, the Israelites in the New Testament era were back in their land although not under their own rule. There were significant changes in Hebrew society. Throughout the Old Testament, foreign rulers had at least a similar mindset in terms of their common Eastern, non-linear mentality. But now Rome was in charge, heavily influenced by linear Greek thinking. The value of community common to the ancient world was now replaced by the rise of the individual at the expense of the majority in a much more decisive way. Israel had been through generations of threat and violence, so when the New Testament era began Israel was caught in a world it did not understand, a world it did not like and a world that did not want God's people (Matthews & Benjamin, 1993).

The Roman emperor believed he was god, although he worshipped many other gods. The family structure of his culture emulated the government so that men were considered gods in their own homes, infanticide was at an all-time high, and the economy was built on the backs of slaves.

The high priest for the Jewish temple was appointed by Rome, and children were at the bottom of the hierarchy, not even referred to as children. The Aramaic term for children in that day was the same term used for slave or servant (McKenna, 1994). The thought of a child-centered family or society, typical of much of contemporary culture, would have seemed absurd. Even Roman children had to achieve adulthood before being considered a free person eligible to inherit the family estate (Long, 1977).

Within the Jewish culture, religious groups had arisen, including the Sadducees and the Pharisees, who were more concerned about personal power than personal purity, and they burdened the people with many rules and expectations, and thus the hope of salvation in any sense was dim. That the Israelite culture was deeply impacted by this was not in question. Jesus repeatedly dealt with those who abused authority, and sought to teach his followers how to respond to their oppressors and yet not become like them. He was a favorite of the children who would seek him out and praise him when others declined to do so. The children had been:

- slaves in Egypt without personal value
- brought into the midst by God and declared valuable through the sanctuary shekel
- portrayed as models of kingdom life through children like Samuel
- acting as mirrors of prayers and hearts, most readily seen in the treatment of the orphan and the fatherless, and
- suffering as martyrs of kingdom rejection.

In the New Testment era, children were forgotten as members of the covenant community; they returned to slave status in both language and life. And then, one day,

Jesus did the unthinkable. After hearing his followers debate over which of them will be the greatest in the kingdom of heaven, Jesus pulled a child from outside their circle and placed him in the midst and says, "I tell you the truth, unless you change and become like little children, you will never enter the kingdom of heaven." Jesus defied both Israelite and Roman culture, and for that matter, every culture in every age. He turned the predominant ethics and values upside-down, and he warned of a severe penalty for anyone who leads a child to sin. The familiar formula, "You have heard that it was said, but I say to you," is not repeated but it is implied. Jesus took the movement in the Old Testament toward a positive view of the child and catapulted it to an ethical ideal that left his disciples silent, and perhaps wondering if they would ever make it into this kingdom of heaven of which Jesus spoke.

Conclusion

What does it mean to become like a child? It means to see children from God's redemptive perspective, and to become like children from the culture's perspective. The child is on the outside, not included in the inner circle of those who think they have the way to God. The child is on the bottom, not considered eligible for recognition or participation and thus does not seek those. The child is powerless, voiceless, defenseless, claimless, forgotten and forsaken. The child is the one who is brought to Jesus, not one who assumes access. The child is the one pulled out of the gutter by a hand that says he does not belong there even when everyone else says he does.

The disciples were called to become as little children. Forget the greatness, the heroics, and the privilege. Walk away from it all. They did not and could not. They could not, until they ran away from Gethsemane and Golgotha. But then Jesus followed after them. He found them along the road. He found them in a room behind locked doors. He found them going back to their old ways, forgetting all that He had accomplished in their lives and considering it all lost. And He once more said, "Follow me." This time they came as children.

Is this relevant? Is this transferable to contemporary culture? Is there room in the ethics and handling of children for this perspective? Is there room in modern churches? Who is distracting whom? Will churches bring children into the midst and keep them there as the model of the kingdom citizen, and mirrors of our own spiritual condition? Will a priority on children set the agenda for church activities and funds? Will God's people embrace the orphan, the fatherless and the endangered? Will there be a humble admission that the rejection of true kingdom life is the real reason children suffer and die? These are difficult questions to answer, not so much because of the answers themselves, but because with any answer given, application is required, and adults need to do some "growing down" to get the message.

References

Crossan, J. D. (1994). *The essential Jesus.* Edison, NJ: Castle.

Gabel John B., Wheeler, Charles B. & York, Anthony D. (2000). *The Bible as literature* (4th ed.). New York, NY: Oxford University Press.

Gore, R. (2001, January). Ancient Ashkelon. *National Geographic Society,* 68–90.

Long, T. C. (1977). *Matthew.* Louisville: Westminster John Knox.

Matthews, V. H., & Benjamin, D. C. (1993). *Social world of ancient Israel 1250–587 BCE.* Peabody, MA: Hendrickson.

McEntire, Mark. (1999). *The blood of Abel.* Macon, GA: Mercer University Press.

McKenna, M. (1994). *Not counting women and children.* Maryknoll, NY: Orbis.

Pritchard, J. B. (Ed.). (1969). *Ancient Near Eastern texts relating to the Old Testament* (3rd ed.). Princeton: Princeton University Press.

Ryken, L., & Longman, T. (Eds.)(1993). *A complete literary guide to the Bible.* Grand Rapids: Zondervan.

Saggs, H. W. F. (1984). *The might that was Assyria.* New York, NY: St. Martin's.

Smith-Christopher, Daniel L. (2002). *A biblical theology of exile.* Overtures to Biblical Theology. Minneapolis: Fortress.

Tatz, C. (2003). *With intent to destroy.* New York, NY: Verso.

Webb, W. J. (2001). *Slaves, women & homosexuals.* Downers Grove, IL: InterVarsity Press.

Williams, D. J. (1999). *Paul's metaphors.* Peabody, MA: Hendrickson.

Wood, John A. (1998). *Perspectives on war in the Bible.* Macon, GA: Mercer University Press.

Chapter Six

Christian Perspectives on Children's Spirituality: Social Science Contributions?

REBECCA NYE[1]

A social science approach to children's spirituality is clearly not everyone's calling. Many with a concern for children's spiritual nature or nurture are primarily practitioners, ministers, theologians or educators. But a perusal of how social science contributes to common interest in children's spirituality can inform everyone. Even though the difficult business of trying to conduct research using social science methods is something the typical person may never do, it is worth knowing how to discern the influence and weigh the quality of research evidence that, rightly or wrongly, may influence any person's work. In the jargon, there is a common need to be "research sensitive" though God forbid everyone becoming social science "researchers!"

First, a rather personal perception of the journey so far in research on children's spirituality will be provided. The current venue represents an initial attempt to ask what specifically "Christian perspectives" might offer this area. It is therefore important to orient to the fact that the majority of research to date has offered a more *general* perspective, dealing with the nature of children's spirituality rather than nurture of the child's spirituality for a specific faith tradition. Most of the empirical research has been to document and describe the rich natural capacity children have for spiritual processing. This has often been neglected by Christian communities, whose concern has been with installing spiritual comprehension software to the awkward hardware with which children are equipped.

---

1. Rebecca Nye conducted ground-breaking research for her doctoral dissertation in England, which later was published in the book *The Spirit of the Child* (1998), coauthored with David Hay. Dr. Nye is now coordinating a children's spirituality research initiative at Cambridge University, and is the research coordinator for the Godly Play approach to children's spirituality. She is in great demand as a conference speaker, and also speaks regularly in churches about the implications of her research and the importance of nurturing the child's spirituality. She has authored several major journal articles on children's spirituality, in addition to several book chapters on related topics.

The second area of this chapter will address the new territory being considered for exploration: *Christian* perspectives on children's spirituality. Taking such a perspective requires more than an isolated—and potentially arrogant—intensification of social science methods applied simply to a narrower subject. To understand the more specific task of researching children's spirituality through Christian lenses, it is important to receive guidance about the nuances of spirituality understood in specifically Christian terms, to be more certain the research questions and approaches are appropriate. This involves the social science contribution deliberately proceeding in dialogue with Christian theology and Christian education, not merely comparing notes as an afterthought. This preparation for applying social science to Christian perspectives on children's spirituality will lead to some hard questions about the wisdom and timelessness of the whole endeavour: What are the costs and benefits of social science studies pursuing an exclusively Christian agenda?

And finally, this chapter will consider the challenges of selecting the appropriate social science tools (sample selection, researcher attributes and methodologies) for the job of developing Christian perspectives on children's spirituality.

Spirituality as a Part of the Child?

About ten years ago I came into this field—the study of children's spirituality—from developmental psychology. I had become bored with the limited focus psychology took on the child's cognitive life when attempting to study their emotional or social psychology. And most of all I was becoming unhappy about the social science methods my research work with children employed.

I sensed that, somehow, despite all the revealing detail disclosed by cleverly designed, "child friendly" experiments to illuminate how some specific cognitive mechanism was functioning in children, something about the essential nature of being a child was being totally ignored. The crunch came when I realised doing my research well was about developing skills that allowed me to persuade each child, in the minimum amount of time possible, to respond to the focus our team wanted to study. Doing it badly meant letting the children get in the way, becoming distracted by something they were interested in or that mattered more to them than my topic of inquiry. This deliberate, skilful avoidance of who each child really was, seemed a bizarre way of seeking to understand childhood more deeply.

Empirical psychology takes to the extreme the practice of looking at just "part" of the child, which is at odds with how spirituality is really the whole of them. It is easy to critique psychology for doing that. But my passionate concern at present is about preventing Christian nurture and education from suffering from the same extremism—developing "parts" of a child's faith—her biblical knowledge here, her moral values there, plus a measure or two of belonging to a supportive community, and the like. The consequences of ignoring spirituality in faith formation are far more serious than mere atomism of disciplines and research. Overlooking the primacy of spirituality develops, in effect, a potentially life-long impression that faith involves just parts of the person, but does not really touch who people really are, and are continually becoming.

Spirituality as a Holistic Category

This holistic approach assumes a particular understanding of what children's spirituality means which has developed through shared debate and scholarship in the last decade, especially in the United Kingdom. What is important about the developing understanding of spirituality in childhood is that it is not synonymous with conventional religiosity, or merely a kinder or more popular way of wrapping and selling religious values and behaviours to the young. Ideally spirituality has a relationship with religion, but in practice "effective" religious education programs can develop religious characteristics that are disconnected from spirituality. And it is too often only in adulthood that this fundamental disconnect is realised, and hopefully restored. Sometimes it is not restored and spirituality-less religion is abandoned as formulaic and simplistic. Walter Wangerin's (2003) experience as a small boy of hearing his class teacher tell the story of Zacheus illustrates this disconnect painfully well. While listening to the story, Walter felt his whole self deeply moved by this story of a small, shy, unpopular figure who nevertheless experienced strong curiosity to know more, to see more, to be involved. When the teacher ended by asking her class, "no doubt out of due concern for their spiritual development, "So what do we learn from this?," Walter recalls feeling utterly let down. The calling of this story to his *whole* being was overwritten with the message that in fact this was just a simple lesson about one *part* of being, and a moral, head-centered part at that.

The opportunity to develop a three-year research project on children's spirituality at the University of Nottingham appeared to be—in many ways—the antithesis of all the angst I had been experiencing with developmental psychology experiments on children's meta-cognition. Here was an area, above all others, that not only did psychology researchers studiously avoid in their dealings with children, but which many assumed was a relatively void category. There had been a comparatively small amount of prior psychological study of children's religion. This had mostly debated the degree to which children at different ages had predictable cognitive difficulties understanding religious material and explanations. Similarly their cognitive development affected their grasp of religious identity and moral reasoning. Children's concepts of God also seemed to show predictable cognitive hallmarks of childhood—children less than twelve years of age apparently struggling with abstract and symbolic conceptualisation when formally questioned. All this evidence of religion's "problematic" nature for children's minds kept questions about *spiritual* capacity hidden under the carpet. In fact, I think researchers are seduced into thinking all this developmental detail about children's intellectual processing of religious concepts *was* the same as their spiritual capacity. This can be compared to saying at a different level that a systematic theologian is necessarily more "spiritual" than the average adult! Even more explicitly Ronald Goldman (1964), whose psychological research on childhood religion influenced decades of Christian education in the United Kingdom, inferred, on the basis of his Piagetian-styled studies of children's religious cognitive psychology, that spiritual experience was "rare in adolescence and practically unknown in childhood."

The legacy of that was twofold. First, it came to be assumed that children could handle only a watered down kind of religious life and by implication spiritual depth and valid insight was an exclusively adult experience; spirituality must be a sequiter to religious understanding which clearly children did not have. The second part of the legacy was that children's expressions on apparently spiritual matters should be treated as cute, accidental, unintentionally meaningful, frequently illogical and a source for adult amusement. The presumption was there was nothing "real" here for study or nurture, just children's characteristic "noise," which of course experimental psychologists and teachers skillfully steer away from as a distraction from their proper focus.

In more contemporary scholarship the case is being made both on theological and empirical grounds for children's spirituality being far from an "empty category." It turns out that children, partly by *virtue* of their distinctive psychological characteristics, have an intriguingly rich capacity for spirituality, for a kind of religious knowing and being which is neither contingent on their religious knowledge nor moral accountability. In fact, in some cases burgeoning religious knowledge may sideline this capacity for spiritual knowing and being. Research evidence on this general spirituality is accumulating fast with a dedicated journal—*International Journal of Children's Spirituality*—annual conferences, some in their tenth year, and other venues. This is not the place for a tour of that developing field, though I shall relate a few insights of my own research concerning this general sense of children's spirituality since these inform the issues to consider for the next step: considering "Christian" perspectives as research scientists.

Interestingly one of the features of children's spiritual life we found in our study of a largely secular group of British schoolchildren is its lack of compartmentalization of spirituality from all that they are and are interested in. Their spirituality was not about studying a novel and discrete *part* of a child's psychology. We had to take the child as a whole to get a feel for her spiritual life, which flies like a bird through their intellectual life *and* their emotional life *and* their social life *and* their cultural life *and* their moral life. It is about their "being a child," as of course someone else called people to notice and learn two millennia ago (Matt 18:2–5).

My Research of Relational Consciousness

My methodology involved interview-based case study research with 40 children (ages 6 through 10) randomly sampled from two schools rather than a special selection of "Christian" kids. I included "all" of their lives as the focus; I analyzed chatter about their sporting activities as closely as I analyzed accounts of explicit religious experience. Additional details related to the methodology employed can be found in my dissertation (Nye, 1998).

Religion Versus Relational Consciousness

I designated "Relational Consciousness" as the core category which united the range of ways children's spiritual lives were expressed, from spiritual experience to mundane chatter. Identifying "relational consciousness" as the unifying theme of the children's data underscores that raw spirituality is indeed something that combined the very basic definitives of human life—one's consciousness and capacity for conscious relationship, not some isolated "part" of how people are created.

Analyzing further instances of this core category of children's "relational consciousness," I found three central themes. First, each child communicated relational consciousness through *an individual signature*, an authentic style of their own—for one child it might be found in an aesthetic appreciation of nature and her inspiration to respond to that appreciation. For another the "signature" might be philosophizing and questioning at every turn and experience. This rootedness of spirituality in individual character resonates with Wangerin's (2003) suggestion that each child might be specially served by a particular story, just for him or her.

Second, children seemed to have a range of predictable as well unexpectedly sophisticated mental strategies through which they serviced their spiritual thoughts and feelings. On one level their conventionally religious reasoning was bootstrapped to their cognitive development, but seeing past this surface layer there was much more going on that suggested profound engagement and motivation, and in an important sense a kind of spiritual maturity which adults often merely feign. When adults read things like "Children's Letters to God" (1991) it is easy to spot youngsters' "literal mindedness" and even laugh at children and not give it any further thought. In my view that says more about *adults* being imprisoned in the literal surface details at the expense of noticing what may be going on for the child at a deeper level. For example, seeing Santa as God's helper might involve more than theologically naivety; it might indicate the child's trust and the reality of her sense that the sacred is a benevolent, child-loving power. It might represent spiritual perception, expressed using the terms and concepts available to the child.

Third, a further insight the analysis yielded was that children recognised their spiritual thoughts, feelings and experiences as profound, significant and inspiring as immediate experience, but assumed they were alone in thinking like this and anticipated being able to grow out of it and moving on to more worthwhile things. So spiritual capacity was not only endangered as they got older and more "developed," but the children thought it must be necessary and desirable to inhibit their natural spiritual thoughts, feelings, and experiences. Many of these had explicitly led them to recognise God, not because they had been *told* that, but because they had discovered, felt, or experienced first-hand God's relation to them.

Interestingly, earlier pilot work indicated that it was unwise at the outset of interviews to indicate that God or religion would be discussed. When *I* brought this up during the pilot studies, the children more often than not treated me to the contents of their heads in terms of religious knowledge—and it was then much more difficult to shift the focus to what was tugging at their hearts. But, leaving the flow of conversation up to them without any prior suggestion of God, there was a surprising amount of spontaneous and more meaningfully used religious and "God talk" brought in by them within discussion of their lives more generally.

Some of this spontaneous "God talk" was positive and associated with enriching or inspiring experiences. But for many of the children, Christian religious language was inadequate for expressing their spirituality. Rather than "spiritual oxygen," such language was more often toxic to discussing spirituality. Listening as the intrigued social scientist to the depth that characterised these children's spiritual lives AND as a Christian hearing time and again that religion was too shallow—made me feel excited and humbled on the one hand, but depressed and defensive on the other. Was it that they really did not understand religion, or was it that adults had not understood children's spiritual acuity?

Examples of Relational Consciousness from My Research

Several examples drawn from my research provide concrete examples of this category of "relational consciousness." They also indicate how the spirituality of children is holistic in nature.

Maggie, age ten, was frustrated about religious language and whether it could be symbolic enough to express her experiences, perceptions and ideas. She commented, *"'Cos sometimes I wonder whether God is just like an answer to all the questions, like how did the war get there and how did the sun, and how are there days and nights and how did the first person get there . . . because it's an easy answer but I don't know whether it's true or not."* God should not feel like a mere answer. Playing that game is too easy; that is not spirituality as known by Maggie.

Bob at age ten was another child readily able to identify and articulate spiritual matters of personal concern—things adults term the major existential issues. These included his sense of unique identity, the soul, thoughts about afterlife, and the apparent metaphysics of self-consciousness. He was also another child for whom the language of the Church seemed too weak to do justice to all this. He was quite an articulate critic of how Christian language failed to serve his spirituality because it left no space for mystery and the unknown. Religion acted like an answer to everything. For ten-year-old Bob ancient Greek religion was perhaps more promising: "*I mean the Greeks they had a god for everything. They have an unnamed God . . . Did you know that, about the Greeks? Because they thought there must be a god we've missed out. So there was another one, the unnamed one, they just prayed to for everything.*" In fact, in a dream, he quite clearly saw the Christian language system as oppressive and entrapping, like cultural rubble. In his dream he saw "*the church caved in on me . . . the spire fell through and then the rest caved in on top of it. All I could see was a little window . . . where's there's like windows in the spire.*" He summed up by saying "*I wouldn't miss them, if everyone knocked every single church in the whole world down. It wouldn't bother me that much.*"

Naturally, most adults are anxious to know what unfortunate experiences of a religious nature these children might have had, how their acquaintance with religious language has become so jaundiced. Suffice to say there was nothing unusually bad about their religious education; it was pretty typical for the United Kingdom where religious education is a compulsory school subject from the age of four, and where there is a compulsory daily act of collective worship in every school, in which Christianity is the mainstay for both the religious education and the worship. The significant thing was that they spoke so honestly, from the heart. My concern was that those children provided with a greater volume of "typical" Christian education and nurture, through a formal connection with a community of faith, lose the ability even to speak so honestly. From a researcher's point of view I took the soft option when I interviewed children outside of a religious context—schools—and without limiting myself to "Christian" children. The harder task would be—and now will be—to find ways to gain access to the spirituality of children who are constrained by a need to say nice, pious things about faith.

So where does this lead if one wishes to study *Christian* perspectives of children's spirituality? If research demonstrates that spirituality is *not* simply a void category in childhood; if it is not bootstrapped to an ability for abstract understanding of religious material; if its source is deeply charged and not just charmingly cute; then there is a long road ahead for Christian thinking, theory and practice.

I wonder if a move from the "whole" to what was mistakenly considered "part" of childhood is likely to result from narrowing the perspective to a "Christian" focus. Can the common language of Christian faith and spirituality make friends with and support the manifest individuality of children, or must the authentic spiritual signature be sacrificed in the cause of Christian spiritual development?

I have had opportunities to present this research at a number of conferences and gatherings over the last few years. But it is exciting to consider the implication that there is a possible new journey in the area of children's spirituality research: a quest for a distinctively Christian view of this area of study.

But to be honest I am more and more awed, perhaps even paralysed, by the complexity of such an expedition. For researchers to explore this new territory there are many likely challenges to consider. Importantly this "shift" from a more general understanding of children's spirituality to an examination of children's spirituality in a *Christian* sense, is not inevitably a "leap into the dark." There is plenty of scholarship on Christian spirituality in an adult sense. This should be mined for guidance as well as developmental theory, educational methodology, and doctrines on child-relevant issues such as baptism and catechesis. The rich tradition of Christian spiritual writings may provide direction by beginning from a very different place in reflecting upon children's thoughts about spirituality, in contrast with the time-honored objections to whether children can be properly "religious" in terms of church membership, moral accountability and comprehension of religious knowledge.

Where to Begin?

When beginning a journey into new territory, it is a good idea to take advice from seasoned travellers. The current Archbishop of Canterbury, leader of the Anglican church worldwide, and eminent theologian, fits that description quite well—he is a seasoned spiritual traveller within the Christian tradition.

In his book on Christian Spirituality, *The Wound of Knowledge*, Rowan Williams (1991) offers a vivid map of Christian spirituality that might help provide direction for researchers.

> "Christian faith has its beginnings in an experience of *profound contradictoriness*, an experience which so *questioned the religious categories* of its time that the resulting *reorganisation of religious language* was a centuries long task. At one level indeed, it is *a task which every generation has to undertake again.* And if "spirituality" can be given any coherent meaning, perhaps it is to be understood in terms of this task: each believer making his or her own engagement with the questioning at the heart of faith . . . the questioning involved here is not *our interrogation of the data,* but *its interrogation of us.* It is the intractable *strangeness* of the ground of belief that must constantly be allowed to challenge fixed assumption of religiosity."

Since this is a provocative and dense picture of Christian spirituality, before going further it may be helpful to savour how this speaks to one's own implicit understanding of what Christian spirituality is about.

An arresting detail is the use of the term "data"—music to the social scientists ears! But of course Williams is referring to the content of faith as "the data" and its special qualities of deep contradictoriness and intractable strangeness—such as an omnipotent God assuming the vulnerability and dependence of a baby—not the clear cut data of empirical reports. In fact as Christian social scientists it is a timely reminder that all research data on children's spirituality is incidental against this bigger picture of *the* data.

William's rich characterization of Christianity's distinctive "profound contradictoriness," the re-birthing effect this has on language, meaning and assumptions, and his sense that spirituality is a personal engagement that allows all this to re-organize in a profound manner *everyone—all* these point clearly to good starting point of the journey. To lose one's way later on might be understandable, but to *start* in the wrong place would be particularly embarrassing, not to mention expensive in terms of research funds.

The Future

First it is suggested that spirituality is *at the heart of every new generation's "task"* so there is support for understanding spirituality—Christian spirituality that is—as a matter of original personal and collective development, rather than imitation or uncritical acceptance of products of older generations of thinking on this subject.

A second question might be whether "new generations" undertaking this task can be stretched to include children. Is it just adults who are sensitive to profound contradictoriness? Perhaps only adults question given categories and play with language so that meaning begins to take root. Perhaps only adults are open enough to let the data of powerful story, action and symbol pull them about. In fact, these capacities suggest things that come naturally to children, and with greater difficulty to adults.

So, very quickly one becomes aware that taking stock of *Christian* spirituality in the terms Rowan Williams offers can help to sharpen questions about Christian childhood nurture. First, how *does* each "next generation" become equipped to pursue this kind of a task and to revel in it? Second, what is the repertoire of skills and conditions that might make such a task either more possible and perceivable to the child, or more difficult and suppressed? Third, how does one enable children to engage with that "intractable strangeness," "the profound contradictoriness" at the heart of faith? How can one ensure that the spiritual task that Christian faith requires, is not overlooked by mistakenly accepting religious categories without engagement and questioning and re-ordering language into the intimate familiarity of a mother-tongue, and at best develop religiosity in place of spirituality? Are the children more likely to reject religion altogether if the language is not engaged?

In turn, this sharpened focus for what Christian spiritual nurture might and might not involve also suggests what might be good or false "leads" for researchers and teachers to follow if they want to pay attention to children living or practicing Christian spirituality. The idea of Christian spirituality grounded in the process of how the data—the Christian story—interrogates people, rather than merely people interrogating it, is particularly helpful. This deserves further exploration.

Thanks to modern education (particularly in science) and cultural style in general, skills with which to interrogate data are precisely what children are encouraged to develop. People frame Bible study as their study of the Bible, rather than using the Bible to study themselves. If routinely children are allowed—even encouraged—to misconstrue the task religious data presents them with, they will naturally turn these valuable interrogative skills to that mistaken task and thus focus on *Christianity's* problems and more often than not reject investing further effort with such a blatantly problematic set of material. Getting the task wrong closes the door to faith for many.

The faith community is understandably anxious, as scientific-type thinking skills impinge on acceptance of faith, and tries to pull rank. So when a child interrogates the data and finds "problems"—such as questioning how literal Jesus' healing miracles were and whether they might not be explained in medical terms these days, or reflecting on a statue of Jesus in shallow water—adults often meet their arguments with more complex counter-arguments to explain things. In other words, adults too suggest the game is "interrogate the data," only adults have more powerful intellectual tools—for the present—than the children. Thus it is a short-term solution and a worryingly unpleasant lesson using power to exert an imperialistic hold over the weak—making interaction with children as perversely unrepresentative of Christian spirituality as one could imagine.

But what if instead, with a more conscious attitude to the spiritual character of the task of faith formation, one's response was to attend to the fact that the child's *question* about "explaining away" healing miracles *was a flashing sign* that the data was "doing something" to them, stirring them up, making them think, disturbing them, questioning their categories, making them become aware of something "strange?" What if, instead of judging or outwitting their attempted explanation, the focus of interaction became the child's desire to wrestle with a problem that the data has inspired for them? Instead of debating, one could say "that's what matters," "this is spiritual engagement, yes you're doing it!"

In fact, by placing the focus on *how the data has affected the child* in this way, the intimacy of subjective engagement with Christian material is protected and affirmed, and it will be easier in that mode for the child to discover that what matters in the end is what this miracle asks of people, rather than objectively analyzing it in terms of historical distance, medical knowledge or evidence of water depth.

If this style—attending to how and when the "data" of faith interrogate the child—is a starting point for seeing Christian spirituality "turned on" in children, then researchers can begin to define the conditions in which this might more easily occur—and so equip adults to take on the "hard option" of studying children's spirituality within Christian contexts—digging beyond "said to please" responses.

In the first place, this suggests, to give children a fair chance, researchers need to study children who have *opportunities* to encounter Christian "data" on these terms, in other words, without misleading lessons in how to interrogate and explain it, but that allow time and space for encounters to do their own powerful interrogative work *in them*. Does this describe how children actually encounter the Christian story, Christian worship, Christian ethics and action? Or are they often robbed of chances to become aware of what their own response is, and its value as spiritual work? Is their spiritual response too often manipulated, pre-determined, or simply not anticipated until they are older? Too often these negative scenarios are unintentionally the reality of Christian nurture and so studying children's spirituality could yield misleadingly thin impressions of children's spiritual capacity and faith.

Next, there is an implication for the *context* that researchers and others provide for children's spirituality. "Being interrogated," especially by material as powerful and intractably strange as religious data, is unlikely to be a straightforward experience in emotional terms at any age. It may be exciting, deep, unhinging, worrying, affirming or undermining work. A context of protected time and a sense of "safe enough" space, and of course relationships, is an essential piece of equipment for studying Christian spirituality, particularly among young children. The location of an encounter with the sacred can be anywhere and any time; researchers and others cannot control that aspect. But it makes sense at least to provide conditions sensitive to the power and depth of feelings the child may have encountered when they re-visit the experience for further processing. So a safe place needs to be provided, as well as enough time for them to find their own pace. And a place needs to be provided where risk-taking is possible, where children can try out ideas that might seem unorthodox—that reorganize religious language and categories in response to its fundamental strangeness. In other words time and space for spiritual play—not cutesy, adult contrived fun—are essential conditions for observing the best of children's spirituality.

One of the most compelling features of Rowan Williams description of spirituality as the process of allowing the data of Christianity to "interrogate us" is the implication that being a person who is *less* familiar with the data may offer a kind of advantage. For children then this data has the potential to shine fresh and new, so perhaps they will be more capable and less numbed to realising its challenging probe into the status quo. Thus, in accompanying children adults may observe and learn from them about the needs of their own spiritual lives, to see how sheer novelty and absence of religious categories helps children become genuinely interrogated by the data, in ways in which adults have perhaps grown immune. Similarly, because of *adult* cognitive style, the primary strategy is to interrogate the data, or to theologize. Young children's psychological advantage—a blessing in fact—is that this kind of capacity is less developed, therefore less dominant or distracting, while their attention to emotion is acute. Watching them everyone can learn again what to do. In another sense, this is about including the children as part of the data of Christian life itself, by noting how attending to and seeking to understand them awakens and interrogates everyone and all experiences of God. Altogether, this makes for an exciting and unusual research agenda—not to mention a radical challenge for Christian nurture.

Advantages and Limitations of Delimiting Christian Spirituality of Children

Are there sufficient grounds for thinking that children's experiences of different faith traditions make a significant difference to their core spirituality? Perhaps by asking more focused "provincial" questions from within a given faith perspective things move forward generally. Rather than trying to seek a universal scholarly language for understanding children's spirituality, researchers and other adults can benefit from looking more closely and critically at particulars within each faith. Thus I hope that Jewish and Muslim colleagues will be encouraged to produce studied perspectives too, and obviously those which do not start from the kinds of premises about spirituality offered by an archbishop of Canterbury! Comparing and contrasting perspectives, approaches to study and findings may be a much more muscular basis for scholarly debate and development both within and between faiths.

In recent times, what might be considered a children's spirituality "field" has emerged, with journals, conferences, books, experts, and the like. It has been, until now, defined by an ethic of tolerance of spirituality in all forms. For some, spirituality has meant a fashionable contrast with the restrictions of religious frameworks—ringing new changes around the letter versus the spirit of the law distinction. Saying "Let's talk about spirituality without using religious language," is a refreshing challenge, but at some point psycho-babble could become a replacement for sacred-ese.

However shifting the focus from general to Christian perspectives risks frightening off some social science interest, because of the kind of language and theory that will be used. Religion has long been a taboo area for social sciences like psychology, despite its founders like William James having special interest in religious psychology. As one takes a "Christian perspective" it is crucial to be overt and comprehensive regarding the specific focus of subject matter and methodologies, as well as connecting empirical study with Christian theology, approaches to Christian education and creating academic dialogue with perspectives from other faiths. Perhaps if Goldman and other stage theorists had engaged more rigorously with Jesus' theology of childhood (see Berryman, 2002), children's spirituality might not be such a novel research area.

On balance then, there are grounds for "going Christian" about empirical research. Unpacking Rowan Williams' perspectives on the distinctive aspects of

Christian spirituality suggests some interesting leads, good places to start looking for data. Clearly, none of this is going to be easy; starting in a good place does not ensure the avoidance of all wrong turns, but it is essential to learn from mistakes that are made. Indeed there are at least three major factors for researchers to consider in embarking on social science research on children's spirituality "from a Christian perspective."

Christian Children?

In terms of empirical work there is nothing simple about limiting the sample to Christian children. First of all, *who* gets to define them as "Christian," using *what* criteria? Is it based upon self-definition, or what a parent states? Is church attendance or other commitment part of the definition? This is not an unfamiliar sampling problem for research with "Christian" adults, but among children it is even more problematic. Child participants cannot as easily define themselves, nor exercise "member checks" to interpretative labels given to them, their statements or behaviours.

In the research I did with David Hay at Nottingham University I did not ask in advance for information about children's religious identity, either from them, their parents or their teachers. It was interesting trying to establish some sense of this from our conversations. One six-year-old boy described spiritual experience as exclusively within, "in my mind, with my mind, in me." He came from a practicing Christian family who had ridiculed him when he said he had seen, externally, the Holy Spirit in his bedroom as "his friend, a bishopy alien." Another six-year-old boy described a conversion type of experience during prayer which occurred in a Church setting—yet his family members were not church members nor was he. A six-year-old defined himself as an atheist, like his mother, yet he had an imaginatively personal sense of God that fuelled his spiritual appreciation of life and love that few of the "Christian" children were able to express. To quote him, *"because God's love never ends, but the Devil's love does end. So Hell is in a square, because as square has a start and an end, but a circle—like heaven—doesn't. I believe in God's love because God made us . . . didn't it . . . God made us and gave us love . . . so we can love each other . . . and that's it."* So, which of these children should be admitted into a research sample as "Christian?"

A research perspective focusing on "Christian" children warrants providing "deep context" about the sense in which a Christian descriptor applies for each child. This implies getting into each child's story, and mitigates against a vast sample size. At least it means providing greater than average detail about the sample. For example, I recently ran some research sessions with "Christian children." All had one parent in seminary and both parents were practicing Christians. The seminary attracts more conservative Anglicans for whom teaching and correct understanding are important values. These children were used to hearing the Bible read as part of family life. I was interested in how they responded to the invitation to be more spiritually imaginative through "Godly Play" (Berryman, 2002). Being aware of the sense in which these children were "Christian,"—scripturally knowledgeable and coming from a context in which "being right" was held in higher esteem than mystery or imagination—would be essential to an adequate understanding of a given researcher's findings. Had a sample of children been drawn from a more liberal, more sacramental but also less family oriented Anglican seminary in Cambridge, I suspect the researchers would have learned very different things about "Christian" children's ability to engage with scriptural stories as spiritually provocative rather than intellectually affirming experiences. Even so, none of this information takes into account what the children studied felt about Christian identity for themselves. Who is researched and how research is reported are fascinating and important variables *within* the Christian research area.

Christian Researchers?

Does it also matter who the researcher is? Does the researcher being a Christian make it more likely that the study of Christian children will be more accurate? In contrast, would an outsider offer more of an objective view? Again, one is confronted with the issue of definition—what is a Christian researcher anyway? These issues are worthy of empirical research and debate. Researchers do bring an influence, so the perspective held does matter, and to appreciate their research those details need to be provided to provide insight about how that "tool" works. Indeed, children's spirituality research from a "Christian perspective" might simply mean that the researcher is a Christian— though the sample of children could be random, multi-faith and secular, and the methods could be traditional social science.

This issue of taking the researcher's religious perspective into serious account crashes into a *double* taboo. The first is the traditional view social science takes of subjectivity, or what might be termed "researcher perspective." Traditionally in research, subjectivity is considered a problem and it should be minimised or neutralised. Owning the characteristics of *faith* one brings to a research study is not what they typically teach in research methods classes! The second taboo is that this is asking Christians to be clear about the differences that lurk beneath the surface harmony of a shared set of beliefs, a Christian shared story. Part of me felt excited that this book, and the conference from which it was derived, brought together so many "like-minded colleagues," Christians sharing my interest in the spirituality of childhood. But another part of me recognizes that a good portion of that like-mindedness could be superficial. For example, in some respects my views of childhood spirituality, faith development and related issues may be closer to those of Jewish, agnostic or even atheist colleagues, than fellow Christians. For example, Christians designing and analyzing studies of children's spirituality might differ substantially on the interpretation of personal salvation and inherent sinfulness as a bridge to be crossed before valid spirituality can be spoken of in children. Likewise different approaches to worship, prayer, symbol and sacrament as adults will doubtless shape perceptions of children's spiritual strengths and limitations.

Thus to pursue social science approaches it will be necessary and enriching—and challenging—to make clear the different motives and assumptions brought as Christian researchers to the studies to be shared with one another. "Findings" cannot be understood fully in isolation of this; the identity of the researcher by itself does not invalidate findings, but describing one's commitments and background will help illuminate and encourage appreciation of each other's contribution on its own terms. But because tackling researcher perspective—even for oneself privately, let alone for public scrutiny—confronts both social science and religious community taboos, one needs to be patient in learning this skill. Furthermore, the researcher's perception of his or her own spirituality and Christian identity may change as a consequence of doing this kind of research. My spirituality continues to be profoundly affected and developed through research with children. For some, perhaps it is only when children are the central focus of attention—"in the midst" (Mark 9:36, King James Version)—that adults start to get close to learning about what the Christian life truly invites everyone to enter.

Christian Methods?

Finally, there is the question of "Christian methods." Might taking a Christian perspective have implications for methodological choices in research? As an example, ethical issues are an obvious matter to consider. One has to be ready for additional ethical demands that arise from one's own Christian perspective, or because faith nurture issues simply arise in the process of the research.

In the course of my doctoral research I thought ordinary ethical standards to protect the child participants from harm would be sufficient. There was no intention to *influence* the children's spirituality, or to develop it along my (Christian) lines nor any lines, I simply wanted to learn about what was "there." However my assumed neutral, non-invasive, methods were taken by many of the children as a developmental opportunity, in which their awareness of spirituality was raised. For these children, coming to the end of our research contact was therefore perceived as negative, a loss, an abrupt end, to a more conscious kind of spiritual life that had only just begun to develop. In fact this led to a major finding of that research project as a whole. As I tried to alleviate the children's sense of betrayal or bereavement when they were told this was their final interview, I tried to help them identify another person—a family member, a schoolteacher, a faith representative—with whom they could go on articulating their spiritual feelings, experience, ideas and values. They laughed at me; no one they felt, least of all the religious people they knew, had time for or interest in spirituality.

The irony was that though my analysis of their data suggested that at the core of children's spirituality was a quality of "relational consciousness," this was being locked away, no doubt withering away in individual isolationism; they were sure no one else felt or thought about things like this. I had to face the fact that for all my ethical safeguards it was crazy to treat spirituality as a feature I could examine without consequences. My study of children's spiritual "nature" (Hay & Nye, 1998) presented unintended ethical problems related to spiritual nurture and "influence." At the same time, using the same child-directed, open-ended interview approach with other children, such as those used with a more authoritative adult style in religious teaching and examination of spiritual matters, could be an undue "liberal" influence in their view.

But beyond ethics, are there other methodological issues for studies of childhood spirituality using a Christian perspective? I worry about characteristics of certain kinds of social science language as a means for fairly representing spirituality. To be able to tell the story of childhood spirituality adequately, despite my training and publications using quantitative methods and language, I have grave reservations about the value of statistics, correlations, analysis of variance, and other quantitative components such as control and experimental groups. The quantitative approach too easily lends itself to becoming numbers about numbers, which for discussing matters of faith and the numinous is a fate even worse than when theology becomes merely words about words. As a relatively new field, and as one unanimously regarded as complex, ambiguous, and surprising, children's spirituality is not adequately delineated to tolerate number crunching. People need the stories, the personal, the descriptions, the creative analyses. I assume spirituality has all these kinds of characteristics and people need to hang on to empirical approaches to research that allow it to be more of what it is—personal, convincing, memorable, unsettling, inspiring. Is there a statistic that is worthy of one's devotion or for which one would die?

So, what are the alternatives, and are these necessarily "Christian?" Qualitative methods and methodology seemed ideally suited to the study of spirituality as I began to consider my research options in this area. For one thing, its "strong" forms, such as grounded theory—which was developed originally by Glaser and Strauss (1967) researching people's experience of dying—permits going rather gently around the researcher's traditional nightmare task: identification of an operational definition of the topic to be studied. Operational definitions can be counterproductive, as exemplified in the attempt to define intelligence by use of an IQ score. How *does* one define observable, reliable and valid criteria for spirituality? And is that "fixing" it arbitrarily, delimiting it, and therefore undermining broader ways it has been implicitly understood long before social science came along? Jack Priestley (1992) suggests that trying to achieve an operational definition of spirituality is like to trying to catch the wind—obviously a metaphor with strong Christian connotations. Priestley goes on to suggest if a researcher *does* catch *something* with definitions and consequent data gathering, the only thing that can be certain is that what's caught *is not* spirituality!

The qualitative research method "grounded theory" is ideal when the researcher is uncertain, or unable, or even unwilling to impose a definition prematurely. Since it is hard enough to define adult spirituality, settling on what will "count as data," a definition of children's spirituality is even more of a challenge. As I entered this research area there were already a few attempts to operationalize what was meant by spirituality in childhood, such as those definitions used within the United Kingdom school system, which regards generalized spiritual development of children as a core educational objective across the curriculum. What was apparent in these definitions was that they used essentially adult criteria, even adult definitions in some cases—but not always—watered down to fit what could be expected of a "mere" child. And no one had checked out the validity of this with real children!

This seemed as illogical and unfair as studying Catholic spirituality by adopting and slightly adapting the terms of references applicable to orthodox Jewish spirituality! Or as non-sensical as determining a preschool child's intelligence in terms of what defines intelligent college educated adults. There is always the possibility that the phenomenon in question might be qualitatively different in children and adults. What I needed was a way for any features of children's spirituality to emerge in their own right. Grounded theory's methods supported that—facilitating a theory to arise from, to grow out of the data, rather than the parameters of an a-priori definition or hypothesis. It is also a rich and exciting way to work with the data, and necessitates collecting rather messy, but authentic "human" data—stories, conversations, observations. It makes a virtue of taking the "noise" and distracting data seriously that plagues traditional child researchers and teachers, in relatively unstructured conditions rather than impose controlled situations set up to produce a certain kind or amount of data. It could be said that there is no experimenter trying to play God here, but rather a space for the spirit to come out to play.

So in this and for all the other reasons I have mentioned so far, I felt there was a kind of Christian compatibility in this research method—allowing me to adopt a non-manipulative approach both to children and to spirituality. I saw parallels with Gospel teachings about childhood in this approach's encouragement to look for *new* theory emerging, rather than understanding children merely through the adult "standard." By observing children in their own right, on their own terms, *adults* may learn some of the most important spiritual lessons—so much so that adults might even find out more about what it really means to "become as little children" (Matt 18:3).

But grounded theory is not the entirely the social scientist's answer to prayer. It turns out that discerning what might be a valid "Christian method" for studying spirituality is just as tricky as the other two points—Christian children and Christian researchers. The problems arise because of the alternative epistemology underpinning most serious qualitative methodology, such as grounded theory. It brings with it an alternative mindset about what "knowledge" and by implication "truth" might be. In typical science using the quantitative paradigm, the epistemology emphasizes facts as "there" to be found by careful science and scientists.

However, in qualitative social science—the kind I used and which I have been suggesting has promise as a Christian kind of a method—truth and knowledge are viewed more as situated, constructed, affected by context and subjectivity; created and shaped by people rather than merely objective "facts." At the level of political equality this is an exciting and biblical direction for social science and theology, as it brings "down the mighty from their seats" (Luke 1:52) and redirects attention to a multitude of voices and realities. What is considered truth, fact and authority that define "reality" are now exposed as being just a position; merely how influential men in the Western church have thought. In contrast, within the qualitative mindset women's experiences, the perspectives held in the developing world, and even children's experiences can claim as much right to be examined as truth-disclosing.

However the research methods derived from this different understanding of knowledge leave Christians with a problem, if at the heart of this there is the implication that ultimate truth and authority are mirages by which people are self-deceived. In various ways Christianity *does* have a place for truth and authority, and for knowledge that is not just subjectively created by humans. In fact that place is found often deep within spiritual life. It is especially in spiritual experience, and exploration of spiritually significant aspects of life, that the perception of what is real can take a form that feels incontrovertible, certain, authoritative and true.

Conclusion

In conclusion, whichever way one "swings" on the quantitative/qualitative methodology issue, either as a researcher, or in the research by which practice is informed, there are caveats of which Christians should be mindful. There is plenty to guide and challenge much needed research dedicated to developing Christian perspectives on children's spirituality, to complement historical, theological and educational enquiries. *Nisi Dominus Frustray!*[2]

References

Glaser, B. G., & Strauss, A. L. (1967). *The discovery of grounded theory.* Chicago: Aldine.
Goldman, R. (1964). *Religious thinking from childhood to adolescence.* New York: Seabury.
Hay, D., & Nye, R. (1998). *The spirit of the child.* London: Fount/HarperCollins.
Nye, R. (1998). *Psychological perspectives on children's spirituality.* Doctoral dissertation, University of Nottingham, UK.
Hample, S. (1991). *Children's letters to God.* New York: Workman.

2. In vain without God!

Priestley, J. (1992). *Bible stories for classroom and assembly*. Norwich, UK: Religious and Moral Education Press.

Wangerin, W. (2003). *The use of story for spiritual formation*. Children's Spirituality Conference: Christian Perspectives, River Forest, IL, June 8.

Williams, R. (1991). *The wound of knowledge: Christian spirituality from the New Testament to Saint John of the Cross*. Cambridge, MA: Cowley.

Chapter Seven

A Sociocultural Perspective on Children's Spiritual Development

WENDY HAIGHT, PH.D.[1]

"I hums to the Lord, and I sings to Him. There'll be a day, I just tells him of my down-and-out-blues." (Coles, 1990, p. 200)

As the comment of this young girl illustrates, spirituality is central to the lives of many children. Beginning in childhood, spirituality can be a source of joy, comfort, meaning and interpretation of life's trials. During their discussions of morality and political issues, Robert Coles (1990) was so impressed with children's spontaneous use and elaborations of their religious beliefs that he embarked on an exploration that became the book *Spiritual Life of Children*. He found that many children of Jewish, Muslim and Christian traditions drew upon their spiritual beliefs to interpret life's joys and complexities from love and birth to accidents, illness, racism and death. Similarly, Sarah Moskovitz (1983) concluded from her study of child survivors of the Nazi Holocaust that a sense of hope for the future rooted in religious faith enabled children to love and behave compassionately towards others in spite of the atrocities they had experienced. Likewise, in her oral history, *Raise Up a Child*, Edith Hudley (Hudley, Haight & Miller, 2003) described human development in a rural African American community as rooted in spirituality. Indeed, scholarship within African American studies portrays spirituality as culturally valued (e.g., Boykin, 1994; Schiele,

---

1. Wendy Haight received her PhD from the University of Chicago where she studied developmental and cultural psychology. She is an associate professor and PhD program director at the University of Illinois, Urbana-Champaign in the School of Social Work. She is the author or co-author of four books: *Pretending at Home: Development in Sociocultural Context, American Children at Church: A Sociocultural Perspective, Raise Up a Child: Human Development in an African-American Family* and *Reflections on Human Behavior in the Social Environment: A Developmental-Ecological Framework for Social Work Practice*. She is the author or co-author of 20 journal articles and numerous book chapters on development in sociocultural contexts.

1996), and central to socialization (Brown, 1991) from slavery through the present (e.g., Hill-Harris, 1998; Lincoln, 1999; Smitherman, 1977; Sobel, 1988).

Yet, developmental psychologists have had relatively little to say about children's spirituality. From the perspective of developmental psychology, the most deeply meaningful experiences of childhood, as described by Edith Hudley, Robert Coles and others, are what Jacqueline Goodnow (1990) has called "homeless phenomena." There is literally no place for them within existing theories of human development (Hudley, Haight & Miller, 2003). Furthermore, much of the existing developmental research on children's spiritual and religious participation is negatively biased. For example, developmental descriptions of children's participation within a European-American church (Zinsser, 1986), and within a private, religiously-based, African-American school (Mehan, Okamoto, Lintz & Wills, 1995), focus on practices which appear antithetical to children's development. Interactions between adults and children are characterized as highly structured and adult-centered with a one-way flow of communication from adult to child. Children are discouraged from questioning, speculating or extending presented material.

Thankfully, there are some exceptions to this picture of neglect and negativity in the developmental psychology literature. In *Stages of Faith,* James Fowler (1981) starts from the premise that nascent capacities for faith are present at birth. He draws upon the classic developmental theories of Piaget, Kohlberg and Erikson, as well as discussions with children and adults, to explore how faith unfolds across the lifespan. In *Religious Judgment*, Oser and Gmunder (1991), examine the development of religious reasoning. After surveying or interviewing over 3,000 Finnish children and adolescents, Kalevi Tamminen (1991, 1994) comments on the emotional depth of religious experiences in childhood. Cindy Clark (1995) in *Flights of Fancy, Leaps of Faith,* explains the connections between children's beliefs related to childhood myths such as Santa Claus, the Easter Bunny, and the Tooth Fairy, and the developmental foundations of religious faith. These remarkable works provide important insights into children's spiritual development, but they have existed at the margins, rarely cited in the mainstream literature on child development.

There are some hints, however, that this situation may be changing. For example, in their edited volume, Karl Rosengren, Carl Johnson, and Paul Harris (2000) argue for a more complex portrayal of children's cognitive development—one that includes metaphysical and theological as well as rational experience. In *African American Children at Church* (Haight, 2001), I describe positive, stimulating, and rich socialization practices within an African American Baptist Church. These practices include verbal narratives, play, song, prayer and call-and-response routines to which children actively contribute: elaborating, questioning and exploring issues of spirituality with teachers and peers in an emotionally supportive setting. In addition, there is a growing awareness that religion and spirituality may illuminate the mysterious quality of "resilience" (Garmezy, 1985). People who are resilient are able to find meaning in their lives even in the face of extraordinary hardship. Robert Coles (1990) provides a memorable example, quoting the words of an eight-year-old girl who helped to deseg-regate a North Carolina school in 1962:

> I was all alone, and those [segregationist] people were screaming, and sud-denly I saw God smiling, and I smiled. . . . A woman was standing there [near the school door], and she shouted at me, "Hey, you little nigger, what you smiling at?" I looked right at her face and I said, "At God." Then she looked up at the sky, and then she looked at me, and she didn't call me any more names.
> (Coles, 1990, pp. 19–20)

Conceptual frameworks for understanding such spiritual experiences, however, are still emerging. Early empirical work on children's spirituality (e.g., Fowler, 1981; Oser & Gmunder, 1991) was heavily influenced by Piaget's theory of intellectual development (see Boyatzis, 2005), and emphasized universal, stage-like aspects of spiritual development revealed through clinical interviews. This work made impor-tant contributions by highlighting children's active search for understanding, and the relationships between spiritual development and other developmental domains. Development was viewed as a complex whole with intellectual, moral and spiritual dimensions in interaction with one another. Children's spiritual understanding was revealed not as a simple copy of adult perspectives, but as an interpretation that is actively constructed by the child.

On the other hand, early empirical work largely ignored context and the various ways in which spiritual meaning and purpose are shared in diverse settings. Recent research reveals that children's religious beliefs affect and are affected by their fami-lies, religious background and other aspects of the sociocultural context (see Boyatzis, 2005; Haight, 2002). These conceptualizations of children's spiritual development as profoundly social are consistent with recent sociocultural theory and research in developmental psychology, which emphasize the child not as a lone seeker, but as born into relationships, family, and community that shape and are shaped by his/her development.

Sociocultural Frameworks for Understanding Development

Spirituality encompasses feelings, ideas, and practices pertaining to a non-material higher force (Boykin, 1994), as well as meaning and purpose in life (Coles, 1995). Spiritual development involves changes over time, as well as the process and causes of those changes. From a sociocultural perspective, spiritual development occurs through the dialectical processes of socialization and acquisition. In brief, socialization is the process by which adults structure the social environment and display patterned mean-ings for the child (Wentworth, 1980; Miller & Sperry, 1987; Haight & Miller, 1993).

Socialization may be direct, as when a pastor preaches a special children's sermon; or indirect, as when parents bring their own religiously oriented reading material into the home. Socialization may be intentional, as when a grandmother escorts her grandchild to Sunday School, or unintentional, as when a child observes her godmother engrossed in prayer. Acquisition is the process through which children interpret, respond to, and ultimately embrace, reject, or elaborate upon the social patterns to which they are exposed (Wentworth, 1980; Miller & Sperry, 1988).

As these descriptions suggest, socialization and acquisition are tightly linked processes. Socialization messages, undoubtedly, impact children's spiritual experiences. Perhaps a Sunday School teacher expressed it most powerfully when she described to me (Haight, 2002) her own relationships with adults as a child:

> I gathered my spirit from them. I saw what they did. I saw them pray. I saw what they were going through. I saw them read the Bible. I saw them sing, and they would sing joyously! (p. 69)

On the other hand, children's acquisition also affects adults' spiritual experiences (see Boyatzis, 2005) and socialization practices. Indeed, at First Baptist Church (Haight, 2002), children are treasured not only as the hope for the future, but for the central role they play in the present as models of love and trust. They are nurtured as future leaders, but also given a place as legitimate community members whose current contributions are meaningful. In this excerpt from his 1992 Christmas sermon, Pastor Daniels quoted Jesus to exhort adults to consider the child both as a symbol of hope for change in this world and also for their current spiritual salvation, "'Suffer the little children to come unto me and forbid them not . . .' Without the little child we will never see God. . . . The kingdom of God is for the childlike. . . . We all need to learn to be childlike." Indeed, Sunday School teachers described not only the effect they had on the lives of their students, but also how routine, sustained contact with individual children deeply affected their own spiritual development.

From this dialectical perspective of socialization and acquisition, spiritual development is embedded within a social and historical context as children actively observe and increasingly participate with others in the routine, everyday practices through which culture is maintained and elaborated (see, for example, Corsaro, 1996; Lave and Wenger, 1991; Rogoff, 1990). For example, at First Baptist Church active participation in the communal worship of God is an important value and socialization goal. Over time, children increasingly participated in, and even shaped, worship services. As toddlers, they sat through worship services with adults for up to 2½ hours with encouragement to clap their hands, sing, and pray—sometimes nap and snack—when appropriate. As preschoolers, they participated in special events such as Christmas programs, and in groups such as the children's choir. During middle childhood and adolescence, children were given increasing responsibilities as they also participated as ushers, and even led devotions as junior deacons and deaconesses.

Embedded within a complex sociocultural context, spiritual development is multidimensional involving the active engagement of intellect, emotion and morality over time. Kalevi Tamminen (1991, 1994) and others have discussed the multiple dimensions of children's religious and spiritual experience. The focus of much of the developmental research on children's religion and spirituality, to date, has been on cognition, which involves thinking, concepts, and religious knowledge, such as a child's knowledge of the Gospels and changing ability to interpret Jesus' parables.

But faith and spirituality have other facets as well. The experiential dimension involves religious experiences, including feeling the nearness of God. It is this more affective component that is so striking in spiritual narratives of African Americans, especially of conversion experiences (see Gates, 1988). During emotionally intense conversion narratives, the protagonist may describe vivid experiences of heaven and hell, complete with visual, auditory and tactile sensations. Spirituality also has an ideological dimension widely shared by members of a cultural community. This is the dimension I emphasized (Haight, 2002) when describing the common beliefs of African-American adults regarding significant spiritual messages to children, such as the inherent worth of each individual as a child of God. Spirituality also has a ritualistic dimension (Ratcliff, 2001), which includes religious practices. This is the dimension emphasized by Edith Hudley (Hudley, Haight & Miller, 2003) when she spoke so eloquently of the comfort and strength she experienced as a child from morning and evening family prayers. The consequential dimension of spirituality is the effect of religiousness on a person's everyday life. Adults at First Baptist Church (Haight, 2002) emphasized this dimension when they expressed that a primary goal of Sunday School, subsequent to bringing the child to Jesus, was to help children to understand and then to apply spiritual teachings to their everyday life.

From a sociocultural perspective, the developing characteristics of spirituality as a multidimensional process are important, empirical issues. Dimensions of spiritual development may be gradual and incremental, or more qualitative and stage-like. Further, some dimensions may progress from less to more complete or competent, while other dimensions may reflect more complex and fluctuating developmental changes. Fowler's (1981) clinical interviews highlighted some changes in cognitive dimensions that occur within a complex, coordinated, stage-like developmental shift moving from less to more competent spiritually. For example, individuals reveal distinct spiritual perspectives as they move through early childhood and into adulthood, and an increasing understanding of religious concepts is linked in a coordinated fashion to more sophisticated moral reasoning.

Other dimensions of spiritual development, however, do not necessarily move forward in a coordinated, integrated fashion from less to more adequate. For example, Tamminen (1991, 1994) found that although spiritual experiences are relatively common in childhood and adolescence, the percentage of children and adolescents who reported experiencing God's nearness decreased with age, most markedly, near puberty (age 13 to 15). At this time, young adolescents expressed doubts about God's existence and about the efficacy of prayer. Thus, at the very time children experience rapid intellectual growth, as well as the understanding and knowledge of religion, the quality of their experience of spirituality arguably declines. It may be that the subjective sense of God's nearness may peak at various other points of the lifespan, for example, during childbirth or before death reflecting a complex, nonlinear developmental function.

Sociocultural Methods

Developing a sociocultural model of spiritual development requires an integration of various social science methods. In recent years there has been an increasing interest in combining developmental and ethnographic methods to study children's spiritual development (see Boyatzis, 2005). The intent of such methodological pluralism is to strengthen both developmental and ethnographic approaches to better understand development in a variety of sociocultural contexts (see Jessor, Colby & Shweder, 1996). Developmental methods include the systematic, often microscopic, description of children's participation in everyday activities and changes in participation over time, as well as in-depth clinical interviews characteristic of early studies of children's religious and spiritual development. Ethnographic methods include the interpretation of the meanings of social practices from participants' perspectives through analyses of a broader context of beliefs, experiences and practices. Thus, the intertwining of developmental and ethnographic methods allows both the identification of the regularities inherent in everyday life, and an interpretation of what such regularities may mean to the participants themselves (Gaskins, Miller & Corsaro, 1992; Sperry & Sperry, 1996).

My study of children's socialization within an African-American church is one example of the combination of ethnographic and developmental methods to further the understanding of spiritual development (Haight, 2002). This study describes the practices, particularly storytelling, through which African-American Sunday School teachers and their students, aged 3–15 years, construct personal meanings from an important cultural resource, the Bible. Detailed observations were contextualized by multiple, in-depth interviews with the pastor, Sunday School Superintendent, and Sunday School teachers to reveal the meaning of these practices to participants. Practices and beliefs associated with Sunday School are further contextualized through description of key events occurring in the larger church community including yearly events such as Vacation Bible School, monthly events such as "youth emphasis" day, weekly events such as the pastor's sermons for children, a variety of other special occasions focusing on children, adult Sunday School classes, and weekly Sunday School teachers' meetings. Observations and interviews are further contextualized through analysis of historical and social background information obtained from a variety of local newspaper articles, historical documents and church publications.

An integration of developmental and ethnographic approaches is important to context-specific conceptualizations of spiritual development. This methodological approach reflects the modern movement in the field of human development away from defining developmental trajectories in universal terms, abstracted from the particular practices within which children develop, and toward the identification and description of various kinds of feelings, beliefs and competences that emerge within particular cultural contexts (Rogoff, 1990). It encourages us to expand the focus from mainstream groups to more diverse groups. This expanded perspective is critical for several reasons. First, African Americans, Hispanics, Native Americans, Asian Americans, members of diverse religious communities worldwide and other groups underrepresented in developmental research are important in their own right. In addition, their inclusion is necessary to disentangle universal from culturally variable aspects of spiritual development. Much of what is presented in the developmental research on children's spirituality is assumed to be "universal," but, in fact, has little supporting empirical research.

Furthermore, an expanded perspective will bring to the fore questions that have not yet been addressed adequately in the developmental literature. For example, in Edith Hudley's (2003) oral history of spiritual development in an African American family, she describes a community in which even young children were allowed to participate with adults in spiritual events in meaningful ways, and their own spiritual experiences were taken seriously. In this context, ten-year-old Edith experienced visions of her recently deceased mother. Adults in her community interpreted these experiences with Edith as meaningful spiritual experiences through which she continued to feel emotionally connected to her mother. Edith's belief that the dead remain available to the living was introduced and reinforced by her father and other adults, but it was she—not they—who actually witnessed the spirits of the dead.

Current developmental theories do not accommodate such mystical experiences, too often reducing the child's experience to a quirk of imagination or cognitive immaturity (Boyatzis, personal communication). Yet such experiences are relatively common in African-American studies. For example, early African American biographers recalled direct communications with God and angels and describe visions of heaven and hell experienced during conversion experiences (Gates, 1988). Such experiences also characterize foundational moments in many religions including indigenous African and Asian religions (Boyatzis, personal communication) and Christianity. (e.g., Moses and the burning bush, Mary with the angel Gabriel).

A developmental-ethnographic strategy increasingly is recognized as critical for understanding children from diverse cultural communities (e.g., Heath, 1996, 1983; Miller, 1982; Philips, 1983; Ogbu, 1974). Moore (1991) argues that an ethnographic approach is particularly important when those involved—the children, the researchers, and the professionals—come from different communities. "The ethnographic approach is a dialectical or interactive-adaptive method in which data, research questions, and analytical categories interact as the study evolves (Hymes, 1982)." Incorporating such ethnographic methods into more traditional developmental approaches forces researchers to understand the meaning of observed behavior from categories emerging from the community being studied, rather than the culture of the researcher.

For example, my ethnographic analysis of adult participants' beliefs about the centrality of storytelling as a tool for supporting children's emerging spirituality, in part, inspired a subsequent developmental analysis of regularities in the ways in which adults actually told stories with children (Haight, 2002). Existing research from other contexts suggested that stories of personal experience would be critical. Personal experience narratives report on events that actually occurred to the narrator. For example, a Sunday School teacher described to the children her own spiritual journey during her recovery from alcoholism. The developmental analyses, however, revealed that "hypothetical narratives"—a much less studied type of story—were as prevalent as stories of personal experience in adult-child interactions in the church I studied. Hypothetical stories allow participants to play with the biblical text or spiritual concepts, discussing what might be or might have been, given the presented or altered circumstances. For example, one Sunday School teacher provided a story starter to the children, "Imagine . . . if you was just lounging on the beach and all of a sudden you took your shades off, looked up, and there was somebody and they were walking on water!" My observations of hypothetical narratives, in turn, motivated a more detailed analysis of adult beliefs about the functions of particular types of stories in the context of Sunday School. For example, adults valued teaching children to apply biblical and spiritual concepts to their everyday lives. They viewed hypothetical stories as a way of helping children to apply important spiritual concepts without getting distracted by, or inappropriately revealing, personal details of their families' private lives.

Methodological Issues

Developmental-ethnographic approaches are diverse, but there are a number of key methodological characteristics designed to enhance rigor and credibility (Patton, 2001). First, rapport building is essential. For example, establishing trusting relationships was prerequisite to gaining entrance into the community at First Baptist Church. I participated with my family at First Baptist Church for one year before approaching the pastor to discuss the study, and I continued with these activities throughout—and beyond—the study. I also worked with community leaders to establish a computer club for children at First Baptist Church. Community leaders were well aware of past abuses of African-Americans by researchers, and several of my colleagues at the university who did not take the time to establish meaningful relationships within the community were denied access for their research. In addition, good rapport is essential to obtaining ecologically valid observations. Participants obviously are aware that they are being observed, so it is extremely important that they be comfortable with the observer. Maintaining a good rapport with participants also facilitates member checking; I was able to go back to participants and discuss if my evolving interpretations were consistent with their understanding.

Second, sustained community engagement is typical of developmental-ethnographic approaches. For example, I detailed the complexities of socialization practices through in-depth, sustained involvement in the church community spanning a four-year period and totaling more than 1,000 hours of direct contact. Gaining access to, and understanding, the perspectives of others is time-intensive. I conducted multiple interviews with each participant to allow him/her time to think over and elaborate upon topics. In addition, repeated observations (a minimum of 10 each) were made in four different Sunday School classes for children. These repeated observations allowed the identification of stable patterns of practice both within and across classrooms, in contrast to temporary fluctuations caused by special events, variations in mood, class composition, and other changes.

Third, naturalistic observation is important to ethnographic-developmental approaches. I examined adults' socialization beliefs and practices, and children's participation within routine contexts familiar and emotionally meaningful to them. Socialization practices and the participation of children were observed within the contexts in which they ordinarily occurred—during Sunday School, church services, other regularly scheduled church activities, and informal church gatherings. I did not attempt to elicit particular behaviors or to structure the situations in any way.

Fourth, triangulation is important to creating a "thick" description as well as establishing rigor and credibility of the data. For example, to balance the strengths and weaknesses of various methods, as well as provide multiple checks on interpretation, I used a variety of data collection strategies including observation, interviews and document analysis. To allow for a more complete account of religious practices, I also observed in multiple contexts including Vacation Bible School, Sunday School, children's sermons, and Easter and Christmas programs. I also used multiple data collectors because characteristics of the investigator influence informants' behavior—both an African-American Spelman College student and I interviewed adults. Using multiple interviewers has the advantage of expanding the audience to which participants addressed themselves and, presumably, the range of topics on which they elaborated.

Fifth, reliability checks, member checking, peer audits and other strategies are necessary to ensure the quality of the data analysis. I conducted extensive inter rater reliability checks on behavioral coding of socialization practices as well as content coding of interviews. Also, community members as well as two other scholars not involved in the research read transcripts and commented on the codes, for example, if they missed important themes or patterns.

Conclusion

In conclusion, much of the developmental work on children's spirituality has focused on children from mainstream communities using stage models of the developmental process and clinical interview methodology, and has provided little information about the contexts that shape and are shaped by spiritual development. This work has made important contributions to understanding children's active construction of spirituality, but urgently needs expansion to incorporate modern developmental theory and adequate methodology. Recent sociocultural research has begun to provide rich descriptions of the contexts that shape and are shaped by children's emerging spirituality. On the other hand, this research is not as strong in its descriptions of children's changing perspectives. From a sociocultural perspective, there is a need to integrate analyses of acquisition and socialization within particular contexts.

In his discussion of the development of faith, Fowler (1981) observes that religious symbols and language are widely available in society. Even in early childhood, youngsters combine fragments of stories and images given by their cultures into their own interpretations of God and the sacred. The question of how children develop their spirituality "in conversation" with others—both adults and children, during everyday routines and special activities—deserves serious consideration from Christian educators, parents, and scholars.

References

Boyatzis, C. J. (2005). Religious and spiritual development in childhood. In R. F. Paloutzian & C. L. Park (Eds.), *The handbook for the psychology of religion and spirituality* (pp. 123–143). New York: Guilford.

Boykin, W. (1994). Harvesting talent and culture: African-American children and educational reform. In R. Rossi (Ed.), *Schools and students at risk: Context and framework for positive change* (pp. 116–140). New York: Teachers College Press.

Brown, D. R. (1991). Religious socialization and educational attainment among African Americans: An empirical assessment. *Journal of Negro Education, 60,* 411–426.

Clark, C. D. (1995). *Flights of fancy, leaps of faith: Children's myths in contemporary America.* Chicago: University of Chicago Press.

Coles, R. (1990). *The spiritual life of children.* Boston: Houghton Mifflin.

Coles, R. (1995). The profile of spirituality of at-risk youth. In R. Coles, D. Elkind, L. Monroe, C. Shelton, & B. Soaries (Eds.), *The ongoing journey: Awakening spiritual life in at-risk youth* (pp. 7–38). Omaha, NE: Boys Town Press.

Corsaro, W. (1996). Transitions in early childhood: The promise of comparative, longitudinal ethnography. In R. Jessor, A. Colby, & R. Shweder (Eds.), *Ethnography and human development: Context and meaning in social inquiry* (pp. 419–458). Chicago: University of Chicago Press.

Fowler, J. W. (1981). *Stages of faith: The psychology of human development and the quest for meaning.* New York: Harper Collins.

Garmezy, N. (1985). Stress-resistant children: The search for protective factors. In J. E. Stevenson (Ed.), Recent research in developmental psychopathology [Book supplement No. 4]. *Journal of Child Psychology and Psychiatry, 26,* 213–233.

Gaskins, S., Miller, P. & Corsaro, W. (1992). Theoretical and methodological perspectives in the interpretive study of children. In W. Corsaro & P. Miller (Eds.), *Interpretive approaches to children's socialization. New directions for child development,* (pp. 5–23). San Francisco: Jossey-Bass.

Gates, H. L. (Ed.). (1988). *Spiritual narratives.* New York: Oxford University Press.

Goodnow, J. J. (1990). The socialization of cognition: What's involved? In J. W. Stigler, R. A. Shweder & G. Herdt (Eds.), *Cultural psychology essays on comparative human development* (pp. 259–86). New York: Cambridge University Press.

Haight, W. (2002). *African American children at church: A sociocultural perspective.* New York: Cambridge University Press.

Haight, W., & Miller, P. J. (1993). *Pretending at home: Early development in a sociocultural context.* Albany: SUNY Press.

Heath, S. B. (1983). *Ways with words: Language, life, and work in communities and classrooms.* New York: Cambridge University Press.

Heath, S. B. (1996). Ruling places: Adaptation in development in inner-city youth. In R. Jessor, A. Colby, & R. Shweder (Eds.), *Ethnography and human development: Context and meaning in social inquiry* (pp. 225–252). Chicago: University of Chicago Press.

Hill-Harris, M. (1998). *Religious socialization and educational attainment among African Americans.* Unpublished Master's Thesis. California State University, Hayward.

Hudley, E., Haight, W., & Miller, P. J. (2003). *Raise up a child.* Chicago: Lyceum.

Hymes, D. H. (1982). *Ethnolinguistic study of classroom discourse: Final report to the National Institute of Education.* University of Pennsylvania, Graduate School of Education.

Jessor, R., Colby, A., & Shweder, R. A. (Eds.). (1996). *Ethnography and human development: Context and meaning in social inquiry.* Chicago: University of Chicago Press.

Lave, J., & Wenger, E. (1991). *Situated learning: Legitimate peripheral participation.* New York: Cambridge University Press.

Lincoln, C. E. (1999). *Race, religion. and the continuing American dilemma.* New York: Hill & Wang.

Mehan, H., Lintz, A., Okamoto, D., & Willis, J. (1995). Ethnographic studies of multicultural education in classrooms and schools. In J. Banks & C. Banks (Eds.), *Handbook of research on multicultural education* (pp. 163–183). New York: Simon & Schuster/MacMillan.

Miller, P. (1982). *Amy, Wendy and Beth: Language learning in South Baltimore.* Austin: University of Texas Press.

Miller, P., & Sperry, L. (1987). The socialization of anger and aggression. *Merrill-Palmer Quarterly, 33,* 1–31.

Moore, T. (1991). The African-American church: A source of empowerment, mutual help, and social change. *Prevention in Human Services, 10,* 147–167.

Morrison, T. (1987). *Beloved.* New York: Plume.

Moskovitz, S. (1983). *Love despite hate: Child survivors of the holocaust and their adult lives.* New York: Schocken.

Ogbu, J. U. (1974). *The next generation: An ethnography of education in an urban neighborhood.* New York: Academic Press.

Oser, F., & Gmunder, P. (1991). *Religious judgement: A developmental approach.* Birmingham, AL: Religious Education Press.

Patton, M. Q. (2001). *Qualitative research and evaluation methods* (3rd ed.). Thousand Oaks, CA: Sage.

Philips, S. (1983). *The invisible culture: Communication in classroom and community on the Warm Springs Indian Reservation.* New York: Longman.

Ratcliff, D. (2001). Rituals in a school hallway: Evidence of a latent spirituality of children. *Christian Education Journal, 5NS*(2), 9–26.

Rogoff, B. (1990). *Apprenticeship in thinking: Cognitive development in social context.* New York: Oxford.

Rosengren, K., Johnson, C., & Harris, P. (Eds.). (2000). *Imagining the impossible: Magical, scientific and religious thinking in children.* New York: Cambridge University Press.

Schiele, J. H. (1996). Afrocentricity: An emerging paradigm in social work practice. *Social Work, 41,* 284–293.

Smitherman, G. (1977). *Talkin and testifyin: The language of Black America.* Boston: Houghton Mifflin.

Sobel, M. (1979*). Trabelin' on: The slave journey to an Afro-Baptist faith.* New Jersey: Princeton University Press.

Sperry, L., & Sperry, D. (1996). Early development of narrative skills. *Cognitive Development, 11,* 443–465.

Tamminen, K. (1991). *Religious development in childhood and youth: An empirical study.* Helsinki: Suomalainen Tiedeakatemia.

Tamminen, K. (1994). Religious experiences in childhood and adolescence: A viewpoint of religious development between the ages of 7 and 20. *International Journal for the Psychology of Religion, 4*(2), 61–85.

Wentworth, W. M. (1980). *Context and understanding: An inquiry into socialization theory.* New York: Elsevier.

Zinsser, C. (1986). For the Bible tells me so: Teaching children in a fundamentalist church. In B.B. Schiefflin & P. Gilmore (Eds.), *The acquisition of literacy: Ethnographic perspectives* (pp. 55–74). Norwood, NJ: Albex.

Chapter Eight

Exploring Scientific and Theological Perspectives on Children's Spirituality

EUGENE C. ROEHLKEPARTAIN[1]

W hat is the state of the field of children's spirituality? Where is it headed? If one were to pose those questions in a room of uninitiated social scientists, some would doubt that it is a definable, legitimate area of study—despite the wealth of knowledge and expertise available, as is evidenced by the chapters in this and other publications. Among those who believe spiritual development is an important domain of inquiry, some would then argue that it only emerges in adolescence.

The reaction would be quite different if the question were posed to a room of religious leaders, theologians, and other scholars. They might see spiritual development as an agenda to be considered within their faith tradition. To them, spiritual development is a religious, not scientific question. And while the scientists might argue that not enough has been written to justify this being considered a field of study, theologians would retort, "We've been studying and debating such questions for thousands of years."

In reality, the questions are legitimate for both the social sciences and theologians. Despite the centrality of spirituality as a force in individual lives and in societies, focused attention on the dynamics of spirituality in children's lives has been rare, both in recent years and historically (see Bunge, 2001). In addition, the efforts that have been made have tended to be either theological *or* scientific, with these two ways of learning and framing knowledge rarely intersecting or learning from each other.

With support from the John Templeton Foundation, Search Institute launched in 2003 a major spiritual development initiative that is beginning to explore these kinds

1. Eugene C. Roehlkepartain is senior advisor to the president at Search Institute, a Minneapolis-based nonprofit organization that provides leadership, knowledge, and resources to promote healthy children, youth, and communities. Roehlkepartain serves as project manager for the institute's initiative on spiritual development. He is author of *The Teaching Church* (1993) and an editor of two recent books on children's spirituality.

of issues. This initiative is initially seeking to map the state of spiritual development in the first two decades of life, then to stimulate new research, dialogue, and application. The goal is not only to advance interdisciplinary understanding, but also to improve spirituality-nurturing practices in families, congregations, and other settings. This chapter describes the work underway and the issues that have surfaced, in hopes that it stimulates new thinking and questions to guide future work.

The Definitional Challenge

In beginning to map this field, the first question that must be addressed is definitional. What is spirituality? How is it similar to or different from religion? Is it something that is so broad that it becomes, essentially, whatever a particular person wants it to be? Or, at the other extreme, is it reduced it to something so specific and narrow that it becomes trivial, irrelevant, or faddish?

Adding to the complexity, spirituality is understood in different ways in different religious traditions and in different disciplines. Some view it exclusively as within their discipline. For example, this perspective might hold that all true spirituality is "Christian spirituality." In contrast, there are those who would argue that spirituality is a completely separate phenomenon from religion. For them, religion most often gets in the way of spirituality. Several helpful articles and books that examine these definitional issues include: Collins (2000), Hill and others (2000), King (2001), MacDonald (2000), Marler and Hadaway (2002), Reich (2001), Stifoss-Hanssen (1999), Wuthnow (1998), Zinnbauer and others (1997), and Zinnbauer, Pargament, and Scott (1999). In addition, much of the definitional work on spirituality has focused on adults, with relatively few scholars (Nye, 1999, being an important exception) articulating definitions for spirituality in childhood.

Given these complex realities, it seems premature—and potentially counterproductive—to propose that a particular definition could adequately capture the richness, complexity, and multidimensional nature of this domain of human life. As Nye (1999) writes:

> Attempts to define [spirituality] closely, and derive an adequate "operational definition" can be sure of one thing: misrepresenting spirituality's complexity, depth and fluidity. Spirituality is like the wind—though it might be experienced, observed and described, it cannot be "captured"—we delude ourselves to think otherwise, either in the design of research or in analytical conclusions (p. 58).

At the same time, remaining open to diverse definitions so that ideas have time to distill does not excuse scholars from articulating their current thinking and assumptions. Thus, for the purposes of this initiative, people examining the current state of the field have drafted overlapping definitions. One grew out of framing social science perspectives on spiritual development (Roehlkepartain, King, Wagener, & Benson, 2006); the other is grounded in the language and themes of theological and religious studies (Yust, Johnson, Sasso, & Roehlkepartain, 2006). While these definitions may be merged as the work advances, both are presented here to highlight particular accents and issues within these diverse disciplines.

Draft of a religious studies definition—"Spirituality is the intrinsic human capacity for self-transcendence in which the individual participates in the sacred—something greater than the self. It propels the search for connectedness, meaning, purpose, and ethical responsibility. It is experienced, formed, shaped, and expressed through a wide range of religious narratives, beliefs, and practices, and is shaped by many forces in society and culture."

Draft of a social science definition—"Spiritual development is the process of growing the intrinsic human capacity for self-transcendence, in which the self is embedded in something greater than the self, including the sacred. It propels the search for connectedness, meaning, purpose, and contribution. It is shaped both within and outside of religious traditions, beliefs, and practices" (Also see Benson, Roehlkepartain, & Rude, 2003).

Neither definition is concise or ideal. We anticipate that each will evolve, perhaps dramatically, as the work progresses. However, they surface several key assumptions or hypotheses that are guiding this work, which are explored here.

Spirituality as an Integral Part of Humanness

Both definitions assert that there is an intrinsic human capacity for spirituality, or transcendence of self toward "something greater." This impulse gives rise to such phenomena as seeking meaning and purpose, the pursuit of the sacred, and embedding one's identity within a tradition, community, or stream of thought. Within the Christian community, spiritual development builds on an understanding of a transcendent and immanent God as well as a community of faithful companions on the journey, all of which bring meaning, purpose, and significance.

Throughout history and across all societies, forms of spirituality have become part of human experience, and it has remained a robust force in life for both individuals and societies, despite numerous predictions of its demise. The scientific evidence for this capacity emerges from several sources, including the growing—but still limited—body of evidence that suggests that spirituality or religiosity has biological or physiological roots (e. g. d'Aquili & Newberg, 1999; and D'Onofrio, Eaves, Murrelle, Maes, & Spilka, 1999).

A Multi-Dimensional Construct

The vast majority of researchers in the field agree that spirituality has multiple domains. For example, Scott (as cited in Zinnbauer, Pargament, & Scott, 1999) analyzed the content of scientific definitions of religiousness and spirituality published in the last half of the 20th Century. Although she found no consensus or even dominant approaches, Scott identified nine content categories in definitions of spirituality: experiences of connectedness or relationship; processes leading to greater connectedness; behavioral responses to something, either sacred or secular; systems of thought or beliefs; traditional institutional structures; pleasurable states of being; beliefs in the sacred or transcendent, and existential questions.

In another study, MacDonald (2000) analyzed 20 measures of spirituality, identifying five "robust dimensions of spirituality" (p. 185): cognitive orientation; experiential/phenomenological dimension; existential well-being; paranormal beliefs; and religiousness. These examples point to the many accents that surface, reinforcing spirituality as a complex, multidimensional phenomenon that scholars have only begun to articulate, much less measure (Benson, Scales, Sesma, & Roehlkepartain, 2005).

Relationship to Religious Development

Both proposed definitions struggle with the relationship between religion and spirituality, with the religious perspectives definition placing more emphasis on theological themes and language. Though many scholars struggle with this issue, Reich's (1996) framework particularly helpful as a way to sort through the options. He identifies four possibilities for describing the relationship: religion and spirituality as synonymous or fused; one as a subdomain of the other; religion and spirituality as separate domains; and religion and spirituality as distinct but overlapping domains. The present initiative has adopted the final perspective. This approach seeks to avoid the polarizations between spirituality and religion that have begun to emerge that undermine the richness of both concepts (see Hill, et al., 2000).

Scholars who focus on spirituality within a particular tradition—such as Christianity—may not see the value of definitional assumptions that seek to be more inclusive. However, finding language that respects and includes a wide range of perspectives not only opens up opportunities for cross-tradition dialogue and learning in a pluralistic nation and world, but it also reinforces the understanding of spirituality as being an intrinsic part of humanness. At the same time, people within specific traditions will likely find value in developing complementary definitions that articulate the distinct accents in spirituality within their own beliefs, narratives, and practices.

Spiritual Development as a Process

The notion of spiritual *development* adds an important dimension in its emphasis on process—spiritual change, transformation, growth, or maturation. Spiritual *development* introduces questions about the nature of spiritual change, transformation, growth, or maturation as well as life phases and stages. For example, Wink and Dillon (2002) argue that spiritual development "demands not only an increase in the depth of a person's awareness of, and search for, spiritual meaning over time, but it also requires an expanded and deeper commitment to engagement in actual spiritual practices" (p. 80).

Through most of the Twentieth Century, spiritual—or, more often, religious—development or change was viewed through stage theory (e.g. Fowler, 1981) or was dominated by nondevelopmental approaches (see Oser & Scarlett, 1991). In the same way that developmental psychology has moved beyond stage theory (e. g. Overton, 1998), spiritual development must also move beyond an overreliance on stage theory, which "implies a certain amount of discontinuity in religious [and spiritual] development, whereas it may actually be a reasonably continuous process" (Hood, et al., 1996, p. 55).

The Search Institute spiritual development initiative approaches spiritual development through a developmental systems lens (Lerner, 2002) that emphasizes a dynamic interaction between ecological influences—family, congregation, school, community—and personal agency. It also addresses developmental trajectory continuity across time, instead of merely emphasizing distinct, predictable, and often disconnected developmental stages. Hence, this initiative spans childhood and adolescence, with an interest in both the pathway across the two decades as well as milestones along the way.

It is important to note, however, that the religious perspectives definition does not include the word "development." To some, this term implies growth from less to more, which is incongruent with the understanding that spirituality is fully formed in a newborn and is too often suppressed, not nurtured, in society. Others note that spirituality is more mystical, relational, and divinely gifted than is suggested by the use of "development," which can imply a sort of inevitability to the process. Coming to terms with the language to suggest both the reality of process as well as these related issues remains an important area for dialogue and discovery.

Embedded in Relationships and Experiences

Many conceptualizations of spirituality have been highly focused on individual experience and impact, thus neglecting the ecological dimension of spiritual development. Mattis and Jagers (2001) note that the vast majority of conceptualization and research in the area of spirituality has emphasized the individual "quest," rather than the social and relational context of spiritual development. However, their research in the African American community and tradition consistently finds that, interpersonal relationships with family, peers, and so on, play a vital role in cultivating and shaping spirituality.

The two working definitions assert that spiritual development is embedded in relationships and experiences, with family as well as peers and adults in neighborhoods, schools, congregations, and other settings. Thus, spirituality is not only an individual quest, but also a communal experience and phenomenon. In addition, the religious studies definition particularly emphasizes the role of narratives, beliefs, and practices in shaping children's spirituality, as well as broader forces in society and culture.

Spirituality as a Life-Shaping Force

Some scholars, particularly theologians, argue that spirituality has intrinsic value in and of itself, thus making any functional impact or value of spirituality irrelevant. One cultivates the spiritual life because God intends or demands it, and any other "benefits" only distract from the central purpose of following God's will.

Though the proposed definitions do not explicitly address outcomes, they imply that spirituality has a powerful effect in life. Spirituality, like religion, can have both positive and negative expressions and outcomes. Some scholars have found that certain forms of religiousness may be more pathological, including a strictly utilitarian or extrinsic religion or spirituality, a conflict-ridden, fragmented religion or spirituality, an impoverished authoritarian religion or spirituality, and spirituality or religion that encourages defense mechanisms that allow people to deny and retreat from reality (summarized in Hill, et al., 2000). But while the field of psychology in the Twentieth century too often emphasized the pathological outcomes of spiritual commitment (e. g. Ellis, 1980), the recent openness to spirituality leans toward only recognizing positive aspects and impact.

While it is important that this trend not lead to defining spirituality as only a positive phenomenon, it is a welcomed development that many fields of science, practice, and policy increasingly recognize the positive contribution that spirituality can make in children's lives. At the same time, an important challenge is to be open to and examine both positive and negative possibilities.

The Emerging Initiative

These definitions, and the assumptions that undergird them, have set the direction for the emerging Search Institute initiative on spiritual development. This initiative is bringing together more than 100 leading scholars from around the world and from many religious traditions, not only to synthesize current understandings of spiritual development, but also to shape the agenda for the future. If successful, this initiative will not only expand theological and scientific study on childhood spirituality, but will also help strengthen an interfaith, international, and interdisciplinary network of scholars and practitioners committed to enriching children's lives.

Expanding Theological Study and Reflection

Within the domain of spirituality in childhood, there has been relatively little systematic attention to conceptualizing and understanding the perspectives that the world's religious traditions bring to the topic. A search of articles catalogued in the American Theological Library Association (ATLA) Religion Database (1993–2003) illustrates the gap in the field. Of the 305,498 articles, books, and dissertations catalogued, only 2,705 include "child" as a key word (and many of these titles are not relevant). Furthermore, only 120 entries include key words of child, youth, and spiritual. Many of these entries are book reviews or are practice-oriented articles, not articles that explore religious or theological themes.

With the exception of books that focus on children within specific religious traditions (e.g. Bunge, 2001), few currently available titles take both theological discourse and children's spiritual lives seriously. Many religious scholars have had few forums for dialogue and learning with others who focus on this age group. As a result, thousands of years of wisdom are overlooked or ignored in current efforts to understand and enrich young people's spiritual lives. As Harold Segura (2002) stated, a theology of children is "in diapers" (p. 1). He explains:

> Children and youth are not given a prominent place within its formal [theological] discourse. Our set of topics revolves around adult priorities and it is from that standpoint that we speak of God and have God speak about those topics. Those who state that our theology has been 'adultcentric' are right (p. 1).

However, there are signs of interest and a growing knowledge base within religious studies. For example, for the first time the American Academy of Religion instituted at its 2003 meeting a focus area dedicated to children. In addition, several conferences on children's spirituality—both within the United States and internationally—have been inaugurated in recent years to bring together scholars and practitioners. In addition, an international dialogue on a theology of childhood among Evangelical Christians has emerged under the leadership of John Collier (2002).

Through the Search Institute initiative, a book is being compiled tentatively titled *Religious Perspectives on Spirituality in Childhood and Adolescence* (Yust, Johnson, Sasso & Roehlkepartain, 2006). This book will create a tapestry of wisdom and insight from the world's major religious traditions on the nature, processes, and practices of spirituality in the lives of children and adolescents. Leading scholars within various faith traditions and from different parts of the world will articulate how their traditions have approached major questions in the field. In the process, the essays will invite reflection and dialogue within and among traditions.

Through this array of diverse contributors, the book will examine a series of questions that grow out of the working definition of spirituality:

- How does a given tradition view children and adolescents? What role do children and adolescents play in the tradition?

- How does a tradition understand the process of spirituality and how it changes across the first two decades of life?

- What rituals, practices, and celebrations within a tradition nurture the inner spiritual lives of children and adolescents?

- What rituals, practices, and obligations of the spiritual life guide young people to meaning, purpose, and ethical action?

- To whom does a given tradition assign responsibility for nurturing spirituality?

- How does a tradition view the major social, political, and cultural forces that influence young people's spirituality?

Expanding Scientific Knowledge and Credibility

How spiritual development unfolds may be as important to personal and social well-being as physical, cognitive, and emotional development. Yet spiritual development is probably the least understood of these human capacities. As evidence, Benson, Roehlkepartain, and Rude (2003) searched two broad social science databases, Social Science Abstracts and PsychINFO, to determine the extent to which religion and spirituality were being addressed in published studies between 1990 and July 2002.

Even with broad criteria—and no effort to screen for quality or depth—less than 1% of the articles on children and/or adolescents cataloged in these two databases addressed issues of spirituality or spiritual development. Even a broader search that included more traditional terms related to religiosity produced only marginal increases in the number of articles retrieved addressing these topics. Furthermore, when compared to other areas of human development—cognitive development, physical development, moral development, and so on—spiritual development lags far behind in the number of articles published.

While spiritual development has not yet emerged as a standard topic in the social sciences, there appears to be growing scientific interest in the area. For example, several special issues of peer-reviewed journals have been published that address spirituality or spiritual development. These journals include *Applied Developmental Science, Annals of Behavioral Medicine, Review of Religious Research, Journal of Health Psychology, Journal of Personality,* and *American Psychologist* (special section). These and other efforts suggest that the broader fields of child and adolescent development may be ready to attend to this overlooked domain.

To this point, however, no one has integrated and synthesized this growing science base in one place. Thus, *The Handbook of Spiritual Development in Childhood and Adolescence* (Roehlkepartain, King, Wagener, & Benson, 2006) is being developed which engages approximately 70 leading scholars in the field from around the world, representing disciplines of psychology, sociology, anthropology, education, medicine, and others. The book—which is expected to be published by Sage Publications in late 2005—examines the following areas:

- The conceptual, theoretical, and scientific foundations of spiritual development;

- The nature of spiritual experiences and practices among children and adolescents from sociological, psychological, and anthropological perspectives;

- The connections between spiritual development and multiple domains of human development, including cognitive, moral, identity, personality, and civic development;

- The ecology of spiritual development, looking at the interaction between spiritual development and multiple socializing influences and systems, including culture and ethnicity, family, peers, education, and religious institutions;

- The developmental outcomes of spiritual development, intentionally highlighting both the positive and negative potential outcomes of spirituality; and

- Future directions for research, policy, and applications in a way that sets forth an agenda and vision for the future of building this field.

This volume will integrate state-of-the-art human development theory and research with major themes in spiritual development. Chapters will not only present the state of the current theory and research, but will also highlight future directions for theory, research, and practice.

Expanding Dialogue across Traditions, Continents, and Cultures

One could devote a lifetime to studying children's spiritual development within a particular culture, religious tradition, or even denomination. Instead, the Search Institute initiative has chosen to be broad in scope, seeking both to understand the unique contributions or accents of a wide range of traditions, cultures, and contexts, while also identifying the common themes across differences. This approach recognizes, in part, that the majority of social science and academic research has been conducted within Christian contexts (see Boyatzis, 2003; Bridges & Moore, 2002), so much less is known scientifically about other contexts and understandings of spiritual development.

Similar patterns appear to hold true in theological or religious studies as well, with relatively few scholars outside Christianity dedicating themselves to exploring children's spirituality. Thus, in addition to including the most commonly studied religious groups and subgroups in the world (e. g. Buddhism, Christianity, Hinduism, Islam, and Judaism), this initiative includes scholars from lesser-studied religious traditions that have unique insights to offer (e.g. Baha'i, Mormonism, and indigenous religions around the world).

Finally, because of its multidimensionality, spirituality does not fit neatly inside any particular domain of social science or theology. Hill, et al. (2000) noted that religion and spirituality inherently involve developmental, social-psychological phenomena, cognitive phenomena, affective and emotional phenomena, and personality. Because of this complexity, no single discipline or research methodology—whether empirical or theoretical, quantitative or qualitative—can, by itself, adequately explore this domain of life.

Furthermore, the range of scientific disciplines does not even address the diversity of religious scholars with insights and contributions, including textual or biblical scholars, theologians, religious educators, ethicists, and others. Thus a multidisciplinary approach with multiple ways of learning and knowing is essential to shed as much light as possible on this important, rich, and complex area of human life.

The challenges in taking such a broad, interfaith, international, and interdisciplinary approach are numerous. First, there are the logistical questions of how to connect with a diverse array of scholars and to develop manuscripts that adequately represent a wide diversity of perspectives. Then, of course, there is the danger of "watering down" traditions in order to find commonality, and at the other extreme, exposing dramatic distinctions in worldviews that make dialogue difficult. Furthermore, broad approaches risk losing the depth, nuance, and distinctiveness of a tightly focused study.

Yet the benefits are believed to outweigh risks and challenges. Perhaps most important, in a time of the shrinking global village and increased concerns about interreligious conflict, respectful dialogue and mutual understanding among faith traditions and cultures can serve as a healing force in society and the world. In an atmosphere of trust and good will, one quickly finds common ground and rich learning from diversity when people from different faiths and perspectives explore together vital issues, such as spiritual development. Though it is certainly appropriate and important to dialogue with others within one's own tradition, it is also critical to model building bridges across differences in healthy and healing ways that enrich mutual understanding. (For more on the potential of interfaith engagement, see Roehlkepartain, 2003.)

In addition, it is unlikely that the field will develop into a cohesive whole that articulates spirituality as part of basic humanity as long as scholarship is fragmented into specific traditions, cultures, and disciplines with little opportunity for shared learning, the exchange of knowledge, and dialogue. Thus the integration effort will seek both to honor the specific accents of different approaches while also cultivating a core of shared understanding.

The international focus is just as important to consider. Given emerging data suggesting that religious and spiritual vitality and salience may currently be most prominent in the developing world (e. g. Gallup International Association, 1999; Jenkins, 2002), it behooves researchers and theologians to seek to learn from non-industrialized and developing contexts in order to enrich both theory and practice. Though it is proving to be logistically difficult, this initiative is building connections to scholars from around the world as active contributors. In the process, learning from those of non-Western cultures is sought, as well as being with them in a way that creates a rich foment of religious and scientific discourse.

Helping to Build an International, Interdisciplinary, Interfaith Network

Several efforts have emerged in recent years to strengthen and deepen the field of spiritual development. This includes the conference on which this volume is based and the related Web site (www.childspirituality.org), the International Conference on Children's Spirituality (www.cwvp.com/site/iccs.html) and its related journal, the North American Conference on Children's Spirituality sponsored by the Child-Spirit Institute (www.childspirit.net), the regular pre-conference sessions at the Society for Research on Child Development, the American Academy of Religion Consultation on Childhood Studies and Religion, as well as others. Through this new initiative, Search Institute seeks to complement these efforts by mapping the state of the field, identifying and linking with established and emerging scholars in various disciplines and contexts, and working with key leaders to identify priorities for future research, dialogue, and utilization of knowledge to improve practice. Out of these initial efforts, it is hoped that a long-term agenda emerges that will allow us to stimulate ongoing learning and application to address the most pressing issues and challenges in the field.

This initiative is only in its initial stage. However, collaborating with other scholars and practitioners in deepening knowledge of spiritual development in childhood is anticipated, as well as strengthening the abilities of families, congregations, and others to nurture children's spirituality more effectively. The challenge is to learn—and share and apply what is learned—so that children will be better supported in their spiritual journeys. In the process, a key goal is to cultivate the sense of meaning, purpose, significance, and belonging that are integral to a life of commitment and contribution.

References

Benson, P. L., Roehlkepartain, E. C., & Rude, S. P. (2003). Spiritual development in childhood and adolescence: Toward a field of inquiry. *Applied Developmental Science, 7*, 204–212.

Benson, P. L., Scales, P. C., Sesma, A., Jr., & Roehlkepartain, E. C. (2005). Adolescent spirituality. In K. A. Moore & L. H. Lippman (Eds.), *What do children need to flourish? Conceptualizing and measuring indicators of positive development* (pp. 25–40). New York: Springer.

Boyatzis, C. J. (2003). Introduction (Special issue: Religious and spiritual development). *Review of Religious Research, 44*, 213–219.

Bridges, L. J., & Moore, K. A. (2002). *Religion and spirituality in childhood and adolescence.* Washington, DC: Child Trends.

Bunge, M. J. (Ed.). (2001). *The child in Christian thought.* Grand Rapids: Eerdmans.

Collier, J. (2002). Report of the Penang [Malaysia] Consultation on Child Theology. Retrieved July 5, 2004, from www.viva.org/tellme/resources/articles/gods_heart/penang.pdf.

Collins, K. J. (2000). *Exploring Christian spirituality: An ecumenical reader.* Grand Rapids: Baker.

d'Aquili, E. G., & Newberg, A. B. (1999). *The mystical mind: Probing the biology of religious experience.* Minneapolis: Fortress.

D'Onofrio, B. M., Eaves, L. J., Murrelle, L., Maes, H. H., & Spilka, B. (1999). Understanding biological and social influences on religious affiliation, attitudes, and behaviors: A behavior genetic perspective. *Journal of Personality, 67*, 953–983.

Ellis, A. (1980). Psychotherapy and atheistic values: A response to A. E. Bergin's "Psychotherapy and religious values." *Journal of Consulting and Clinical Psychology, 48*, 635–639.

Fowler, J. W. (1981). *Stages of faith: The psychology of human development and the quest for meaning.* San Francisco: HarperCollins.

Gallup International Association (1999). *Gallup international millennium survey.* Retrieved September 9, 2002, from www.gallup-international.com/surveys1.htm.

Hill, P. C., Pargament, K. I., Hood, R. W., McCullough, M. E., Swyers, J. P., Larson, D. B., et al. (2000). Conceptualizing religion and spirituality: Points of commonality, points of departure. *Journal for the Theory of Social Behavior, 30*, 52–77.

Hood, R. W., Jr., Spilka, B., Hunsberger, B., & Gorsuch, R. (1996). *The psychology of religion: An empirical approach* (2nd ed.). New York: Guilford.

Jenkins, P. (2002). *The next Christendom: The rise of global Christianity.* New York: Oxford University Press.

King, U. (Ed.). (2001). *Spirituality and society in the new millennium.* East Sussex, UK: Sussex Academic.

Lerner, R. M. (Ed.). (2002). *Concepts and theories of human development* (3rd ed.). Mahwah, NJ: Erlbaum.

MacDonald, D. A. (2000). Spirituality: Description, measurement, and relation to the five factor model of personality. *Journal of Personality, 68*, 157–197.

Marler, P. L., & Hadaway, C. K. (2002). "Being religious" or "being spiritual" in America: A zero-sum proposition? *Journal for the Scientific Study of Religion, 41*(2), 288–300.

Mattis, J. S., & Jagers, R. J. (2001). A relational framework for the study of religiosity and spirituality in the lives of African Americans. *Journal of Community Psychology, 29*, 519–539.

Nye, R. M. (1999). Relational consciousness and the spiritual lives of children: Convergence with children's theory of mind. In K. H. Reich, F. K. Oser, & W. G. Scarlett (Eds.), *The case of religion, Vol. 2: Psychological studies on spiritual and religious development* (pp. 57–82). Lengerich, Germany: Pabst.

Oser, F., & Scarlett, W. G. (Eds.). (1991). *Religious development in childhood and adolescence.* San Francisco: Jossey-Bass.

Overton, W. F. (1998). Developmental psychology: Philosophy, concepts, and methodology. In W. Damon & R. M. Lerner (Eds.), *Handbook of child psychology* (5th ed., Vol. 1). *Theoretical models of development* (pp. 107–188). New York: Wiley.

Reich, K. H. (1996). A logic-based typology of science and theology. *Journal of Interdisciplinary Studies, 8,* 149–167.

Reich, K. H. (2001, April). *Fostering spiritual development: Theory, practice, and measurement.* Paper presented at the International Conference on Religion and Mental Health, Teheran, Iran.

Roehlkepartain, E. C. (2003). Making room at the table for everyone: Interfaith engagement in positive child and adolescent development. In R. M. Lerner, F. Jacobs, & D. Wertlieb (Eds.), *Handbook of Applied Developmental Science* (vol. 3): *Promoting Positive Youth and Family Development* (pp. 535–563). Thousand Oaks, CA; Sage.

Roehlkepartain, E. C., King, P. E., Wagener, L. M., & Benson, P. L. (Eds.) (2006). *The handbook of spiritual development in childhood and adolescences.* Thousand Oaks, CA: Sage.

Segura, H. C. (2002). *"He put him in the midst of them."* A working paper prepared for the Understanding God's Heart for Children international initiative. Retrieved July 5, 2004, from www.viva.org/tellme/resources/articles/gods_heart/theology.html.

Stifoss-Hanssen, H. (1999). Religion and spirituality: What a European ear hears. *International Journal for the Psychology of Religion, 9,* 25–33.

Wink, P., & Dillon, M. (2002). Spiritual development across the adult life course: Findings from a longitudinal study. *Journal of Adult Development, 9*(1), 79–94.

Wuthnow, R. (1998). *After heaven: Spirituality in America since the 1950s.* Berkeley: University of California Press.

Yust, K. M., Johnson, A. N., Sasso, S. E., & Roehlkepartain, E. C. (Eds.). (2006). *Religious perspectives on spirituality in childhood and adolescence.* Lanham, MD: Rowman & Littlefield.

Zinnbauer, B. J., Pargament, K. I., Cole, B., Rye, M. S., Butter, E. M., Belavich, T. G., et al. (1997). Religion and spirituality: Unfuzzying the fuzzy. *Journal for the Scientific Study of Religion, 36,* 549–564.

Zinnbauer, B. J., Pargament, K. I., & Scott, A. B. (1999). The emerging meanings of religiousness and spirituality: Problems and prospects. *Journal of Personality, 67,* 889–919.

Chapter Nine

Children in Wesleyan Thought

CATHERINE STONEHOUSE[1]

I n their foreword to *The Child in Christian Thought*, Don S. Browning and John Wall (2001) claim, "Contemporary theologians have on the whole neglected childhood as a serious intellectual or moral concern" (p. xi). John Wesley, the father of Methodism, stands in stark contrast to such contemporary theologians. Throughout his long life and ministry, Wesley demonstrated concern for children, "their well-being in general and their religious and moral growth in particular." (Willhauck, 1992, p. 9)

The Importance of Children to Early Methodists

Wesley studied what the scholars of his day had to say about the education and upbringing of children. His journals record the religious experiences of children, his interactions with them, and their responses to him, indicating that he observed the children, seeking to understand what was best for them. Although some of Wesley's rules for schoolchildren seem austere to us, accounts of his interactions with children show a deep sensitivity, tenderness, and love for them. On one occasion, after preaching, Wesley took some children for a ride on his "rig." Another time a child had been denied the Lord's Supper, and when Wesley discovered this, he took her on his knee and gave her communion. These accounts reveal a man attentive to children and desiring to meet their needs (Gill, 1936).

---

1. Catherine Stonehouse received her MRE from Asbury Theological Seminary and her PhD in Education from Michigan State University. She has served as a Director of Christian Education in local churches, in curriculum development and in denominational Christian education leadership positions within the Free Methodist Church. Currently she is Orlean Bullard Beeson Professor of Christian Education at Asbury Theological Seminary. Stonehouse is the author of *Patterns in Moral Development*, and *Joining Children of the Spiritual Journey: Nurturing a Life of Faith*. She also has contributed chapters for three books, essays in Christian Education dictionaries, and has published several scholarly journal articles.

Society in Wesley's day had no child-welfare system, but Wesley and the early Methodists took a deep interest in children, particularly the children of the poor. They invested in caring for the whole child, physically, socially, mentally, and spiritually. Methodists established schools, orphanages, and a children's center in London (Gill, 1936). Wesley also prepared resources to be used to teach children in Methodist schools as well as in the home (Willhauck, 1992). The Methodists also supported the growing Sunday School movement (Reed & Provost, 1993).

As Wesley observed children he came to believe that many experienced genuine faith during their formative years (Willhauck, 1992). This belief fueled his investment in the spiritual instruction and nurture of children. He also believed that the continuance of the Methodist revival depended on bringing children to faith. He required Methodist preachers to preach to and instruct children, whether or not they felt gifted to do so. Ministry with children was an essential part of being a Methodist preacher (Wesley, 1984). What he required of his preachers, Wesley did himself. He not only catechized and preached to children, he noticed them when visiting in homes, made a practice of giving a sixpence to the children he met, spent time with schoolchildren, and corresponded with young people (Byron, 1903).

What led to this important focus on children in early Methodism? Answers to this question can be found in Wesley's personal formation through his mother's investment in the spiritual nurture and education of her children. Susannah taught them systematically, stressing the importance of educating both girls and boys. She spent time with each of her children individually every week. Wesley valued Susannah's methods and sought her wisdom as he guided the education of children in the Methodist movement. In addition, Wesley's theology is "child friendly." It describes grace as it relates to all of life, from birth to death, and this calls for understanding how God is at work in the lives of children. Wesley's understanding of salvation, sin and grace, baptism, and conversion, influenced intentional ministry with children. This chapter will also consider how children were nurtured in the home, the school, and in the Methodist societies, and reflect on some implications for ministry with children in the twenty-first century.

Children in Wesleyan Theology

When doing theology, Wesley took into account the whole of life from birth to death. He sought to understand God's work in human hearts and how that had an impact on the lives of persons of all ages. He ordered his description of God's saving, transforming work in what he called the *via salutes*, or the way of salvation. In his sermon, "The Scripture Way of Salvation," Wesley described the potential for a lifelong journey in a relationship with God. He believed God initiates that relationship, reaching out to every human being in grace. God does not wait until a certain "age of accountability" to extend grace to the young, nor does God wait to hear a person cry out for help before offering grace. Instead, Wesley believed that God's grace is "implanted at birth" (Wesley, *Works*, Vol. 7, 1984, p. 43). From the beginning of life God is at work seeking to draw everyone into a relationship with Him.

The effects of God's grace along life's journey are experienced in different ways. Wesley referred to these different experiences of grace as prevenient, justifying, sanctifying, and glorifying grace. Prevenient grace is God's uncalled for, seeking, wooing love, when in repentance, individuals respond to God's gracious drawing and experience the forgiveness of sins and justifying grace. God's Spirit then begins to transform, making believers more and more like Christ, doing the work of sanctification. Glorifying grace is given at the time of death and refers to the total healing of the scars of sin and the limitations of our humanness.

Wesleyan theology understands salvation, not as an event in one's life, but as a lifelong, maturing relationship with God. Along the spiritual journey there are crucial events of response to God; however, those events must be understood in the light of God's work that begins early and continues through all of life. Therefore, to understand the spirituality of a child from the perspective of Wesleyan theology a snapshot of an event is insufficient; a video of the child's relationship with God is needed. In that video the action of God is seen as well as the response of the child, the actions of the child and the response of God. The wonder of grace and the reality of sin is revealed. To see a child's spirituality through Wesley's eyes, it is helpful to explore his understanding of sin and grace, of baptism and conversion.

Sin and Grace

In Wesley's writings there is discussion of three aspects or kinds of sin: original sin, involuntary sin—of ignorance or sin resulting from infirmity, and willful sin against God's known law. Inherited original sin, involuntary, and willful sin are all sin in need of Christ's atonement. However, Wesley believed that God's gracious, atoning response to the different types or expressions of sin varies. He affirmed that God does not hold people responsible for inherited sin or sins of ignorance. One faces condemnation only for willful acts of rebellion against God, if the person does not repent of those acts and receive God's forgiveness (Borgen, 1988). But, as reflected in Wesley's view of grace, he believed that early in life every human being has an inner awareness of right and wrong. To go against that inner awareness willfully is an act of rebellion against God, sin for which all are accountable.

Wesley described original sin as an inherited bent toward sinning, a disease that infects the nature of every child, even the children of godly parents. This disease of sin causes human beings to be susceptible to the pull of evil and this inclination leads to intentional sin (Wesley, 1984). Even though sin infects everyone from birth,

Wesley believed in the power of grace that was also at work from the beginning of life (Willhauck, 1992). God does not leave humanity at the mercy of sin, for in the heart of every person God plants prevenient (or as Wesley called it, preventing) grace (Im, 1994). Wesley declared:

> No man living is entirely destitute of what is vulgarly called *natural conscience*. But this is not natural: It is more properly termed, *preventing grace*. Every man has a greater or lesser measure of this, which waiteth not for the call of man . . . and everyone . . . feels more or less uneasy when he acts contrary to the light of his own conscience. So that, no man sins because he has not grace but because he does not use the grace he has. (Wesley, 1984, p. 512)

Through prevenient grace, God takes the initiative and makes it possible for children, even very young children, to respond to God's seeking love.

What is this prevenient grace that is at work within the life of every child? What are the evidences of it? The above quote states that it is grace that comes before a person has any awareness of the need for God or calls out to God for help. It is the first expression of God's grace in the human soul, and is initiated by God. Wesley believed that what seems like a natural sense of right and wrong within a child is not simply an innate characteristic of human beings, but is an expression of prevenient grace. Wesley labeled "all the drawings of the Father"—a person's first desire for God, and instances of "light" or awareness of God's will that comes to all people (John 1.9)—as evidence of prevenient grace (Outler, 1964). It is the grace that provides the ability to respond to God (Scanlon, 1969).

Prevenient grace, then, is extended to every child. From infancy God draws the child in love. As children respond to the grace-inspired desire to know God—even though they may not be able to name the desire—that desire grows and leads them on. However, grace may be resisted or its influence stifled through neglect, lack of nurture, distractions, or an unwillingness to respond. Generally, people stifle the convictions, desires, or insights the Spirit of God brings to their hearts, and "after a while forget, or at least deny, that ever they had them" (Wesley in Outler, 1964).

Because of prevenient grace, children have an early openness to God. Wesley saw this in the children of his day. He observed children whose faith seemed to "know no barriers or doubt," and believed that their faith was not some weak imitation of real faith but a model of what God wants to bring to rebirth in adults. Twenty-first century parents and adult friends who listen to children hear them early in life expressing a desire to know about God. They also note the ease with which children lovingly respond to God. Some children may continually respond positively to God's drawing love and come into a maturing relationship with God, having no memory of not knowing and loving God. However, through yielding to the pull of sin, most children lose that open responsiveness to God and find themselves in need of God's justifying grace (Willhauck, 1992).

Another function of prevenient grace is to bring people to an awareness of personal sin and to plant within their hearts a longing to be forgiven. Children and adults alike may come in repentance and faith to Jesus and through justifying grace receive forgiveness, peace, and joy. This is not simply a legal transaction through which God considers the child or adult justified because of Christ's atonement. It is that, but it is more. Wesley understood grace in all its expressions as God's love being present and active in a person's life. As God's love forgives, God's Spirit begins the work of sanctifying grace, the work of bringing about real change, and making it possible for Christians to become more and more like Jesus (Outler, 1964).

These understandings of prevenient, justifying and sanctifying grace are taken from Wesley's sermon on the "Scripture Way of Salvation." Although he is not speaking specifically of the child's experience in this sermon, Wesley apparently saw these expressions of God's grace active in the lives of children. Similarly, children today experience God's grace in these ways.

A Wesleyan view of spirituality, not only of children but adults as well, calls for understanding the dynamic interaction of sin, grace, and the means of grace. In Wesley's plan for spiritual formation and growth he emphasized ordinary and sacramental means of grace. Participation in the faith community—the Methodist societies, classes, and small accountability groups called bands—was an ordinary means of grace. God's grace could come to someone through other Christians, and in the faith community persons could find the encouragement needed to keep responding and growing in love for God and others. Prayer and Bible reading were also encouraged as ordinary means of grace.

For Wesley the Sacraments were used by God to mediate grace. Wesley encouraged Methodists to meet Christ in Holy Communion as frequently as possible. He also instructed parents to bring their children to receive grace through infant baptism.

Infant Baptism and Conversion

Within denominations that claim a Wesleyan theology there is much debate about infant baptism. Many churches baptize infants, while others have set aside the practice in favor of infant dedication and believer's baptism, and yet others let parents choose whether their child will be baptized or dedicated. Some Wesleyans who baptize infants seem to limit the significance of the baptism in order to emphasize the importance of the children's later conversion. But what were Wesley's beliefs concerning infant baptism and the conversion of children?

In his "Treatise on Baptism" Wesley identified the benefits. Through baptism:

1. Original sin is washed away.

2. One enters into a covenant with God.

3. One is admitted into the church.

4. Believers are adopted by God and become God's children.

5. People are made heirs to the kingdom (Wesley, 1984).

In this treatise Wesley discusses at length why he believes that these benefits of baptism belong to infants as well as to adults. He argues that since infants bear the stain of original sin, they need to be washed of that stain through baptism.

Wesley also argued for infant baptism through his understanding of biblical covenant relationships, for he saw a parallel between the covenant-making described in Deuteronomy 29 and infant baptism:

> You stand assembled today, all of you, before the LORD your God—the leaders of your tribes, your elders, and your officials, all the men of Israel, your children, your women, and the aliens who are in your camp . . . to enter into the covenant of the LORD your God, sworn by an oath, which the LORD your God is making with you today; in order that he may establish you today as his people, and that he may be your God. (Deut 29:10–13, New Revised Standard Version)

Wesley hypothesized that if the little ones of Israel could stand with their parents before God and be included in the covenant made with the Lord, then present-day children can be brought by their parents for baptism to enjoy a covenant relationship with God. A covenant is a two-way commitment, not a magical guarantee of blessing. The relationship is real and meaningful, and God calls children and adults to live according to the covenant laws, to live in God's ways. In baptism parents commit their children to live the covenant and promise to help them learn how to live out their covenant.

The circumcision of male infants was the seal of the covenant relationship between the Jews and God. Therefore, Wesley concluded, if Hebrew infants could be marked with the sign of the covenant, then within the Christian church children should be marked by the sign of baptism and welcomed into the family of God.

Wesley also turned to the words of Jesus to support his belief in bringing children to Christ through the act of baptism:

> Then little children were being brought to him in order that he might lay his hands on them and pray. The disciples spoke sternly to those who brought them; but Jesus said, "Let the little children come to me, and do not stop them; for it is to such as these that the kingdom of heaven belongs." (Matthew 19:13–14)

In these verses Wesley heard Jesus inviting children to come to him and proclaiming them to be heirs in the Kingdom of God, as recognized through baptism (Wesley, 1984).

From this discussion one gains the impression that for Wesley, infant baptism was more than an act of the parents, more than a ritual designed to strengthen the parents' resolve to teach their children the ways of God so that later in life the children could come to know Christ. He saw infant baptism as a means of grace, a transaction in which God washes away the stain of original sin and welcomes the child into the family of God, the church.

Christians often speak of baptism as an outward sign of God's inward work. Some would say that this understanding excludes infants and young children from the sacrament since they cannot repent and by faith receive forgiveness of their sins through Christ. I would claim, however, that infant baptism is also an outward sign of an inward work. God's prevenient grace is at work in the heart of the child, washing clean the stain and guilt of original sin even before the child can call out to God for aid. God is making a covenant with the child and welcoming him or her into the family of God as a present member, not just a future or potential one.

However, Wesley did not see this very real and gracious work of God as an unconditional lifetime guarantee of intimacy with God or as eternal salvation. Earlier it was noted that Wesley understood salvation as a way, a journey with God across a lifetime. Along the way God continually offers grace and waits for response, giving each person the freedom to accept or reject that grace. To understand Wesley's view on infant baptism, his perspective on grace and sin in the lives of children must be examined, as well as what he has to say about children and conversion.

Walter Wangerin (1986) refers to the child's relationship with God as a dance with God that begins in the mist. In the child's earliest misty awareness, God holds her through the loving arms of a parent or nursery worker. God gives joy to a little boy as he watches the wind swirl the leaves, or hears the words, "Jesus loves you," whispered in his ear. God initiates this dance, graciously reaching out to children through the experiences of life, drawing them to himself. Children respond in love and desire to know about God. But in this fallen world another dynamic is at work as well, sin. The sins or brokenness of those caring for children, the hectic chaotic pace of life, or the lack of others joining the children in the dance with God can make it difficult for the children to hear the inviting music of grace and to respond. Although the guilt of original sin is atoned by Christ's blood and the washing of the baptismal water, the infection of sin is still present making it easy for children to yield to the temptation of destructive and self-centered choices.

Although God's grace is mediated to the infant or child in baptism, Wesley believed that baptismal grace could be lost or "sinned away," making it necessary for the child to be reborn to continue on the way of salvation. Wesley stated that he had sinned away the "washing of the Holy Ghost" by the age of ten (Willhauck, 1992). Because of the infection of original sin creating the human tendency toward sin, and the presence of evil in the world, Wesley believed that most children were in need of spiritual rebirth (Willhauck, 1992). He also affirmed that rebirth through justifying faith was available to young children:

> Justifying faith implies . . . a sure trust and confidence that Christ died for *my* sins, that he loved *me*, and gave himself for *me*. [At whatever time] a sinner believes, be it in *early childhood* [emphasis mine], in the strength of his years, or when he is old, God justifieth that ungodly one. (Wesley, 1984, p. 60–61)

Wesley observed children who discovered Christ's great love for them personally, who believed that Christ died for their sins, and who through justification were reborn. Such children convinced Wesley that boys and girls have great religious potential, and consequently he came to believe that all children should be encouraged to experience God's justifying grace (Willhauck, 1992).

From her extensive study of Wesley's writings, Susan Willhauck (1992) came to see Wesley as one who held in dynamic tension perspectives that others debate as "either/or" positions. Wesley held together a belief in the mystery of God's grace at work in the child's heart and the reality and power of sin and evil. He underscored the importance of infant baptism and the need for conversion. He encouraged Christian instruction for children in the church (society), home, and school; instruction that would continue to foster a child's responses to God or would prepare children to experience God's love, repentance, and rebirth, bringing them back into a relationship with God.

Early Methodists and the Nurture of Children

Wesley was a keen observer of real life and designed the practices of Methodists to provide what real people needed to walk with God in a real and often difficult world. As he watched the results of the Methodist revival, Wesley discovered that an initial response to God's grace was not enough to launch most people on a continuing journey of maturing faith and holy living. With deep concern he saw that most seekers or new Christians who were left on their own were soon "faster asleep than ever" (Wood, 1967, p. 188). Wesley realized that people needed an environment that nurtured and supported them in their responses to God's gracious work in their lives. For these reasons, he established Methodist societies, classes, and bands where people, awakened to their need for God, learned what it meant to be a Christian and discovered how God wanted them to live. In these small group meetings, believers shared their successes and failures in living the Christian life and found the support needed to cooperate with God's transforming work in their lives.

Wesley focused his attention not only on the discipling of adults but also on establishing nurturing environments for children and providing instruction to help them respond to God's grace and enhance their spiritual formation. Susan Willhauck (1992) believes that what impressed Wesley most in the children he observed was their "deeply felt experiences of God." Fear that children might lose their beautiful relationship with God, or never come to know God, motivated Wesley to encourage parents, teachers, and preachers to take seriously the religious instruction of children. He believed children were more likely to respond to God's grace and to continue to grow in grace when adults instructed children and shared their faith with them.

Methodists and the Sunday School

As noted earlier, Wesley instructed preachers on the attention they should give to the children in Methodist societies. They were to keep a list of the children and, if children showed evidence of a genuine relationship with God—"awakening"—they were to be accepted as members of the society. In some Methodist settings societies for children were established (Willhauck, 1992).

One way in which Methodists expressed their care for the souls of children was through the Sunday School. Although Robert Raikes is credited with founding the Sunday School movement in 1780, the Methodists had been conducting "Sunday Schools" long before that. For example, during Wesley's mission to Georgia, he began a Sunday School in 1736; and a plaque at Christ Church in Savannah names him as the founder of the Sunday School. In 1770 Hannah Ball, a Methodist lay woman, reported to Wesley that she had been meeting with the children twice a week. There is evidence that Raikes got the idea for Sunday School from a Methodist preacher's wife, Sophia Bradburn, and consulted with Hannah Ball as he began implementing his plan (Willhauck, 1992).

Family Religion

Early Methodists nurtured children in their societies and through their outreach. Wesley, however, seems to present the home as the most important setting for the spiritual care and formation of children. Wesley instructed parents to offer more than a series of lessons to be delivered or propositions to be taught. He challenged parents to set an example of godly living for children to follow. In his sermons on child rearing, Wesley called families to lives of orderliness, simplicity, and moderation (Willhauck, 1992). These were core values of the Methodist movement and Wesley assumed that they could be passed on to the next generation if children had the opportunity to live out these values in their homes. He realized that the lived faith of the adults and the values they acted on day by day gave meaning and integrity to their words of instruction.

Two sermons, both published in 1783, clearly articulate Wesley's views on how to rear children to become strong Christians who live holy lives. In these sermons, Wesley challenged both parents with responsibility for the instruction of children. The sermon, "On Family Religion," called Methodists to adopt the "wise resolution" of

Josh 24:15: "As for me and my house, we will serve the Lord." Wesley charged fathers with the spiritual care of their children, the latter whom he described as: "Immortal spirits whom God hath for a time entrusted to your care, that you may train them up in all holiness, and fit them for the enjoyment of God in eternity. This is a glorious and important trust" (Wesley, 1984, p. 79). Similarly, in the sermon "On the Education of Children," Wesley highlighted the important role of mothers. They are the ones who provide care for young children and in that care lays amazing potential for education and spiritual formation (Wesley, 1984, pp. 95–98).

Wesley began his discussion of family religion with what it meant to serve the Lord. He called parents to a service of the heart involving worship, faith, love for God, and love for others. He challenged parents to walk consistently in God's ways, doing God's will from the heart (Wesley, 1984). Before Wesley laid out the "how-to's" of family religion, he highlighted the heart, the being of the parents, and the life they lived before their children. Wesley showed parents that their relationship with God and the life they lived would be more important than all the verbal instruction they could provide.

After laying this foundation, Wesley moved on to identify what parents can do so that their children will serve the Lord. The first task is to *restrain* children from outward sin:

> Your children, while they are young, you may restrain from evil not only by advice, persuasion, and reproof, but also by correction; only remembering that this means is to be used last—not till all other have been tried, and found to be ineffectual. And even then you should take the utmost care to avoid the very appearance of passion. Whatever is done should be done with mildness; nay, indeed, with kindness too. Otherwise your own spirit will suffer loss, and the child will reap little advantage (Wesley, 1984, p. 80).

Notice the process Wesley lays out for parents. They are to begin with advice, persuasion, reproof, and, only after all else has failed, to correct. But Wesley acknowledged that more than words are needed at times to restrain children from evil. Although Wesley did not oppose the use of physical punishment, notice the cautions and emphasis on kindness in the act of correction. He identifies the purpose of correction: for the advantage of the child, not simply for punishment. Furthermore, he points out that the spirit with which parents discipline their children has an impact on the effectiveness of the correction and the spiritual well being of the parent. These were probably radical words to many Methodist parents who were just learning what it meant to live the Christian life.

The second responsibility of parents is *instruction*. The father is to be sure that everyone in the home has the "knowledge . . . necessary for salvation." This involves giving everyone the opportunity to attend worship and being sure that every day everyone in the family has "time for reading, meditation, and prayer." Wesley encouraged the practice of a daily family devotional time and even published prayers for families and for children to use (Wesley, 1984; Wesley, *Works*, Vol. 11, 1984). These practices and opportunities are the context for further instruction.

> Wesley offers interesting guidelines for teaching children. Instruction is to begin *early*—From the first hour that you perceive reason begins to dawn. Truth may then begin to shine upon the mind far earlier than we are apt to suppose. And whoever watches the first openings of the understanding, may, by little and little, supply fit matter for it to work upon, and may turn the eye of the soul toward good things, as well as toward bad or trifling ones. (Wesley, 1984, p. 81)

Parents were taught to begin early and to pace their instruction with the child's readiness. This is also seen in the admonition that instruction is to be *plain*, couched in words children would use themselves, and starting with what the child knows. Wesley provides an example of how he would implement this principle:

> Bid the child look up, and ask, "What do you see there?" 'The sun.' "See how bright it is! Feel how warm it shines upon your hand! Look, how it makes the grass and the flowers to grow, and the trees and everything look green! But God, though you cannot see him, is above the sky, and is a deal brighter than the sun! It is he, it is God that made the sun, and you, and me, and everything. It is he that makes the grass and the flowers grow; that makes the trees green, and the fruit to come upon them! Think what he can do! He can do whatever he pleases. He can strike me or you dead in a moment! But he loves you; he loves to do you good. He loves to make you happy. Should not you then love *him?*" (Wesley, 1984, p. 82)

In spite of his rather shocking statement, "He can strike me or you dead in a moment," which I would not include in a conversation with a young child, Wesley's focus is on the greatness and the love of God. His description gives wise and practical guidance for parents.

Wesley realized that teaching must be given to children *frequently*, as frequently as every meal. Furthermore, effective teaching calls for parents to *persevere* in their instruction. Lessons of life are not learned quickly. Wesley realized that effective spiritual instruction calls for an immense amount of patience. And Wesley reminded parents that only God can provide the patience they need, and only God can take their words, "apply them to the child's heart," and cause the light of understanding to dawn. Parents should pray as they instruct and guide their children, trusting God to be the ultimate, transforming teacher (Wesley, pp. 82–86).

In his sermon, "On the Education of Children," Wesley stated that the "grand end of education" is to cure the general disease of human nature. He offered parents encouragement and practical suggestions for helping to cure their children's diseases of atheism, willfulness, pride, love of the world and material things, falsehood, anger, and injustice. In his discussion on pride, Wesley asked what parents could do in order to "check [pride] until it can be radically cured" (Wesley, 1984). This comment seems to imply that an important but only partial cure is possible through education. Only God, by sanctifying grace, can provide the "radical cure," but parents can serve their children well by "checking" their sinful tendencies. Wesley believed that if parents taught children the importance of doing well, youngsters could be kept from evil.

When Wesley addressed the cure for each disease, he called parents to look carefully at how they responded to their children. He pointed out the ways in which parents teach what they do not mean to teach. For example, when parents give in to a child's persistent, willful cry, they "pay him for crying," and reinforce the behavior. Or, when they laugh at their children's "witty contrivances to cheat one another" parents teach injustice. Wesley also cautioned that unreasonable severity in discipline could cause children to lie, an outcome not intended by the parent (Wesley, 1984).

Wesley believed strongly in the power of life experiences to teach and he showed parents how to weave instruction into the everyday life of the family. The "diseases of human nature" can be cured, or at least checked, by the way parents and children live their lives together. For example, if parents talk with their children about everything but God, they foster atheism. Therefore, Wesley called parents to celebrate with their children, from their earliest days and in all of life, who God is, what God does, and God's great love for them. Wesley believed that talking about God and worshiping God in the flow of life is the antidote for atheism and the food of faith. Even the eating habits of a family Wesley viewed as formative behavior. For Wesley food should only serve the purpose of nourishing the body, but if it is used to reward or make a child happy, it teaches the child to seek for happiness in material things rather than in God (Wesley, 1984).

Wesley stressed the conquering of the child's will as a key factor in spiritual formation during childhood. From his mother, Wesley came to believe in the importance of children submitting to the will of their parents. For Susannah Wesley, religion was "a matter of breaking the will" so that one could submit to God's will. The earlier the will was broken, the better. By learning to submit to their parents, children were being prepared to submit to God and God's will. Wesley warned against always giving in to their child's wishes. He believed such coddling strengthens the child's will and leads to selfish willfulness that becomes increasingly difficult to change (Wesley, 1984).

To many twenty-first century ears, talk of breaking a child's will sounds harsh and destructive, given that research in the area of moral development has demonstrated the important role strength of will plays in moral action. Even though it takes a strong will to cause a child to disobey, it also takes a strong will for a child to do what is right when pressured to do what he or she knows to be wrong (Kohlberg, 1984). In many cases, for children to live out God's will requires a will strong enough to resist peer pressure. While valuing the strength of will that gives children the courage to do what is right, as with Wesley we long to see children, and adults, surrender their wills to God. Submission to God, however, often requires a resistance to peer pressure for children and teenagers.

Wesley was also concerned about children learning how to live a life of love. He instructed parents to curb any expressions of "unmercifulness" in children. Children should not be allowed to cause pain to siblings or to animals (Wesley, 1984). Although Wesley did not make a place for play when designing the educational plan for his schools, in comments from the sermon, "On the Education of Children," he pointed to the importance of what goes on during times of play with other children and with animals. Children are formed through all the practices and patterns of their lives. Wesley called parents to establish an environment in the home that would help children live in ways that can prepare them to understand, through experience, the goodness of God. Instruction and boundaries contribute to this healthy environment.

> Consider the ending of Wesley's sermon "On the Education of Children": Ye that are truly kind parents, in the morning, in the evening, and all the day beside, press upon your children to "walk in love, as Christ also loved us, and gave himself for us"; to mind that one point, "God is love; and he that dwelleth in love, dwelleth in God, and God in him." (Wesley, 1984, p. 98)

In these final words, Wesley focused again on the importance of the life lived by parents. Wesley held before them the goal of being truly kind at all times. He also reinforced their responsibility to instruct their children and pointed to the most important theme of that teaching, God's love. For even though Wesley believed that moral instruction had value, he also believed that the best safeguard against rebellion is a deep-seated confidence in God's love. Therefore the most important goal for Christian teaching in the home, the church, and the school, is to help children grasp the greatness of God's love for them.

Schooling

For Wesley, education held great importance, both the education that took place in the home and further education in the school. He charged parents to choose carefully a school for their children, both their girls and their boys. The most critical component in a good school, Wesley believed, was a God-fearing master or mistress (Wesley, 1984).

Wesley held a very negative view of the schools for children in his day and the options open to Methodist parents. The content of basic education was inadequate and religious content almost nonexistent in the schools. Teachers did not provide a model of godly character and most students came from godless homes creating an environment that could lead children into sinful practices. In the light of these conditions, Wesley decided to establish a school (Wesley, 1984). He purchased property in Kingswood, a few miles out of Bristol. The Kingswood School was to be a boarding school so that its influence on the students—fifty boys—would be continuous. Wesley planned that the boys would not go home until they left the school permanently.

Children between the ages of six and twelve were admitted to Kingswood. In this policy Wesley's perspective on spiritual formation during childhood is reflected. He chose to invest in what he considered to be the most formative period of life. He wanted to prevent "bad habits and ill principles" from taking root in a child's heart and believed that work was best done before the age of twelve. Not just any child could enroll at Kingswood; requirements for admission were that the child have some awareness of God, at least a beginning desire to know God, and parents who wanted a rigorous spiritual education for their child.

Wesley's goals for the Kingswood school involved "Forming [the children's] minds, through the help of God, to wisdom and holiness, by instilling the principles of true religion, speculative and practical, and training them up in the ancient way, that they might be rational, scriptural Christians" (Wesley, 1984, p. 293). The rules at Kingswood were very strict and the schedule intense. From four o'clock in the morning when the children got up until eight o'clock in the evening when they went to bed, they were continually engaged in study, classes, prayer, meditation, work, or walking, with no play allowed. And the curriculum was rigorous, including reading, writing, arithmetic, English, French, Latin, Greek, Hebrew, history, geography, and the like. Wesley made certain that the children read only the best books that presented purity, strength, eloquence of language, and useful ideas.

At Kingswood, Wesley wanted to build a home "to have therein a Christian family; every member whereof, children excepted, should be alive to God, and a pattern of all holiness. Here it was I proposed to educate a few children according to the accuracy of the Christian model" (Wesley, 1984, pp. 301–302). He placed great importance on the character of the schoolmaster and all the adults who worked at the school. For effective education, Wesley realized that the teachers' lives needed to demonstrate what they taught. Finding schoolmasters whose lives modeled the holiness Wesley wanted the children to see and learn, proved difficult and he was disappointed with the effectiveness of Kingswood. The religious formation and basic education Wesley hoped for at Kingswood did not happen. His plan contained worthy goals and positive elements in the design, but his understanding was limited regarding what children need and the factors that contribute to their formation.

Implications for Ministry with Children Today

In the 21st century, what does Wesley have to say to persons concerned about the spiritual formation of children? In her presentation at the Children's Spirituality Conference in June of 2003, Marcia Bunge (see chapter three) challenged her audience to study history and, through critical retrieval, learn from the past. History offers us the light of what God has revealed to past generations. And yet centuries of additional research and study of children have provided many insights that Wesley did not have. In the light of what has been learned about children since Wesley's day, the limitations of some of his approaches are clear, and some beliefs Wesley held are not acceptable, such as discouraging play, never praising children in their presence, limiting any form of commendation, and at an early age teaching children that they are "fallen spirits" (Wesley, 1984). However, there is much in Wesley's writing to highlight—significant insights to guide ministries with children and their families. These insights and the practices of early Methodists provide at least four insights and questions for church ministry today.

Wesley saw great importance in the spiritual formation occurring during childhood. He encouraged beginning the nurturing of infants as soon as the child responds, and believed that between the ages of six and twelve some of the most significant formation takes place. Note that it is the leader of the Methodist movement who placed this high value on children and their spirituality. In churches today, how are children viewed? Do leaders believe in the importance of what God wants to do in the hearts and lives of children? What priority is given to the spiritual nurturing of children in the context of the church and the home? What practices demonstrate the importance placed on the spirituality of children? Which practices indicate that churches and parents do not expect significant Christian formation to happen before the teen years? How could church leaders be encouraged to grasp more fully the importance of respecting and giving serious attention to the spiritual life of children?

Wesley took Scripture seriously, declaring himself to be a man of one Book. Although Scripture was his main source of insight and guidance, he was open to learn from many sources. He studied the prominent educators of his day as he sought to understand children, taking guidance from some and disagreeing with others. Parents and church leaders today should also desire a strong biblical base for ministry with children and be open to what can be learned from educators and psychologists who invest their lives in the study of children.

Aware of the profound teaching and learning that takes place in the flow of life, Wesley highly valued the role of parents in the spiritual nurture of their children. He provided settings for the spiritual growth of parents and also gave them guidance and instruction regarding parenting. Are young parents finding contexts in churches where they can be known and nurtured? Are they finding mentors, fellow pilgrims, instruction, and answers to their questions about being an effective Christian parent?

Wesley saw the importance of infant baptism as a means of grace, believed that most children would experience conversion at some point along their spiritual journey, and desired to help establish an environment in the home and in the faith community where children would be nurtured over time. In today's churches is there a focus on one means of bringing children to Christ by baptism, conversion, *or* nurture? Or do ministries with children reflect a "both/and" understanding similar to that of Wesley? In the words of Marcia Bunge (in chapter three), is there a "complex richness" in the understanding of how God works in the lives of children? Are there meaningful rituals of infant baptism (or dedication) and nurturing environments in which children come to know Jesus and continually respond to his call, "come, follow me, be my disciple?"

As we reflect on twenty-first century ministries, Wesley's words are clearly relevant: Children are "immortal spirits whom God hath for a time entrusted to [our] care, that [we] may train them up in all holiness, and fit them for the enjoyment of God in eternity. This is a glorious and important trust" (Wesley, *Works*, Vol. 7, 1984, p. 79).

References

Borgen, O. E. (1988). John Wesley: Sacramental theology no ends without the means. In J. Stacey (Ed.), *John Wesley: Contemporary perspectives* (pp. 67–82). London: Epworth.

Bunge, M. J. (Ed.). (2001). *The child in Christian thought.* Grand Rapids: Eerdmans.

Byron, G. (1903). Notes and queries: Children's sermon by J. Wesley at Bolton. *Proceedings of the Wesley Historical Society, 4,* 119–90.

Gill, F. (1936, October 15). Wesley and the children. *The Methodist Recorder.*

Im, S. (1994). *John Wesley's theological anthropology: A dialectic tension between the Latin Western patristic tradition (Augustine) and the Greek Eastern patristic tradition (Gregory of Nyssa).* Unpublished doctoral dissertation, Drew University.

Kohlberg, L. (1984). *The psychology of moral development: Essays on moral development, Volume 2.* San Francisco: Harper & Row.

Outler, A. (Ed.). (1964). *John Wesley.* New York: Oxford University Press.

Reed, J. E., & Prevost, R. (1993). *A history of Christian education.* Nashville: Broadman & Holman.

Scanlon, M. J. (1969). The Christian anthropology of John Wesley. Dissertation Abstracts International, 30(06A), 261. (UMI No. 6919692). Ann Arbor: University Microfilms.

Wangerin, W., Jr. (1986/1996). *Orphean passages.* Grand Rapids: Zondervan.

Wesley, J. (1984). *The works of John Wesley: Complete and unabridged* (3rd ed., Vols. 5–10, and 13). Peabody, MA: Hendrickson.

Willhauck, S. E. (1992). John Wesley's view of children: Foundations for contemporary Christian education. Dissertation Abstracts International, 53(03A), 765.

Wood, A. S. (1967). *The burning heart: John Wesley, evangelist.* Grand Rapids: Eerdmans.

Chapter Ten

Children's Spiritual Experiences and the Brain

SCOTTIE MAY

The spiritual experiences of children reflect the wide variety of ways they can respond to different environments. Intense, stimulating settings usually energize and activate children, which can provide the context for exuberant praise. Yet in a slow-paced setting conducive to reflection, youngsters may be transfixed in wonder and awe, a very different and often more meaningful spiritual experience for youngsters.

In this chapter the nature of children's spiritual experiences will be explored by examining recent research of spirituality and neurological correlates of these experiences. These findings provide useful insights into the spiritual experiences of children, and thus practical implications of these perspectives will be considered at the conclusion of the chapter.

What Are Spiritual Experiences?

The term "spirituality" is used in many ways in modern society, and writings on the spirituality of children also vary widely in their descriptions and assumptions about spiritual experience.[1] A key reference point for this chapter is the work of Rebecca Nye (2003; Hay & Nye, 1998), who describes children's perceptual experiences as a state of heightened attentiveness and awareness related to profound wonder. Hay and Nye emphasize that spiritual sensitivity can be categorized as *awareness sensing* which emphasizes the "here-and-now" aesthetic experience or meditation, often marked by focusing in which there is undivided, intense concentration on the present moment.

---

1. It may be that the different areas of the brain are related to different kinds of spiritual experience. Thus, the careful mapping of brain activities that occur during different kinds of spiritual experiences may produce greater accuracy in defining these experiences. Perhaps the specific associations discovered in this manner can result in a taxonomy of spiritual experiences, reflecting the spectrum and wide variety of such experiences, based upon different patterns of neural activity (Newberg & Newberg, 2006).

Spiritual experiences of children could also be considered *mystery-sensing*, mysterious because they are associated with life's ultimate mystery, characterized by wonder, awe, and/or a highly imaginative state far beyond what is typically experienced in daily life. A third category found in children's descriptions of their spiritual experiences is *value-sensing* characterized by a quest for meaning, trust in life, and affirming ideas of value or worth expressed in feelings of delight or despair. These three categories may reflect distinct spiritual experiences, or conversely may be combined to some extent. Regardless, the three categories point to a core category of *relational conscious-ness*, with "relational" denoting the importance of God, other people, things, or self as the focus of attention, while "consciousness" emphasizes the heightened perception, awareness, and reflective aspects of spiritual experience.

Spiritual experiences, in Nye's view, occur in children regardless of religious training or lack of such. In this respect she follows Robert Coles's (1990) research of children's spiritual experience. Nye emphasizes that spirituality is, in this sense, quite distinct from religion. She makes clear that spiritual experiences are relatively common early in life, although they tend to be less frequent—or at least reported less frequently—as children move into late childhood and adolescence.

Spiritual experience is often powerfully influenced by the immediate environment. Certain contexts may be more conducive to quiet reflection and experiences of awe and wonder than others. Sophia Cavalletti (1992) developed a specific curriculum, building upon Maria Montessori's prior work, to help children to be more receptive to such experiences. Cavalletti's approach forms the core of what is now termed "Catechesis of the Good Shepherd," as well as the increasingly popular adaptation known as "Godly Play," developed by Jerome Berryman.[2] Their carefully prepared environments give evidence that the setting may affect children responses. Context and preparation are important, but not determinative—spiritual experience is never guaranteed by any specific method, but certain contexts and methods may help the child be more open to such experiences.

As I have watched children in these prepared environments, I have wondered what is happening within the child that appears to make a difference in their actions and attitudes. What might they be feeling or thinking? Neurological research in recent years provides helpful insights.

Neurological Aspects of Spiritual Experiences

Linking brain activity to the spirit, mind, or soul has a long history filled with endless speculation, but a relatively short history in terms of research. For example, some of the ancient Greeks believed the soul was in the ventricles (hollow areas of the brain

2. See also Stewart and Berryman (1989), and Stewart (2000).

that contain cerebral spinal fluid), while Descartes felt the self or mind connected to the brain in the pineal gland (MacKay, 1980).

Social scientists from many areas of research are intrigued with child spirituality because of escalating emotional and behavioral problems seen in one fourth of North American children. A significant study suggests "the human child is 'hardwired to connect.' We are hardwired for other people and for moral meaning and openness to the transcendent. Meeting these basic needs for connection essential to health and to human flourishing" (Commission on Children at Risk, 2003, p. 6). The findings of this study demonstrate that "nurturing environments, or lack of them, affect gene transcription and the development of brain circuitry" (p. 17). A strongly nurturing context may reduce or reverse the effects of genes that lead to anti-social or negative emotional behaviors. The study also reveals that positive spiritual development and religiosity may have the same effect as primary nurturing relationships because they influence well-being in significant ways.

While research cannot directly measure spirituality—by its very nature "spirit" is immaterial—there have been recent investigations that suggest that certain patterns in neural activity tend to correspond with the experiences of a spiritual nature. Before exploring this research, it is worthwhile to consider the overall geography of the brain and how researchers currently understand the neural activities in the brain. It must be emphasized that research in this area is very recent and tentative conclusions today may be modified considerably by additional research in the years to come.

The Triune Brain

There are three general areas of the brain, and thus the one may speak of the "triune brain" (MacLean, 1974; Caine & Caine, 1994). Neurons to and from every area of the body arrive at the base of the brain—located at the top of the spinal cord—at the *brain stem*. This part of the brain, particularly a section termed the "reticular system," is associated with basic arousal and filtering of neural data. Thus, sleep and wakeful periods are directly associated with the functioning of this part of the brain, as are hyperactivity and lethargy in children. Often the cerebellum, closely related to balance and coordination, and the thalamus which is a hub for most sensory data are collectively termed the "lower brain" (Myers, 2001) because of their lower and more central location, but also because this part of the brain is also found in lower species of life.

A second general area is found between this lower brain and the uppermost sections of the brain, termed the "limbic system." This region, which includes the amygdala and hypothalamus, is involved in emotions, basic motives, aggression and fear, and basic bodily activities such as hunger, thirst, body temperature, and sexual response (Myers, 2001). Of particular interest for Christians is the observation made by neurologist Antonio Damasio (Interview with Damasio, n.d.), Professor of Neuroscience, Psychology and Philosophy at the University of Southern California, that moral behaviors such as compassion have emotional grounding involving the limbic system as well as other parts of the brain. Therefore, the functioning of the brain has relevance for those in ministry who seek to encourage compassionate behavior.

The uppermost part of the brain is termed the "neocortex," the "neo" or new reflecting the assumption by some that this area is the product of more recent evolutionary development. The cerebral cortex, as it is sometimes termed, is found only in higher species of animals and humans, is divided into two halves or "hemispheres," and is associated with thought and perception of sensory experiences, as well as control of muscles.

While it may be tempting to apply the biblical concept of humans being made in the image of God (Gen 1:27) by comparing the triune brain with the triune God, such comparisons tend to be elusive and oversimplify brain function. They can also reveal an inadequate understanding of God.

Spiritual experiences, as described by Nye, involve all areas of the brain. Her emphasis upon a different level of awareness suggests the possibility of the reticular system being involved. Sensory input must be passed on from the sensory receptors (eyes, ears, skin, and so on) for the child to be influenced by the immediate environment to be more receptive to spiritual experiences. Similarly, spiritual experiences are understood and articulated through the functioning of the left cerebral hemisphere, while the more intuitive and artistic aspects of spiritual experience relate to right hemisphere functioning. Yet, for the purpose of this chapter, the focus will be upon the more emotional aspects of spiritual experience linked with the limbic system (primarily the amygdala), as this has been the focus of recent research of spirituality and brain function. The limbic system constitutes an important linkage between the upper (thinking) part of the brain and the lower (arousal and attention) part of the brain.

The Three Sections of the Limbic System

The limbic system is made of three components. The amygdala is associated with the physiological response to an emotional situation, arousal that can produce aggression or fear (Myers, 2004, Golden, 1981). This part of the brain is associated with early memories created prior to the use of language that can trigger emotional responses later in life through nonverbal cues such as smells touches, sounds or visual sensations. Such "memories" are not recalled as specific events, yet they may produce intense emotional associations (Goleman, 1995). The amygdala is also associated with being calm and quiet, such as the response of an infant when being comforted (Diamond & Hopson, 1998, p. 126). Thus, the amygdala is probably involved in the quiet spirituality of reflection and wonder as described by Nye (1998) and Berryman (1991).

In contrast, the *hippocampus* is involved in the storage and processing of cognitive memories. While the amygdala is more directly associated with emotion, the hippocampus can help with recalling the circumstances where emotion was experienced (LeeDoux, 1996). The encoding and recalling of linguistic memories involves the hippocampus, although the actual memories are stored in the cerebral cortex.

A third part of the limbic system—the *hypothalamus*—is associated with hunger, thirst, sexuality, and pleasure. While one must be careful not to oversimplify a complex issue, it is interesting that fasting from food and/or water, sexual abstinence (or expression), and deep pleasure all have been associated with adult spiritual experiences, both in the Christian faith and other religions.

Yet these three components of the limbic system are interdependent, and there are vast interconnections between the limbic system, the cerebral cortex, and the lower brain as well. Goleman cites evidence that "feelings" are essential for making rational decisions. He comments, "The emotional brain is as involved in reasoning as is the thinking brain" (p. 28). In other words, the brain functions in a manner that is not purely limbic or cortical Unfortunately, when churches and religious schools emphasize cognition as the key to a child's religious development responses, they have opted for less than a complete spirituality.

The Limbic System and Emotions

Goleman's groundbreaking work (1995) in emotional intelligence identifies the role of emotions in the development of the person and the significance of the limbic system in that process. He explains that an infant learns appropriateness of emotions from the responses of the primary caregiver. The infant mirrors that person's mood, thereby learning to be passive and depressive or animated and responsive. The child attunes to the primary caregiver when the emotions are met with empathy, accepted, and reciprocated. These interactions connect to the limbic system through emotion-specific neurons. Because the emotional brain is as involved in decisions of the growing child as the thinking brain, Goleman believes that it can even overpower the thinking brain. He finds that young children soon learn whether or not empathy is an acceptable value. If it is not, the young child quickly refrains from showing empathy. This may become a long-term coping strategy in that relationship. Emotions and feelings originate in the limbic system, as do some aspects of personal identity and memory functions, according to Goleman.

Paul D. MacLean (1974) emphasized that the neocortex dominates the lower levels of the brain and suggested that the limbic system—because of its link with emotions—can "hijack" the higher mental functions on certain occasions. As he understood it, the limbic system tends to be the seat of our value judgments, instead of the more advanced neocortex. The limbic system decides whether the neocortex has a "good" idea or not, whether it feels true and right (Johnson, 2004; Caine & Caine, 1994). Joseph LeDoux (1996) expresses gratitude to MacLean for his pioneering work in identifying the limbic system as the emotional center of brain as does Chauncey Leake (1975), though LeDoux feels he overstated and simplified what is very complex and not yet verifiable.

A Connection to God?

Neuropsychologist R. Joseph (2001) goes so far as to say that "the limbic system may well be the seat of the soul or may serve as the neural transmitter to God" (p. 133). This view is supported by Andrew Newberg, Eugene d'Aquili, and Vince Rause (2002) in their work, *Why God Won't Go Away*. They studied the spiritual experiences of Buddhist monks and Franciscan nuns. These experiences for this population were associated with observable neurological activity. The researchers developed a theory of neurotheology "that provides a link between mystical experience and observable brain function. In simplest terms, the brain seems to have the built-in ability to transcend the perception of an individual self" (p. 174). The intent of neurotheology is to attempt to understand the link between brain function and aspects of religious experience (p. 175).

> These mystical experiences occur on a continuum. At the far end of this continuum are the profound states of spiritual unity described by saints and mystics. But the same complex brain function that makes such powerful states possible also enables us to feel much milder, and more 'ordinary' sensations of spiritual connection—the sense of uplift or absorption you feel during moments of prayer or contemplation, for example, or while joining in with your congregation to sing a hymn (p. 175).

The experiences of "flow," meditation, and "focus" mentioned by Rebecca Nye in her theory, that to some extent parallel such mystical experiences.

Damasio (2003) suggests an alternative perspective: "I do not favor the attempt to neurologize religious experiences, especially when the attempts take the form of identifying a brain center for God or justifying God and religion by finding their correlates in brain scans (2003, p. 284). These experiences are mental activities which means that they are highly complex biological processes. Damasio finds no reason to avoid describing them neurobiologically, yet always emphasizes the limitations in doing so. Christians must always keep in mind the distinctives of their faith—the realities that make Christianity unique such as the Holy Spirit, grace, sin, and forgiveness. Damasio states, "Accounting for the physiological process behind the spiritual does not explain the mystery of the life process to which that particular feeling is connected. It reveals the connection to the mystery but not the mystery itself" (p. 286).

If the data presented in *Why God Won't Go Away* is valid, it provides neuro-biological evidence for the significance of Nye's concept of spirituality as "relational consciousness." Experience and encounters with "Other" (for present purposes, "Other" is God) are at the core of these concepts. It is important to note again the evidence that areas of the brain other than the limbic system play a role in spiritual experience, such as the temporal lobe of the cerebral cortex (see Britton & Bootzin, 2004). Even in spiritual experience, the brain tends to function as a holistic unit, not as isolated modules.

Though much more is known today about the complex interrelated workings of the brain, this does not necessarily provide guidance on how to construct learning experiences or encounters with God for spiritual formation, nor does it "prove" that learning will happen. This information may never lead directly to "correct" pedagogy, but there is greater certainty that emotion plays a significant role in learning (Wolfe and Brandt, 1998).

Language and Spiritual Experience

The emotional component of spiritual experience needs to be clearly distinguished from the language about spiritual experience, as these two aspects of religious and spiritual life are relatively dichotomized in the brain. Too often spirituality has been associated with language, either learning the correct language or articulating the desired language.[3] Unfortunately, as has long been known, words do not always match deeds in the religious realm. What is perhaps less recognized is that feelings and related spiritual experiences also may be disconnected from words.

The separation of language from spiritual experience highlights an important distinction between *connatural knowing* and *speculative knowing*. Connatural knowing is an *encounter* with what is to be known. Initially infants learn language and sounds in this manner. Speculative knowing is *detached*, rational, theoretical, propositional—the more traditional "schooling" approach. To illustrate this distinction, Christopher Renz (1998) did a study on attitudes toward confirmation among Catholic youth which involved traditional religious education focused on speculative knowing. By the early adolescent age of confirmation, Catholic children have had years of experience

---

3. Research underlying stage theories—such as that of Piaget, Kohlberg, and many religious development theories—requires that children listen and understand stories, questions or instructions, as well as make verbal responses. Thus the stages that are central to such theories maybe more a function of language abilities than children's thinking. If children are cognitively able to think about a matter, they still may be unable to express that thought in language because of limitations in vocabulary or other aspects of language expression. Furthermore, the child may not even be given the opportunity to think about a subject because of inadequate understanding of what was stated by the examiner, because the query did not fir the child's vocabulary or other aspects of language receptivity. Both receptive and expressive language limitations can mask genuine cognitive capabilities. Thus, stage theories may reflect shifts in language abilities more than the child's thinking abilities or spiritual development (Ratcliff, 1988).

with speculative knowing. Renz found that these children are bored, tuned out during confirmation classes, and drop out of church once the rite is achieved. Renz suggests purposefully altering traditional religious education by introducing connatural knowing to young children so that they may *encounter* God rather than being taught about him. Renz feels that consistent early experiences *with* God will allow the desire to know *about* him to grow. This proposed sequence of knowing seems to parallel a child's knowing about her parents: connatural knowing comes first, with the desire for speculative knowing gradually coming later. Thus, a relationship with God may be established with positive emotional grounding.

In *Godly Play*, Jerome Berryman (1991) writes about the significance of language and experience for the young child. His carefully prepared environment, adapted from Cavalletti's Catechesis of the Good Shepherd, seeks to create space to allow children to begin to formulate and ask existential questions—questions such as "What happens when someone dies?" "Mommy, what if you don't come back?" or "What should I be when I grow up?" The environment must create opportunity for interplay between experience and language which at first the child lacks. If experiences of God are provided, language to describe those experiences may develop. Language shapes experience; experience shapes language (p. 153). But helpful language must be used. The language of religion, of spiritual formation, is the language of mystery and of relationship. As the child enters into symbols, parables, and narratives, the presence of God may be experienced (p. 148). But language may also be spiritually deforming, introducing fear or mistrust of God or even irrelevance. Language may keep us from coming closer to God—if God is defined with detail and precision, if self is described in conditional terms, or if the sense of awe and wonder is removed from worship.

Berryman also considers the role of laughter with children: carnival laughter versus godly laughter (1991, p.16). Godly laughter is that of creation and play. Carnival laughter is raucous, mocking, deriding, easily trivializing religion or turning into "magic" that the child may try to control. Yet, at the time of this writing, a fun-oriented, carnival-like atmosphere is becoming increasingly common in many children's ministries.

Along with the importance of language, Berryman (2003) also identifies the necessity of nonverbal experience. An awareness must be developed to recognize nonverbal limbic response as well as verbal neocortex response because, in Berryman's words, "falling in love [with the Lord Jesus] through grace" happens through the limbic system, whereas it is spoken about through the left hemisphere of the neocortex.

Other scholars concur with Berryman's position. Kevin Reimer and James Furrow (2001) write, "Cognitively, the child's relational experience precedes the development of spiritual narrative, and then mediates a recursive process of interaction between narrative and new experiences of person, objects, or the divine" (p. 10). The nonverbal "inner speech" may become the foundation for spirituality. As speech is linked with an internal experience of God, the child is then able to slowly personalize spirituality. The child uses symbols from narratives or a concrete experience as the basis for relational consciousness not unlike the concept of bonding (p. 20). As the child integrates the meaning of the symbols with circumstances, identification with God and self as other may take place in relational terms.

Lee Kirkpatrick (1997) also sees attachment or bonding as significant in religious formation. Issues of infant attachment through the availability and responsiveness of the primary caregiver who serves as a haven and a secure base is considered a fundamental dynamic underlying Christianity and many other theistic religions. Consistent with object relations theory, separation from the human attachment figure causes distress. When attachment shifts positively from the caregiver to God, "the mere knowledge of God's presence and accessibility allows a person to approach the problems and difficulties of daily life with confidence" (p. 117). Though the human parent has limitations, the idea of God as the absolute adequate "attachment figure," the protective parent, is always reliable and available when the child is in need. Since early communication between the very young child and her caregiver is a key component of this process, insights from awareness of the functions of the limbic system may perhaps enable adults to facilitate communication between God and the young child.

James Loder (1998) provides an alternative perspective. He writes that it is important "to make the crucial distinction between a person whose god is created out of the self and parental images and one whose image of God is derived from *an actual encounter* with the living God to whom humans do not give birth" (emphasis added). When a child understands God only from human images, Loder feels that the image of God understood in this way "deprives the spirit of the person of the transcendence and the 'beyond-one's-self' toward which it drives."

If Loder is correct, a major barrier that needs to be overcome is the assumption that cognitive concepts indicate a child's spirituality (see Chapter 6). Observing a young child's affective, expressive, and artistic responses may give evidence of that child's spirituality more so than verbal articulation about spiritual matters. Established speculative Christian religious language fails to supply life to the child's spirituality— the relational consciousness.

David Hay, Rebecca Nye, and Roger Murphy (1996) write: "Over the past thirty years the dominance of cognitive developmental theory in the field of religious education has led to a severe neglect of the study of the spirituality of the child and to a distortion of what goes on in the religious education classroom" (p. 47). This undoubtedly is caused in part by the challenge of finding appropriate research methodologies (see Chapter 11). Another factor is the narrowness of developmental stage theories that come "near to dissolving religion into reason and therefore childhood religion into a form of immaturity or inadequacy" (p. 56, also see Chapters 6, 7, and 20). Children's ability to experience the spiritual has been seen as flawed, whereas, in reality their cognition "includes those components which are quintessential to spirituality—skills which are actively pursued by adult practitioners of spirituality" (Levine, 1999, p. 137). If cognitive development is central (the left hemisphere of the neocortex), this emphasis precludes the profound religious faith of mentally retarded people—those who have found group ritual as the significant way in which the relationship with God is sustained. "Could it be that particular cultures, secular or perhaps 'over-cognitively religious,' hamper the development of the expression of spirituality because of preconceptions about children's competencies, or more commonly, their lack of competence?" (Hay, et al., p. 64).

Truth as Heart Experience versus Intellectual Affirmation

Parker Palmer (1993), using Jesus' own words in John 14:6, describes the quest for truth as encountering the Person who claims that he *is* Truth. Therefore, it may be said that for the Christian truth is not so much an intellectual activity as it is an experience. Cognitive affirmations of propositional statements can easily be dichotomized from one's way of life and the will (attitudes, felt values, dispositions).

Renz describes a child's spiritual life as beginning with love. "One cannot love what one does not know. A human moves toward God in love because there is a first experiential encounter with God. . . . Connatural knowledge is knowledge always directed towards an end. For the human, it is the source of a creative loving response to God's first offer of love"[4] (p. 59). Renza goes on to state that effective formational education for the child must have both connatural and speculative experiences but that connatural knowing should happen first.

Renz (1992) explains that through Catechesis of the Good Shepherd, Cavalletti seeks "to create an holistic environment in which the child can be in relationship with God." This space is called an atrium: "An ensemble of elements—few and essential—was slowly delineated, which the child showed that he knew, not in an academic way, but as if they were a part of his person, almost as if he had always known them" (p. 22). The atrium experience includes silence—a full silence rather than an empty one. It is a critical part of every atrium. Children love it. It is during times of silence that they sometimes "discover they have an inner life" (Lillig).[5]

Cavalletti comments that in the atrium young children, though usually wordless, "speak loudly through their attitudes and bodies" (North American Montessori Teachers' Association, 2000). Key values that Cavalletti has identified from observing the children are—

- *Joy*, deep, peaceful, serene that is evident in their posture, focus and contentedness in being in the atrium.

---

4. "We love because he first loved us," I John 4:19.

5. In a recent research project, children at a community center who had experienced this type of environment verbalized their desire for quiet in what is usually a rather noisy setting. A sixth grader said, "When it's quiet, He [God] just comes to mind."

- *Dignity* from the ability to have a personal relationship with God, accompanied by wonder, amazement, freedom, and independence.

- *Essentiality*, which means eliminate frills and fluff because otherwise the young child may be lost in a cluttered, busy environment.

"The spiritual life is to determine what is *essential*," Cavalletti has commented (North American Montessori Teachers' Association, 2000). Therefore, the child is the teacher. Watch the child's reaction and growth to determine what is essential. Through the parable of the Good Shepherd, the story that profoundly satisfies the younger child's hunger for relationship with God, the young child is most struck that the Shepherd calls the sheep by name. In contrast, adults are drawn to Shepherd laying down his life for the sheep. Give the essentials in word and materials; then step aside letting the Holy Spirit bring the child to the Shepherd to live together in relationship.

Cavalletti (1992) continues: "God is the God of the covenant." Covenant and relationship are synonymous. God is the God of the relationship—the I-Thou. "The child seems to reach completion of his being in relationship with a personal God, being a partner of the covenant" (p. 21). A sense of belonging often flows from that covenant relationship.

Damasio describes recent neurological insights in an interview conducted by Steven Johnson that provide physiological support for Cavalletti's insights and observations. Damasio notes that parts of the brain operate at different speeds: the cognitive system can be trained to function faster and faster because the neurons are myelinated.[6] But the unmyelinated emotional system works at a slower pace, and "[t]here is no evidence that the emotional system is going to speed up" (Johnson, p. 49). He fears that as cognition continues to speed up, emotional neutrality may result. This underscores the need Cavalletti sees for children to have space where they can be present thoughtfully and slowly in order to provide emotional grounding and a desire for an ongoing relationship with the Good Shepherd, the "Other."

Spiritual Experience Is More Than Brain Function

Spiritual experience is clearly related to brain functioning, yet a description of that functioning does not adequately convey the richness of that experience. There is a sense of awe and/or fear; the experience of the Holy Otherness of the moment.

Rebecca Nye, Robert Coles, and many other researchers, consider spiritual experience to be a universal across religious faiths. Nye and others suggest that even small children have spiritual encounters and that the religious language of theology is added as a descriptor of that experience. These spiritual encounters are marked by awe and a sense of something uncanny.

6. Myelinization refers to the addition of a thin coat of myelin around the nerve which causes impulses to move faster and more efficiently through the nerve.

The awe-filled experience of the young child is supra-rational—but not irrational—in that the experience is inexpressible and undefineable by the child. Experiences such as these cannot be taught nor initiated by human will; the numinous can only be awakened and evoked. Some children may "tremble" in such an experience, a physical response that goes beyond normal fear. For some children there is an element of fascination that draws them or woos them to the Holy Other. This type of experience is described as occurring to some people in Scripture as well as throughout the history of the Christian church.

These experiences can serve as an essential complement to rational theology, as without them one only has ideas *about* God (or speculative knowing, as mentioned earlier), while the awe-filled experience is an encounter *with* God (described as con-natural knowing earlier in the chapter).

Conclusions and Recommendations

If the argument presented here is accurate—that the awe-filled spiritual experience and its corollary limbic system functioning plays a crucial role in the spirituality of the child—then, scholars and practitioners alike have significant work to do. Both liturgical and non-liturgical churches tend to rely heavily on words to communicate the Christian faith to children. Yet brain research, as well as reflection upon the ways God expresses himself suggest the need for a more holistic approach in which emotions and experience should be the result of educational and corporate worship, not mere words.

One of the first tasks should be to help restore a child's corporate sense of wonder. Current children's ministry can diminish a child's wonder. Mathew Woodley (2000) writes, "Wonderless living has become the norm" (p. 26). Citing Abraham Heschel, he says: "We teach children how to measure, how to weigh. We do not teach them how to revere, how to sense wonder and awe." This amazes Woodley because he feels that if the Lord God is present, that place should be alive with wonder. The inner experience of wonder can emerge from outward visual, tactile, or verbal contexts and experiences. They may involve unusual states of awareness (lower brain), powerful emotions (the limbic system), or intuitive/verbal components (right and left hemispheres of the cerebral cortex respectively).

Cavalletti's guidelines (1992) provide insights particularly for Americans ministering with children: Watch the child's attitudes and actions to learn what is essential; then adjust accordingly. (More adult involvement is usually not better in this context; intervene only when it is essential.) Allow wonder, amazement, freedom, and appropriate independence. Create experiences so the child can relate to God; provide and promote a sense of belonging.

Nelson adds that we must "help them to know their own soul and provide or perfect the rituals and forms" that give meaning to their lives (1990, p. 117). For this to happen, we must protect children from the world's clamor and its call for them to fulfill their desires by buying "stuff." We must help them "touch the places of life's mysteries and give them back meaning—not a sentimentalized meaning but a meaning that they will never outgrow" (p. 117).

Experiences that encourage internal dialogue, connatural learning, or emotional connectedness, seem critical for the spiritual formation of children given the research presented. This has significant implications for curriculum development. By the very nature of congregational life, the faith community may be the best place for children to hear spiritual and biblical narratives. "Curriculum largely overlooks the potential for the narrative contribution of local faith communities and may circumvent it altogether with an individualistic approach to spiritual appropriation in children" (Reimer and Furrow, 2001, p. 21). Children need settings where narratives are shared, as well as settings for personal reflection (see Chapter 19 on narrative education).

For generations, language has been the focus in ministry with children, the cognitive left hemisphere of the neocortex. In recent decades the creative right hemisphere of the neocortex has received increasing attention, all the while recognizing that there is cross-communication between hemispheres. Given the evidence presented here about the limbic system, it seems crucial to take seriously the possibility that children's experiences or encounters with God can be facilitated by preparing environments that allow connatural knowing and relational consciousness to emerge. Nye's relational consciousness is powerfully relevant for ministry praxis in the spiritual formation of children. The child's spirituality should influence the form ministry takes rather than merely following a cultural trend or cognitive theory.

A new curriculum paradigm is recommended, using "curriculum" in its broadest, most holistic sense. Just as is sometimes found in public education, this new curriculum is based on core commonalities—qualities essential for accomplishing the goals. Consider the paradigm model that follows which is based on Christian commonalities.

Core Commonalities for Children's Christian Spiritual Formation

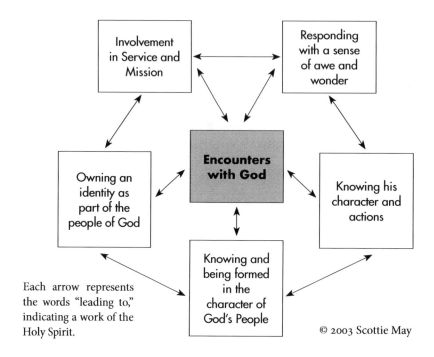

Each arrow represents the words "leading to," indicating a work of the Holy Spirit.

© 2003 Scottie May

Undoubtedly each of the "leading to" phrases points to or requires an act of the Holy Spirit—some type of conversion—a new or renewed turning toward the Lord Jesus, a deeper way of allowing Christ to be formed within. In many churches children can be enabled to encounter God from their earliest years in ways that will become the very fabric of their lives. As a result, they may become eager, life-long learners about the God who made them because they have *experienced* him. We who minister with children must provide opportunities for living encounters with the living God!

References

Berryman, J. (1991). *Godly play: An imaginative approach to religious education.* Minneapolis: Augsburg.

Berryman, J. (2003). *The importance of children's spirituality.* Presented at Conference on Children's Spirituality: A Christian Perspective, River Forest, IL.

Britton, W. B. & Bootzin, R. R. (2004). Near death experiences and the temporal lobe. *Psychological Science, 15,* 254–258.

Caine, R., and Caine, G. (1994). *Making connections.* New York: Addison-Wesley.

Cavalletti, S. (1992). *Religious potential of the child.* Chicago: Liturgy Training Publications.

Commission on Children at Risk. (2003). *Hardwired to connect: the new scientific case for authoritative communities.* New York: Institute for American Values.

Damasio, A. (2003). *Looking for Spinoza: Joy, sorrow, and the feeling brain.* Orlando: Harcourt.

Diamond, M., & Hopson, J. (1998). *Magic trees of the mind: How to nurture your child's intelligence, creativity, and healthy emotions.* New York: Plume.

Goleman, D. (1995). *Emotional intelligence.* New York: Bantam.

Hay, D., Nye, R., & Murphy, R. (1996). Thinking about childhood spirituality: Review of research and current directions. In L. Francis, W. Kay, & W. Campbell (Eds.), *Research in religious education* (pp. 47–71). Macon, GA: Smyth & Helwys.

Interview with Antonio Damasio (n.d.). Retrieved July 6, 2004, from http:// www.harcourtbooks.com/authorinterviews/bookinterviews_damasio.asp

Johnson, S. (2004). Antonio Damasio's theory of thinking faster and faster: Are the brain's emotional circuits hardwired for speed? *Discover, 25*(5), 45–49.

Joseph, R. (2001). The limbic system and the soul: Evolution and the neuroanatomy of religious experience. *Zygon, 36*(1), 105–135.

Leake, C. (1975). Human purpose, the limbic system, and the sense of satisfaction. *Zygon, 10*(1), 86–94.

Kirkpatrick, L. (1997). An attachment-theory approach to the psychology of religion. *International Journal for the Psychology of Religion, 2,* 3–28.

LeDoux, J. (1996). *The emotional brain: The mysterious underpinnings of emotional life.* New York: Simon & Schuster.

Levine, S. (1999). Children's cognition as the foundation of spirituality. *International Journal of Children's spirituality, 4*(2), 121–140.

Lillig, T. (1998). *The Catechesis of the Good Shepherd in a parish setting.* Chicago: Liturgy Training Publications.

Loder, J. (1998). *The logic of the Spirit.* San Francisco: Jossey-Bass.

MacLean, P. D. (1974). *Triune conception of brain and behavior.* Toronto: University of Toronto Press.

Myers, D. (2004). *Psychology* (7th ed.). New York: Worth.

Nelson, G. (1990). Christian formation of children: The role of ritual and celebration. In E. Bernstein (Ed), *Liturgy and spirituality in context: Perspectives on prayer and culture* (pp. 114–135). Collegeville, MN: Liturgical.

Newberg, A., d'Aquili, E., & Rause, V. (2002). *Why God won't go away.* New York: Ballantine.

Newberg, A. B., & Newberg, S. K. (2006). A neuropsychological perspective of spiritual development. In P. Benson, E. Roehlkepartain, P. King, & L. Wagener (Eds.), *The handbook of spiritual development in childhood and adolescence* (pp. 183–96). Thousand Oaks, CA: Sage.

North American Montessori Teachers' Association (Producer). (2000). *Discovering the real spiritual life of children* [videotape]. (Available from Liturgy Training Publications, 1800 North Hermitage Avenue, Chicago, Illinois 60622-1101).

Nye, R. (1998). *Psychological perspectives on children's spirituality.* Doctoral dissertation, University of Nottingham. Wetherby, West Yorkshire, UK: British Thesis Service.

Palmer, P. (1993). *To know as we are known: Education as a spiritual journey.* San Francisco: Harper.

Ratcliff, D. (1988). The cognitive development of preschoolers. In D. Ratcliff (Ed.), *Handbook of preschool religious education* (pp. 7–29). Birmingham, AL.: Religious Education Press.

Reimer, K. & Furrow, J. (2001). A qualitative exploration of relational consciousness in Christian children. *International Journal of Children's Spirituality, 6,* 7–23.

Renz, C. (1998). Christian education and the confirmation debate: Towards a theology of catechesis. *Journal of Christian Education, 41*(1), pp. 53–65.

Stewart, S. (2000). *Following Jesus.* Louisville: Geneva.

Stewart, S. & Berryman, J. (1989). *Young children and worship.* Louisville: Westminster John Knox.

Wolfe, P., & Brandt, R. (1998). What do we know from brain research? *Educational Leadership, 56*(3), 8–13.

Woodley, M. (2000). The wonder of it all. *Discipleship Journal, 119,* 25–28.

Chapter Eleven

How Shall We Study Children's Spirituality?

CHRIS J. BOYATZIS AND BABETTE T. NEWMAN[1]

We (the authors) begin with the assumption that children are spiritual beings and have experiences, cognitions, and emotions about their relationship to the transcendent. The purpose of this chapter is to describe and examine critically many research methods used to study children's spirituality. A recent review on the psychology of religion and spirituality declared that any "single disciplinary approach is incapable of yielding comprehensive knowledge of phenomena as complex and multifaceted as spirituality" (Emmons & Paloutzian, 2003, p. 395). The remedy suggested by these prominent psychologists of religion is a "multilevel interdisciplinary paradigm" that entails the collection of different kinds of data and multiple levels of analysis. This chapter endorses this position and emphasizes throughout the need for a multi-method approach to children's spirituality.

Throughout this chapter, we briefly describe a number of studies whose methodologies may stimulate advances in the understanding of children's spirituality.[2] Some

1. Chris Boyatzis is Associate Professor of Psychology at Bucknell University. He received his Ph.D. and M.A. degrees from Brandeis University and B.A. from Boston University. Boyatzis has organized and edited several special issues devoted to religious and spiritual development, and has written chapters on the topic for many major handbooks. In addition, he has published about 40 articles and chapters in academic journals and books. In 2001, he organized the first pre-conference at the biennial meetings of the Society for Research in Child Development on religious and spiritual development. This pre-conference will have its third meeting in 2005. Boyatzis is married to an Episcopal priest, has two daughters, conducts parenting programs at churches in many denominations, and is active at a local and national level in religious education.

Babette T. Newman received her Bachelors degree in Psychology from Thiel College and her Masters degree in Clinical Psychology from West Virginia University. She is currently pursuing her Ph.D. in Child Development at Virginia Polytechnic Institute and State University where she is an adjunct instructor. Her primary research interest is the spiritual development of children and adolescents. She has worked as a psychologist in community mental health and in physical rehabilitation, as well as a neuropsychometrist with children and adults. She is also married and the mother of two young men.

2. The roundtable discussion chaired by Don Ratcliff (Ratcliff, 2003) included participants Holly Allen, Karen Crozier, Donna Habenicht, Dana Hood, Gary Newton, and Eileen Starr. The roundtable

of these studies employed multi-method strategies or involve adaptations of existing measures to make them more suitable for assessing children's spirituality. In addition, we point readers toward particular sources that offer especially helpful critiques of certain methods. We also highlight aspects of children's spirituality that warrant empirical inquiry and suggest concrete ways researchers could determine which of their multiple and diverse methods may provide findings that are likely to be redundant with previous studies, in contrast with methods that tend to provide unique and different insights. Finally, we note that although this book's theme is Christian spirituality, we are confident our chapter's methodological review and working definitions of spirituality are not restricted to children in Christian faith communities or cultures significantly influenced by this faith, but may be applied to children anywhere. Before discussing methodology, we turn to the task of defining spirituality.

Recent Attempts to Define Spirituality

Spirituality is difficult to define, and thus it has been given various and nuanced meanings (Ramsey & Blieszner, 1999). Within the conference roundtable on methodology there was little consensus on how to operationalize "spirituality" (Morgenthaler, 2003). Newman (2003) identified over 17 essential qualities in an array of definitions that have been used in research. Though there is some evidence that people distinguish between "religious" and "spiritual" (see Walker & Pitts, 1998; Zinnbauer & Pargament, 2005), the constructs are surely interrelated in theoretical substance and in lived experience, as most Americans consider themselves to be religious *and* spiritual (Zinnbauer & Pargament, 2005). Thus, we caution against forcing a false dichotomy between "religion" and "spirituality," and at points in this chapter we will alternate between the terms.

Amidst this semantic fluidity, roundtable discussants (Morgenthaler, 2003) emphasized the need for scholars to make explicit their working definition of "spirituality" within their particular studies and communications of those works. Here we offer a brief review of definitions from major scholars within the psychology of religion and the emerging field of religious and spiritual development. In rich qualitative work with children, Rebecca Nye (Hay & Nye, 1998) and others (Reimer & Furrow, 2001) have identified the core of spirituality as "relational consciousness"—a marked perceptiveness in the child of his or her relationships with other people, God, or the self.

Some developmental scientists have described spiritual development as growth in the orientation to transcend oneself and commit to helping others (Lerner, Dowling, & Anderson, 2003) and "the process of growing the intrinsic human capacity for

discussion chaired by Shirley Morgenthaler (Morgenthaler, 2003) included Chris Boyatzis, Katherine Jonas, Joyce Mercer, Babette Newman, Wendy Norwood, Sara Pendleton, Gene Roehlkepartain, and Karen-Marie Yust. Throughout this chapter, any mention of ideas or findings from roundtables refers to these discussions with citation (by Chair) of the specific session in which the point was made.

self-transcendence, in which the self is embedded in something greater than the self, including the sacred" (Benson, Roehlkepartain, & Rude, 2003, p. 205). Some scholars' definitions emphasize the relationship with the sacred. For example, Pargament (1999) has described spirituality as the search for and relationship with whatever one takes to be holy or sacred, and Hill et al. (2000, p. 66) defined spirituality as the "feelings, thoughts, experiences, and behaviors that arise from a search for the sacred," with sacred referring to whatever the person takes to be a divine being or object or an "Ultimate Reality or Ultimate Truth" (p. 66). Spirituality has also been characterized as "a sacred, unifying principle that expresses itself in a sense of wonder and inspiration, a feeling of connectedness with people and nature, and a reverence for life" (Quick, 1999, p. 413). All of these definitions make clear the centrality of *relationship* and *self-transcendence* in spirituality. Indeed, to transcend oneself is to move in relation to another, whether the transcendent entity is divine (e.g., God), or nature, the cosmos, love, or other people individually or collectively.

The Value of a Multi-Method Approach

It is a major challenge to study children's sense of the transcendent and their inherent connectedness to the "something more" (see James, 1902/1986; Johnson & Boyatzis, 2005). Children's feelings, beliefs, attitudes, and experiences regarding the transcendent make spirituality a multidimensional construct. To understand children's spirituality in a valid and complete way, methods must account for the multiple ways children perceive, experience, and express spirituality. Measures of spirituality should ideally be able to account for spiritual change over time. We encourage the development and use of multiple measures, both qualitative and quantitative, to provide diverse windows into children's spirituality. In one conference roundtable discussion (Ratcliff, 2003), the reliance on a single method to study children's spirituality was compared with attempting to get a sense of a panoramic scene with many photographs—all taken from only one camera angle.

Multiple measures reveal different insights into the same topic. For example, Barrett and Keil (1996) found that participants' God concepts were somewhat different when responding to a Likert scale of God attributes than to vignettes about God. In their study of parent-child communication about religion, Boyatzis (this volume; Boyatzis & Janicki, 2003) used two measures—a survey for parents with Likert scales to measure the frequency, content, context, and triggers of discussions about religion, and a diary in which parents recorded their actual conversations with children about religious and spiritual matters. Results indicated that the quantitative survey and the qualitative diary produced different images of parent-child communication about religion. The authors asserted that surveys may be ideal for tapping parents' *global* schemas of family communication whereas diaries capture *actual* conversations. The important point here is not that different measures fail to converge on a single conclusion, rather, the key insight is that *different measures yield different impressions of the same phenomenon under study*. Thus, multiple measures of any variable may provide a more comprehensive picture.

Although we have emphasized methods over design issues, research by Catherine Stonehouse (2001) provides a strong example of a between-group, post-test study of children's spirituality. Stonehouse assessed the impact on children of a popular religious education curriculum, Godly Play (Berryman, 1991), on children in a Christian church; some were enrolled in Godly Play classes and were compared to a matched sample of children, from similar churches in the area, who were not in Godly Play classes. This kind of quasi-experimental design is rare in research on children's spiritual and religious growth and we hope more researchers will consider this and similar designs. This study also featured a remarkably eclectic set of measures: children's drawings of God, Jesus, and their favorite Bible story; conversations with children about their artwork; discussions about the children's favorite Bible stories; a semi-structured interview with children about their religious experiences and sense of God; and parent interviews. Stonehouse analyzed the children's art and verbal comments and found that children in Godly Play classes expressed significantly richer and more mature ideas and feelings than control children on most variables, including creative engagement with religious issues, meaningful insights, curiosity about religion (e.g., utterances such as "I wonder about . . ."), and expression of pleasure while discussing God.

Together, the studies above illustrate a multi-method approach that is valuable for the study of the multidimensional nature of children's spirituality. Doing so will have many benefits, such as allowing analysis of the findings from the disparate measures to learn what unique insights are offered by each and what is common across measures.

Research Methods

Specific methods on how to study children's spirituality need to be critically examined. Retrospective accounts from adults about their childhood experiences will be omitted, though such reports have been valuable for confirming that children do have spiritual experiences and for unfolding the varieties of religious and spiritual experience (e.g., Robinson, 1983). This omission is due in part to space limitations, but primarily reflects our higher priority on research that explores children's spirituality by studying *children directly*.

Interviewing Children about Spiritual, Religious, and Metaphysical Concepts

Researchers need to explore ways to encourage children to be active participants in research in general and, specifically, in the interview process. Techniques that encourage authentic responses from children are essential. In one conference roundtable on interview methods (Ratcliff, 2003), some discussants claimed that playing with children helps create a comfortable and safe context in which children could express their spirituality. Other means include allowing the child to explore the tape recorder before the interview or providing the child the opportunity to play with clay or to draw. Authentic responses from children are also facilitated by terminology that is familiar to the individual child. Researchers should not only pilot test their interview protocols for general age-appropriateness but ask individual children early in interviews what particular words they commonly use for God, heaven, and/or other key terms relevant to a given study. Some interviewers avoid introducing specific terms (e.g., "spirit," "religion," "religious experience") until the children themselves use the terms (Hay & Nye, 1998), and others have found that the phrase "not alive" was preferable to "dead" when interviewing preschoolers about the afterlife (Bering & Bjorklund, 2004). Repeating or paraphrasing children's responses in interviews gives the child an opportunity to reflect on his or her own ideas, which often gives rise to new ideas that are deeper than initial ones. Finally, multiple responses to the same or similar questions allow the interviewer to gauge the consistency of the child's thinking on an issue.

The relationship between interviewer and child highlights the need for researchers to consider personal issues such as rapport, candor, trust, and authenticity, as well as the more epistemological issues of objectivity and neutrality. Excellent treatments of these matters are offered in Coles (1990), Hay and Nye (1998, chapters 5 and 6) and Heller (1986, chapter 2). When talking with a relatively unfamiliar adult (i.e., the typical interviewer) about God or other intimate spiritual matters, children may not disclose much of the depth and nuance of their relational consciousness and moments of transcendence. Recollections by both adults and children about their earlier spiritual experiences often reveal a reluctance to discuss their experiences with parents or other adults, who are likely to dismiss or challenge children's experiences (Hardy, 1979; Hoffman, 1992). Scholars should be inspired, then, by the rich qualitative works in which children reveal complex, detailed thoughts to researchers who spend extensive time with children, get to know them well, are humble and authentic in their self-presentation, and treat children as conversation partners rather than interview subjects. Sometimes the most revealing data emerge in informal conversations rather than more formal interviews. Some interviewers talk with children in the company of their peers, which can increase some children's comfort level as well as create a more interactive synergy from which new ideas may spring (Coles, 1990; Hay & Nye, 1998). Regardless of the interpersonal context, acknowledging children as the experts on their own spiritual experiences and positions—where they are the teachers and re-searchers the learners—can result in richer data from children. These attitudes toward the child allow the interview to become a collaborative effort with children who know that their stories are valued (Grover, 2004).

One method for creating a more open, collaborative interview was described by Holly Allen in a roundtable discussion (Ratcliff, 2003). At the end of one of her interviews with a child, she asked if the child had any questions of her. The child then asked Allen one of her own questions, and Allen answered the question honestly and sincerely. As a result, the child then continued discussing the topic and provided more information than he had previously. As a result of this serendipitous discovery, Allen modified her subsequent interview technique to include more of her own spiritual experience and found that many children she interviewed were more forthcoming than prior to using this technique.

Researchers may have to go to even greater lengths to gain the trust of children. While she was a college student, developmental psychologist Stephanie Carlson inves-tigated the attitudes of Mennonite children and parents toward fantasy play (Carlson, Taylor, & Levin, 1998). To earn the trust of adults and children in the rural Mennonite community of central Pennsylvania, Carlson volunteered at a Mennonite school for about 6 months, dressing and acting as Mennonite women would (i.e., dressing plainly with hand-made clothing and no makeup, jewelry, or adornments, and comporting herself very modestly). Only after this time and effort to gain the community's trust could Carlson begin interviewing children and parents for her research. Though ex-treme, Carlson's work illustrates the extent to which scholars may need to go to build trust with some populations in order to learn about their spirituality.

Interviews rely, of course, on children's verbalizations. This can be problematic in some ways. First, some spiritual experiences may not be amenable to linguistic expres-sion. Many adults know that their own experiences can surpass their ability to convey them verbally. Children's sense of the transcendent and inherent connectedness to the "something more" may have an "ineffability" (James, 1902/1986) that overwhelms the ability to verbalize such consciousness.

Second, verbal exchanges can create an expectation for the child's direct and perhaps rapid response. However, providing speedy answers may be antithetical to the nature of spirituality. To counter this problem, contemporary scholars may resus-citate an interesting method devised a century ago (described in Hay & Nye, 1998) of "experimental introspection." In this technique, the researcher asks children questions ("What is the nature of prayer?" "What is God like?") and then invites them to close their eyes and reflect on the topic before answering. A simple between- or within-group design comparing children's responses would indicate if children's spirituality reveals itself differently in the standard and reflective formats.

Third, a reliance on children's verbalizations may create an interpretive context in which researchers study the *language* used to describe experience rather than the experience itself (see Boyatzis, 2001). Three issues are of concern here: possible limitations in receptive language skills (understanding questions), expressive language skills (responding and describing), and the possibility of giving memorized answers (see Ratcliff, 1997, n.d.). As the conference roundtable participants emphasized, it behooves scholars using interviews both to think carefully about what exactly is being received from youngsters, especially young children, and to employ supplementary measures for fuller illumination of the children's spirituality. A small methodological safeguard would be to assess children's productive language skill—through a standard measure of expressive vocabulary development—to learn if it is correlated with children's descriptions of spiritual experiences or beliefs. This would provide a statistical check on the notion that the limits of a child's language reflects the limits of the child's spiritual experience.

In his superb work, *The Spiritual Life of Children*, Robert Coles (1990) made use of qualitative style interview techniques in which he talked with children—sometimes alone and sometimes with peers, but always at length—on multiple occasions, and in locations comfortable to the children. Part of his procedure included asking children to draw pictures and discuss them. Coles offers long excerpts of the conversations, exchanges that convey Coles' age-appropriate and respectful engagement of children in serious talk about the spiritual. Coles the interviewer is simultaneously a learner and a fellow spiritual pilgrim sharing the child's search for meaning. Such in-depth qualitative methods impose costs and challenges for the interviewer but surely engender remarkably authentic insights into children's spirituality.

Drawing Tasks

As noted in the Coles study, children's artwork related to spiritual or religious themes is a valuable age-appropriate, nonverbal measure for exploring spirituality. Children's drawings provide two valuable kinds of data. The obvious one is the actual drawing itself, and the other is children's verbalizations about the artwork produced while they are drawing and after they have finished drawing. Recording children's comments about the artwork is important because the act of drawing often gives rise to new insights about the spiritual topic in the picture (Gunther-Heimbrock, 1999). In addition, children's comments provide the researcher the children's interpretations of their own work (Ratcliff, 2003).

Children's artwork was a major measure in early work on children's God concepts (Harms, 1944; Pitts, 1976). Pitts analyzed school-children's drawings of God for their content and anthropomorphic depictions of God. God was most anthropomorphized by the Mormon, Mennonite, and Lutheran children (all very similar in their scores), followed closely by Roman Catholic and Methodist children (who had identical scores). Jewish children drew the least personified pictures of God, and Unitarian children's scores fell between Jewish children's and the other groups'. Roman Catholic children's drawings had the highest ratio of religious-to-nonreligious symbolism, Unitarian children's art had the lowest, and Jewish children's drawings were often abstract and non-representational. These findings reveal that children's notions of a transcendent divinity can be conveyed in a drawing task and that these depictions seem to correspond well to the children's denominational doctrines and imagery.

Though revealing, it may be risky to take children's drawings at face value and we offer some caveats here. First, a drawing is unlikely to convey the child's actual God image or other transcendent entity in a veridical way or having isomorphic correspondence. This is because the artistic product will always reflect the constraints of the medium as well as—or even more than—the child's actual God image (an apropos admonition here: "the map is not the territory"). Asking a child to draw God increases the odds for an anthropomorphized deity, especially by young children (see Barrett, 1998; Hyde, 1990). In addition, analyzing children's art is not a simple process (see Boyatzis & Watson, 2000), and interpretation *by* the child may be very helpful, especially with older children. Consider Hood's (2003) astute observation that if a child draws a picture of God with large hands, the drawing may reflect the child's mental image of an anthropomorphized, human-like God—or the large hands may instead serve to express the child's belief that God has a uniquely divine power to create. One child drew diamonds on the roads of heaven, which may not be the child's actual image of heaven but her symbolic way to express its beauty. Finally, task characteristics may affect drawings; when asked to draw God first and a person second, children's drawings of God were more abstract and the person pictures included more religious imagery (Pitts, 1976). Helpful discussion of children's art and their comments about it is in Coles (1990, chapter 8) and Cavalletti (1983, appendix).

Structured Tasks

Scholars have long used semi-structured interviews, often incorporating stimulus materials. "Transformational narratives" were used in one creative approach by Margaret Krych (described in Loder, 1998, chapter 8), who told 8- to 11-year-old children Gospel stories during a 6-week class. Krych would begin a particular story with Jesus in it, setting up the characters and situation, but then stop and ask the children what Jesus would do at that point in the story. Children created various responses, expressed verbally and through drawing. Though the point of the exercise was religious education, researchers could use this technique to assess children's spiritual conceptions.

In another study, Scarlett and Perriello (1991) collected prayers of youths and college students in response to hypothetical situations the researchers provided (e.g., a friend is dying; what would you pray?). Future researchers may assess prayers from children in response not only to hypothetical situations but also actual ones.

A between- or within-subject comparison would indicate if the different procedures reveal unique or similar impressions of children's understanding and use of prayer and their images of the transcendent entity to whom they pray.

Structured tasks are also prominent in research on the development of forgiveness, a topic being studied by Susanne Denham and her students (e.g., Denham, Neal, & Bassett, 2004) and Beverly Wilson and her students (e.g., Pickering & Wilson, 2004). Both research groups are collecting data from multiple measures of multiple informants—the children and their peers, teachers, and parents. Denham et al. have designed the Children's Forgiveness Inventory, with a series of pictorial vignettes depicting peer transgressions in various interpersonal situations. Children then answer questions (e.g., "Would you forgive your friend? if your friend did it on purpose? by accident? if your friend felt really bad?") that tap their notions about the affective responses, behaviors, and cognitions associated with forgiveness. Pickering and Wilson have also devised a new, pictorial measure with follow-up probes to assess children's different motivations for forgiving others. In both research groups' measures, these hypothetical tasks are complemented with questions about actual incidents of forgiveness in the children's families. These new measures could prove to be important methodological contributions to the field.

Quantitative Surveys

Thus far, we have emphasized qualitative measures to study children's spirituality. Surveys may provide some additional tools for the task. A recent encyclopedic handbook of religious measures (Hill & Hood, 1999) devotes a section to measures of spirituality, but the instruments were developed and normed on adults in college and beyond. Most extant surveys are not helpful regarding standardized instruments with children. Peatling (1973) offers an older instrument with extensive reliability and validity data, although subsequent research indicated some theological bias in it (Degelman, Mullen, & Mullen, 1984). This predicament calls for scholars to develop new measures that are valid and age-appropriate for children. A recent quantitative measure, the Daily Spiritual Experience (DSE) Scale (Underwood & Teresi, 2002), has been validated on several samples, but only one included youth and the youngest of those were 15 years old. Nevertheless, researchers could examine surveys to identify questions that could be adapted for children and administered in age-appropriate ways. The DSE, for example, includes items such as "I feel God's love for me, directly," "I desire to be closer to God," and "I feel thankful for my blessings." Such items are amenable to adaptation for use with children.

One measure may, with modifications, be useful with children. Saur and Saur (cited in Hill & Hood, 1999) developed a projective measure of 11 black-and-white photographs of people in "postures that may be construed as prayerful" (Hill & Hood,

p. 372). The photos are shown to subjects, who are asked to tell a story about each card and suggest what the main character is feeling and perhaps praying. Prompts are asked, with questions intended to elicit children's open-ended impressions to be analyzed for spiritual content, affect, imagery, and so on. Although this measure has not been used with children and seems to have had limited usage in general, young children might respond well to its pictorial stimuli and projective nature. Researchers could adapt this measure to involve other stimuli (line drawings, art by children and/or adults, photos, sculptures) as projective measures to tap children's relational consciousness and connectedness to a transcendent.

An excellent adaptation of an existing measure was conducted by Jonas and Norwood (Morgenthaler, 2003), who modified the widely-used Religious Problem Solving Scale to make it appropriate for school-age children. Given the role that religious coping can play in children's lives (see Pendleton, Benore, Jonas, Norwood, & Herrman, this volume), this is an important methodological contribution to the field. Other researchers could modify various existing (adult) scales on different constructs. When modifying scales, researchers must conduct the necessary statistical assurances, such as demonstrating the new measure's construct validity, internal consistency, factor structure, test-retest reliability, and so on.

Congregational Research and Participant Observation

Several scholars in this volume (e.g., Allen; Haight; Mercer, Matthews, & Walz) have studied children's spirituality within congregational settings. For example, Mercer et al. analyzed three congregations through a multi-method effort, conducting participant observations, interviews, focus groups, and oral histories. To assess children's perspectives on their congregational experience, Mercer et al. had children conduct tours of the physical church space and use video cameras to describe their relationships within their churches. These innovative methods are marvelous for illuminating different facets of children's church experience. Researchers could also provide children with cameras for each of them to create a photo album of the meaningful places and experiences of their congregational context (Mecum, 2001, has done this to study spirituality outside the church context).

As part of congregational studies, researchers could conduct multi-method assessment of children's emotions, beliefs, and experiences around organized religions' rituals and sacraments. Important Christian rituals or sacraments include baptism, first communion, confirmation, confession, and so on. Children also often assume different physical positions in worship services and liturgies. How does children's participation in these rituals, sacraments, and duties enhance their sense of transcendent connectedness, both to the holy and sacred as well as to the community around the child? We know that from the perspectives of the religions, children are changed profoundly by these sacraments, but do *children* feel transformed by them? Qualitative and ethnographic work will be most important here (see McLaren, 1993, on such a study conducted in a Roman Catholic school). For the Christian faith, serious issues include grace and redemption, sin and salvation, faith and good works, the Trinity, the power of divine figures to forgive or punish or heal, and so on. Researchers need to carefully and creatively analyze if and how children's relational consciousness is expanded as they explore these weighty matters within their faith community.

For some spiritual constructs, observational methods may yield rich data. For example, researchers can watch and record children's behaviors in the midst of congregational activity, either as part of formal worship or faith-community events or their own informal activity. This is particularly true when the observer has become an accepted part of the community and the children no longer feel that they must act a certain way (Morgenthaler, 2003).

In participant-observation, researchers are an active part of the community they are studying. In participant-observation work, researchers may also simultaneously function as teachers, aides, ministers, and so on (Morgenthaler, 2003). This dual role gives researchers different but integrated perspectives—as researcher and as participant—on children's spirituality and what occurs around them as they systematically reflect on their observations through their own theoretical or empirical lenses.

While these observational methodologies have their advantages, they also pose challenges. A specific concern, raised by many roundtable discussants, is the need for researchers to minimize the typical risks associated with observation and participant-observer dynamics that may alter the behavior of adults and children in the congregation (Morgenthaler, 2003; Ratcliff, 2003). Researchers must take appropriate steps to allow congregation members to habituate to their presence and express proper respect for members' congregational experience.

Spiritual and Religious Play at Home

As theologian Jerome Berryman (this volume) has argued, play creates a sense of openness and wonder that is at the heart of spirituality. Indeed, some religious education approaches emphasize play with religious materials (Berryman, 1991; Cavalletti, 1983). Play—especially play that involves pretense—may provide an indirect, symbolic realm in which to study children's transformation of mundane and sacred objects, space, and identities. Although many theories highlight the value of play in development, "religious play" has been ignored. Young children often associate God with play (Heller, 1986), and qualitative researchers (Hay & Nye, 1998, chap. 7) and theologians of childhood (e.g., Cavalletti, 1983) have given serious attention to play as a facilitator of and window into religious development.

Two anecdotes shared with the first author highlight the promise of studying religious play. One woman, raised Roman Catholic, described how she would "play communion" with her sisters by cutting small pieces of white Wonder bread and compressing them into flat discs. She then gave these "communion wafers" to her younger siblings, with Welch's grape juice (in gaudy wine glasses) served as the Eucharistic blood of Christ. In a striking parallel, another woman recalled her childhood ritual of making white-bread communion hosts and using the family's microwave as a tabernacle (where Roman Catholics store consecrated communion bread) from which she served communion to herself and her siblings.

The research literature is quiet on playful and spontaneous expressions of spiritual significance and religious ritual. Scholars must study the link between children's religious play and relational consciousness or connectedness to the transcendent. Thus, new measures might include interviews and surveys of children and family members, or direct observation and videotape of children during religious play to learn about the nature and function of religious play. More indirect or expressive measures include story-telling, use of props, and artwork accompanied by children's descriptions. Because religious play is likely to occur at home, research should examine whether parents' responses—either supportive or discouraging—to children's playful experimentation with the sacred is associated with children's sense of the divine and the broader function of religion in their lives.

Conclusion

We have urged researchers to study children's spirituality with a multi-method approach. Nothing less than this approach will be sufficient to understand children's sense of relationality to what transcends the self—the divine, nature, other people, love. We have emphasized qualitative approaches that, while not free from challenges and limitations, situate the child at the center of the research inquiry and allow the child's own words, activities, and creations to be the primary source of insight (see Grover, 2004). This methodology, long ago championed by William James to learn about adults' spirituality, is crucial today to grasp the depths and varieties of children's spirituality. With this continuity will come change (see Boyatzis, 2005, for discussion of future research directions). A future version of this chapter, perhaps just several years hence, will surely describe brain imaging techniques that provide glimpses into neurological substrates of children's spirituality (see May, this volume).

Amidst this broad spectrum of evolving methods, researchers must ensure rigor in their approaches to children's spirituality. The unease with which the behavioral sciences have approached religion and spirituality (see, e.g., Boyatzis, 2003) makes it necessary that research on children's spirituality meets or surpasses the threshold for acceptable scientific methods. Such rigor must be achieved if the work is to be taken seriously by a wide scholarly audience and if it is to have maximum value for families, congregations, schools, and communities. This chapter's emphasis on qualitative methodology, often seen as "soft" from traditional vantages, might only make it tougher for the field to advance into the mainstream. However, we believe that scholarship on children's spirituality will gain scientific legitimacy *and* be of maximum applied value if researchers strive for creative and authentic understanding of children while meeting accepted standards for scholarly inquiry. The use of multiple methods, yielding both quantitative and qualitative data at many levels of analysis, will help accomplish this.

This emerging field has enormous potential to achieve a key task—to understand the child as a meaning maker, a spiritual pilgrim who grows outward in small steps or sudden spurts toward the transcendent while growing ever more deeply in his or her innermost parts. The good news is that many scholars—such as those described in this chapter and those contributing to this volume—exemplify impressive integration of both rigor and creativity, tradition and progress, and thus help us move forward to understand the child.

References

Barrett, J. L. (1998). Cognitive constraints on Hindu concepts of the divine. *Journal for the Scientific Study of Religion, 37*, 608–619.

Barrett, J. L., & Keil, F. C. (1996). Anthropomorphism and God concepts: Conceptualizing a non-natural entity. *Cognitive Psychology, 31*, 219–247.

Benson, P. L., Roehlkepartain, E. C., & Rude, S. P. (2003). Spiritual development in childhood and adolescence: Toward a field of inquiry. *Applied Developmental Science, 7*, 204–212.

Bering, J. M., & Bjorklund, D. F. (2004). The natural emergence of reasoning about the afterlife as a developmental regularity. *Developmental Psychology, 40*, 217–233.

Berryman, J. (1991). *Godly play: A way of religious education*. San Francisco: Harper.

Boyatzis, C. J. (2001). A critique of models of religious experience. *The International Journal for the Psychology of Religion, 11*, 247–258.

Boyatzis, C. J. (2003). Religious and spiritual development: An introduction. *Review of Religious Research, 44*, 213–219.

Boyatzis, C. J. (2005). Religious and spiritual development in childhood. In R. F. Paloutzian & C. L. Park (Eds.), *The handbook for the psychology of religion and spirituality* (pp. 123-143). New York: Guilford.

Boyatzis, C. J., & Janicki, D. (2003). Parent-child communication about religion: Survey and diary data on unilateral transmission and bi-directional reciprocity styles. *Review of Religious Research, 44*, 252–270.

Boyatzis, C. J., & Watson, M. W. (Eds.). (2000). Symbolic and social constraints on the development of children's artistic style. *New Directions for Child and Adolescent Development, no. 90*. San Francisco: Jossey-Bass.

Carlson, S. M., Taylor, M., & Levin, G. R. (1998). The influence of culture on pretend play: The case of Mennonite children. *Merrill-Palmer Quarterly, 44*, 539–563.

Cavalletti, S. (1983). *The religious potential of the child*. New York: Paulist.

Coles, R. (1990). *The spiritual life of children*. Boston: Houghton Mifflin.

Degelman, D., Mullen, P., and Mullen, N. (1984). Development of abstract religious thinking: A comparison of Roman Catholic and Nazarene children and adolescents. *Journal of Psychology and Christianity, 3*, 44–49.

Denham, S. A., Neal, K., & Bassett, H. H. (2004, April). "You hurt my feelings pretty bad": Parents' and children's emotions as contributors to the development of forgiveness. In S. Denham (Chair), *Children's forgiving in behavior, cognition, and affect.* Symposium conducted at the biennial meeting of the Conference on Human Development, Washington, DC.

Emmons, R. A., & Paloutzian, R. F. (2003). The psychology of religion. *Annual Review of Psychology, 54*, 377–402.

Grover, S. (2004). Why won't they listen to us? On giving power and voice to children participating in social research. *Childhood, 11*, 81–93.

Gunther-Heimbrock, H. (1999). Images and pictures of God: The development of creative seeing. *International Journal of Children's Spirituality, 4*, 51–60.

Hardy, A. (1979). *The spiritual nature of man: A study of contemporary religious experience.* Oxford: Clarendon.

Harms, E. (1944). The development of religious experience in children. *American Journal of Sociology, 50*, 112–122.

Hay, D., & Nye, R. (1998). *The spirit of the child*. London: Fount.

Heller, D. (1986). *The children's God*. Chicago: University of Chicago Press.

Hill, P. C., & Hood, R. W., Jr. (1999). *Measures of religiosity*. Birmingham, AL: Religious Education Press.

Hill, P. C., Pargament, K. I., Hood, R. W., Jr., McCullough, M. E., Swyers, J. P., Larson, D. B., & Zinnbauer, B. J. (2000). Conceptualizing religion and spirituality: Points of commonality, points of departure. *Journal for the Theory of Social Behavior, 30*, 51–77.

Hoffman, E. (1992). *Visions of innocence: Spiritual and inspirational experiences of childhood.* Boston: Shambhala.

Hood, D. K. (2003, June). *Six children seeking God: Exploring childhood spiritual development in context.* Paper presented at the meeting of the Children's Spirituality Conference—Christian Perspectives, River Forest, IL.

Hyde, K. E. (1990). *Religion in childhood and adolescence*. Birmingham, AL: Religious Education Press.

James, W. (1902/1982). *The varieties of religious experience*. New York: Penguin.

Johnson, C. N., & Boyatzis, C. J. (2006). Cognitive-cultural foundations of spiritual development. In E. C. Roehlkepartain, P. E. King, L. Wagener, & P. L. Benson (Eds.), *The handbook of spiritual development in childhood and adolescence* (pp. 211–223). Thousand Oaks, CA: Sage.

Lerner, R. M., Dowling, E. M., & Anderson, P. M. (2003). Positive youth development: Thriving as the basis of personhood and civil society. *Applied Developmental Science, 7*, 171–79.

Loder, J. E. (1998). *The logic of the spirit: Human development in theological perspective.* San Francisco: Jossey-Bass.

McLaren, P. (1993). *Schooling as a ritual performance* (2nd ed.). New York: Routledge.

Mecum, S. (2001). *God's photo album*. San Francisco: HarperSanFrancisco.

Morgenthaler, S. (Chair). (2003, June). *The roundtable on children's spirituality research methods: Observations and surveys*. Session at the meeting of the Children's Spirituality Conference—Christian Perspectives, River Forest, IL.

Newman, B. T. (2003, June). *Illuminating definitions of spirituality*. Paper presented at the Conference on Children's Spirituality—Christian Perspectives, River Forest, IL.

Pargament, K. I. (1999). The psychology of religion *and* spirituality? Yes and no. *The International Journal for the Psychology of Religion, 9*, 3–16.

Peatling, J. H. (1973). The incidence of concrete and abstract religious thinking in the interpretation of three Bible stories by pupils enrolled in grades four through twelve. *Dissertation Abstracts International, 34*(12A), 7604. (UMI No. 74-12859)

Pickering, S. R, & Wilson, B. J. (2004, April). Forgiveness in first grade children: Links with social preference, aggression, social problems, and reciprocal friendships. In S. Denham (Chair), *Children's forgiving in behavior, cognition, and affect*. Symposium conducted at the biennial meeting of the Conference on Human Development, Washington, DC.

Pitts, V. P. (1976). Drawing the invisible: Children's conceptualization of God. *Character Potential, 8*, 12–24.

Quick, S. (1999). Spirituality. In C. A. Smith (Ed.), *The encyclopedia of parenting theory and research* (pp. 413–415). Westport, CT: Greenwood.

Ramsey, J. L., & Blieszner, R. (1999). *Spiritual resiliency in older women*. Thousand Oaks, CA: Sage.

Ratcliff, D. (n.d.). Child-assisted data collection and analyses in children's spirituality research. Retrieved July 12, 2004, from http://don.Ratcliff.net/childspirituality/child.htm.

Ratcliff, D. (1997) Conducting research with children: Methods and potential applications in educational ministry contexts. Retrieved July 12, 2004 from http://don.ratcliff.net/childspirituality/kids.htm.

Ratcliff, D. (Chair). (2003, June). *The roundtable on children's spirituality research methods: Interviews and adult retrospective studies*. Session at the meeting of the Children's Spirituality Conference—Christian Perspectives, River Forest, IL.

Reimer, K. S., & Furrow, J. L. (2001). A qualitative exploration of relational consciousness in Christian children. *International Journal of Children's Spirituality, 6*, 7–23.

Robinson, E. (1983). *The original vision: A study of the religious experience of childhood*. New York: Seabury.

Scarlett, W. G., & Perriello, L. (1991). The development of prayer in adolescence. In F. Oser & W. G. Scarlett (Eds.), *Religious development in childhood and adolescence* (pp. 63–76). *New Directions for Child Development, no. 52*. San Francisco: Jossey-Bass.

Stonehouse, C. (2001). Knowing God in childhood: A study of Godly Play and the spirituality of children. *Christian Education Journal, 5*(2), 27–45.

Underwood, L. G., & Teresi, J. A. (2002). The Daily Spiritual Experience Scale: Development, theoretical description, reliability, exploratory factor analysis, and preliminary construct validity using health-related data. *Annals of Behavior Medicine, 24*, 22–33.

Walker, L. J., & Pitts, R. C. (1998). Naturalistic conceptions of moral maturity. *Developmental Psychology, 34*, 403–419.

Zinnbauer, B. J., & Pargament, K. I. (2005). Religiousness and spirituality. In R. F. Paloutzian & C. L. Park (Eds.), *The handbook of the psychology of religion and spirituality* (pp. 21–42). New York: Guilford.

PART II

Encouraging Children's Spirituality in the Home

Chapter Twelve

The Co-Construction of Spiritual Meaning in Parent-Child Communication

CHRIS J. BOYATZIS[1]

On an Easter Sunday afternoon years ago, my wife and I were driving home from church with our oldest daughter, Janine, who was then 8 years old. Spontaneously and most sincerely, from the backseat Janine uttered:

> "What if this is all just a story? About Jesus, I mean. What if he wasn't real, if there's no God, that there's no point to it?"

I almost drove off the road.

Perhaps all parents know from experience that their children can engage them in serious discussions about faith, and these discussions feel like crucial "engines" in the children's and the parents' spiritual and religious development. Though it takes a village to raise a child, the family is surely "the first village" of religious development. Parents' practices and beliefs constitute a "personal religious community" (Cornwall, 1987) that conveys a "religious salience" to children (Hoge & Zulueta, 1985) and provides "cognitive anchors" (Ozorak, 1989) for their thinking and worldviews. Despite ample evidence of parents' influence on children's religious and spiritual development (e.g., Acock & Bengston, 1978; Bao, Whitbeck, Hoyt, & Conger, 1999; Hoge, Petrillo, & Smith 1982), little is known about *how* parents influence children, and even less is known about how children influence their parents' spiritual growth.

Parent-child conversations are rich contexts for religious socialization. These events often occur within regular family interactions and rituals (Maslak 2001) and become "embedded routines" important to a family's religious experience (Wuthnow 1999). Whether the conversations occur during structured events or spontaneously, they can enhance growth of spiritual meaning in families. Early in Scripture

1. [Chris Boyatzis' background was provided in chapter 11.]

The author thanks the participating families who shared their conversations, The Rev. Robin Jarrell for being a partner in spiritual parenting, and, most of all our daughters, Sedona and Janine.

parent-child conversations about religion are deemed critically important. On the plains of Moab, Moses describes the laws that must be heeded for a good and fruitful life and then exhorts his people to share these laws of faithful living with their children: "And you shall teach them diligently to your children, and shall talk of them when you sit in your house, and when you walk by the way, and when you lie down, and when you rise" (Deut 6:7, Revised Standard Version).

Parents have a scriptural call to search for the sacred all day and night, in all contexts. These talks can happen anywhere. Once, while my youngest daughter was taking a bath when she was 3–1/2 years old, she cupped a bar of soap in her hands and asked me to pour water over her hands to "*bathtize* the soap." This prompted a discussion about the girl's own baptism three years earlier. Since that bath, we have had countless conversations about her baptism.

In these conversations, she and I reminisce about how the church had gathered at a parishioner's farm that Sunday morning for the annual Rogation Sunday service, when in rural Pennsylvania people bless the farm land, the crops, the farm animals, even the tractors. We talked about how the priest held her at the pond's edge, how her Godmother—my sister—stood nearby to dry her off with the towel that I, the baptized child's father, had been wrapped in after my own baptism decades earlier. What this child, now 8 years old, knows and feel about her baptism—this crucial sacramental transformation—has arisen entirely from family conversations. Her parents have reconstructed the baptism for her and in the telling reconstructed it for ourselves, too, and find new layers of meaning in that important sacrament. My hope here is to lay bare a mundane process that is vitally important for spiritual growth and meaning: How children and parents talk with each other about religious and spiritual matters.

Unfortunately, an assumption that pervades the social science literature is that such exchanges feature a *unidirectional parent-to-child transmission* of religious beliefs and practices. This literature depicts children as relatively passive and embryonic recipients shaped by their parents.

In actual conversations, what might a unidirectional transmission style sound like? To illustrate, here is a diary entry from the present study, a father-child conversation. Note that it is initiated by the father, consists largely of "who" and "what"—so-called "test" questions to determine what the child knows (Olsen-Fulero 1983), and concludes with the father's mild correction of the child ("yes, but"). The boy does not ask questions or offer his views beyond what the father requests:

F: "Do you know who God is?"

C: "The man who put people on the earth."

F: "What does God do?"

C: "God watches over us with the angels."

F: "Who is God's son?"

C: "Jesus."

F: "Do you know what Jesus did for us?"

C: "He watches over us."

F: "Yes, but he also died on the cross for us."

Surely many such conversations occur in homes, and their didactic and Socratic style is helpful to convey certain information. But it is possible to conceptualize a rather different style of communication, one that reflects children's active role in their religious socialization. Clearly, children possess complex ideas about spiritual and religious concepts, ask questions that provoke parents' reflection, and draw religious meaning from symbols and actions around them (e.g., Coles, 1990; Hay & Nye, 1998; Wuthnow, 1999). As Robert Coles has argued, beginning at surprisingly early ages children ask the very metaphysical and existential questions that philosophers, theologians, and less cerebral types have been asking for millennia: "Where did we come from?", "Where are we going?", and "What are we doing here?" Coles suggests that children be viewed as "spiritual pilgrims." Indeed, it could be said that children are but a short version of *homo poeta*, "man the meaning maker."

Parent and child work together to create meaning about God, heaven and the afterlife, good and evil, and so on. In this view, communication has a *bi-directional reciprocity* in which children and parents are mutually active. In this family milieu, children and parents both participate actively in conversations, speak often, initiate and terminate conversations, express their doubts, show frustration when they fail to understand, struggle with epistemological complexities, challenge each other, and point out logical discrepancies or attitudinal hypocrisies. In this conversational style, parents and children develop communication orientations motivated toward open and mutual discussion of ideas wherein parent and child express their own views and incorporate the other's, even when those views conflict, rather than strive for family congruence wherein children must agree with parents (Krcmar, 1996; Ritchie, 1991).

In this reciprocal style, parents try to cultivate rather than indoctrinate their children. Parents could ask open-ended solicitations (e.g., "What do you think heaven is like?") rather than closed-ended "test" questions (e.g., "Who built the Ark?") to which the parent knows the factual answer (see Olsen-Fulero, 1983). To promote mutual exchange, parents often may not correct their children's views and may place a low priority on conveying their own views. Here is one conversation that illustrates these features. The child initiates the conversation, asks many questions, and gets annoyed at times and insistent at others. The parents and child both have a role in guiding the conversation; parents and child draw out each other's views. The child (C) carrying the conversation is six years old. While finishing dinner, her mother (M) was nearby reading and the father (F) was casually reading aloud the 10 Commandments from the Bible to the child and her older sister.

C: "Did God have a wife? A baby? A son?"

F: "He had a baby boy—Jesus."

C: "But does God have a wife? (*sounding troubled*) If God wants Jesus to be born, he can't have eggs. Only baby ducks do! If God wanted Jesus to come, he couldn't cuz there was no wife around."

M: "An angel came around, Gabriel, and said to Mary, 'Would you be Jesus' mommy?' So God put Jesus in Mary's tummy, and God was taking care of Jesus in Mary's tummy."

C: "He would actually come out with a cross on his forehead."

M: "Why?"

C: "Because he's special."

M: "Special, why?"

C: "Cuz everybody really loves him, and thinks he's special. But God is so big. How could he fit in Mary's tummy? All squished up?"

M: "Because God wanted to be with us. That's why God came as Jesus, to see what it's like to be a person. God's not (*in deep authoritarian voice*) 'I'm a God above everyone,' but lives with the people. Do all these things—get sick, play—to know what it's like to be a person."

C: "God looks like—he has a big, like, thingie, like a trident, except it's not a trident, a stick like gold with a green thing. God is holding that now, a red and sort of dark green and a gold jewel that's his hat. The costume he's wearing matches his hat. (*Pauses for several seconds . . . then in exasperated tone*) Can we change the subject?"

M: "Sure."

C: (*indignantly*) "Cuz I know a lot about God, and you told me things I already knew." (*All is quiet for about 5 seconds, everyone else reading silently . . .*)

C: "Mom, does God have a house? Does he read books?"

M: "I don't think so. I'm not sure."

C: "Is God a girl or man?"

M: "I think both."

C: "How can one side be a girl and the other side a man? (*Sounding excited . . .*) I know—sometimes God does boy things and sometimes girl things. (*Pauses several seconds . . .*) I think God is a girl."

M: "You may be right."

F: "Why do you think God is a girl?"

C: "I don't know. Girls might think God is a girl, and boys might think he's a boy. (*Exasperated* . . .) Can we change the subject, fast-forward to another thing."

M: "OK."

This verbatim example illustrates many features of a reciprocal communication style in which the child is active. It also indicates that the analysis of actual parent-child conversations is a promising method for research on religious socialization. One method used (Boyatzis & Janicki, 2003) required parents to record specific aspects of family behavior over a designated period of time. Though not a trouble-free method, diaries have illuminated parent-child conversations about other topics (Bradbard, Endsley, & Mize, 1992; Callanan & Oakes, 1992). The diary method generates a corpus of *actual* parent-child conversations about religion. Such qualitative data make a novel contribution to a literature replete with retrospective reports from teens and adults. Social science publications tend to rely on quantitative surveys that most likely tap parents' *global perceptions* of communication. Thus, diaries may be most valuable for shedding light on the specific dynamics of parent-child conversations about religion and spirituality.

Quantitative methods have converged on one conclusion about family life: Mothers are the primary religious socializer (Acock & Bengston, 1978; Myers, 1996), even in interfaith families (Nelsen, 1990). The mother's prominence may be due to several factors. Some work (Wuthnow, 1999) indicates that mothers turn to religion more than fathers to help them with the emotional troubles of parenting, although fathers also can frame their roles in terms of their faith (e.g., Dollahite, 2003). In retrospective accounts from adults, women recall seeing their mothers pray more than their fathers (Wuthnow, 1999). Mothers spend more time with their children (Myers, 1996), which increases verbal interaction with children (Clark-Stewart & Hevey, 1981). In addition, children rate their mothers higher than fathers as a confidant and self-disclosure partner (Buhrmester & Furman, 1987). Thus, mothers may be especially involved in religious communication with children.

The Diary Study of Parent-Child Conversations

The information presented here is part of a larger study (see Boyatzis & Janicki, 2003, for an extended report). Participants were 23 families with two parents in the home and a child or children between 3 and 12 years of age, who were recruited from churches, parochial schools, and preschools in central Pennsylvania. The mean child age was 7.6 years ($SD = 2.74$) with similar numbers of boys (54.5%) and girls (45.5%). Mothers' ages ranged from 27 to 48 years ($M = 37.2$ yrs; $SD = 6.08$), and fathers' from 31 to 54 years ($M = 40.7$ yrs; $SD = 5.50$). Almost all fathers (97%) were employed full-time outside of the home, and most mothers (60.7%) were employed at least part-time outside the home. Most (57%) children were enrolled in a parochial school, 9.5% in a religiously-affiliated preschool, and 4.8% received no religious education outside home; 28.6% regularly attended Sunday School classes. All participants were White, and almost all parents were Christian (63.0% Catholic, 22.4% Protestant; 11.5% other Christians).

Families were asked to participate for two 1-week periods in 1998: 1 week in late October or early November, and 1 week in early December. During these periods, parents were asked to complete the Parent-Child Communication Diary. Parents received blank pages for their actual diary entries with spaces for the date and time, location, people present, and situation. Parents received sample entries in dialogue format as concrete examples for their own entries. To avoid biasing parents, the samples included conversations on different religious and spiritual issues and in different conversational styles. Parents were instructed to complete their diary entries as verbatim and soon as possible after actual conversations.

Diary entries were then typed and content-analyzed. Table 1 presents diary data from both phases on select variables that were coded; these and other variables analyzed were chosen based on our own judgments of potentially informative aspects of family discussions. Reliability for diary analysis was tested by comparing the author's coding of variables with the coding by a trained psychology student. Interrater reliability was very strong on all variables (see Boyatzis & Janicki, 2003, for details).

Of the 23 families who participated in the first phase, 15 (65.2%) completed diaries during the second phase. Entries from both phases were combined for subsequent analyses. Across both phases combined (a 2-week period), families wrote an average of 5.4 (SD = 2.7) entries. One family wrote only 1, another family wrote 12. The average conversation lasted close to 3 rounds of back-and-forth exchanges, though some lasted 9 rounds. As Table 1 shows, the typical entry addressed 2 religious topics. Conversations typically occurred in the evening and in random situations in the home; meals and bed time were also common contexts. Conversations were often triggered by daily routines or religious rituals. Surprisingly, Sunday School or worship services were infrequent prompts of conversations about religion, and conversations about religion rarely occurred en route to or coming from worship services.

Frequencies were not used for the diary variables because they would have yielded very low figures on many variables. Diary variables were analyzed in terms of the proportion of times a particular variable was cited relative to the total number of diary entries provided by a family. For example, if a family wrote four entries and discussed the topic "Bible stories" once, the family's proportion score on the "Bible stories" variable was .25.

In these Christian families the most common topics were God, Jesus, and prayer (see Table 1). Some topics were rarely discussed: angels, the devil, Hell, and miracles. The coming Christmas season affected family discussions: Compared to phase 1 in the fall, in phase 2—in December—families' conversations about Jesus more than doubled, as did discussion about worship services; conversations about heaven tripled; discussion of the meaning of holidays increased by 15 times. Based on the diaries, it appears that religious discussions occur within the natural ebb and flow of family life. These conversations occurred mostly in the evening but throughout the day in various contexts: at meals, bedtime, prayer, and in random situations around the home. Given the religious nature of this sample, it is surprising that so few conversations were prompted by worship services and so few occurred going to and from worship.

Support for a Bi-Directional Co-Construction in Parent-Child Communication

A major focus of the analyses was the structure of conversations: Were they mutual and bi-directional between parent and child, or more of a top-down, unilateral transmission from parent to child? The data revealed a bi-directional reciprocity. Children initiated half of all diary conversations. Close to two-thirds of families had children who initiated at least 50% of conversations, and in 11% of families the children initiated all of the conversations. Diaries also revealed that the proportion of child-to-parent words in diary entries was .9, suggesting that parents and children said virtually the same number of words in each diary. Also, parents rarely corrected their children (.4 corrections per conversation, though in some entries there were as many as 3 corrections in a single conversation) and they asked more open-ended requests for information than test questions. In the analysis of who terminated the conversations, children and parents had similar proportions (.4 vs. .6, respectively). Overall, then, children asked questions about religion and spoke about as much as parents did; they regularly initiated and terminated conversations; parents did not often correct their children much; and they asked for children's ideas more than they asked for answers to "test questions." These data are understood to collectively demonstrate that parent-child communication about religion is marked by a more reciprocal and bi-lateral style rather than a unilateral transmission style.

One way to describe parents' behavior in such conversations is to view it as "conversation management" in which parents create scaffolding to facilitate their children's involvement and understanding. This developmental scenario is consistent with a framework of cognitive growth which posits that knowledge is first *inter*personal and later, through mechanisms such as discussions with parents, becomes internalized and *intra*personal for the child (Vygotsky, 1978).

On each diary entry parents were asked to give a specific interpretation of their conversation to convey if parents are concerned more with transmitting their beliefs or creating a more open communication climate for co-construction of meaning. Parents indicated the degree to which they felt they actually conveyed in the conversation their personal position on the topic. After each entry, parents expressed this feeling on a 5-point scale, with a higher number indicating that the parent more strongly conveyed his or her position. These were called "conviction ratings." If parents had high conviction ratings, it suggested they were truly trying to transmit knowledge or beliefs to their child. On the other hand, more modest conviction ratings might reflect the parents' openness to the child's position or reticence to impose their own views. The average parents' conviction rating across all of the diaries on the 5-point scale was a 3.7 ($SD = 1.1$). That is, parents felt *somewhat* certain that they had expressed their beliefs to children. The large standard deviation and use of the full range indicate that parents varied widely across conversations in how much they conveyed their actual beliefs.

Parents' conviction ratings varied with the types of questions they tended to ask their children. For example, these conviction ratings were inversely correlated with the proportion of requests for information they made ($r = -.46$, $p < .05$). In other words, the more parents solicited their children's ideas through asking questions, the less certain they were that they had conveyed their own beliefs. This interesting finding could be interpreted in different ways. For example, it could mean that parents are not very sure of what they believe or what they are talking about and thus ask children more open-ended questions. Or perhaps parents are sensitive to their child's level of comprehension and simplify the message, and in the process making it something less than what they actually believe about the matter. In addition, this finding could also indicate that parents were creating a bi-directional and mutual communication climate. This constellation of results—parents' average conviction rating was not very high, and the more parents asked open-ended requests to learn what their children think the less concerned they were with making their own positions known—supports the view that parents were attempting to create a co-constructive atmosphere in religious and spiritual communication.

This image of an active child is highlighted in part to serve as an antidote to the research literature's ubiquitous depiction of the child as a passive recipient of parents' transmission. (On the child's active agency in the family, see Cummings and Schermerhorn, 2003.)

Mothers and Fathers in Religious Communication

As in the conversations above, mothers were integral. Mothers recorded virtually all diaries (96% in phase 1, 98% in phase 2) and were much more involved than fathers in conversations. In 42% of the families, fathers did not participate in any diary conversations (all mothers participated at least once), whereas in 87% of families the mothers participated in all of the diary conversations (this occurred for fathers in only 5% of families).

Although affective tone in the conversations was not analyzed, it was clear that mothers were crucial for creating meaning for their children within a faith framework.

Here is an evening conversation between a mother and child after the father left for a business trip.

C: (*teary-eyed*) "I miss Daddy."

M: "I miss Daddy, too. Do you know who is gonna take care of Daddy and be with him in Chicago?"

C: "Who?"

M: "God."

C: "But I miss Daddy."

M: "I do too, Sweetheart. God will take good care of Daddy while he's away from us. Do you know how?"

C: "He'll watch over him."

M: "That's right."

Here is an entry that brings to life many of these coded variables. A mother and child were sitting in their kitchen after dinner and discussed whether they would adopt a cat.

C: "Are we going to keep the kitty forever?"

M: "We'll keep the kitty if she likes it here at our house." (*Then the child placed his hands together and prayed out loud*: "Oh please, God, let this kitty like it here. Oh please, God, let this kitty like it here.")

M: "Do you think that will work?"

C: "Yep, don't worry."

This brief exchange is revealing. First, through her behavior, the mother models Christian kindness in welcoming the (feline) stranger and caring for God's creation. But beyond that, after the child prayed, the mother's words ("Do you think that will work?") create dialogue on the act of prayer and the nature of faith. In a way, the question poses a stiff challenge—does prayer work?—and the parent thus helps the child grow in faith through deed (the praying) but also in thought and word.

These diaries provide evidence of a specific mechanism through which mothers play a major role in their children's religious development. Mothers, relative to their husbands, talk a great deal with their children about religion and spirituality. In addition to earlier explanations for this difference, children seem to seek out their mothers for talks about religion, as suggested by the percentage of conversations that children initiated with their mothers. The father's conspicuous absence from religious communication in this study may be a methodological artifact: Fathers may be less inclined than mothers to record events in diaries. On the other hand, perhaps fathers and children find faith in action in some situations where mothers might not. The family is watching a football game on TV.

> C: "Dad, why did that guy make the sign of the cross when something good happened?"
>
> F: "Why do you think he did?"
>
> C: "To, like, thank God for . . . what?"
>
> F: "Well, probably for helping him receive that good pass."
>
> C: "Oh!"

From one perspective, the mothers' centrality could be a developmental advantage for the children. On non-religious topics, the more mothers use elaborative statements and frequent elicitations about past events, the better their children remember them (McCabe & Peterson, 1991). It is likely that mothers' (and fathers') bi-directional and mutual conversation style may enhance the child's religiosity in positive ways. Research using retrospective recall data indirectly supports this prediction (Dudley & Wisbey, 2000; Okagaki & Bevis, 1999).

Co-Construction of Spiritual Meaning

The central elements of Christian faith—God, Jesus, prayer—were also the most common themes in these (Christian) families' conversations about religion. Throughout the conversations parents and children work together toward increasing understanding about these issues. Diaries showed exchanges about God's personality, appearance, omnipresence, origin, and role in people's lives. Surely parents, not just children, wrestle with these issues. Parents who discuss religious and spiritual issues with their children may come to think of their children as partners in the search. Aquinas famously defined theology as "faith seeking understanding." Mothers and fathers and sons and daughters are working out this theology project together.

God was a stable topic across the time span in this study, but some topics might be sensitive to idiosyncratic events. For example, it would be surprising if in the aftermath of September 11 families did not discuss faiths other than their own much more often than they did during this study, in which the diary theme of "faiths other than one's own" appeared in *less than 5%* of diaries. And given the recent ubiquitous attention to terrorism and violence, more frequent discussion of the after-life and the soul could be expected, topics that were rare in the diaries from the present study. Of course, our sample confirmed that a family does not need global worries to make such concerns real, as the following discussion illustrates.

Playing in their kitchen after dinner, this family had a serious discussion triggered by a minor accident. The parents help the children understand some fundamental truths about life and faith. The family's infant (here referred to as "Baby") just bumped his lip and bled for perhaps the first time, and an older sibling begins the conversation with a concern:

C1: "Do babies ever die?"

C2: "Of course they do."

F: "Well sometimes they do unfortunately." C1: "Why does God make a baby die?"

M: "Well, honey, everything God does is to help us learn about how much he loves us. I don't know why he would make a baby die."

C1: "Could (Baby) die?"

M: "(Baby's) boo-boo is fine and he is a good, strong, healthy baby. We all should pray everyday for God to keep us and everyone we love safe and happy.

Here is a conversation from another family, between a mother and child while riding in their car.

C: "Does God hear me wherever I am?"

M: "Yes, He does."

C: "Can he hear me talk to him?"

M: "Absolutely. He hears you and He knows when you are talking to him."

C: "How can he hear me through the roof of the van?"

M: "Anytime you need to talk to him, He is there for you. If you are feeling sad, or happy, or worried."

C: (*looking up*) "Okay, I'd like you to bring me a new black and white soccer ball and new jeans and . . ."

M: "Hey, wait a minute—who are you talking to?"

C: "Santa!"

M: "I thought you were talking about Jesus and you were asking about Santa!"

C: "Mom, you're silly—can I still talk to Santa?"

M: "Let's write him a letter."

Throughout many conversations, parents and children negotiate the constraints of a human mind in understanding a metaphysical being. Such conversations demonstrate how children work to comprehend different ontological categories of beings-in-the-world and beings-not-of-this-world (God, angels, etc.). Developmental psychologists have recently turned attention to these cognitive processes (see, e.g., Rosengren, Johnson, & Harris, 1999; Woolley, 1997). Parents might reflect on the ways they help children understand how different worlds, the empirically known and the intangible relate to each other (see Harris, 2000). Children spend much of their time wrestling with these ontological and epistemological distinctions, more time than adults and parents might realize they do, and surely children can have experiences or insights that parents might find odd, anomalous, or "inappropriate" to reason or faith. Rather than dismissing such events, parents might carry an attitude of openness to the varieties of children's religious and mystical experience. Indeed, this attitude could be vital for fostering the child's faith in those sacred figures and traditions that are central to religious faiths (see Clark, 1995). Jesus, too, emphasized that children's experience must be respected (see, e.g., Matthew 18; 21:14; Luke 18:15). Social scientists have much work to do in the study of children's felt and lived experiences in the religious and spiritual realm (Boyatzis, 2001). Future work on family communication might examine conversations about different types of ontological beings and topics.

In many conversations with children, adults provide different forms of testimony and ways of thinking. Parents have probably realized that in the process of such discussions, they arrive at deeper understanding of the spiritual and metaphysical complexities. Part of this comes directly from sharing in children's joy and wonder when dealing with mystery, an open and wondering epistemological stance that might be at the heart of spiritual growth (see Berryman, 1991; Matthews, 1980; Stonehouse, 1998).

The mysterious nature of the divine seems to capture much of children's (and adults') attention. Here are two conversations that reflect children's struggle to know God. The first is with an eleven-year-old girl speaking with Robert Coles about the skin color of Jesus (Coles, 1990, pp. 57–58):

> "My daddy says there weren't any cameras then, so there's no picture of Him . . .
> I know that in the black churches they'll tell you Jesus is black; he's colored.
> Our maid told us that's how He looks in her church—the pictures of Him—so
> there's the difference. I asked my grandma who's right, and she said . . . 'Honey,
> I don't think it makes any difference up there—skin color.'"

Here is another conversation, one I had with my oldest daughter when she was 8–1/2 years old. We focused on God's omniscience and on prayer and communication with God:

F: "The other day you asked mom if God knows everything. What made you ask?"

C: "Well, it's hard to say because . . . I just thought about how people think God is perfect, but do they mean He *knows* everything is perfect. So I just wanted to ask if people know that God knows everything."

F: "Hmm. Do *you* think He knows everything?"

C: "I don't know. I think we might find that out when we go to heaven. But, um, I sort of think there's somethings that He might not—or *She*—might not know."

F: "So you think we find out when we go to heaven."

C: "Yes, cuz I think that's where you can talk to God and that's where you can ask God lots of questions."

F: "Is there any other way to talk to God *now*, here on earth?"

C: "If you pray. People usually think praying is like talking to God. But when I pray, I'm . . . ah, I just, I'm very impatient. When I can't hear God I go, I go (*in mock upset and whiny tone*), 'Mommy, It's *not talking to me!* It's *not talking to me!*' See, cuz I just can't hear God very well."

F: "When you pray, what do you expect to hear? Do you think you'll hear God?"

C: "Oh, I expect to hear . . . I expect to hear . . . I expect to hear somebody going (*in deep voice*) 'OK, thank you for that prayer.' If I ask any questions, I expect to hear the answers later on, next time I pray. But unfortunately I can't really hear the voice. I don't know if God's talking to me and I just can't hear it, or if God's not talking to me."

F: "I think it's hard to know what God thinks."

C: (*emphatically*) "You just *don't know*."

The conversation continued a while later, discussing a different aspect of God:

C: "God might not be a he or she; it might be something else that's never lived; it might be, uh, something we've never had on this earth."

F: "So God's something that—"

C: "I'm saying it *might* be, I'm not saying it definitely is."

F: "Do you think it's hard to know, definitely, what God is?"

C: (*solemnly*) "Yes, it's hard."

F: "Because a couple of times you've said 'God *might* be this, God *might* be that.' I think you realize that it may just be impossible to ever really know what God is, whether it's a he or she, and that's why you say it's an 'it,' or before you said God could be a table or a chair. Why did you say it could be a table or chair?"

C: "Well, that's sort of an example of saying it might be something that we nev-er . . . He might be made out of *wood* or something."

Parents must respect children's earnest negotiation and interpretation of the myriad ideas and images that fill the enigmatic gap between the tangible and the non-actual. This is an important psychological and transitional space (Winnicott, 1953) in which children maneuver, and with openness and faith child and parent can grow and learn together in that space.

I recall a lovely question from my youngest daughter when she had just turned 7 years old. At bedtime one night, she suddenly asked, "Daddy, what does *your* God look like?"

Future Directions

There are some important limitations of this study, one being the small and primarily Roman Catholic sample, most of whom had children in parochial school. Future work must study different kinds of families from different denominations to know how widely our characterization of communication can be generalized. Nevertheless, the results are helpful for articulating a style of family communication that respects the child as an active meaning-maker and that reveals a more open and reciprocal process than the "transmission" model suggests.

The study has methodological value, too. The diary measure is a novel and innovative tool. We believe it obtains ecologically valid, authentic information on family's *actual* religious and spiritual communication, in contrast to retrospective self-reports or data from surveys that may reflect general perceptions or memory-impaired depictions of family communication. Of course, the diary method has drawbacks. First, social desirability or privacy concerns may have led some parents to omit or edit certain conversations, and some entries seemed embellished by parents to read like a "theologically correct" conversation. Second, during weekly telephone check-ins, parents said they had difficulty recording every religious conversation. Thus, the diary data may underestimate the actual frequency of parent-child communication about religion. With modifications, the diary promises to be an important window into family communication for future research.

There are many important questions to investigate. First, to what degree does parent-child communication actually *influence* children's and parents' spiritual growth? Systematic analysis is necessary to learn how conversational style and content may not only *reflect* but also *affect* parents' and children's beliefs. Another factor in parent-child communication is the degree to which parents sanctify their role or see their work as parents as holy and sacred (e.g., Boyatzis & Tunison, 2002; Mahoney, Pargament, Murray-Swank, & Murray-Swank, 2003). Would parents who see themselves as "doing God's work" as parents be more—or less—reciprocal and mutual in their conversations with their children?

Do families use different communication styles depending on the topic? Conveying the story of Noah's Ark may call for one style, but wrestling with the problem of evil in a world created by a loving and omnipotent God calls for another. In addition, research could address parents' and children's goals in particular conversations. A parent compelled to describe the Biblical mandate against stealing might use a distinct unidirectional style, whereas a parent trying to help a child understand the concept of the Holy Trinity might employ a more bi-directional style with open-ended questions. It should be noted here that parents might discuss some topics in an open, flexible fashion because they themselves may not fully comprehend them or be resolved in their own thinking about them.

Some research indicates that mothers (McCabe & Peterson, 1991) and adolescent girls (Beaumont 2000) have distinct communication styles. Researchers should develop ways to think about children's distinct "religious-communication styles." As parents know, some children have a high tolerance for ambiguity, and their faith may grow best in a milieu of ongoing open-ended exchanges that prioritize questions and doubt over answers and certainty; other children who prefer closure and certainty might find the didactic transmission of information from parents more comforting and educational. Research could address how these styles are related to children's and parents' religious beliefs. Longitudinal designs will clarify two important issues: Are childhood styles nascent forms of religious orientations that continue into adulthood, and does growing up in a family with a particular communication style predict specific religious beliefs, attitudes, and faith orientations later in life? All of these questions lay out a research agenda for a more genuine understanding of family communication about religion in childhood as well as how childhood experience is related to spirituality in adulthood.

Concluding Thoughts

Beyond such questions, a more complete understanding of parent-child communication about religion requires a better understanding of how children influence their parents. Our data make clear that the child is an active figure rather than a passive religious *tabula rasa*. In some families, there may be clear roles—parent-as-mentor and child-as-naíve apprentice—but in other families parent and child may be more like partners in the co-construction of religious and spiritual meaning. In still other families, parents may even view their child as a "spiritual savant," one serving as the parents' teacher. More than a few times friends have said that their children have "come here to teach us something," and presumably something more profound than the joys of diapering or orthodontia.

Without minimizing parents' responsibility for raising faithful children, it behooves parents, scholars, clergy, and educators to respect the role children play in a family's or congregation's experience of religion. Consider the words of the great Teacher who said "Let the children come to me, do not hinder them; for to such belongs the kingdom of God. Truly I say to you, whoever does not receive the kingdom of God like a child shall not enter it" (*Mark 10:13*). While one ponders what Jesus meant by "like a child," it is clear that spiritual reflection and faithful action can emerge in small moments. One night in a darkened room, when our youngest daughter, Sedona, was

2–1/2 years old, she knelt by her parents' bed, clumsily interlaced her small fingers, and slowly began to move her lips in inaudible whispers. Her parents, taken aback by this toddler's spontaneous act, knelt on each side of her, and then her older sister joined the family in prayer. This small act by a toddler effected an important family ritual that continues years later.

When Moses told his people to talk with their children about faith and God throughout the day and in various settings, Moses was also unwittingly telling researchers where to look for a crucial context of spiritual socialization and growth. Perhaps this chapter will inspire continued inquiry into the complex dynamics between child and parent to understand how they are teacher and student to the other.

References

Acock, A. C., & Bengston, V. L. (1978). On the relative influence of mothers and fathers: A covariance analysis of political and religious socialization. *Journal of Marriage and Family, 40*, 519–530.

Bao, W-N., Whitbeck, L., Hoyt, D., & Conger, R. C. (1999). Perceived parental acceptance as a moderator of religious transmission among adolescent boys and girls. *Journal of Marriage and the Family, 61*, 362–374.

Beaumont, S. L. (2000). Conversational styles of mothers and their preadolescent and middle adolescent daughters. *Merrill-Palmer Quarterly, 46*, 119–139.

Berryman, J. W. (1991). *Godly play: A way of religious education.* San Francisco: HarperSanFrancisco.

Boyatzis, C. J. (2001). A critique of models of religious experience. *The International Journal for the Psychology of Religion, 11*, 247–258.

Boyatzis, C. J., & Janicki, D. (2003). Parent-child communication about religion: Survey and diary data on unilateral transmission and bi-directional support styles. *Review of Religious Research, 44*, 252–270.

Boyatzis, C. J., & Tunison, S. (2002, August). *Religiosity and interpersonal aggression and corporal punishment in Appalachian parents and children.* Paper presented at the annual meeting of the American Psychological Association, Chicago.

Bradbard, M. R., Endsley, R. C., & Mize, J. (1992). The ecology of parent-child communication about daily experiences in preschool and day care. *Journal of Research in Childhood Education, 6*, 131–41.

Buhrmester, D., & Furman, W. (1987). The development of companionship and intimacy. *Child Development, 58*, 1101–1113.

Callanan, M. A., & Oakes, L. M. (1992). Preschoolers' questions and parents' explanations: Causal thinking in everyday action. *Cognitive Development, 7*, 213–233.

Clark, C. D. (1995). *Flights of fancy, leaps of faith.* Chicago: University of Chicago Press.

Clark, C. A., Worthington, E. L., & Danser D. B. (1988). The transmission of religious beliefs and practices from parents to firstborn early adolescent sons. *Journal of Marriage and the Family, 50*, 463–472.

Clarke-Stewart, K. A., & Hevey, A. (1981). Longitudinal relations in repeated observations of mother-child interaction from 1 to 2 1/2 Years. *Developmental Psychology, 17*, 127–145.

Coles, R. (1990). *The spiritual life of children.* Boston: Houghton Mifflin.

Cornwall, M. (1987). The social bases of religion: A study of factors influencing religious belief and commitment. *Review of Religious Research, 29,* 44–56.

Cummings, E. M., & Schermerhorn, A. C. (2003). A developmental perspective on children as agents in the family. In L. Kuczynski (Ed.), *Handbook of dynamics in parent-child relations* (pp. 91–108). Thousand Oaks, CA: Sage.

Dollahite, D. C. (2003). Fathering for eternity: Generative spirituality in Latter-Day Saint fathers of children with special needs. *Review of Religious Research, 44,* 237–251.

Dudley, R. L., & Dudley, M. (1986). Transmission of religious values from parents to adolescents. *Review of Religious Research, 28,* 3–15.

Dudley, R. L., & Wisbey, R. L. (2000). The relationship of parenting styles to commitment to the church among young adults. *Religious Education, 95,* 39–50.

Harris, P. L. (2000). On not falling down to earth: Children's metaphysical questions. In K. S. Rosengren, C. N. Johnson, & P. L. Harris (Eds.) *Imagining the impossible: Magical, scientific, and religious thinking in children* (pp. 157–78). Cambridge: Cambridge University Press.

Hay, D., & Nye, R. (1998). *The spirit of the child.* London: Fount.

Hoge, D. R., Petrillo, G., & Smith, E. (1982). Transmission of religious and social values from parents to teenage children. *Journal of Marriage and the Family, 44,* 569–579.

Iannaccone, L. R. (1990). Religious practice: A human capital approach. *Journal for the Scientific Study of Religion, 29,* 297–314.

Krcmar, M. (1996). Family communication patterns, discourse behavior, and child television viewing. *Human Communication Research, 23,* 251–277.

Mahoney, A., Pargament, K. I., Murray-Swank, A., & Murray-Swank, N. (2003). Religion and the sanctification of family relationships. *Review of Religious Research, 44,* 220–236.

Maslak, M. A. (2001). A community of education: Nepalese children living and learning religious ritual. *Culture and Religion, 2,* 61–77.

Matthews, G. B. (1980). *Philosophy and the young child.* Cambridge: Harvard University Press.

McCabe, A., & Peterson, C. (1991) Getting the story: A longitudinal study of parental styles in eliciting narratives and development narrative skill. In A. McCabe & C. Peterson (Eds.), *Development of narrative structure* (pp. 217–257). Hillsdale, NJ: Erlbaum.

Myers, S. M. (1996). An interactive model of religiosity inheritance: The importance of family context. *American Sociological Review, 61,* 858–866.

Nelsen, H. (1990). The religious identification of children of interfaith marriages. *Review of Religious Research, 32,* 122–134.

Okagaki, L., & Bevis, C. (1999). Transmission of religious values: Relations between parents and daughters' beliefs. *Journal of Genetic Psychology, 160,* 303–318.

Olsen-Fulero, L. (1983). Informational functions of mother-child discourse: Knowing them when we see them. *Child Language, 10,* 223–229.

Ozorak, E. W. (1989). Social and cognitive influences on the development of religious beliefs and commitment in adolescence. *Journal for the Scientific Study of Religion, 28,* 448–463.

Ritchie, L. D. (1991). Family communication patterns: An epistemic analysis and conceptual reinterpretation. *Communication Research, 18,* 548–565.

Rosengren, K. S., Johnson, C. N., & Harris, P. L. (Eds.). (2000). *Imagining the impossible: Magical, scientific, and religious thinking in children.* Cambridge: Cambridge University Press.

Stonehouse, C. (1998). *Joining children on the spiritual journey: Nurturing a life of faith*. Grand Rapids: Baker.

Vygotsky, L. S. (1978). *Mind in society*. Cambridge: Harvard University.

Winnicott, D. W. (1953). Transitional objects and transitional phenomena. *International Journal of Psychoanalysis, 34*, 89–97.

Woolley, J. (1997). Thinking about fantasy: Are children fundamentally different thinkers andbelievers from adults? *Child Development, 68*, 991–1011.

Wuthnow, R. (1999). *Growing up religious: Christians and Jews and their journeys of faith*. Boston: Beacon.

Table 1: Descriptive Data from Diary Entries in Phase 1 and 2

Coded Variables and Response Categories	Phase 1		Phase 2	
	M^a	SD	M^a	SD
When conversations about religious issues occur.[b]				
Evening	.41	.35	.53	.38
Afternoon	.25	.16	.16	.25
Morning	.18	.14	.14	.26
Where conversations occur				
Random location/situation in the home[c]	.35	.30	.25	.37
Bed time	.20	.14	.14	.27
Meal time	.18	.26	.18	.29
Praying	.13	.26	.09	.16
Storytelling	.08	.17	.04	.07
Traveling	.07	.15	.13	.28
Watching TV	.04	.09	.07	.15
Returning from worship services	.04	.10	.09	.21
Dropping off child at school/Sunday School	.04	.10	.02	.09
Bath time	.02	.07	.00	.00
Picking up child from school/Sunday School	.02	.07	.07	.19
Going to worship services	.00	.00	.10	.04
Topics of religious conversation				
God	.48	.37	.54	.84
Jesus	.30	.30	.63	.33
Prayer	.27	.29	.27	.32
Faith as it relates to other issues	.29	.26	.13	.25

Coded Variables and Response Categories	Phase 1		Phase 2	
	M[a]	SD	M[a]	SD
Bible stories	.19	.25	.04	.11
Heaven	.09	.15	.28	.32
Afterlife and the soul	.08	.13	.06	.19
Angels	.06	.11	.06	.15
Worship services	.06	.13	.13	.32
Faiths other than that of your family	.04	.10	.02	.06
Meaning of holidays	.03	.08	.45	.36
Devil	.03	.15	.00	.00
Miracles	.02	.07	.00	.00
Hell	.00	.00	.00	.00

Prompts of religious/spiritual conversation

	M[a]	SD	M[a]	SD
Daily routine	.27	.32	.44	.33
Religious routine/ritual	.27	.15	.24	
Something learned at school/Sunday school	.13	.17	.03	.10
Birth, death or other major event	.12	.16	.11	.16
Spontaneous initiation of discussion	.12	.14	.25	.39
Praying	.11	.20	.07	.16
Instruction or discipline	.11	.25	.03	.10
Something observed at worship services	.07	.15	.15	.24
Religious/spiritual issues in the media	.05	.12	.14	.23

a. Rated on percentage scale; each score is proportion of times item was cited relative to total number of entries by family.

b. Some entries did not include time, so Ms for these variables do not = 100%.

c. Parents' reference to location not in defined categories.

Chapter 13

A Child's Concept of God

JOYCE E. BELLOUS, SIMONE A. DE ROOS AND WILLIAM SUMMEY[1]

S elf-esteem is a popular educational issue and refers to the value people have of themselves. Many Christian parents and teachers want the young to think well of themselves and they are interested in teaching children about God by passing along faith traditions to them. Research on religiosity suggests that children's self-concepts form alongside concepts they have for God. That is, the God concept is important in the formation of the self-concept. Drawing on this research, we (the writers) will argue that self-concepts and God concepts emerge through processes of attachment that characterize infancy and childhood. Appropriate self-esteem is a by-product of drawing close to God; it is an act of faith grounded on believing a person is valuable to God.

This chapter will investigate and evaluate psychological processes involved in forming God concepts and psychological research that assesses connections between

1. Joyce E. Bellous is Associate Professor of Lay Empowerment and Discipleship at McMaster Divinity College where she has taught since 1993. She has published over 30 essays on education, ethics and culture as book chapters and journal articles. Her current research is focused on children and spirituality and she was a Conference Respondent at the fifth annual International Conference on Children's Spirituality in Lincoln England. Her Ph.D. is in the Philosophy of Education from the University of Alberta, her M.A. is in Policy Studies and Multicultural Education while her B.Ed is in Education, both from The University of Calgary, and her B.A. is in Psychology and Philosophy from the University of Alberta.

Simone A. de Roos obtained her Ph.D. at the Catholic University in Nijmegen in the Netherlands in Developmental Psychology. She is currently a researcher in Religious Education at the Department of Philosophy and History of Education at the Free University Amsterdam. She is also an internal school consultant at the Christian elementary school Johan Weststeijn in the Netherlands. She has published several journal articles and has two chapters published in books written in German.

William Summey has an M.Div. and Ph.D. in Religion from Vanderbilt University. He is Editor in chief of the parenting magazines *ParentLife* and *BabyLife* as well as several children's devotional magazines, all produced by LifeWay Christian Resources. He is also adjunct professor of religion at Belmont University.

attachment theories (and corollary object relations theories) and a child's religiosity. In discussing self-esteem and God concepts, connections will be made among concepts the young have of themselves, of other people and concepts they have of God. Parents and teachers must grasp the significance of their encounters with children and the influence of their own God concepts on the development of a child's attachment to God. There is evidence that an emergent self is shaped by an unfolding God concept; the need for others grounds a positively felt attachment to God. A focus of concern on childhood is a way to encourage the growth of an integrated sense of self and a healthy view of God.

Forming God Concepts

Ana-Maria Rizzuto studied the theory of object relations that emerged from Sigmund Freud's thought. Freud wanted to know how people come to possess actual belief in the existence of God (Rizzuto, 1979, p. 41). The theory of object relations addressed that question. Object relations theory is limited to what can be observed about human experience. While it is limited, systematically observing human phenomena remains one plausible way to make human experience more understandable, bearable, and open to transformation. What is strange about this aspect of Freud's theory is its elimination of mothers from the formation of God concepts. Rizzuto addressed the omission of mother-child relations and the significance of those relationships to God concept formation (Rizzuto, 1979; 1998), as did John Bowlby (1988) in his description of attachment theory, which is a particular interpretation of object relations between mother and child.

In general, object relations theories explain the need for others, since they are "theories about our relations to the 'objects'-people and things-to which we are attached and which give meaning to our lives" (Klein, 1987, p. xv). In writing about object relations, Rizzuto's aim was to demonstrate how object relations theories illuminate the formation of God concepts, and to point out limitations in Freud's application of his theory. Hers is not a book on religion; rather it asserts that religious education must negotiate the mental mythologies each child brings to the classroom. This chapter will focus on the relationship between meaningful 'objects' and the formation of God concepts in a child by examining Rizzuto's views first, then Bowlby's theory, followed by analyzing the formation of concepts for God on the basis of research carried out by de Roos and her colleagues. This investigation will be concluded by reconciling children's God concepts with formal religious education. At the center of this inquiry is an explication of what it means to have a God concept and to maintain a concept of God.

To begin with, the phrase God concept designates the union of ideas, feelings and images each person associates with God. Images and ideas are acquired early in life: the "first conscious God representations appear between the ages of two and three" (Rizzuto, 1979, p. 178). A concept of God blends feeling-charged images with intellectually rich ideas to form a concept that has cognitive as well as affective dimensions. Rizzuto asserts that every human being constructs a concept for God so that there is no such thing as a human being without a God concept. In the course of development, "each individual produces an idiosyncratic and highly personalized" concept derived from object relations, evolving self-representations, and environmental systems of belief. Once formed, a God concept "cannot be made to disappear; it can only be repressed, transformed or used" (Rizzuto, 1979, p. 90).

Other research posits that God concepts form in a space carved out between mother and infant in their mutual relationship. The "early stage in this development is made possible by the mother's special capacity for making adaptation to the needs of her infant, thus allowing the infant the illusion that what the infant creates really exists" (Rizzuto, 1979, p. 177). That is, God concepts form in a space between infant and mother that is its own reality and that contributes to a child's sense of being real and living in a real world. Illusion does not signify something false. Illusion is not delusion. All art, science and religion depend on illusion for their existence. Illusion is the bedrock of learning and all learning is organizing experience.

This space of experiencing is located between two elements necessary for normal functioning: an inner psychic or soul reality-which people often situate in the mind, head, belly, heart or some other physical part of the body, as a simple way to express its identity and explain its function-and also an external reality, the people and objects outside the psychophysical entity called a human being. Experiencing takes place in the 'space' between the mother and child (Winnicott, 1971, p. 53), a space that has the potential to house the healthy "illusions" of life.

Erik Erikson (1950) elaborated what happens in these encounters between infant and mother, in terms of the development of trust or its deficiency. Trust forms primarily through one's experience of parental attentiveness. Due to the very 'human' potential involved in the child and mother relationship, "attention is the central reinforcement of [that] sensory process" (Stern, 1985, p. 43), through gazing—an interaction that has no need for words (of which the infant is incapable). Attention is linked to expectation; if conditions are favorable and the mother consistently meets the child's needs, the child develops a sense of what experience is like and that it is pleasant. Stern (1985) identifies in these encounters what he calls the building of trace memories, *Representations of Interactions that have been Generalized or RIGs*. Children register a trace memory of the mother with a general sense of mother responding to needs in a way that is pleasant. The need for repetition of these interactions for trace memories to form may relieve parents who worry that infants are irreversibly harmed by a few inappropriate responses (Stern, 1985, pp. 97–99).

Like Stern, Rizzuto was interested in children's subjective experience, an unconscious weaving of images, feelings and ideas that converge in the process of elaborating a concept of God (Rizzuto, 1979, preface). She found that representational memories, woven together to form the concept of self and one's objects, are retrieved consciously or unconsciously to reassure one's self in times of lowered self-esteem or to enhance an existing feeling of self-worth. For example, the person who briefly plays with his hair, may be unknowingly remembering a parental caress (Rizzuto, 1979, p. 56). Her research is evidence for a correlation between the experience of one's parents and one's view of God, through her carefully constructed case histories. God is, in this sense, the ultimate parent who is viewed as highly capable either of meeting needs, being loving by providing consolation and protection, or alternatively, is entirely incapable of providing the necessary resources for living. She was also interested that Sigmund Freud chose to see God as not providing these resources, as he did not believe in God. Rizzuto made a careful study of his reason for rejecting God and in doing so provides many more clues to the significance of object relations in the formation of God concepts. She is clear: God concepts remain entwined in a complex way with one's experience of parents, as Freud reveals (Rizzuto, 1998). God concepts may be repressed or transformed but they do not go away. That is, children learn through experience whether or not to trust God. Parents, teachers, significant others, as well as salient things (e.g., church buildings, television programs) are influential in constructing a child's expectation that God is dependable, good and kind (or the opposite of these), whether or not the child has formal religious training.

Learning as Organizing Experience

When children—even those with *no* experience of religion—are asked to give an account of God, they may do so in words or by drawing a picture. During research into their spirituality, the young demonstrate readiness to use religious language to express spiritual insight. As an example, Katie (age 6), told researcher Rebecca Nye that she had recently become the owner of a Bible, but said she had never been inside a church. Rebecca asked her what she thought about God, and Katie replied: "I don't know yet, because I haven't read it very long." Question: "Did you know about God before you got your Bible?" Response: "No, not at all." Katie had little coherent understanding of formal religion. However, earlier on in the conversation with Rebecca, she said to Rebecca when discussing a picture of a starry sky: "You couldn't even reach that high, no one can except God." At another point in the conversation, when she was asked: What sort of things could somebody know about themselves that nobody else could know, she replied: "God knows everything." And in another moment, reflecting on how we know things, she said that her moral knowledge of when she's being good or bad was God-given. In addition, she decided that other kinds of knowledge are beyond human understanding, but might be special knowledge, available to God, such as the mystery of "like . . . um . . . how we get alive." (Hay & Nye, 1998, pp. 103–104).

Katie's story is not unique; people who have no formal religious training have a concept for God, a phenomenon repeated in other research, as far back as William James's (1960/1890) exploration of the varieties of religious experience. And current spirituality research asserts that God concepts form in every human being (even when parents are non-believers—see Tamminen, Vianello, Jaspard, and Ratcliff, 1988). They form in an intermediate 'space' between infant and the outside world. In this location, between inner and outer reality, "illusions" form and meaning is created. This third place, which is neither the self nor the world but is influenced by both, is the genesis of the spiritual aspect of human life. The spiritual is an intermediate space between the personal and the material. It is a mid-point reality between subjective and objective realities. Objects form here as a child experiences the self and the world. These objects or concepts focus a child's ongoing perceptions of everything. The intermediate space is an area of experiencing, "to which inner reality and external life both contribute," and which, in turn, acts back on a child's perception and understanding of outer and inner reality. It is an unchallenged space that an individual creates in the "perpetual human task of keeping inner and outer reality separate yet interrelated" (Winnicott, 1971, p. 2). The spiritual aspect of human beings integrates experience and forms embodied concepts to live by. These embodied, emotionally laden concepts can shift their shape with changes in experience. Keeping up with new experience is a spiritual task. Sanity depends upon the activity of interrelating yet separating material and personal realities implied in this place of illusory experiencing.

In this intermediate space, organizing occurs. These illusions are not false but rather idiosyncratic and useful as organizing principles for ordinary living. Throughout life, children (and adults) test the world and self on the basis of concepts formed during early years of life. The objects, representations, or concepts that flourish in the intermediate space between self and world are called "transitional phenomena" (Winnicott, 1971, p. 4) or transitional objects of perception. These objects—images, feelings, ideas—are the stuff of thinking; they are experience-rich and assumption-laden. God takes the form of a transitional phenomenon or transitional object in this sense.

Transitional objects, formed in the margins between inner personal experience and outer material reality, explicate the theological insight that people are made in God's image. Human experience inevitably forms a concept of God. It was a concept Cain had for God that prevented their intimacy, just as his brother's concept allowed Abel unhindered access to the Almighty. It is striking that God met Cain in his resentment and tried to open up his experience to hope. Cain did not accept the offer; instead, he killed Abel. Cain's pattern is often repeated. It is as if Cain could choose to reconsider his idea of God, or sin, but did not seem to hear what God was offering. He sinned (Gen 4:1–16). This is sin's educational role-although its lessons come at a high human cost. Spiritual maturity is not accomplished solely by acts of the will, rather, it is accomplished through experiencing. It is by seeing and hearing God's own way of Being that people test their assumptions about God, which tend to be inadequate, confused, and incomplete. Spiritual maturity is a by-product of seeing God in new ways, as Job (in contrast to Cain) testified at the end of his suffering and as a result of it (Job 42:1–6).

The psychological idea of 'experiencing' is similar to the educational concept of experiencing described by Hegel and used later by John Dewey. In particular, Dewey described experiencing in *Art as Experience* (1980). Dewey was concerned to describe what artwork accomplishes in the intermediate space between person and actual object. 'Knowing' art, not its material alone, is aesthetic experience. In this intermediate space, idea and emotion are stirred: aspects of art are felt and known. Dewey distinguished the spiritual and the ideal from the material (Dewey, 1980, p. 6). The quality of material objects is felt and known spiritually in the margins between inner and outer reality. Experiencing takes place in the relationship between a person and her or his environment.

Dewey explored the relationship people have with their environments using aesthetic experience as a model, and noted the following elements in the interrelationships and separations that are necessary for mature thought to emerge and for learning to be transformational. In the relationship to the environment, he pointed out what he called a rhythm of loss and recovery that is essential to enjoying harmony with life. People become conscious of themselves, their concepts and the world, through the rhythm of loss and recovery. Emotion is the conscious sign of a break, actual or impending, in the union with the world and perceptions of it. The discord caused by emotion is an occasion that induces reflection. A desire to make peace with the world converts mere emotion (such as fear) into interest in objects that might restore harmony between the understanding of the world and the self (Dewey, 1980, pp. 13ff).

For example, a child who is terrified of spiders may choose to do a class project on them. Somewhere in the depth of curiosity, fear dissolves. Inner harmony between the ways one thinks the world is, and how it seemed to be moments before, returns when the self, the concepts and the knowledge of outer reality are again in concert. Losing and recovering the world leads to transformational growth: concepts in the margins between the material world and a child's personal world shift their shape. It is this same process of loss and recovery that Job's life demonstrated as he strove to understand God. The book of Job is a narrative that shows how God concepts shift and change in the light of God's actual Being, in concert with human experience. By working out emotions inherent in loss and recovery, a child is organizing experience into a meaningful whole, or mental mythology, one that seems to be in place by the time a child is nine years old. By the time children are nine or ten, they begin to use the cues they receive from the outside world "from that point forward to confirm or challenge an existing perspective" or worldview that is firmly formed (Barna, 2003, p. 58).

"Experiencing" God

Rizzuto explains how the process of loss and recovery is necessary for the growth and maturing of God concepts. She identified four primary God concepts through her research. She studied patients as well as hospital personnel to arrive at her analysis, since she wanted to "extract from psychopathology what might be of benefit to normal psychology," as Freud also intended to do (Rizzuto, 1979, p. 181). The four God concepts are demonstrated by people:

- Who have a God whose existence they do not doubt

- Wondering whether or not to believe in a God they are not sure exists

- Amazed, angered, or quietly surprised to see others deeply invested in a God who does not interest them

- Who struggle with a demanding, harsh God they would like to get rid of if they were not convinced of his existence and power (Rizzuto, 1979, p. 91).

Religious educators are wise if they treat children differently depending on the God concept that is already formed in a child's mind, based on object relations experience.

For example, in the space between mother and child, generalized representations form from a host of experiences common to infancy. In this space children play with reality, inner and outer, and form object relations, transitional objects that constitute the mental mythology each human being lives by. The child's sense of self develops in relationship to the mother's sense of the child. If the child perceives itself as wonderful and worthy in its mother's (or other primary caretaker's) eyes, life is good enough for the child to flourish because the child can relax. But if the image formed is of a bad child, if the child has not been able to fulfill the conditions that inhere in the narrative parents told themselves about the child before its birth, there is likely to be a conflict of being. The child senses that what is wrong is not what the child *does* but what he or she *is*. The child cannot please parents or his or her God except by becoming a different sort of person. The child can never relax (Rizzuto, 1979, p. 188).

The most powerful implication of Rizzuto's research for religious education is that all four God concepts that she identified cause people difficulty in the absence of transformational learning. Her central thesis is that "God as a transitional representation needs to be recreated in each developmental crisis if it is to be found relevant for lasting belief" (Rizzuto 1979, p. 208). Further, she noted that God concepts are linked to self-concepts; there is a dynamic, sometimes dangerous link between self-concepts and God concepts. As a consequence, "the task of teaching religion to children demands exquisite attention to the experience of the child as well as to what [teachers present to children]" (Rizzuto, 1979, p. 211). The child's creation of the God concept is a private process that takes place in silent exchanges between parents and the child, exchanges that are not based on words, *per se*. Later on, educators, pastors and authority figures will contribute to the shape of that God concept. But it is not simply what these people say but what they are and do that is used as children reshape their understanding of God according to their personal needs (Rizzuto, 1979, p. 210).

That is, the "child's and the adult's sense of self is affected by the representational traits of the individual's private God" so that "consciously, preconsciously, or unconsciously, God, our own creation, like a piece of art, a painting, [or] a melody" will, in "reflecting what we have done, affect our sense of ourselves" (Rizzuto, 1979, p. 179). Once created, "our God, dormant or active, remains a potentially available representation for the continuous process of psychic integration" and can be used for religious purposes because God concepts are "beyond magic" in the sense that all transitional objects are never under magical control. Similarly, internal objects are under manipulative control, while outside objects are not, one's parents, for example (Rizzuto, 1979, p. 180). For this reason, if children have negative or frightening concepts, interventions from religious educators that take no account of what is already in play in the child's mental mythology, can produce an effect that is more than a child is able to tolerate (Rizzuto, 1979, p. 199).

As children age, there is an interrelationship between God concepts and a sense of self, such that crises in experience influence both God concepts and self-concepts. Throughout the formation of God concepts, the attachment to other people, particularly mothers and fathers is central to healthy spiritual development.

Conceiving God in the Need for Others

Developmental studies show that it is necessary for an infant to be in consistent, loving relationship with a caregiver that consistently meets physical, emotional and psychological needs. This is support on which the infant's survival depends. Studies of attachment and loss highlight this relationship. John Bowlby, a child and family psychiatrist in London, developed the concept of attachment, in which he asserts that attachment of an infant to a parent is necessary for survival; removal of parental support has dramatic negative effects upon the child. Emotional closeness and availability establish the parent as a secure base for the child. Secure attachment to parents persuades the child that the parent will be helpful in the future. Under more rather than less optimal conditions, the child is able to anticipate a loving response to distress and develops a set of expectations for the future based on hope. By contrast, children who experience an absence of help or whose life is characterized by loss act out in anger (Bowlby, 1988, pp. 1–38). If deprived of holistic support and human interaction, children grow inactive, depressed and become uninterested in their environment (Galatzer-Levy & Cohler, 1993, pp. 36–37).

While environment is significant in the attachment processes of infancy and childhood, it would be mistaken to think of children as passive recipients. Infants experience the world in subjective ways that are largely shaped by biology (e.g., temperament) but they are also co-creators of what they experience. Attachment is reciprocal. Infants take part in communicating with caretakers and are able from birth to elicit responses to their needs: "Environment profoundly influences development, but the environment that is so influential is largely determined by how the infant takes in the surroundings, a process that in turn is profoundly influenced by biological endowment" (Galatzer-Levy & Cohler, 1993, pp. 44–45).

The environment is initially apprehended for the child through the process of mirroring, based on gaze behavior, usually between mother and infant. While Freud invented object relations theory, he ignored the foundational role that women usually play in helping construct a child's concept of God. This bedrock role is best described as mirroring, in which a mother gazes at her baby, the look on her face is related to what she sees in her baby. A baby begins to see itself as it is seen. An infant's need is to be seen as worthy, wonderful and attractive. If infants do not receive the blessing of a mother's gaze, the effects of the loss are felt deeply. But, as noted, even a tiny baby is not helpless.

Gaze behavior between a mother and child is called "affect attunement." The mother and the baby work out their relationship without using words. They use a form of communication that relies on making sounds and gestures, but especially relies on the eyes. Even little infants can initiate, sustain and terminate an encounter by using their eyes alone. Babies can look at their mother's face, turn their heads and look at an object in the room, so that they get their mother's attention focused on that object with them. Then, their eyes change until their mother realizes the episode has come to an end. The mirroring functions in infancy are achieved through emotional interchanges in which

> Babies live in a world where the emotional comprehension of their states and the provision of needed emotional supports are essential to their well-being and development. . . . By emotionally understanding and supporting the baby, essential others create an environment in which the baby can grow in her interest in the world and in herself. A central competence of babies and parents is the ability to create this experience, which centers on a unified emotional, sensory, and motor way of being in the world. If things go well, the baby comes though with a sense of vitality and effectiveness-a feeling that the world is sensible and manageable-and with an enthusiasm for experience. (Galatzer-Levy & Cohler, 1993, p. 63)

The relation between mother and child is a rich experience of affect attunement (Stern, 1985). One of its aspects, gaze behavior, helps an infant form the most basic beliefs they hold about themselves and the world, and also helps form mental representations for God. Mirroring is the first step. In gaze behavior, when mother and infant interact, if the mother's face is unresponsive, the mirror (her face) is a thing to be looked at and not into. To create a healthy sense of God's identity, and a positive self-concept, the infant's gaze must pass through the mirror (a mother's face) to where the real mother dwells (Rizzuto, 1979, p. 187). The child needs to sense there is something more than a face to look at: behind the face is a person who has an interior (a soul). This complex experience also grounds children's belief in their own personal interior. A foundational result of a positive experience with affect attunement is the formation of hope and trust in a child's heart. It is through attachment to another person that self-concepts (Kohut, 1984, pp. 172–210) and God concepts develop.

Testing Attachment Theory and a Child's God Concept

Simone de Roos and her colleagues conducted research on attachment theory to explore the effects of the quality of parent/teacher interactions on young children as well as the effects of religious socialization on children's religiosity. For both questions, they wanted to concentrate on one aspect of religiosity, the formation of God concepts. While past work on the relationship between attachment theory and God concept formation has relied on adult and adolescent samples, they chose to study kindergarteners for several reasons:

- God concepts are formed early in life and exert great influence on later religious inclinations (Kirkpatrick, 1999).

- Young children spend a lot of time with parents and teachers, and, therefore, early attachment is proposed to have stronger influence on God concepts of young children than on those of adolescents and adults.

- Entering kindergarten is a major transition and creates a potential secondary attachment.

These researchers focused on the Western Christian tradition, and examined two attachment hypotheses in the prediction of individual differences in young children's God concepts. In particular, they were interested in studying the formation of God concepts that were centered on God as a loving, comforting, caring, powerful presence, versus God as a punishing presence.

They examined two hypotheses. First, the correspondence hypothesis suggests that people's view of God will parallel their images of their early parent-child relationships (Kirkpatrick, 1999). They proposed that children with a less optimal care-giver relationship will develop a more negative, stern, punishing, less positive concept of God and that children with an optimal experience with parents will develop a loving, comforting concept of God. The second hypothesis, the revised correspondence hypothesis, incorporates parental religiosity and socialization in the prediction of God concepts (Granqvist, 1998). The second hypothesis supposes that secure childhood attachment influences God concepts through the socialization process itself. The God concepts of securely attached children should correspond to their attachment figure's God concepts, rather than to the security of their relationship. That is, securely attached children are more likely to be successfully socialized into and subsequently adopt parts of the attachment figure's system of religious behaviors and beliefs than insecurely attached children (Granqvist & Hagekull, 1999). Two aspects of religious socialization were studied: caregivers' God concepts and their goals for religious education.

In a previous study, de Roos and her colleagues tested the correspondence theory among kindergarteners and examined the effects of the mother-child attachment relationship as well as the quality of the teacher-child relationship on children's concepts of self, others, and God (de Roos, Miedema, & Iedema, 2001). Their results supported the correspondence hypothesis in the case of the teacher-child relationship. A more optimal teacher-child relationship was connected to a more loving concept of God in the kindergarteners. Furthermore, this connection was mediated by the child's self-concept. That is, young children with a close, open, and harmonious relationship with their teacher showed positive emotions, high involvement in groups and had high self-esteem, which was associated with a loving, caring God concept. This finding confirms the idea that through positive interactions with significant others positive self-concepts and God concepts develop (Rizzuto, 1979). This result of de Roos and colleagues may also be interpreted in terms of the revised correspondence hypothesis (cf. Granqvist, 1998). The children came mainly from non-believing families; the mothers of these children were agnostic. In contrast, the majority of teachers were religious. A correspondence between a more optimal teacher-child relationship and children's God-concepts (such as a loving God) was found. In a more optimal caregiver-child relationship, children were more inclined to adopt their care-givers' religious beliefs and behaviors than in a less optimal caregiver-child relationship (e.g., less open, more conflict-ridden).

In other research, de Roos's team worked with parents that were mainly non-church affiliated, and open, liberal Christian parents. In this study they found an indication that the mother-child relationship may be important for children's concepts of God, since mother's concepts influenced children's views of God as a loving friend or father/parent; the more mothers perceived God as a friend, the more their kindergarteners viewed God as a father or loving friend (De Roos, Iedema, & Miedema, 2001). In the same research, teachers' God concepts were found to have effects on young children's answers to open-ended questions about God. The more teachers—who were predominantly open and Christian—experienced God as a father or friend and the more they associated God with positive feelings, the more their pupils referred to biblical words and stories in their descriptions of God. Among a more orthodox Christian sample, it was shown that mothers who have a loving idea of God have preschoolers who view God as powerful, loving and caring (De Roos, Iedema & Miedema, 2003; Hertel & Donahue, 1995).

Several conclusions can be drawn from the team's research. The first hypothesis proposed that the content of people's God concept will parallel early parent-child relationships. If they had optimal child-parent relationships, children would be more likely to have a positive view of God; under less than optimal conditions, they tend to have a view of God as harsh and unloving. The first hypothesis hoped to show a correspondence between early parental experience and the content of a child's God concept. The team found no support for the first hypothesis. Religious socialization must be taken into account to explain children's God concepts, because the situation is more complex than the first hypothesis allows.

In contrast, the revised correspondence hypothesis was partially confirmed. Children can cognitively learn about a powerful and comforting, helpful God from their parents and teachers, *even in an environment in which all relationships with these significant others are experienced as negative.* However, in such a surrounding they do not emotionally acquire a concept of an intimate, personal bond with God. Children that have negative relationships with all their caregivers are not reinforced to view God as someone that loves them, will make them happy, is nice and is a friend. When children experience a lot of conflict and feel little openness and warmth in all relationships with their caregivers, God is not perceived as a close, personal, and warm entity. A remarkable finding in the study is that faulty relationships with mother, father, or teacher can be compensated for by other relationships, thus fostering an intimate relationship with God among young children. That is, even when a child has negative relationships with both parents, a teacher can positively influence the development of a perception of God as a loving, kind friend.

The third conclusion suggests that religious socialization is an important contributor to children's God concepts. The more mothers, fathers, and teachers stressed the value of traditional goals for religious education, the more their kindergarteners perceive God as a powerful, helping, and loving entity. The traditional goals for religious education tend to include objectives such as:

- to become good Christians
- to get converted
- to be in awe of God
- to get to know stories from the Bible
- to learn to pray.

Caregivers' God concepts affected children's God concepts as part of the process of reaching these goals. That is, caregivers' ideas of God as loving, comforting, powerful, and strict as well as punishing, led them to pursue traditional goals for religious education which in turn influenced the children's view of God as powerful, helping, and loving.

Children referred more often to God as a loving than as a punishing presence and their punishing God image could not be predicted by any variable. These results suggest that, for children at the present time, a loving God concept is more salient than a punishing concept, and the origin of the negative God image is uncertain.

The traditional goals for religious education carried out in an environment of other people's positive view of God influences a child's concept of God. Regardless of its content, every child develops a mental mythology, a world view that shapes the child's interpretation of "the world as a whole" (James, 1960, p. 104). If this personal world view encounters the Christian world view, broadly conceived and positively conveyed, the child's own perspective can expand, grow and provide the child with the necessary means to go on living in a world that generally gets more complex as the child grows older. This educational process requires more than getting the child to make "a decision for Jesus," although volition is important to the Christian tradition; the child needs to sense differences between personal concepts for God and formal understandings. The assumption here is that healthy dialogue between personal and formal world views liberates children from misconceptions that are endemic to childhood, without disdaining or dismissing the value and insight that inhere in their personal constructions.

Living Narratively

The research conducted by de Roos focused on Western Christianity, as already noted. The words of Jesus of Nazareth might summarize the position of this chapter thus far. With regard to a link between adults as meaningful 'objects' in a child's life, Jesus gave the following warning: "But if any of you causes one of these little ones who believe in me to sin, it would be better for you to have a large millstone hung around your neck and to be drowned in the depths of the sea. Woe to the world because of the things that cause people to sin! Such things must come, but woe to the person through whom they come!" (Matt 18:6–7, New International Version) In light of this research, Jesus' warning may imply the following:

- Parents and teachers play important roles in the formation of children's God concepts.

- God concepts continue to influence people over the course of their lives.

- God concepts can encourage or hinder attachment to a loving God.

- Encounters with God concepts create an effective learning environment.

- There is a direct relationship between God concepts and self-concepts.

- Self-esteem is affected by the God concepts people hold.

- Educators must take children's experience seriously if they wish them well.

Thus there is a need to re-envision religious education to take advantage of these insights. A better understanding of the processes of attachment can help caregivers and teachers improve children's connection to God through experiences that help children reflect on their own God concepts in an environment that is conducive to perceiving God as loving, kind and willing to be in personal relationship with them. Having a concept of God is different from having a personal relationship with God. A personal relationship sustains a human being through the inevitable crises of ordinary living.

God concepts are personal constructions that form independently of formal religious instruction. Children have a reality that persists in shaping perceptions of the world, other people and the self. As a result, a God concept has power to act as an idol situated in the inner shrine of a human heart as a stronghold unmoved by scripture or formal understandings of God. As part of earlier Christian training, it was common to accuse children of placing themselves on the heart's throne. Some readers may remember the image of an inner throne on which stubborn, selfish children placed themselves, instead of choosing to do the right thing, which is to place God on "the heart's throne." That approach to the child's religiosity neglects how children construct God concepts in the first place. Perhaps primary teachers can be forgiven for their lack of insight; most have not attempted to apply object relations theory to Sunday School.

Often the will is the central focus for Christian education. This presumes that the occupant "on the heart's throne" is there by independent, conscious, intentional choice and can be removed by another independent, conscious, intentional choice. A second assumption takes it for granted that God *might not be on the throne,* hence the child has to put God in God's place. A third assumption presupposes a uniform concept of God, one that is unproblematic. Parents and teachers may assume that the God concepts they hold are the same as the child's. If their God concept causes a teacher no trouble, it is unlikely to occur to them that a God concept could cause trouble for a child. Are these accurate assumptions to make about children's experience?

It is important to note, in contrast to focusing solely on the child's will, that the greatest concern for formal religious education is to help children discern the concept of God that reigns in their hearts. Inadequate, hurtful, inaccurate concepts of God are a more serious threat to spiritual maturity than is self-centeredness, though perhaps the two obstacles are related. A concept of God is inadequate or hurtful if it is incapable of sustaining a healthy response to life because it cannot address a child's actual experience and the theological questions children begin to ask. Children need to have a larger view of God than their existing concept can assimilate, if God is to remain an attractive attachment. Children must come to understand that religion is a serious business (Pratt, 1956, p. 102) and that God is more than they can easily imagine.

As an example, Rizzuto showed that even an apparently positive concept (e.g., God is good, kind, loving) may interfere with the capacity to mature in faith. For example, she analyzed the experience of those people who "domesticate" God. To some, God is a homey, safe divinity of simple human characteristics and lacking the powerful dimension of transcendence (Rizzuto, 1979, pp. 105–107). The transcendent God, the God understood to be larger than existing concepts, is revealed through the normal crises of doubt and disbelief that accompany adolescence, and that inevitably include self-examination, self-searching and self-revision. To get too comfortable with God is to be ignorant of God. The self-examination implied in spiritual crises draws a believer toward humility and grace, and away from ignorance and arrogance. God must become a problem during adolescence before God is a solution to the spiritual quest-and its destination in adulthood.

The significance of this point is central. It is not by casting one's self off the "heart's throne" that maturity begins. Rather, obtaining a fresh and enlivened vision of God's own Self enables people to grow up in the faith. God can be perceived through the kindness of others. Until concepts of God are revised in light of scripture, communal knowledge, self-examination, and experiencing God "face to face," God concepts are merely products of imagination. The accuracy of God concepts must be addressed to mature in the faith. What does this mean?

As one thinks about others, there is an internal conversation. While it seems real and to that extent satisfying, it is imaginary. One invents the self and the other in that conversation with self about another person-motives, words, admissions and all. The only way one can know another person is to have a real conversation in which they can speak for themselves. One needs the other to know the other; all else is imagination.

This example illustrates what must be accomplished to facilitate the growth in God concept. The narrative told to the self about God must be explored, followed by a decision regarding whether this is the story that is desired. Rizzuto explains the dialogical nature of the human mind by describing the entrance of a child into a social world that has already mythologized a child's meaning in advance of his or her birth (Rizzuto, 1979, p. 183). The child enters a narrative that is already there and in the first few years of life constructs a God concept that must be reckoned with throughout life. Parents also have preconceived ideas about their infants, shaped by a lifetime of experiences, including their own childhoods. These ideas hang together in a narrative that makes sense to the parent. Parents who are flexible and attentive to their youngsters respond to their actual baby rather than their preconceived fantasies about them. Part of "good enough" parenting is the willingness to hear one's own narrative about life and also listen to the child's perspective. In this process of telling and retelling our stories, God must be allowed to speak for Himself. But first there needs to be a sense of the role imagination plays in forming the thought-life, and narratives about God.

Thinking is powerful. Letting God speak and be heard allows the young to come to God fully and freely. But who is this God who is speaking? What is God's tone of voice? What is the look on God's face when a child inclines herself towards God? As the parable of the ten talents, five talents, and one talent reveals, it is the concept of God that provides courage to put personal gifts to use, just as it is a concept of God that frightens people into burying them. In Matthew, Jesus encourages individuals to weave together our human value with God's divine value. Jesus said: "Are not two sparrows sold for a penny? Yet not one of them will fall to the ground outside your Father's care. And even the very hairs of your head are all numbered. So don't be afraid; you are worth more than many sparrows" (Matt 10:29–31). He also said: "But store up for yourselves treasures in heaven, where moth and rust do not destroy, and where thieves do not break in and steal. For where your treasure is, there your heart will be also" (Matt 6:20–21).

The heart can be full of tension when the subject of God is raised, especially for abused children but also for those whose lives have been relatively peaceful. Personal God concepts must grow up to engage the God who lives above mere human concepts. The internal and personal concept people hold of God is a post-modern equivalent of idolatry that, unless transformed, limits learning. Until one understands how these concepts form, it is difficult to make progress in establishing a healthy view of God. Since concepts of God made from experience are personal and private, and if formal understanding is to be acquired, wise teachers take account of personal, private concepts that constitute the bedrock of individual belief. That is, Christian educators must find ways to connect the God of scripture to the child's personal, private God. Without these connections, learning does not produce the transformations that personal, private concepts must undergo if they are to sustain people through the inevitable crises of ordinary life and lead them toward Christian maturity.

Given the theoretical framework and the practical empirical application of attachment theories, three final questions remain:

- How does a God concept form in a child's heart? Is it by independent, conscious, intentional choice?

- Is there a concept for God in every child's heart?

- How do parent/teacher concepts influence a child's God concept?

Recall that God concepts are personal rather than accurate. They are made from primary experience. As a result, an education to help children chart their way toward happy self-concepts and healthy God concepts must allow them to name their current concepts and observe what scripture reveals about God through the person and work of Christ. The child is asked to compare what is held in the heart—the center of human willing, thinking, feeling and acting—with what is revealed in scripture, without ridicule, and through the help always available from the Holy Spirit. Self-knowledge and the experience of God are educational outcomes of this form of theological reflection. Allowing Jesus more room to flourish in the heart is the way forward to growing up in God's grace.

The point of growing up authentically is to be in conversation with socially generated stories each person entered at birth and to tell a life long narrative of what one wants to and will be. The working out of identity is a conversation. Children and adults need not reject other people and God in order to be authentic selves, contrary to Sigmund Freud. To be in conversation is not to capitulate. Nor is authenticity expressed by silencing other voices in a human landscape that is one's relational homeland until only one's own voice is heard asserting itself, with its hollow echo reverberating in spaces left empty by the absence of loved ones—again as Freud did in his own life (Rizzuto 1998). One engages in conversation because other people are needed to know who one is—conversations that are emotionally loaded and to that extent, rich with meaning. Conversing with God in community with others helps people know God. Knowing the self as beloved by God provides an open door to authentic human potential that does not forget its need for other people and their esteem and does not disdain the limitations God set with what it means to be human.

Conclusion

Children need to be with other people who perceive God as friend in order to see God positively and imagine that a personal relationship with God is a possibility for them. Informal, relational religious education can lead to a positive, conscious choice about God and God's value in their lives, a decision and commitment based on healthy dialogues with others.

Learning about God is dialogical. The young need to sense how they conceive God at a given time in their lives and dialogue with their own perception by comparing it with the tradition and texts of faith. They need time and opportunities to express in a concrete way what they currently think about God. They need to have their questions answered. They need to know others intimately who think of God as friend and who are hopeful about the future.

References

Barna, G. (2003). *Transforming children into spiritual champions.* Ventura, CA: Regal.

Baumeister, R. F. (1986). *Identity.* New York: Oxford University Press.

Baumeister, R. F. (1991). *Escaping the self.* New York: Basic Books.

Baumeister, R. F. (1994). Self-esteem. In V. S. Ramachandran (Ed.), *Encyclopedia of human behavior* (Vol. 4, pp. 83–87). San Diego: University of California, San Diego, Academic Press.

Baumeister, R. F. (1997). *Evil: Inside human cruelty and violence.* New York: Freeman.

Baumeister, R. F. (Ed.). (1999). *The self in social psychology.* Philadelphia: Psychology Press.

Bowlby, J. (1988). *A secure base: Parent-child Attachment and healthy human development.* New York: Basic Books.

Derber, C. (2000). *The pursuit of attention.* New York: Oxford University Press.

De Roos, S. A., Iedema, J., & Miedema, S. (2001). Young children's descriptions of God: Influences of parents' and teachers' God concepts and religious denominations of schools. *Journal of Beliefs and Values, 22,* 19–30.

De Roos, S. A. (2003). Effects of mothers' and schools' religious denomination on preschool children's God concepts. *Journal of Beliefs and Values, 24*, 165–181.

De Roos, S. A., Miedema, S., & Iedema, J. (2001). Attachment, working models of self and others, and God concept in kindergarten. *Journal for the Scientific Study of Religion, 40*, 607–618.

Dewey, J. (1980). *Art as experience.* New York: Perigee.

Erikson, E. (1950). *Childhood and society.* New York: Norton.

Galatzer-Levy, R. M., & Cohler, B. J. (1993). *The essential other: A developmental psychology of the self.* New York: Basic Books.

Granqvist, P. (1998). Religiousness and perceived childhood attachment: On the question of compensation or correspondence. *Journal for the Scientific Study of Religion, 37*, 350–367.

Granqvist, P. & Hagekull, B. (1999). Religiousness and perceived childhood attachment: Profiling socialized correspondence and emotional compensation. *Journal for the Scientific Study of Religion, 38*, 254–273.

Hay, D & Nye, R. (1998). *The spirit of the child.* London: Fount.

Hertel, B. R. & Donahue, M. J. (1995). Parental influence on God images among children: Testing Durkheim's metaphoric parallelism. *Journal for the Scientific Study of Religion, 34*, 186–199.

James, W. (1960). *The varieties of religious experience.* London: Fontana. (Orig. pub., 1890).

Klein, J. (1987). *Our need for others and its roots in infancy.* London: Tavistock.

Kohut, H. (1984). *How does analysis cure?* Chicago: University of Chicago Press.

Kirkpatrick, L. A. (1999). Attachment and religious representations and behavior. In J. Cassidy and P. R. Shaver (Eds.), *Handbook of attachment: Theory, research, and clinical applications* (pp. 803–822). New York: Guilford.

Pratt, J. B. (1956). *The religious consciousness* New York: MacMillan.

Rizzuto, A.-M. (1979). *The birth of the living God.* Chicago: University of Chicago Press.

Rizzuto, A.-M. (1998). *Why did Freud reject God?* New Haven: Yale University Press.

Stern, D. (1985). *The interpersonal world of the infant.* New York: Basic Books.

Tamminen, K., Viannelo, R., Jaspard, J-M., & Ratcliff, D. (1988). The religious concepts of preschoolers. In D. Ratcliff (Ed.), *Handbook of preschool religious education* (pp. 59–81). Birmingham, AL: Religious Education Press.

Taylor, C. (1991). *The ethics of authenticity.* Cambridge: Harvard University Press.

Winnicott, D. W. (1964). *The child, the family and the outside world.* Baltimore: Penguin.

Winnicott, D. W. (1971). *Playing and reality.* London: Tavistock.

Chapter Fourteen

From Doctrine to Practice:
The Influence of the Doctrine of Original Sin on Puritan Child Rearing

TIMOTHY A. SISEMORE[1]

Children are a delight! There is something special about children that draws adults to them. It is easy, then, to assume them to be innocent, free from the responsibilities of living a moral life, buds that, given adequate care, will blossom into beautiful adults. After all, 73% of Americans believe children are born good (Ellingsen 2003). Do children have a sin nature? As modern heirs of the Enlightenment, the Christian tradition may be betrayed by seeing children as only good and innocent. And if this is done, the stakes are higher than what might be presumed.

A vital uniqueness for Christian theology is seeing children *before* God, not just relative to adults. John Calvin (1559/1960) astutely framed his *Institutes* around the intertwining of the knowledge of God and the knowledge of self, for knowledge of self must lie in relation to the knowledge of God and be properly understood in that light lest the result be a less than adequate theological anthropology. Children stand before God tainted with original sin.

Ormerod (1992, p. 6) observes, "The doctrine of original sin does not stand in some splendid theological isolation in the Christian view of the world. Indeed it stands in profound relationship to theologies of grace and redemption. To reject the doctrine of original sin would be to call into question much of Christian faith and theology." How might this be? The way original sin is viewed will impact how human nature is understood, as well as how the nature of children is perceived. Are they naturally

---

1. Timothy A. Sisemore, Ph.D., is Professor and Dean of Clinical Activities at the Psychological Studies Institute in Chattanooga and Atlanta, specializing in counseling children and adolescents. He received his M.A. in theology and Ph.D. in clinical psychology from Fuller Theological Seminary. Dr. Sisemore is author of *I Bet . . . I Won't Fret*, a guide for children with anxiety disorders, *Of Such is the Kingdom: Nurturing Children in the Light of Scripture*, and numerous journal articles. He is also a husband and father.

innocent? Are they "blank slates" morally speaking, or naturally good until corrupted by adults, or do they have a bent toward sin? The answers that are assumed will drive one's understanding of the tasks of parenting, education, and ministry.

This crucial issue will be explored by tracing the line of thought on original sin from the Bible, through Augustine and Calvin, to the Puritans, focusing on Jonathan Edwards as the last bastion of this tradition in America. This view impacted their treatment of children in the family, church, and community in their day, and similarly have implications for ministry to children today.

The Biblical Foundations of the Doctrine of Original Sin

The primal couple was sinless and enjoyed perfect harmony with God and creation. This *is* the way it was meant to be—to borrow from the title of Plantinga's (1995) perceptive book. It would not last long. Genesis 3 details the sin of Adam and Eve, and the resulting fall of humankind. The story is well known, but one that has sparked many controversies, not the least of which is whether Adam and Eve were literally persons who breathed, walked, and ate forbidden fruit. Blocher (1997) suggests some approaches to reconciling the Genesis story with scientific theory, and he preserves the view that the first parents were literal persons. Undoubtedly this was the view of Augustine, Calvin, and the Puritans. To judge the story of the Fall as mere myth can easily lead to a cascade of changes in orthodox Christian doctrine that may jeopardize the faith (Ormerod, 1992).

Humankind's original parents were cursed for their sin, though the prospect for redemption is immediately held out by God, and this storyline comprises the rest of the Bible. Some contend that the teaching of Rom 5, which compares the sin of Adam and the obedience of Christ, stands alone in drawing from the story of the Fall to imply lessons about its impact on subsequent human nature. Yet, Blocher (1997) traces the echoes of the primal sin throughout Holy Writ.

Ezekiel evidently draws parallels from the Eden story to the fate of the king of Tyre (Ezek 28:12–19). The Psalms make allusions to the punishment of Adam (Ps 73:5; 82:7), and echoes of Eden can be seen in the wisdom teaching of Prov 8 (see particularly verse 36). Job 15:7–8 and 31:33 hark back to the Genesis story, the latter apparently reflecting upon Adam's efforts to hide his sin. Blocher (1997) comments that recent interpreters have seen Ecclesiastes as an orthodox exposition of the first three chapters of Genesis, with 12:7 and 3:20 being obvious references to the fate of Adam in Gen 3:19. Ecclesiastes 7:29 refers to the sequence of original righteousness and its corruption.

The New Testament provides many more references to the Fall of Adam and Eve. Jesus' reply to the Pharisees in Matt 19:4–8 (and parallels in the other Gospels) shows a creation-fall-redemption pattern; clearly something occurred after Genesis 1–2 to harden people's hearts. The Fall is easily inferred as the cause of bloodshed from Abel forward (Matt 23:35). Blocher cites evidence to support Luke's juxtaposition of Jesus' genealogy (3:23–38) with the temptation narrative (4:1–13) as reflecting an Adam-Christ typology, Jesus standing firm against temptation whereas Adam succumbed to it. John looks back to the serpent of Genesis as the devil (e.g. Rev 12:9; 20:2), and Jesus pointed back to this event in calling the devil a liar and murderer (John 8:44). These themes form a backdrop against which to consider Jesus' frequent comments regarding the blessings of children, as the importance he places on children lies apart from their spiritual purity (see Sisemore, 2000, pp. 38–54).

Paul refers to the deceit of the devil that led Eve astray (2 Cor 11:3; 1 Tim 2:14), leading to implications that care be taken that other people not suffer the same fate. In Rom 8:20 Paul notes creation's fall from its original state being not by its own choice. Paul may allude to Gen 1–3 in the hymn of Phil 2:6ff, but makes clear reference to the Fall in 1 Cor 15, with verses 21–22 on death coming through Adam leading directly to Rom 5:12, the classic text on original sin.

Indeed, Rom 5:12–19 is the text where original sin is most clearly developed by Paul. I have summarized the major points of the passage elsewhere (see Sisemore, 2000, p. 48–54), but here I will offer a few thoughts regarding its role in the development of the doctrine of original sin.

Moo (1996) stresses the importance of considering the context of this section in the flow of the entire book of Romans, particularly noting that the earlier distinctions of Jew and Greek disappear here as Paul's focus turns to the corporate nature of humanity. It does not, however, directly develop a doctrine of original sin. "The universal consequences of Adam's sin are the *assumption* of Paul's argument; the power of Christ's act to cancel those consequences is its *goal*" (p. 315, italics his). Paul takes for granted that all humans in some sense are participants in Adam's sin. It may nonetheless be seen that the idea of imputation of sin from Adam tainting all of his descendents establishes the principle of the imputation of the righteousness of Christ described in verse 18: sin that derives from Adam is cured by righteousness derived from Christ.

Moo observes that church fathers such as Calvin and Luther assume a corrupted human nature. Psalm 51:5 is an example of texts that support people being born in sin since Adam, being "by nature children of wrath" (Eph 2:3, New American Standard Bible). Moo rightly notes that "the folly, degradation, and hatred that are the chief characteristics of human history demand an explanation" (p. 329) which Paul provides in showing universal solidarity as persons in Adam, however this might be explained. Though the mechanism by which original sin is transmitted has been debated, for most of church history theologians argued for original sin. The implications of this for understanding children was not missed by the early believers.

Original Sin in the Theology of Saint Augustine

Smith (1994) traces the development of the theology of sin through church history, and observes the notion that Augustine would later term original sin (*peccatorum originate*, in *Ad Simplicianum*; see Rigby, 1999) developing through Irenaeus of Lyons who saw it as a function of human solidarity with Adam, and even Chrysostom who left place for it in his theology. Ambrose of Milan, Augustine's mentor, was pivotal in the development of the doctrine, seeing sin as a state rather than merely particular acts. Rigby (1999) finds Origen, Tertullian, and Cyprian to be sources also used by Augustine in developing his position.

Augustine was the one who codified the ideas before him into a systematic understanding of original sin. The great saint understood original sin as separate from the particular sins of the individual, referring to Adam's sin as "the one sin in and by which all have sinned since all were in that man" (412/1971a, p. 19).

Augustine followed five lines of argument through his works to support his position. The scriptures themselves were his primary argument. Second, "if Paul had been forced to prove his assertions on original sin, Augustine believed he would have turned his readers' attention, as Augustine did, to the extent of suffering in the world" (Brown, 1967, p. 394). Augustine also offered himself as proof, as seen in his memorable autobiography, *The Confessions* (397–400/ 1960). Augustine's fourth line of proof was tradition as he drew from his predecessors in the faith as noted above. Tradition tied into the practice of infant baptism, his final realm of evidence. He saw the baptism of infants as cleansing original sin, but not "the sin which they themselves committed in their life" (Augustine, 1971a; p. 23).

In sum, Augustine (1971b) saw children born in original sin, something which made them worthy of condemnation, though he argued unbaptized infants who died would receive the "mildest condemnation of all" (p. 23) and babies were cleansed by baptism. Yet, the sinful nature remained and would erupt into sin when the hands grew strong enough to do what the will intended. This meant that parents were vigorously admonished to baptize their children. Stortz (2000), accusing Augustine of overly moralizing and theologizing childhood, seems optimistic in stating that today "[w]e take the narcissism of an infant more lightly, hopeful that the child will grow out of it" (p. 100). The great saint would likely respond that such hope is theologically unfounded and based in a humanistic optimism that he, along with the biblical writers and the church fathers, did not share.

Yet, Augustine would see the sinful nature of children as requiring moderated discipline. While he was brutally honest about his own sinfulness, he also questioned the harsh discipline used on him in childhood and implies that sin can be managed without such excessive punishment. One of his earliest prayers was that he would not be beaten at school (397–400/1960, I.10), realizing that the adult issuing the beating was not necessarily driven by better motives than he. If Augustine had advised parents, he would have warned of the dangers of sin and admonished parents to train children in the faith, but he most likely would not have advised beatings (though he probably would have approved of milder punishments). Monica, his persistently loving mother, might serve as a model for modern parents in her prayers and admonitions for her wayward son.

Original Sin in the Theology of John Calvin

The Church largely upheld Augustine's views, but the doctrine was refined and changed. Cyril of Alexander (376–444) held that people do not sin in Adam, but because of his sin, everyone inherits his corrupt nature (Smith, 1994). Anselm of Canterbury (ca. 1033–1109) agreed that infants were born with original sin, but that this was not as guilt-producing as personal sin. Thomas Aquinas (ca. 1227-ca. 1274) made further refinements by emphasizing that original sin existed in the soul but not the flesh, with its impact including negative consequences to human reason. The esteemed reformer Luther was an *Augustinian* monk, and maintained the great African's basic posture on original sin.

But the line from Augustine to the Puritans runs through Calvin. Calvin held firmly to the doctrine of sin. Calvin (1559/1960) situated his section on original sin in the *Institutes of the Christian Religion* in the context of knowing the self accurately. What was given at creation is lost, with Adam's fall leaving humanity in a "miserable condition" (II.1.1). People blindly love themselves, yet "God would not have us forget our original nobility, which he had bestowed upon our Father Adam, and which ought truly to arouse in us a zeal for righteousness and goodness" (II.1.3).

People are defiled at birth, says Calvin. "The natural depravity which we bring from our mother's womb, though it brings not for immediately its own fruits, is yet sin before God, and deserves his vengeance: and this is that sin which they call original" (Calvin, 1984, p. 200). He affirms nonetheless that the guilt borne by infants is "not of another's fault, but of their own. For even though the fruits of their iniquity have not yet come for them, they have the seed enclosed within them" (1559/1960, II.i.8). Young children are sinners in the same sense as apple trees are apples trees before they bear fruit, inevitably bearing apples when they mature. This inherited depravity is "diffused into all parts of the soul" (II.i.8), affecting all aspects of life.

Yet original sin is less evident in little ones. Pitkin (2000, p.165) points out that in Calvin's thought, "although young children are corrupted by original sin, when compared to older children and adults, they demonstrate a lack of malice that their elders ought to emulate." Calvin held tenaciously the doctrine that children bear the image of God, and treated them with respect while not overlooking their sinfulness. Calvin insisted that children be viewed as gifts from God (Psalm 127), warning that "unless men regard their children as the gift of God, they are careless and reluctant in providing for their support, just as on the other hand this knowledge contributes in a very eminent degree to encourage them in bringing up their offspring" (Calvin, 1559/1960, I.xv.3). Parents are not to neglect caring for precious little ones, but are to nurture and discipline them with love and firmness, given their inclination to sin.

Calvin ministered as pastor to children and families in Geneva. His approach to regulation of the church, his writing two catechisms, and his promotion of school reforms demonstrated his care for youngsters (Pitkin 2000), in spite of being born in sin. His care extended doubtlessly to parents who grieved the deaths of their blessed children in a time of a 30–50% child mortality rate.

Here, then, is a good model of a theologian who does not miss the biblical teaching on original sin, yet who offered much positive care to the little ones of his flock. This is a point often missed by those who argue belief in original sin necessarily leads to harsh and even cruel treatment of children. It is the Puritans who have particularly been disparaged on this account.

Original Sin in Puritan Theology

Calvin's theology quickly spread throughout Europe and found a home among the English, particularly among the Puritans. These believers suffered considerable persecution for their views on doctrine and living the Christian life. Because of this, they invested considerable resources in training their children in the faith (Sisemore, 2000). Many eventually made their way to the New World seeking freedom to live out their faith.

Puritan thought on original sin is exemplified by Reynolds' (1593–1676) comments on the twofold nature of original sin. He commented, "the privation of that righteousness which ought to be in us; and the lust or habitual concupiscence, which carrieth nature unto inordinate motions" (1996, p. 248).

Though many Puritan authors addressed the issue, it is best described by the "last" of the Puritans, Jonathan Edwards (1703–1758), a "Puritan born out of time" (Packer, 1990, p. 310) or a "Modern Puritan" (Introducing: The Modern Puritan, 2003, p. 9). There is precedent for seeing Edwards as representing Puritan thought when it comes to children (Brekus 2001), and his depth of thought on the issue reflected in his last work (finished May 1757), *The Great Christian Doctrine of Original Sin Defended*.

Edwards's work on original sin has been hailed as "possibly the foremost book ever written on the subject" (Murray 1987, p. 429), citing Cunningham as seeing the book as one of the most valuable possessions of the church, but also quoting Lecky as believing it to be "one of the most revolting books that have ever proceeded from the pen of man" (p. xxiii). Several themes from Edwards' important work will be surveyed to illumine some of the emphases this Puritan presented in his discussion of original sin.

Edwards surveys numerous biblical references regarding the sinful nature of persons to conclude that wickedness is a "property of the species" (Edwards, 1974, p. 187). "Why should man be so continually spoken of as evil, carnal, perverse, deceitful, and desperately wicked, if all men are by nature as perfectly innocent, and free from any propensity to evil, as Adam was the first moment of his creation?" (p. 188). The biblical language reflects the daily realities of the inhumanities perpetrated by humans against humans.

Edwards also emphasizes Jesus' great commandment of loving God and neighbor as summing the duty of love. Yet, even when people do not directly offend God or neighbors by malicious acts, everyone falls short of the love that God requires. Thus, in Matthew 25 Jesus can rightly condemn those who did not reach out in compassion to their neighbors, and Paul is correct in faulting those who fail in love (1 Cor 13; 16:22). This requirement even goes to human motives. "If we love not God because he is what he is, but only because he is *profitable* to us, in truth we love him not at all" (p. 156, italics his). Edwards sees the selfish interests of the infant, as observed by Augustine, as reflecting original sin because of the failure to love.

Johnson (2002) argues the demise of the Puritan era can be attributed in large part to the belief in original sin. But Edwards did not agree as he saw in the nature of original sin a tendency for faith to fade in generations subsequent to a work of God, and indeed saw this as a *proof* of the doctrine, not a disproof. He cites the biblical examples such as the deterioration of the human condition within 50 years of Noah's death, despite the flood (p. 170). Indeed, he even mentions the decline of New England in the same context. Despite the promises to children of believers, original sin makes us aware that revivals may not last.

Edwards also draws attention to the biblical use of terms like "flesh" and the need to be "reborn" as showing that it is not just that acts need to stop, but character needs to change. He also notes the universality of death as a consequence of the guilt of original sin, even the death of children. Edwards states, "We may well argue from these things, that infants are not sinless, but are by nature children of wrath, seeing this terrible evil comes so heavily on mankind at this early period" (p. 175).

The Doctrine of Original Sin in Puritan Practice

Original sin is a logical predecessor of the great doctrines of grace that the Puritans held so dearly. Edwards (Brekus, 2001) saw children as both sinners and saints, tainted with original sin, yet capable of genuine faith. Thus, a balance must be maintained: Children are gifts and blessings with hope for salvation, yet born in sin and inclined toward evil. How, then, does such doctrine work out in practice?

Parenting becomes a vital task. They were to bear in mind, as Baxter (1996, p. 430) admonished, "that your children's original sin and misery is by you." Original sin was thus the theological foundation for the Puritan emphasis on child training (Ryken, 1986), though the importance of parenting also derived from the covenant theology most Puritans held, wherein children were received into the community of faith as members of the covenant of grace through believing parents. It meant "children belong to God and are entrusted to parents as a stewardship" (Ryken, p. 78). How does this important task work out in practice? Oliver Heywood (1629–1702) posits four major duties of parents to their children (Heywood, 1999; orig. 1660):

Provision

Parents were to care for the physical needs of their youngsters with care and responsibility. Idle or neglectful parents could be prosecuted in Puritan New England (Morgan, 1966). Laziness was not tolerated in children, so it clearly was not an option for parents.

Correction

Puritan belief in original sin meant that parents anticipated wrongdoing in their children and that they were obligated to correct it. There is little doubt that some took advantage of this responsibility and were excessive, although exaggerated critiques that are oblivious to nuance, such as those of Greven (1990) and Johnson (2002), merely perpetuate false stereotypes of Puritan parenting and mistakenly conclude that all original sin meant was an excuse to unleash the rod upon their children without mercy. Brekus (2001), for example, observes that Greven takes merely "fragmentary evidence" of abusive discipline by Edwards on his children to perpetuate false stereotypes. Puritan discipline included restraining sinful impulses, but would embrace a "gentle rod" and "gentle discipline" according to the child's nature (Ryken, 1986), and was not necessarily harsh (Packer 1990). Brekus concludes this could create an atmosphere of fear for children, but it was a fear to teach biblical fear the fear of God. Ideally this correction was to be done in an atmosphere of love. The Puritan "counselor" Baxter advised parents that children should be governed "as children, making them perceive that you dearly love them, and that all your commands, restraints, and corrections are for their good and not merely because you will have it so" (Baxter, 1996, p. 450).

Instruction

Puritans were very aggressive in educating their children, both in matters of faith and in general. The children learned early of their sinful state. "Original sin was no fairy story with which to frighten little children; it was an unpleasant but inescapable fact, and the sooner children became acquainted with it, the better" (Morgan, 1966, p. 93).

Part of instruction was example, and parents "recognized the importance of example as well as instruction" (Braund, 2000, p. 161). Catechizing was practiced, with the goal of learning the meanings of basic doctrines and not just facts. Children were taught the Bible and encouraged to study it. A major educational method was family worship. Edwards (Brekus, 2001) demonstrated the role of the pastor in teaching the children of the flock as some of his sermons were specifically targeted for children, balancing fear of God with the joyful prospects of heaven. Instruction was not just religious, but was intended to prepare children to serve the family and the community, and in the process form habits that gave little place to the promptings of original sin.

Prayer

Parents would be remiss in their duties to their children if they failed to pray faithfully for them. Heywood (1999, p. 493) observes, "This is a natural duty, and a general relief to the aching hearts of pious parents, not only for obtaining children, as in the case of Hannah, but for grace in children, when they go astray." The Puritan's life was a godward life, and it was to God that parents would appeal for grace in the lives of their children. Clearly the doctrine of original sin shaped the parenting of the Puritans, yet what does this imply to Christians who minister to children in the 21st Century?

Implications of the Doctrine of Original Sin for Ministry to Children Today

Many things have changed dramatically since the days of the Puritans. Belief in original sin is now a minority view among Christians. The Enlightenment has prompted many believers to have greater faith in humanity apart from God. Children are seen as born morally neutral at worst, but more often as born basically good, losing their innocence due to the pressures of adult society. Such views influence public policy, education, parenting, counseling, and ministry to children. But it is perplexing to realize how often these more "humane" views are assumed and are not the product of serious theological reflection. Many who believe in the innate goodness of children do so without knowing why.

For all the arguments in favor of original sin offered thus far, the best may simply be the "raw data" of observing children. Selfishness is natural, and does not have to be taught. Even lying seems to come naturally. Lewis, Stanger & Sullivan (1989) studied children about three years old to determine the ability to "mask their emotional expression." These young children were effectively able to mask their misbehavior by using verbal and facial deception that was organized and integrated. In other words, they could lie convincingly. If such behavior is learned, one is left to wonder to how much deception so many young children had been exposed. Though children are often kind and thoughtful, one is struck by how much more naturally they do wrong. Moreover, they live in a world populated by adults sharing the same problem. "Human wrongdoing, or the threat of it, mars every adult's workday, every child's school day, every vacationer's holiday" (Plantinga, 1995, p. 8).

Original sin still seems to fit, and it is affirmed by a respectable line of thinkers. If embraced today, it will have a major impact on how parents work with their children. Here are a few ways believing in original sin will affect ministry with children.

The Duties of Parents

Christian parents today are often adrift as they seek direction in raising their children. Parents easily assume they are to raise their children to have a lot of possessions so they can entertain themselves and be happy, with God being the Christian's advantage over others who are pursuing similar goals (see Dawn, 1997, and Sisemore, 2000,). Confused parents have much to learn from the godward focus the doctrine of original sin gave to the parenting of the Puritans.

Education

Puritans believed it vital to instruct their children in the faith and in life skills, all of this targeting the central goal of the glory of God. Christian parents today often neglect the religious education of their children, and Christian education programs often seek to entertain and often fail to teach. Catechizing still has value. Bible memorization is still a good thing. A Christian worldview that encompasses every field of study is a very worthy outcome of education (Murray, 1987). Education has a moral element, and all knowledge is to be related to a knowledge of God. Parents and teachers working from this perspective will not teach children that an education is merely the best way to make a lot of money someday, but is a way of being equipped to love and serve God and others more faithfully.

Discipline

Many parents and educators naively assume that children will become self-disciplined by merely accepting their behaviors. Letting children do as they please throughout the day does not promote self-control, much less holiness. Yet, many have become afraid of their children, believing that their children will not love them if they set limits on their behavior. Discipline is not only necessary for shaping proper behavior, but for children to learn skills needed to adapt and survive in the real world.

It cannot be denied that the approach to Scripture taken by the authors that have been reviewed leads to acceptance of the use of "the rod," but this is not to endorse abuse, or even inordinate physical discipline. The misuse of corporal punishment is not necessarily cause for its disuse. It has a place in a broader disciplinary strategy that offers positive incentives (as God does to his people in Scripture) and negative consequences other than spankings (Sisemore, 2000). The Puritans understood discipline more broadly as building pro-social and godly habits of behavior in their children, supplanting the inclinations of the sin nature. The same applies today.

Work

With so many conveniences available today, children are not needed by the family in the same sense that they were in Puritan times. This may account for the feelings of boredom and alienation so common among teenagers. The Puritans would advise today's parents that original sin bears fruit in idle minds and hands, and would suggest to us that regular chores be established for children from around age seven. This serves to structure time, but also to help them feel like a relevant part of the family. This will teach work as valuable in itself, not as a means to financial advancement.

Self-esteem

Psychology has convinced many that feeling good about one's self is the goal of life, and a lack of self-esteem underlies most of the problems people have. Yet, some psychologists are seeing the error of this assumption (e.g., Seligman 1995) and learning that merely feeling good about one's self does not produce happiness or health. Yet many Christians see building self-esteem as a primary objective of their work with children. Augustine, Calvin, and Edwards would all be appalled at such a thought, and say the Apostle Paul would be, too. For them, pride is the essence of sin, and the doctrine of original sin promotes its opposite, humility. Rather, children are to find joy, meaning, and fulfillment in Christ. Christian joy is far richer and deeper than secular self-esteem.

Counseling

Much Christian counseling fails to account for the biblical nature of persons, and accepts psychological assumptions about the nature of persons without careful biblical critique (Sisemore, 2003). If original sin is affirmed, counseling becomes an active process of helping children cope with their struggles and guiding parents in how to facilitate this (see chapter 22). The answers are not latent in children's "good natures," waiting for the opportunity to come out. Instead, one will seek to move the child's family in a godward direction, knowing that God's grace is essential in positive change.

Children in Church

As many churches drift from their roots in tradition, the liturgies and practices that address original sin are disappearing, and many churches lack a systematic grasp of who children are and what should be the church's ministry to youngsters. Knowing adult obligations to children as the Puritans did, clearer policies will be developed on church membership, baptism, communion for children, children's church, Sunday School curriculum, and the deeper goals of ministry which involve guiding children to God while making them part of the community of faith and teaching them to serve others.

Children in the Community

Ellingsen (2003) develops a fascinating argument as to how original sin impacts the world in which everyone lives, and thus adults will be more alert to its influence. Regarding children in particular, Ellingsen paints a rather grim picture of the sins parents inflict on their children due to their own sinfulness, including maltreatment, desertion by "deadbeat dads," and the decline of the "traditional family" through unwed pregnancies and divorce. Poverty and homelessness inflict injuries on children in the community, as do the aggressive marketing techniques aimed at bored children and their indulgent, guilt-ridden parents who show more interest in their careers than parenting.

Believing in original sin will create a realism about the laws and policies needed to protect children from exploitation in the community, and protect children from the dangers of inadequate supervision and neglect. Parents, too, will grasp that "Augustinian Christians are people who know that parenting is nothing more than the joyous experience of being a vehicle of the will of God" (p. 156) and standing up for this purpose when the fallen world contradicts these goals.

Conclusion

Callahan (2003) observes that each sickness encountered is a reminder that humanity is under the curse of death, and will inevitably succumb to its power. Similarly, the sins that children commit point us to their spiritual death, the death associated with original sin. As surely as medicines are sought out for little ones, the grace of the Great Physician should be sought for the sickness of soul that is born in them (and adults!). Symptoms of a disease ignored can be fatal, and the symptoms of sin can be spiritually fatal for children. It is easy to be self-deceptive by overlooking personal sin as well as that in our children. Love must not blind adults to their moral pain and need of a Savior. It is important to teach them good "spiritual hygiene" to combat original sin and equip them to grow in holiness, learning self-control and to walk in the ways of

God. Ultimately, sin was overcome on the Cross, and the greatest joy children can know is being forgiven, and living in a loving relationship with the God who is greater than all sin. The masquerade that hides sin must be set aside even though it is tempting to consider the self and children to be good, knowing that "the phenomenon of self-deception testifies that we human beings, even when we do evil, are incorrigibly sold on goodness. At some level of our being we know that goodness is as plausible and original as God, and that, in the history of the human race, goodness is older than sin" (Plantinga, 1995, p. 112).

References

Augustine (1960). *The confessions of Saint Augustine.* Garden City, NY: Image Books. (Orig. pub. ca. 397–400)

Augustine (1971a; orig. 412). On the merits and remission of sins, and on the baptism of infants. In P. Schaff (Ed.), *The Nicene and post-Nicene fathers* (Vol. 5, pp. 12–79). Grand Rapids: Eerdmans.

Augustine, (1971b; orig. 418). On the grace of Christ, and on original sin. In P. Schaff (Ed.), *The Nicene and post-Nicene fathers* (Vol. 5, pp. 214–257). Grand Rapids: Eerdmans.

Baxter, R. (1996; 1673). *A Christian directory.* Morgan, PA: Soli Deo Gloria.

Blocher, H. (1997). *Original sin: Illuminating the riddle.* Grand Rapids: Eerdmans.

Brekus, C.A. (2001). Children of wrath, children of grace: Jonathan Edwards and the Puritan culture of child rearing. In M. J. Bunge (Ed.), *The child in Christian thought* (pp. 300–328). Grand Rapids: Eerdmans.

Brown, P. (1967). *Augustine of Hippo.* Berkely: University of California Press.

Callahan, C. (2003). Visions of eternity. *First Things, 133,* 28–35.

Calvin, J. (1984). Commentaries on the epistle of St. Paul to the Romans. In H. Beveridge (Ed.), *Calvin's Commentaries, Vol. 19.* Grand Rapids: Baker.

Calvin, J. (1960; 1559). *The institutes of the Christian religion (2 vols.)* (J. T. McNeill, Ed.). Philadelphia: Westminster.

Dawn, M. J. (1997). *Is it a lost cause? Having the heart of God for the church's children.* Grand Rapids: Eerdmans.

Edwards, J. (1974; 1758). The great doctrine of original sin defended. In *The works of Jonathan Edwards* (Vol. 1, pp. 143–233). Carlisle, PA: Banner of Truth Trust.

Ellingsen, M. (2003). *Blessed are the cynical: How original sin can make America a better place.* Grand Rapids: Brazos.

Greven, P. (1990). *Spare the rod: The religious roots of punishment and the psychological impact of physical abuse.* New York: Vintage.

Heywood, O. (1999; 1660). *The family altar.* Morgan, PA: Soli Deo Gloria.

Introducing: The Modern Puritan. (2003, Winter). *Christian History,* 22(1), 9.

Johnson, G. G. (2002). *Puritan children in exile: The effects of the Puritan concepts of the original sin, death, salvation, and grace upon the children and grandchildren of the Puritan emigrants leading to the collapse of the Puritan period.* Bowie, MD: Heritage.

Lewis, M., Stanger, C., & Sullivan, M. W. (1989). Deception in 3-year-olds. *Developmental Psychology, 25,* 439–443.

Moo, D. (1996). *The epistle to the Romans.* Grand Rapids: Eerdmans.

Morgan, E. S. (1966). *The Puritan family.* New York: Harper & Row.

Murray, I. H. (1987). *Jonathan Edwards: A new biography.* Carlisle, PA: Banner of Truth Trust.

Ormerod, N. (1992). *Grace and disgrace: A theology of self-esteem, society, and history.* Newtown, Australia: Dwyer.

Packer, J. I. (1990). *A quest for godliness: The Puritan vision of the Christian life.* Wheaton, IL: Crossway.

Pitkin, B. (2001). "The heritage of the Lord": Children in the theology of John Calvin. In M. J. Bunge (Ed.), *The child in Christian thought* (pp. 160–193). Grand Rapids: Eerdmans.

Plantinga, C., Jr. (1995). *Not the way it's supposed to be: A breviary of sin.* Grand Rapids: Eermans.

Reynolds, E. (1996; original ed. 1826). *A treatise on the passions and faculties of the soul.* Morgan, PA: Soli Deo Gloria.

Rigby, P. (1999). Original sin. In A. D. Fitzgerald (Ed.), *Augustine through the ages: An encyclopedia* (pp. 607–614). Grand Rapids: Eerdmans.

Ryken, L. (1986). *Worldly saints: The Puritans as they really were.* Grand Rapids: Zondervan.

Seligman, M. E. P. (1995). *The optimistic child.* New York: Houghton-Mifflin.

Sisemore, T. A. (2000). *Of such is the kingdom: Nurturing children in the light of scripture.* Geanies House, Scotland: Christian Focus.

Sisemore, T. A. (2003). Christian counseling for children: The five domains model. *Journal of Psychology and Christianity, 22,* 115–122.

Smith, D. L. (1994). *With willful intent: A theology of sin.* Wheaton, IL: Bridgepoint.

Stortz, M. E. (2000). "Where or when was your servant innocent?": Augustine on childhood. In M. J. Bunge (Ed.), *The child in Christian thought* (pp. 78–102). Grand Rapids: Eerdmans.

PART III

Encouraging Children's Spirituality in the Church

Chapter Fifteen

Six Children Seeking God: Exploring Childhood Spiritual Development In Context

DANA KENNAMER HOOD[1]

"I tell you the truth, anyone who will not receive the kingdom of God like a little child will never enter it." (Luke 18:17, New International Version)

These words from Jesus call all Christians to a profound respect for children. Sofia Cavalleti (1992) demonstrates this type of respect in her book, *The Religious Potential of the Child*. She calls the reader to enter the mystery, joy, and wonder of the child's relationship with God. This requires more than a casual interaction with children. What is necessary is an in-depth relationship.

> Jesus was calling us to a life-long journey of growth and transformation—of continually turning and changing and becoming always more like them, but I believe he was first calling us to look at them. In order to become like them, we must first come to know them. We must first find out who they are and, especially what their relationship with God is like. (p. 14)

This was what I sought to do in this study. It was my goal to research children's perceptions of God, drawing on the contextualist perspective as a theoretical framework. In my study, I explored this issue with six kindergarten children who were all part of the same faith community. This study was conducted in context, including as informants all possible participants in the process of the child's religious development, including parents, Bible class teachers, and the children's minister. Through interviews and observations conducted in the child's religious setting, I sought to include an

---

1. Dana Kennamer Hood received her Ph.D. from the University of Texas in Austin. She currently serves as Associate Professor of Education at Abilene Christian University. In addition to several journal articles and book chapters, Dana has published the book *Beautiful in God's Eyes,* a study of women in the Bible for young teenage girls. She has done extensive work in curriculum development with David C. Cook Publishing Company and presents at national conferences on various topics including childhood spiritual formation and childhood brain development.

in-depth view of context that was missing from previous research. The results of this study strongly support the assertion that context cannot be ignored in understanding children's religious concepts.

Limitations of Developmental Perspectives

Developmental perspectives, particularly the theories of Jean Piaget and James Fowler, have been very influential in research on children's religious and faith development (Basset, 1990; Elkind, 1978; Fowler, 1981; Goldman, 1964; Nye & Carlson, 1984). These views, however, focus primarily on the cognitive abilities of young children. Often emphasized are the universal stages that affect development in this area. These theoretical perspectives have several drawbacks when discussing children's religious and spiritual concepts.

First, the application of these theories in the areas of religious and faith development tends to emphasize the *limitations* of young children (Tamminen, Vianello, Jaspard, & Ratcliff, 1988). Robinson (1977) adds that the "starting point of all Piaget's thought about childhood is the incapacity of children to see the world as adults see it" (p. 9). He further challenges researchers to consider the child's *experience* of God as being equally important as the child's understanding of Him. God is in many ways beyond understanding (Burke, 1999; Levine, 1999).

As researchers have explored children's perceptions of God from a developmental perspective, they have often described the thinking of young children as magical in quality. (Fowler, 1981; Harms, 1944; Steele, 1990). Rather than viewing this as a limitation, Levine (1999) asserts that it is precisely these "cognitive capacities"—not limitations—of children to look beyond what is "real" to what is imagined "which are quintessential conditions for the experience of the spiritual" (p. 122). Burke (1999) also supports a respect for imagination, stating that God is "unseen." To imagine, she comments, is to form an image of something that is not seen. So therefore, "how could we form an image of God *except* through the faculty of the imagination?" (p.10).

Finally, universals can be helpful, but they sometimes prevent us from looking deeper. Very little attention is given to the family, religious, and social contexts in which these very personal beliefs and ideas are emerging. To fully understand a child, context must be considered.

The Contextualist Perspective

Susanne Johnson (1989) asserts that "spiritual formation simply is not intelligible apart from the communal context and faith tradition in which people are formed" (p. 19). Westerhoff (1976) applies this same idea to his discussion of religious socialization. He states that children learn faith and theological concepts through "participation in the life of a tradition-bearing community with its rites, rituals, myths, symbols, expressions of beliefs, attitudes and values, organizational patterns, and activities" (p. 121). This assertion is similar to Rogoff's (1990) description of "guided participation in which care givers and children collaborate in arrangements and interactions that support children in learning to manage the skills and values of mature members of their society" (p. 65).

This perspective does not negate the importance of cognitive developmental level. On the contrary, the contextualist perspective as described by Rogoff (1990), Bronfenbrenner (1979) and others recognizes that the developmental and personal characteristics of the child will play a significant role in the shaping of the context in which the child participates.

Bronfenbrenner's Ecological Theory of Development

Bronfenbrenner characterized developmental psychology as the "science of the strange behavior of children in strange situations with strange adults for the briefest possible periods of time" (1997, p. 19). This has often been the case in studies of childhood faith and spirituality. The omission of authentic contexts in research leaves us with an incomplete understanding of children's perceptions of God.

Bronfenbrenner describes context as a "nested arrangement of concentric structures, each contained within the next" (p. 22). The innermost level, the microsystem, refers to activities and interactions in the child's immediate surroundings. These include the child's family, school, and in this study, the child's church. The relationships in this microsystem are reciprocal. The behavior of the adult influences the behavior of the child, and the child's unique characteristics influence the behavior of the adult. The mesosystem surrounds the microsystem and represents the interactions between the child's various immediate settings. The parent's relationship with the church will carry over into the home. The third layer is the exosystem. This refers to the settings that do not contain the child but that do affect the child's experiences in the immediate setting. This might include the parent's work context or a class attended by the parent. The fourth layer includes the belief systems and customs of a culture that influence the child's interactions in the other levels. Bronfenbrenner has labeled this the macrosystem.

Description of the Study

This paper will examine the results of a qualitative research study exploring the ideas about God held by six kindergarten children within the contexts of their families and their faith community. Bronfenbrenner's conceptualization of context provided the theoretical framework for this study.

All participants in the study were members of Windway Church of Christ, (all names are pseudonyms), a congregation of about 2500 members. The Church of Christ is a conservative protestant Christian denomination with a strong emphasis on Bible study and the need to remain true to scripture. The church affirms the Bible as the inspired word of God and encourages individual members to engage in personal study of the scriptures so that they will be able to discern whether theological and doctrinal teachings are scripturally accurate (Allen & Hughes, 1981).

The informants for this study included six kindergarten children (Jeremy, Amy, Jessica, Ryan, Katie, and Jonathan), their parents, and their Bible class teachers. With the assistance of the Children's Minister and the Bible class teachers, the children were selected from families with high levels of involvement in the life of the congregation. The rationale for this selected sampling (Erlandson et al., 1993) was to focus the study on children of parents who highly value involvement in the faith community.

The researcher used a variety of methods to collect data for the study. Children were observed in their Sunday School classes and in the corporate worship service as they participated in the children's sermons.

Results and Discussion

The influence of multiple layers of context was evident in the responses of the children, their parents, and their teachers. These contextual influences will be discussed using the following categories: (a) the family; (b) the faith community; (c) the broader community; (d) the child as an active participant; and (e) the study as context.

The Family

The family exerts the primary influence on a child's development. This is as true for religious and spiritual development as it is for cognitive or social development. All of the parents in this study indicated that they take an active role in sharing God with their children. Their perspectives were often reflected in the children's responses.

Jeremy, for example, was the only child to suggest that God is both masculine and feminine, "a boy and a girl." In fact, he stated that this "had to be!" Jeremy's view is quite different from children's perspectives in previous research. Heller (1989) concluded that boys were uncomfortable with the possibility that God could be female. Dickie and others (1997) indicated that young children, both boys and girls, perceive God to be like the father, possessing primarily masculine traits.

Jeremy's parents spoke strongly about being committed to teaching him about gender equity and believed that this probably contributed to his conclusion that God must be both male and female. This illustrates the innermost layer of context as described by Bronfenbrenner (1979). As the children interact in their families in their microsystems, they learn particular ways of thinking.

All of the children regularly spoke of God's presence in their lives. They all expressed the belief that it makes God happy to be with them and they are happy knowing he is there. For Jessica, God's companionship means that Jesus accompanies her throughout the day. They discover butterflies and rainbows together. He goes with her to school and likes to play "ring-around-the-rosies" with her. Katie described her ongoing conversations with God. She talks with Him about everything while she plays. He likes to listen and to watch her have fun.

These six children appear to have images which are different from those of the children in a study by Graebner (1964). He concluded that children saw God as the God of the Bible rather than in personal terms. The children in his study perceived God as watching, but distant from humanity.

These differences between the children in Graebner's study and the current study may plausibly be attributed to religious socialization. The parents in this current study emphasized God's love and care. Several indicated that they want their children to know that God loves them *specifically*. They want them to know that God is with them at all times.

Heller (1989) indicated that the youngest children in his study, ages 4 to 6, often associated God with play and gaiety. This was evident in the responses of the children in my study as well. However, it is important to note that contextual as well as developmental issues contributed to this association. The parents in my study often supported this view of God in their interactions with their children. For example, Ryan's mother emphasized that God likes to have fun and to laugh. She taught Ryan that God created laughter and that He enjoys it when we laugh.

An avoidance of God's wrath, along with the focus on God's love and care, guided the parents' interactions with their children. This often intentional exclusion of the negative aspects of God was clearly seen in these six children's overwhelmingly positive view of God. The children in this study did not readily attribute the emotion of anger to God, in contrast with Graebner's (1964) research in which the children often described God as the one who punishes evil persons. Ryan, Jonathan, and Jessica emphatically stated that God never gets angry, and when Jessica was asked if there is anything that God never does, she replied, "God never, never, never, never gets mad." When people do things that displease God He is sad, but never angry.

Parents in the study had made a conscious decision to emphasize the loving and accepting attributes of God rather than the wrathful and judgmental attributes of God so often taught and experienced in their previous churches. In choosing Windway Church they selected an environment which taught God's unconditional love. This illustrates the complex and interrelated nature of context. The faith community had an impact on the parents who, in turn, were impacted in the way they shared God with their children.

This demonstrates Bronfenbrenner's (1979) second level of context, the mesosystem. The child is affected by the parents' interactions with the faith community. It also demonstrates that different settings of a particular context cannot always be clearly divided. The influences of family and faith community in the lives of these children are inextricably connected. As Vergote (1981) points out, it is difficult to determine what comes from the child's relationship with the parent and what comes from the faith community culture. This is particularly true for families, such as those in this study, for whom faith community life is a large part of family life.

It is also important to understand the differences in the nature of interactions that take place in these two very important contexts—the family and the faith community. Anderson (1999) points out that it is sometimes difficult to identify clearly the influence of parents on children's beliefs. It is much easier to see the influence of the faith community. He states that this is because interactions within the family about faith issues are often incidental and spontaneous. The faith community, on the other hand, intentionally teaches children specific concepts about God.

This could be seen in the responses of the parents in this study. Almost all stated that they share God with their children "along the way" and "as it comes up." They indicated that they do not have organized devotionals or Bible lessons at home. They make God part of everything they do.

Another difficulty in identifying clearly the influence of parents in this study involved the methods used. Through classroom observations, children were seen responding to activities and Bible teaching in Sunday School. However, in order to know about parental influences in the home, personal interviews had to be conducted. Parents then recounted memories of their children asking questions or making statements about God, yet very few parents were able to recall specific examples.

The Faith Community

Children at Windway Christian Church attend Bible class and corporate worship, but the primary setting for participation in the faith community is through the Bible class setting. The experiences of corporate worship are, for the most part, not designed to actively include them.

Violent Bible stories and information about God's judgment were intentionally excluded from the children's formal Bible classes much as they were from interactions with their parents. The teachers emphasized God's love and felt that discussions of God's anger were not appropriate for young children. The teachers often reminded the children that they were special to God. One song the children sang described Jesus as "a friend next to you." Therefore, family and faith community worked together in the lives of these six children as they came to know a God who loved and cared about them.

Heller (1986) stated that young children often described two deities, one all good and one all bad. He explained this based on the child's emotional need to deal with evil in the world. In the current study, the children's descriptions of a loving God appeared to be a reflection of what Heintz (1999) referred to as "congregational culture."

The language the children used to describe God was at times the same language found in songs and lessons in their Bible classes. Lesson material described God as "big" and "strong." The teachers indicated that they used language the children would understand. They also chose songs with lyrics that would make sense to young children. Here the interaction between the context and the individual is obvious; the teachers selected language in response to the children's developmental level. Therefore, the children used that language to express their emerging ideas about God.

The children's ideas were not only influenced by their participation in Bible classes, but also by participating in the larger faith community. Amy's parents specifically stated that they do not talk about the crucifixion with her. In the children's Bible classes, emphasis on the crucifixion comes in the first grade. However, when Amy was asked to draw a picture of her favorite story about God, she drew Jesus on the cross. She evidently attempted to understand Biblical teachings discussed in other faith community settings, such as corporate worship.

The influence of the faith community on the children's ideas about God cannot be limited to the teachings of the church. Windway Christian Church is more than Bible classes. Windway is a gathering of people where one person's life experiences can impact many others. This was seen in several of the children's repeated references to Kasey, a ten-year-old girl at Windway who had died of cancer the year before. They mentioned several times that while they could not see God, Kasey could.

Kasey's illness and death greatly affected the children. The children prayed for her faithfully in Bible classes and at home. However, the impact that her death had on the children was surprising to the parents. Kasey's experience caused the children to think in new ways about heaven, angels, and seeing God. After all, a little girl that they knew from their church had seen angels and was now in heaven with God.

The Broader Community

While the family and the faith community were strong influences in their lives, the children participated in other contexts as well. They attended school, watched television, played sports and spent time with friends. The origin of some of the ideas expressed by the children appeared to come from sources other than their participation at Windway.

Both Jeremy and Jonathan talked about God making dinosaurs before he made people. According to the teachers, this was not a topic addressed in the Bible school classes. Instead, these boys seemed to be integrating their understandings of God with information they were learning in their public school kindergarten classes and through the media. Their perceptions of God were taking shape within the interactive settings in the mesosystem, which included home, school, and church.

This is another example of how children's experiences in other contexts interact with their emerging ideas about God. As Katie discussed God's power, she mentioned fairies. She said that God's power was greater than the fairies. Again, this was not a topic discussed in the children's classes at church.

Katie's discussion of fairies could be misinterpreted as simply a reflection of the "fairy-tale stage" of religious understanding described by Harms (1944). However, through continued conversation, I was able to see that her view of God was complex and emerging. Katie clearly stated on several occasions that God does not have human qualities; He is eternal and ever present. When I asked her to draw a picture of God she chose instead to draw Jesus. She told me that she "imagined" God with a beard and a mustache, but if she drew him that way people would think he was just a man. During one interview she obviously struggled with the idea of God's eternal nature.

Dana: Where do you think God came from?

Katie: Well . . . [silence] Uh Oh! [giggles]

Dana: What do you mean, "Uh Oh?"

Katie: Well, everything comes from God but I don't know where God comes from. He's always been there. I know where Jesus came from. Jesus was a little boy. But God . . . that's weird.

Dana: So Jesus was a little boy, but you don't know where God came from.

Katie: Nope. Jesus was a little boy but God is . . . God is just God, I guess.

Katie's struggle is not unique to children. The fact that God has always existed even challenges adults. As I explored these and other issues with children I was reminded of Robert Coles' (1990) view of children in his book, *The Spiritual Life of Children*. He characterizes children "as seekers, as young pilgrims well aware that life is a finite journey and as anxious to make sense of it as those of us who are farther along in the time allotted us" (p. xvi). The children in this study were clearly "seekers."

The Children as Active Participants

It is important to remember that the children do not passively absorb information about God. They actively participate in their families and in the church. They bring to this process their developmental levels, individual personalities, interests, and concerns. Each has a unique approach to life that contributes in shaping their understandings of God.

Individual interests. Children have individual preferences and interests. The things that intrigue them can impact their thoughts and questions about God. For example, Jeremy had an avid interest in muscles, bones, and his own physical strength. This was manifested in the questions he asked about God and his descriptions of Him. When I asked Jeremy if there was anything that he wondered about God, he told me that he wondered how God made people. "I know what He put on them. He put muscles and bones and legs and arms and a tummy, but I wonder how He did that."

Jeremy's parents told me that he was fascinated with his muscles and bones. He liked to identify his bones by their real names—tibia, femur, and clavicle. On one occasion Jeremy asked his parents if God has bones. His interest in this topic clearly focused at least some of his thoughts about God in a particular direction. In addition, this interest framed many of the conversations he had about God with his parents as they responded to his questions.

Individual personalities. These six children were all unique. Their particular ways of thinking, feeling, and interacting had an effect on their questions, concerns, and perceptions about God. Jessica had a determined, strong-willed personality. This affected her thoughts about God in very distinctive ways. She was at times extremely frustrated that she could not see God and would not accept her parents' explanations for why she could not see Him. Seeing God face-to-face was her strong desire and she did not understand why God would not grant this wish.

Ryan, on the other hand, brought his more cautious nature to the process of coming to know God. His parents shared that Ryan was unsure in unfamiliar situations, particularly with adults. He wanted to make sure he would be able get something right before he decided to join in. This was reflected in my interactions with Ryan. As Ryan talked about seeing God on earth, he said that he would be embarrassed. His father also shared that at one time Ryan did not want to pray because he "couldn't." Apparently Ryan felt uncertain about his ability to pray acceptably. Ryan's approach to learning about God was clearly different from that of the children who are less cautious.

After our first interview I learned that Ryan didn't want to continue helping me. Ryan felt unsure about some of the questions and was worried about having the right answers. I tried to help Ryan become comfortable with me. I made an extra effort to visit with him as I observed the Bible classes. While these interactions with Ryan helped, he still seemed unsure. I decided to show Ryan how much he had already contributed by letting him see the transcript of our first interview. When Ryan saw the nine page transcription of the conversation, he said proudly, "I said all that? Wow!"

Unlike Ryan, Jonathan loved to joke and ask questions. Both of these qualities were evident in his comments about God. He would often give joking and playful answers to my questions. At other times he would become very reflective, asking himself and God very serious questions. Jonathan's sense of humor combined with his inclination to ponder issues about God will most certainly impact his image of God.

This was evident in the following conversation with Jonathan. During one interview, I asked him what God does in heaven. He began his response in his characteristic joking manner. Then he became very serious as he really thought about what it might be like to see God in heaven.

Dana: What do you think they are doing in heaven?

Jonathan: They are doing the Mamba in heaven.

Dana: They are doing the Mamba?

Jonathan: Naw, I was just joking. [He stopped talking to draw for awhile and then looked at me with a serious face and continued.] I want to see God—really see him. I think that will be cool. But I want to wait 'till I am old to see him cuz you have to be dead to see God. So I want to get really old and then die and then see God. [He continued drawing and then looked up to the ceiling and asked God a question.] God are you invisible? I think you are invisible. Yeah . . . you are invisible.

Dana: You think God is invisible.

Jonathan: But not in heaven. You can see Him in heaven.

Dana: What do you think it will be like to see God in heaven?

Jonathan: Really different.

Dana: What do you mean really different?

Jonathan: I won't be able to see anything else because He will be all around me—you know like the air we breathe is all around us.

Individual Ideas. For many of the ideas expressed by the children, there existed no clear connection to what they had been taught. These thoughts seemed to be original for them. This was evident in Jonathan's description of seeing God and in Katie's depiction of heaven. She described heaven as having a rainbow sky (see Figure 1).

Figure 1

Ryan expressed a unique idea about the Bible being in heaven. He said that everyone in heaven would be reading the Bible. They would be gathered around a really big Bible in the middle of heaven (see Figure 2). "This is the really big Bible. It has to be big so everybody can see it." I asked Ryan why he thought people would be reading the Bible in heaven. He told me that the Bible tells all about God and in heaven everyone wants to know about God. "The Bible," he told me, "is the most important book."

Figure 2

As research is focused on context, it is important to remember that children have thoughts that are truly their own. Not every belief that they have comes as a direct result of something they have been taught. Developmental psychology states that children construct their own understandings and bring these understandings to contribute to the context of which they are a part. More importantly, God's word affirms that He is speaking to their hearts as well (Psalm 8:2).

As children participate in a context, they are not blank slates (Bronfenbrenner, 1979). Instead, they influence the context just as the context influences them. The relationship between the child and the context is not one-sided; it is reciprocal. This reciprocal relationship was evident in the findings of this present study.

The Study as Context

In many ways the study itself became a context for the children's developing ideas about God. This could be seen in the responses of the parents, the children, and in the children's drawings.

According to Manning (1997) qualitative researchers have a responsibility to demonstrate the authenticity of their results. Authenticity is defined as a set of criteria for judging the quality of a study's findings, attending to the value of participating in the study for the informants. This includes what she describes as ontological authenticity which asks if the informants of the study experienced growth in understanding due to participation in the study. Interactions between the researcher and the informants should not be one-sided. Rather, these interactions should be collaborative and open. This view of authentic findings guided my interactions with the children, their parents, and their teachers. Through these respectful, collaborative encounters all participants, myself included, experienced growth through our interactions with one another.

For the parents. Because of their participation in the study, some of the parents discussed issues with their children that might not have been discussed otherwise. One mother told me about one such conversation she had with her daughter, Jessica. Curious about Jessica's ideas and thoughts about God, her mother asked, "What does God look like?" Jessica replied that she did not know, but that she did know what Jesus looked like. Then Jessica clarified her thoughts by saying, "Well, I don't really know what He looks like. I have just seen pictures that other people drew, but they don't know either." After a little while Jessica continued, "But my heart knows what they both look like cuz they live together in my heart." Jessica's mother indicated that she was moved by Jessica's insights.

As the parents considered their children's responses, they at times questioned their approach to teaching their children about God. For example, I described the children's responses related to God's lack of anger. Some parents wondered if their choice to completely exclude issues related to God's wrath had been inappropriate.

> I think that it is probably a little unfair. . . . It seems like they ought to know about God's wrath in some situations. Because they are going to learn about it some how, some time. And we don't need to pretend it doesn't exist. . . . Um, and I think, what do we need to tell children when? Are they going to think, "They are not telling me the whole truth about God" (Ryan's mother).

Some of the parents were obviously challenged to rethink the things they were teaching their children about God. Their participation in the study caused them to evaluate their approach to their child's religious socialization.

For the children. The interviews gave the children an opportunity to reflect on new ideas. In response to my question about God's origins, Katie indicated that she had never thought about that.

Jonathan had new thoughts about the omnipresence of God. During a conversation he first told me that God was everywhere. I then asked him if God was in the room with us. "Nah!" he replied and continued drawing. Then suddenly he dropped his crayon, threw his hands to his face, opened his eyes wide, looked all around the room, and said, "Oh no! Yes! Yes! He *is* here. He is *right here!*"

Even though Jonathan quickly responded that God is everywhere, it was in the context of our conversations that this became real to him. He had often heard that God is everywhere, but until he was given the opportunity to personally reflect on this idea, it was not clear to him.

In the children's drawings. As the children drew pictures of God and heaven, it was clear that the actual process of drawing provided a particular context for them to express their ideas about God. This approach to interpreting children's drawings is expressed very effectively by Gunther-Heimbrock (1999).

> For theological and educational reasons, and proposing to direct our view in another direction, I generally assume that we may take children's pictures not only as reproductive but also as a productive and creative process that shapes their own personal religiosity and builds their world view, their religious ideas and practice—all intertwined with their own subjectivity (p. 55).

The children's drawings provided a perfect example of this "productive and creative" process. As the children drew pictures of their images of God they used language that indicated that their art was a way to communicate. They would say things such as, "I gave him . . ." or "I made him . . ." The children were clearly expressing ideas by "giving a painting rather than just telling us the message by words" (Gunther-Heimbrock, 1999, p. 55).

The children often drew pictures of God with human characteristics. Past research has asserted, based on drawings, that young children have anthropomorphic images of God (Hyde, 1990). However the children in this study often expressed the idea that God is definitely not human. They all stated that no one knows what God looks like. This challenges the validity of studies such as that by Harms (1944), which used children's drawings to draw conclusions about children's perceptions of God without the benefit of the children's explanations.

Burke points out, "an image of God is really only an approximation of the experience of God" (Burke, 1999, p. 9). These children used the symbols available to them to convey their images of God. This symbolic process was evident in the children's descriptions of their drawings of God.

When Jonathan drew his picture of God, he was not saying that God has "big hands." He "*gave* him really big hands" in order to symbolize God's power to create (see Figure 3). Jeremy drew God "behind a cloud cuz he's too big to draw" (see Figure 4). On the sides of God's mostly bald head he placed some "hair spots" to represent the fact that God is "very, very, very, old."

Figure 3

Figure 4

Gunther Heimbrock (1999) also challenges the strict interpretation of children's pictures of God based solely on content and not process. When researchers view children's pictures as a direct representation of a child's ideas, they are demonstrating a limited understanding of children's thinking and of their art.

More importantly they also reveal their own limited concept of picture, taking pictures to be a mere translation or reproduction of what is first developed by children in their minds. The underlying assumption here is that children begin by completely building up their inner images of God and then copy that image onto paper. This seems to be a rather naive concept of a picture which could be called, in theoretical terms, a direct representation (Gunther-Heinbrock, 1999, p. 54)

As children draw, they imagine, create, and explore. Their drawings are often metaphors to represent ideas. Gunther-Heinbrock calls researchers to remember that drawings of God are "not snapshots." They are not always representations of an existing world, but rather a world that in many ways is just coming into being as the child draws or paints.

This was particularly evident in the children's drawings of heaven. Ryan's Bible and Katie's rainbow sky were attempts to communicate ideas that they have about this yet unseen place. Amy pictured heaven as a house with jewels and diamonds (see Figure 5). She said, "It's like a happy, happy song there." Jonathan drew diamonds on the road to represent the beauty of heaven and added the rainbow because it is "a happy place" (see Figure 6).

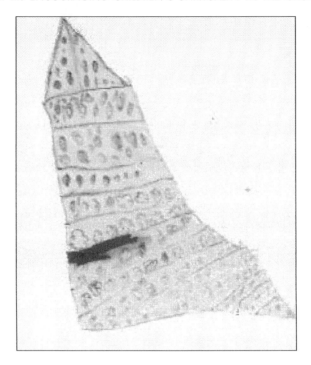

Figure 5

Figure 6

In the interpretations of the children's drawings it is necessary to consider more than the content. It is also important to consider the "relationship between the picture and the child" (Gunther-Heimbrock, 1999, p. 55). The act of drawing or painting becomes a context for expressing feelings, thoughts, and even questions. It is also helpful to remember that it is not an everyday occurrence to be asked to draw a picture of God.

Implications of the Study

It was not the goal of this study to discover findings that would be generalizable to other contexts. I sought to explore six children's concepts of God in context. It is the reader's responsibility to determine if findings from a study could be applied or adapted for his/her context. This study, however, does demonstrate that to understand children's perceptions of God, it is necessary to consider context seriously. It is not possible to interpret children's concepts appropriately without an understanding of the contexts in which those concepts have developed.

For those interested in helping children come to know God, this study has several implications. First, it is important for the adults in a child's life to reflect on ways in which their own experiences are shaping what they tell children about God.

Second, this study demonstrates the power of talking *with* children, rather than just *to* them. The children's answers to my questions were never corrected or redirected. As was the case with Jonathan's epiphany about God's presence, this gave the children the opportunity to make sense of ideas on their own.

If this study is applied in any way, my hope is that it will be applied through the manner in which the reader listens to children's ideas about their most sacred beliefs. I would encourage the adults in children's lives to avoid dismissing a child's ideas as simple reflections of their immature thinking but urge them to listen with anticipation as children have something meaningful and personal to share.

References

Allen, L. C. (1991). *Discovering our roots: The ancestry of Churches of Christ.* Abilene, TX: ACU Press.

Anderson, D. W. (1999). Children's spirituality and family relationships. In S. K. Morgenthaler (Ed.), *Exploring children's spiritual formation: Foundational issues* (pp. 231–246). River Forest, IL: Pillars.

Basset, R. L. (1990). Picturing God: A nonverbal measure of God concept for conservative Protestants. *Journal of Psychology and Christianity, 9,* 73–81.

Bronfenbrenner, U. (1979). *The ecology of human development.* Cambridge: Harvard University Press.

Burke, P. (1999). The healing power of the imagination. *International Journal of Children's Spirituality, 4,* 9–18.

Cavalleti, S. (1992). *The religious potential of the child.* Chicago: Liturgy Training Publications.

Coles, R. (1990). *The spiritual life of children.* Boston: Houghton Mifflin.

Dickie, J., Eshleman, A., Merasco, D., Shepard, A., Wilt, M., & Johnson, M., (1997). Parent-child relationships and children's images of God. *Journal for the Scientific Study of Religion, 36*(2), 25–43.

Elkind, D. (1978). *The child's reality: Three developmental themes.* Hillsdale, NJ: Erlbaum.

Erlandson, D. A., Harris, E. L., Skipper, B. L., & Allen, S. D. (1993). *Doing naturalistic inquiry: A guide to methods.* London: Sage.

Fowler, J. W. (1981). *Stages of faith: The psychology of human development and the quest for meaning.* New York: Harper & Row.

Goldman, R. (1964). *Religious thinking from childhood to adolescence.* London: Routledge and Kegan Paul.

Graebner, O. (1964). Child concepts of God. *Religious Education, 59*(3), 234–241.

Gunther-Heimbrock, H. (1999). Images and pictures of God: The development of creative seeing. *International Journal of Children's Spirituality, 4*(1), 51–60.

Harms, E. (1944). The development of religious experience in children. *American Journal of Sociology, 50,* 112–122.

Heintz, K. (1999). Clarifying congregational culture. In S. Morgenthaler (Ed.), *Exploring children's spiritual formation: Foundational issues* (pp. 213–218). River Forest, IL: Pillars.

Heller, D. (1986). *The Children's God.* Chicago: University of Chicago Press.

Hyde, K. (1990). *Religion in childhood and adolescence.* Birmingham, AL: Religious Education Press.

Johnson, S. (1989). *Christian spiritual formation.* Nashville: Abingdon.

Lawrence, P. (1965). Children's thinking about religion: a study of concrete operational thinking. *Religious Education, 60,* 111–116.

Levine, S. (1999). Cognition as the foundation of spirituality. *International Journal of Children's Spirituality, 4*(2), 121–140.

Manning, K. (1997). Authenticity in constructivist inquiry: Methodological considerations without prescription. *Qualitative Inquiry, 3*(1), 93–115.

Nye, C.W., & Carlson, J. S. (1984). The development of the God concept in children. *Journal of Genetic Psychology, 145,* 137–142.

Robinson, E. (1977). *The original vision: A study of religious experience of childhood.* New York: Seabury.

Rogoff, B. (1990). *Apprenticeship in thinking: Cognitive development in social context.* New York: Oxford University Press.

Steele, L. (1990). *On the way: A practical theology of Christian formation.* Grand Rapids: Baker.

Tamminen, K., Vianello, R., Jaspard, J., & Ratcliff, D. (1988). The religious concepts of preschoolers. In D. Ratcliff (Ed.), *Handbook of preschool religious education* (pp. 59–81). Birmingham: Religious Education Press.

Vergote, A. (1981) The parental figures: Symbolic functions and medium for the representation of God. In A. Vergote & A. Tamayo (Eds.), *The parental figures and the representation of God* (pp. 169–184). New York: Mouton.

Westerhoff, J. H., III. (1976). *Will our children have faith?* New York: Harper & Row.

Chapter Sixteen

Children in Congregations: Congregations as Contexts for Children's Spiritual Growth

JOYCE ANN MERCER, DEBORAH L. MATTHEWS, AND SCOTT WALZ[1]

What *congregational* practices support and nurture the faith of children? Much of the current discourse on children's spirituality focuses on the practices of individuals involved in the faith formation of children, such as parents or teachers. This paper examines the practices of congregations as communal contexts in which children grow in faith. It comes out of the "Children in Congregations"[2] research at San Francisco Theological Seminary, a congregational studies project involving three Protestant churches in the San Francisco Bay area.[3] This research explores various practices in

1. Joyce Ann Mercer is Associate Professor of Practical Theology and Christian Education at San Francisco Theological Seminary. She has a Ph.D. from Emory University, a D.Min. from McCormick Theological Seminary, an M.S.W. from the University of Connecticut Graduate School of Social Work, and an M.Div. from Yale Divinity School. An ordained minister with the Presbyterian Church (USA), she is also a licensed independent clinical social worker. She has written 18 journal articles and is the author of a *Welcoming Children: A Practical Theology of Childhood* (St. Louis: Chalice, 2005).

Deborah L. Matthews holds an M.Div. and a Diploma in Spiritual Formation Studies from San Francisco Theological Seminary, as well as an M.A. in Christian Spirituality from the Graduate Theological Union. She is a candidate for ordination in the Presbyterian Church (USA), and has published one journal article.

Scott Walz has an M.A. in Early Childhood Education from Concordia University in River Forest, Illinois and an M.Div. from Pacific Lutheran Theological Seminary in Berkeley, California. He is currently working on an M.A. in Liturgical Studies at the Graduate Theological Union and Pacific Lutheran Theological Seminary. Scott is ordained in the United Church of Christ.

2. The Children in Congregations Project, and our participation at this conference, both take place through the generous support of the Louisville Institute. We are grateful for their ongoing commitment to our project and to fostering connections between academic work and congregational life through their grant programs.

3. All three congregations were Presbyterian Church (USA) churches. Our intention is not to generalize from these three congregations to others (i.e., we are not proposing this as a representative sample in any way), but to suggest that these three particular churches may evidence practices and

worship, education, family support, and mission, through which the three particular congregations studied shape the faith lives of children. We (the researchers)[4] will focus on three specific congregational practices through which the congregations nurture children's spirituality. These practices do exist not in isolation but within a larger and more comprehensive framework of congregational practices with children.

The "Children in Congregations" Project: Research Methodology

Two guiding questions shape the "Children in Congregations" study: (1) "How do congregations with vital ministries with children welcome children, contribute to their thriving, and nurture them in the practices of Christian faith?" and, (2) "How do children contribute to the vitality of congregations: what impact does the presence of children have upon the lived theology and practices of a particular community of faith?"

"Congregational studies" refers to a method of research developed by James Hopewell and further refined by scholars such as Nancy Ammerman, Carl Dudley, and others,[5] using social science methods, such as participant-observation, in-depth interviewing, demographic and environmental studies, and survey research, in the study of religious communities. Our project entails studies of three congregations in the San Francisco Bay area evidencing some form of vitality in their ministries with children. Each of these congregations—all Presbyterian, described in detail later—is distinctive from the other two in terms of size, socio-economic and demographic situation, and theological orientation. Over a nine month period, team members spent 12–15 hours a week participating in the life of their assigned congregation, in worship, education, governance (e.g., session meetings, children's ministry committee meetings), retreats, fellowship, and mission work.

In addition to the naturalistic inquiry afforded by participation in what the church already was doing, our team conducted various activities as part of the research, including congregational "time lines" (an oral history activity commonly utilized in congregational studies); "space tours" with children and adult members of the congregations (a walk through the facilities in which persons can tell the place-based stories of their experiences in the congregation, sometimes including video); interviews and neighborhood walks with local business, education, and town planning officials; and focus groups with children and adults. Throughout the process, we have

---

dynamics similar to many others and therefore warrant close attention.

4. Use of the collective pronouns "our" and "we" in this paper refer to the research team for the Children in Congregations Project, who together are the collaborative authors of this paper.

5. Works detailing actual studies of congregations are too numerous to cite here. See Hopewell (1987); Ammerman, Carroll, Dudley, and McKinney (1998); Eiesland (2000); and Foster and Brelsford (1996), for examples.

worked out of a methodological commitment to seek not only patterns of coherence in action and meaning, but also discrepancies and gaps such as the differences between a congregation's stated desires concerning children's presence in worship and its actual practices of inclusion and exclusion. Consequently, in the preliminary analysis of congregational practices offered in this paper, we look both affirmingly and critically at particular practices with children, with the deepest respect for and gratitude toward the three congregations participating in the study. One limitation of the present paper concerns the preliminary nature of the research and its exploratory character: We are not attempting to prove the efficacy of practices, but simply to note what was observed and to suggest some possible meanings and implications, to be explored in future analysis and in further studies of congregations.

The Concept of Practices as a Guiding Perspective for Research

"Practices are those shared activities that address fundamental human needs and that, woven together, form a way of life . . . Christian practices are things Christian people do together over time in response to and in the light of God's active presence for the life of the world" (Bass 1997, pp. xi, 5). Orienting congregational research to this concept of practice means we have paid attention to those activities done in community over periods of time that form persons into a community of faith and a people who make meaning in the world through their actions in response to God.

Two aspects of Christian practices deserve special attention in relation to this project: their communal nature and their faith-forming capacities. Christian practices were and are formed in community interactions in response to the things God does in the world. "Enter a Christian practice and you will find that you are part of a community that has been doing this thing for centuries . . . It is ancient, and larger than you are; it weaves you together with other people in doing things none of us could do alone" (Bass 1997, p. 7). Practices are not actions people merely perform by themselves, for individual perseverance will fail and insights will be too limited (Bass 1997, p. 196). Even communities are subject to these hazards, and deeper wisdom must be drawn from the larger context of Christian community in order to understand how Christian practices form the community.

Of course there is an individual element to practices. Participation in practices involves variety and multiplicity: people vary in their interpretations and performances of practices, as well as in the extent of their conscious and intentional constructions of meaning in relation to particular practices.[6] Similarly, practices involve people in mul-

6. Consider for example the practice of participating in the Eucharist in a congregation. For one adult, this action may be a deliberately chosen, meaning-filled event, engaged in from sensory/kinesthetic and consciously reflective levels of experience as an encounter with the Sacred. A second adult in the same moment may be coming to the Table, engaging in the same practice non-reflectively and

tiple levels of engagement and response (e.g., kinesthetic, linguistic, logical-cognitive, musical) such that persons may be participating in the same practice at the same time yet in quite different ways and with differing meanings they attribute to that practice. A constitutive aspect of practice, however, is the social framework in which these individually instantiated modes of participation take place; practices necessarily involve some shared sphere of action and meaning by those engaging in them.

At the same time, differences within any given practice, like encounters with alternative practices, express the dynamic and transformational potential of practices, as these differences call into question attempts to render a single, fixed meaning to a practice. Thus, in addition to being bearers of tradition, practices are also sites for resistance, transformation, and change (Chopp, 1995, p. 17). This critical dimension often finds expression in that aspect of a practice that does not mean what, at face value, it appears to mean. Congregational practices of offering children's sermons in worship provide a good example. Congregations often identify their explicit intention in this practice as offering something special just for children rendering the substance of the day's message understandable at a child's developmental level, when such practices may also operate implicitly to marginalize or exclude children by segregating them from the worshiping community as a whole and trivializing their ways of knowing through moralisms.[7] Clearly, intentionality alone does not guarantee a particular effect in relation to a practice. For example, one cannot claim that just because a congregation "intends" the inclusion of children in worship with its practices of children's sermons and activity books, children necessarily *are* more included than in a congregation that does these things haphazardly. However, when congregations do exercise intentionality in their practices with children, they create "webs of meaning" and action that form a more comprehensive matrix to nurture children that—it seems to us—increases the opportunities for children to be shaped by those practices.[8]

Taken all together and performed together with others, Christian practices form a way of life, a way of being Christian as the person of faith participates in them. Practices, by their very nature, teach. That is, certain kinds of knowledge are presupposed by a practice and are reinforced and/or corrected in enacting the practice. Participating in practices over time teaches persons the necessary knowledge for the practice, in addition to creating a context in which persons can both develop their "skills" or competence in the practice, and further internalize or identify with the communal meanings and values embodied by a practice.

If children are likewise formed in faith by engaging in church practices, then passing along the practices of the faith necessarily takes place in the context of the

---

habitually while constructing their weekly grocery list in their mind.

7. For more on the critique of children's sermons, see Mercer (2002); Ng and Thomas (1981); and Pritchard (1992).

8. For perspectives on the importance of intentionality in educational ministries, see Sara Little (1983).

community that continues to shape and to share those practices. Studying how children are welcomed and nurtured in practices of the faith means discovering how children are formed into people of God as well as how doing this work shapes the congregations engaged in it.

Christian Education at Shepherd of the Hills[9]

Shepherd of the Hills Presbyterian Church is a 50-year-old, 2100-member church in an affluent suburb of San Francisco. On a typical Sunday 900 worshipers attend Shepherd of the Hills' three services, and over 100 children pass through the nursery and Sunday school classrooms. The constituency of the church reflects its social context—overwhelmingly Euro-American and affluent, a mix of Baby Boomer parents with young children and older couples whose children are grown. The church is known for its mission giving and participation, and for high quality music and education for adults and children. Besides a growing number of volunteers, several personnel for children are on staff including one full-time pastor, a full-time Director of Children's Ministry, and two part-time staff devoted to children's ministry and co-coordinating childcare.

Educational ministry as a whole at Shepherd of the Hills is a congregational practice encompassing a variety of specific and smaller practices. It strives to be a shared, transformational, pedagogical endeavor that critiques social and theological reality as it shapes it. Many people are involved in the endeavor, including teachers, pastors, and custodial staff, all organized under a guiding vision that Christian education is important to the whole congregation. Being involved in this practice of educational ministry with children forms people in a Christian way of life. This is the church's stated goal for children, yet the adults who participate (including parents) report that their involvement has helped them integrate their faith with their daily lives—by learning stories, listening to the children, and talking about the process with each other. It is the contact with the practice that teaches them about the practice. And having been shaped by the practice of educational ministry, participants understand and act in the world in new ways, becoming part of a critique of their larger theological and social reality.

The focus here will be on the congregational practice of teaching and learning biblical interpretation, a practice that takes place within the wider umbrella of educational ministries. The primary form of Christian education the church offers children is Godly Play classes during each of the Sunday services. This Montessori-based curriculum teaches children to use religious language through a format similar to the structure of worship, from gathering together ("getting ready"), to hearing and

---

9. Except where we have permission to use the actual identities of congregations and/or persons within them, we have changed their names and certain other identifying information as necessary to respect a covenant of anonymity in the research process.

responding to the Scripture (through a story and "wondering questions"), to having a feast and receiving a blessing.[10] The format and content challenges young learners to make their own meaning out of the stories of the Christian tradition in an environment that honors individual meaning-making while it teaches a way to be in Christian community. By using this educational curriculum, Shepherd of the Hills makes the statement that children ought to be learning how to use religious language and how to be in a particular kind of Christian community.

One Sunday, in the third through fifth grade class, a new story format was used, that of side-by-side parables. The storyteller told the Parable of the Sower, and asked its wondering questions. She asked children to think about whether there was anything in the next parable that would help them understand the first one. She then told the Parable of the Mustard Seed and asked a few of its wondering questions (see Matt 13:1–9 and 13:31–32 for the related biblical text).

The children's attention to the first story was heightened this day, and they immediately moved into the wondering. Several children, including a visitor, offered a group interpretation of the parable, each adding to what others said. Others watched and listened closely. At the end of this wondering time the group's interpretation included:

> The seeds were people.

> The birds were bullies or other people who kept people from going to church, maybe by distracting them.

> The seeds that fell on rocky ground symbolized people who only went to church a few times so it "didn't take."

> The seed falling among thorns represented people who came to church a little more but things got in the way of them coming.

> The seed that grew in the grass represented people who came to church all the time.

Using the "manipulables" that are part of the Godly Play storytelling method, the storyteller moved the harvest baskets around, asking the children where they should go. The children maintained their joint interpretation that seeds falling on good soil would yield the greatest harvest. The storyteller then moved on to the next parable, saying, "You probably already know which one it is" as she pulled out the yellow felt underlay. Several children exclaimed, "The mustard seed!" After the story,

---

10. For more information about these elements, see Berryman (1991; 1995). "Wondering questions" are designed to help the children enter the story and think analytically about the story before applying the story to their lives. For example, the questions for sacred stories are "What did you like best?", "What do you think is most important?", "Where are you in this story?", and "Is there a part of the story we could leave out and still have all the story we need?"

the wondering immediately began again as the children made connections between the parables. Comments included:

"The birds in the mustard seed belong in the sower story. They were bullies too."

"No, they ate the seed, but lived in the mustard plant."

"If they lived in the mustard plant, they weren't bullies anymore; they were changed."

"The mustard plant was like a family and the birds were part of the family."

"The mustard plant was part of the large harvest."

"The sower had planted the seeds and the mustard seed."

"Maybe the birds were happy when the sower sowed seeds."

"Maybe the sower was happy when the birds ate the seed."

"Maybe the sower sowed seeds so the birds could eat them."

Almost all the children spoke during this part of the wondering time, each again listening to each other, and adding ideas with respect and kindness. The circle of children had been safe enough and the stories engaging enough that even the newcomer and those who did not come regularly added to the interpretation of the stories.

Here, the children connected biblical stories to their own lives, with an overarching theme of church as a community of belonging (e.g., the importance of "getting to church") and of encounters with those who threaten spiritual/ physical well-being (e.g., connecting birds to bullies), all in an atmosphere of respect for each other's ideas. After six months together they had internalized the lessons of the circle (where everyone is listened to) and of the process of the story and the wondering in order to learn to use religious language for making meaning. This represents the effectiveness of the Godly Play form of education in achieving its goals in this church's context. It also shows the powerful way in which practices in one area of congregational life shape and reflect the implicit values and messages of the institution: these children already have begun to internalize the high value this particular church culture places on church attendance, which has a decisive impact on their interpretation of the parable.

In teaching with the Godly Play method, Shepherd of the Hills models the priority it attributes to teaching children the central Christian practices of interpretation of scripture texts and meaning-making with religious language, even from a young age. The wondering questions begin the children's foray into this practice, so that as they get older they will be able to continue making meaning of the texts they hear in worship and educational events. Thus, the children are "apprenticed" in one of the basic formational practices of the Christian faith for this community through the congregation's practice of teaching and learning biblical interpretation within the bounds of a way of being Christian together.[11]

An irony presents itself, however. The children are included in the practice of interpretation within the Christian education classes, but they are structurally excluded from the primary community sites for enacting this Christian practice in the worship and the proclamation of the Word that takes place there. The congregation offers education for children during every worship service. Children begin the worship hour with their families in the sanctuary. A few minutes into the service, they are invited to stay with their families or go to Godly Play. Presumably, parents and children could worship together during one hour, and then take part in some form of Christian education for the other hour, as there are adult education events on occasion, or adults could teach during this hour and participate in an adult event during the week. In practice, families only attend one service, and choose to worship together or be separated for the hour. Thus, most children who attend Godly Play do not participate in the congregation's worship life.

Many Sunday school teachers and parents have expressed frustration that the children do not attend worship, and that they are excluded from the core ritual expressions of the Christian faith in which they could be taught to participate. In spite of that exclusion, children demonstrate through their connections between getting to church and one's growth in faith that they understand worship as the primary place for the community's interpretation of texts.

Another irony in this practice with children relates to children's visibility to the congregation. Although not occurring in the church's primary space for congregational practices—the sanctuary during worship—the resources the church invests in training, teaching and providing resources for Godly Play are extraordinary. The church has in a sense "hired out" the education of its children, and the children of the church end up in a kind of protected zone. People who care deeply about ministries with children give their best energies to them and so the children benefit immensely. Yet this protected area is a wall that isolates the children from the rest of the congregation, demonstrated in their absence from congregational worship (in contrast see chapter 17). The congregation has little knowledge of what the children are doing and therefore little interest in receiving back from them what they have learned. But in its support for the program, its commissioning of those so gifted to work with and for children, and the presence of buildings, materials and staff for Godly Play, the whole church participates in the action of educating children in

11. For a study from an Evangelical perspective on Godly Play's ability to enhance the spirituality of children, see Catherine Stonehouse (2001). Stonehouse compares children in Godly Play and those experiencing "a variety of worship experiences not based on any particular plan" (p. 31). From her data, she concludes that Godly Play "helps children creatively engage the stories and discover meaning in them" (p. 39); "may be a factor that enhances a wondering, searching spirit in children" (p. 41); and "gives children a quiet place and time to hear the stories of God and reflect on them" (p. 43). This underscores our observations about how Godly Play functions educationally at Shepherd of the Hills.

faith. And those adults in the congregation who become Godly Play teachers speak of how their own lives of faith become transformed as they come to "inhabit" the stories they tell each week in teaching children.

Music and Mission at Bethel Community Presbyterian Church

Bethel Community Presbyterian Church is a congregation located in the multi-cultural urban village of San Leandro, California. Local people who wanted to have a Sunday School for their children established the congregation in the 1940s. The social and economic makeup of the community began to change in the 1970s as people from non-European ethnic cultures moved into the area. By the 1990s the congregation had dwindled to a few dozen members and considered merging with another congregation or disbanding, but has now become a redevelopment congregation with a permanent pastor. Since entering the redevelopment process, Bethel has seen new growth and vitality. It now has 83 members and an average worship attendance of 70 people. The ethnic makeup of the congregation has become more diverse in recent years. An average Sunday worship service includes African, African American, Euro-American, Chinese American, Indonesian and Palestinian worshippers.

The new pastor has brought a strong interest in children's ministries. The congregation embraced this interest and reexamined their congregational practices with children. Service to children now figures prominently in the church's mission. For example, several members engage in the practice of volunteering at an elementary school located across the street. The most significant practice for serving the children in the community, and the pride of Bethel, is that of gathering children from the community alongside their own members' children on Friday afternoons to participate in music, art and literacy activities followed by dinner with parents and caregivers.

On one particular Friday afternoon at the end of November, the children gathered in preparation for choir rehearsal. As the children entered the sanctuary, they began to fill in the first three pews at the front left hand side, in front of the piano. "Nancy," the music director, began by asking the children where they should be sitting. Some of the children spoke the answer out loud. "In the first three rows." Nancy asked the children if they remembered singing at the "Miracle on East 14th Street" event last year. (This is a December holiday event that is sponsored by the local Chamber of Commerce.) Some children said "yes." Nancy reminded them of the songs they sang at this event and mentioned that they had received chocolate for their participation. She said that they have been invited to sing again this year. She told the children that she needed to teach them some Christmas music other than the music from their Christmas musical, because the music from "The Grumpy Shepherd" probably was not the most appropriate music to sing at this event. She then stated that they were going to sing one of the songs they sang last year, "Sing Noel." She demonstrated a rhythmic body percussion using clapping and patting on the thighs. The four beat pattern was "pat-pat-clap-rest." The children joined in. Sam and Tony began chanting "We will, we will rock you." All of the children were able to do this pattern, even the children not involved in the Christmas musical. Once the pattern was established, Nancy moved to the piano and sang the song while those children who knew the song joined in. The children who did not know the song either did not sing or caught what words they could as the song progressed.

When the song was completed, Nancy said the children's singing was good. She acknowledged that some of the children did not know the song, but assured them that it is easy to learn because there are only two words in the song, "sing" and "noel." Someone asked what "noel" meant. Nancy asked if any of the children knew what the word meant. After some incorrect guesses, Nancy asked the children at what time of the year they sing this song. They replied "at Christmas" and Nancy told them that "noel" means "Christmas." Some of the children started singing the song again with the words "Sing Christmas" and Nancy said it should be "Sing about Christmas." Nancy continued the rehearsal with some other musical selections for the event.

This brief glimpse inside a Friday afternoon children's choir rehearsal exemplifies the interconnectedness of practices and how a congregation shares its valued congregational practices with children. As in many Christian congregations, communal singing is a regular congregational practice experienced in the wider practice of worship at Bethel, where the congregation's faith is nurtured and expressed through the practice of singing together in congregational song, hymnody, and choirs. One way children from outside the worshipping community of the congregation learn this practice is in the educational event on Fridays.

This practice has a transformative, critical edge. At face value, the church appears to be engaging in an educational practice that benefits children, welcoming and mentoring them into the congregational practice of singing in worship. And yet many of those engaging in the practice that Friday, like most other times, were children and families who were not members of the congregation. On the one hand, this practice of welcoming children and educating them in the practice of Christian hymn singing affords no apparent tangible benefit to the church in terms of increased membership. On the other hand, what became obvious to us was the way these missional practices with community children in fact, have contributed to the congregation's revitalization. Whereas in previous years the church was more focused on its internal needs, this practice with children has begun to refocus the congregation to look outside itself. The church reallocated many of its resources to engage in this ministry, and an ordained minister with musical skills directs the children's choir and hand chimes ensemble. Congregation members are either paid or volunteer staff members, and donate food for the dinner. The money from several of the fundraisers held throughout the year is designated to support this Friday event with children. Furthermore, when children from the wider community do participate in congregational worship, as the children's choir does once a month, the visual presence of the children engages the youngsters in worship while it reinforces the congregation's interest in continuing the practice.

Thus, the children's presence and the church's engagement with children in this multivalent practice have an unexpected pedagogical feature for the congregation. By engaging in the activity of teaching Christian music and the Christian practice of hymn singing, Bethel learns to be missional; to share itself with the community, and congregants learn to work together to accomplish something that none of them could do alone. It is not a perfect solution to the congregation's struggles with survival, nor is there uniform embracing of the congregation's involvements with children by every member of the community. Still, after experiencing and learning from its practice of caring for children, Bethel has begun to talk about other ways of caring for the community, such as supporting a transitional housing program for unemployed families. The practice of welcoming community children to Bethel is teaching the congregation to be an open, caring and compassionate church community.

Calling Each One By Name: The Practice of "Singing the Children Up" at First Presbyterian Church

San Anselmo, California is a small town about twelve miles north of San Francisco's Golden Gate Bridge. The one hundred year old First Presbyterian Church of San Anselmo, like the town in which it ministers, is a small community of mostly European-Americans of upper-middle or upper-class socio-economic standing. The church is across the street from the local elementary school, whose nonsectarian aftercare programs are operated by the church through its preschool director. A residential facility for developmentally disabled persons is within walking distance for its residents, some of whom are church members. While the higher income of many church members affords some protection from the impact of economic decline, quite a few of this congregation's professionals have been unemployed for a year or more.

The town and church are also home to a Presbyterian Church (U.S.A.) theological seminary, whose students and their families bring both racial-ethnic and socio-economic diversity to these communities. "First Friendly," as the church is nicknamed, brings approximately 250 worshippers together on a given Sunday morning, and its staff includes a pastor, associate pastor for families, children and youth, associate pastor for older adult ministries, a weekday preschool director and teachers (who also happen to be the paid nursery childcare staff for many church functions including Sunday morning worship), music director, organist, and administrative/clerical staff persons.

On a recent Sunday morning this congregation gathered for worship amidst the sounds of children's chatter, adult laughter, and babies crying over the organ music as people found their seats. In the narthex as persons entered, adults were greeted by the "official greeters" who welcomed them to the church. In addition to a handshake, children coming into the church received a special greeting from "Jack," who also asked them their names and made sure they each had a worship packet (a Ziploc bag with crayons, children's activity sheets, and a children's bulletin). Jack gathered the names of all the children who came into the church that morning, as he does every Sunday. Then, during the congregation's rite of passing the peace, Jack walked almost imperceptibly up to the front of the sanctuary, handing a small piece of paper to the pastor. As the congregation sat down again, "Pastor Charles" picked up his guitar and began to sing the refrain of a song, printed in the bulletin, which the whole congregation then joined in singing as children throughout the sanctuary perched on the edges of their seats or moved to the ends of the pews, waiting to hear:

> Come, come, come and sit down. We are a part of the family.
> We are lost and we are found. We are a part of the family.[12]

A few children went immediately to sit on the chancel steps along with the other adult worship leaders upon hearing the opening chords of the song. But following the refrain, the pastor continued to sing, one by one singing out the names of all of the children in the congregation, including those names of visitors or children who attended less frequently, given to him on the slip of paper provided by Jack a few moments earlier. Most children could be seen listening carefully for their names. Some like Julie jumped with delight upon hearing her name sung, running forward with excitement to sit on the steps as the song continued. Nathaniel stood beside parents in the pew, rocking back and forth until finally hearing his name, and then walked forward in a dignified and gentle way. Some children arrived in the chancel area accompanied by an adult. Others, moving forward after hearing their names sung, joined some adults by taking a seat in a lap or leaning against a shoulder.

The pastor's singing of the names ended on this day, as it always does, with the call for "all of our visitors too" to come forward. Then the congregation joined together in the final singing of the refrain, which ended as the pastor put aside his guitar, sat among the children, and began engaging them in the "time with children."

The congregational practice of "singing the children up" (as it is referred to in worship planning meetings), like all practices, is a composite entity, involving pastoral musical leadership, congregational singing, adult companionship of children, and children's listening, singing, and movement. The practice also reflects composite and multiple levels of meaning, as it is a liturgical practice simultaneously operating as a gathering rite, a practice of hospitality, and an enactment of the valuing of children by the whole community. As a gathering rite situated after the passing of the peace and preliminary to the children's sermon, this musical practice transforms the process of getting children to the front of the sanctuary from an awkward movement *en mass* that tends to reinforce negative perceptions of children's presence in the sanctuary in terms

12. The hymn is an adaptation of "Part of the Family," by Jim Manley (1985).

of noise, to a liturgical dance in which the entire congregation participates as each child moves to the front when called by name. Corporately bringing the children into the congregation's presence through a liturgical action of naming them is significantly different than a simple verbal invitation to children in general to come forward.

This practice would not function well were it isolated from the other liturgical actions of the congregation, by being a separate form or quality of music designed for the children and unlike the rest of the worship service. Its power to operate as a congregational practice of welcoming children and including them fully in the community occurs precisely because the practice fits the larger liturgical practices of the congregation, with its variety in musical styles cast in a traditional Reformed order of worship.

But perhaps most significant is the power of this worship practice to shape the religious imaginations of children by constructing over time a notion of church simultaneously tied to, yet bigger than, their personal experiences of "family." The whole congregation sings the song, and children come from all kinds of families—"traditional" nuclear families, blended families, extended families, single parent families, same-sex parent families, multiracial/cultural families, interfaith families—responding to the singing and to the call of their names in worship. This liturgical practice, unlike similar practices that seek to directly engage children in worship, does not require young children to engage in analogical thinking or in making cognitive connections that compare the love of God to a never-ending circle of toothpaste squirted out on newspapers or seeing in everything Jesus did or said some message about obedience to parents and other authorities. Instead, as a practice situated in liturgy that does not constantly seek to explain itself, the whole congregation sings the names of the children as it populates their imaginations with the notion that "we are part of the family."

As a practice of hospitality, "singing the children up" actually begins when Jack welcomes the children at the door, makes a relational connection with them, and learns their names. This hospitality then extends into the worship space as the practice invites rather than restricts children's movement and voice, and as it implicitly "expects" that they will be listening and will therefore hear their names. Parents, as well as other adults in the community, spoke in interviews and informal conversations about the power of this particular congregational practice to constitute the worship space as hospitable for children.

Notably, however, their comments reflect the ways in which the liturgical practice of singing up the children by name also creates a hospitable worship environment for adults who live in a geographical area marked by lifestyles shaped by anonymity and individualism in which participation in a faith community is an exceptional behavior rather than a normative one. Here, pastors in their opening words of welcome to the worshipping community often invite everyone to sign the "friendship pads" registering their attendance at the service in the face of a culture in which few people may be known by name. Singing the children's names reminds everybody that they too have names and identities, an important reminder in the "dot-com" telecommuter context of this northern California community. Older members of the congregation frequently commented on their enjoyment at seeing the children come forward in response to hearing their names, and therefore the pleasure they get from participating in the congregational singing of the song.

There is an ongoing debate about the negative potential of children's sermons displaying children for adult gratification versus the positive potential to communicate the importance of children and to offer children a simplified message. While we do not want to become enmeshed in that debate, our research suggests that one of the most important positive impacts of this congregational practice of gathering the children together in worship is its visual power. Children, generally smaller than the sanctuary furniture and the adults with whom they sit, can easily be rendered invisible in most Christian worship spaces. At First Presbyterian Church, the practice of gathering the children together through song provides visibility to the children, creating the possibility of their recognition by adults. The fact that they are gathered by name creates, in addition, the possibility of their being known by name by many adults in the congregation.

In addition to these child-affirming aspects of the practice, First Presbyterian's congregational practice of singing the children up into the chancel also reveals and critiques several discrepancies in the larger life of the church regarding children's visibility. While the children's names are markedly significant, adult visitors virtually can be ignored in this small-town church where members tend to meet, greet, and congregate with their friends. Many adults do not greet children or know them by name in the ordinary places of encounter such as the coffee fellowship time or upon their arrival at the church. Also, the fact that this practice is the prelude to the children's exit from worship to their Christian education classes (they are present for the whole service once every five weeks) points out the double message given to children about their inclusion and belonging in worship: as two practices carried out over time in this congregation, the extravagant inclusion of the singing practice may or may not offset the ritual exclusion of the children from worship for most of the services. In addition, the practice of calling persons by name always teeters on the brink of inadvertent exclusion of someone who is present but unnamed in the singing.

Bourdieu's (1977) assertion that practices function critically in that they often embody meanings other than their commonly accepted and explicitly articulated ones may be apropos here. In the case of the congregational practice of gathering the children through singing, it is possible to interpret the practice as *appearing* to be about the valuing of children when it in fact may contribute further to their marginalization by legitimating their exclusion from other arenas of congregational life. In spite of such variant and discrepant meanings and the issues they raise for this practice with children, First Presbyterian Church focuses on the earlier mentioned, positive elements as it embraces the practice of singing the children's names in virtually every worship service.

Some Preliminary Implications from this Study of Congregational Practices

As mentioned earlier, congregational practices are activities by a community over time. Such practices shape and critique the life of the congregation in addition to their potentially transformative impact on individuals. In this study of the three congregations participating in the "Children in Congregations" project we are currently at a very preliminary stage of analysis, one that involves articulating the questions that emerged during the study. These include three questions related to the three examples of congregational practices discussed above: How does the congregation's structuring of educational ministry contribute to children's faith development? How does the presence of children in the congregation affect its mission and identity as a community? What practices in worship engage the religious imaginations of children?

As we begin to reflect on and analyze congregational practices with children, several themes emerge. First, many of the congregational practices with children that we experienced, including those discussed above, take into account children's developmental proclivities toward impulsivity and physicality. In some cases, the practices constructively engage the impulsivity through body movement. Many congregational practices with children invite children to move, such as processionals or gathering rituals; dance and music; and roaming in the aisle or parents rocking and nursing infants.

In other cases, these practices take children's impulsivity and physicality into account by allowing children to choose how they will participate in the community's activities from a variety of acceptable modes of participation. For example, children in worship may sing hymns with adults, draw, notice imagery in stained glass windows, play with toys, "wonder" as encouraged by Godly Play, or move around on the floor below the pews, all within the range of what that community deems an acceptable norm for children's participation. In all these practices, children's agency is honored and encouraged in age-appropriate ways. One mark of a congregation's capacity to welcome and nurture the spirituality of children may be its creativity in constructing positive communal practices that make room for a variety of levels and types of engagement rather than prescribing a fixed type—such as listening with full cognitive comprehension to the sermon—as necessary for legitimate participation.

Second, a critical element in the vitality of each of the three congregation's practices with children is their dedication of significant resources—space, people, financial, programmatic—to a wide array of children's ministry activities. That is, these congregations do not limit the resources allocated to children's ministries to a single area, such as the purchase of Sunday school materials, but instead resource children's ministries throughout the life of the congregation. Nor are all their resources monetary. In several instances, more tangible financial resources followed rather than preceded personal and communal commitments of time, skills, and energy—as, for example, at Bethel when the congregation began a community time of watching movies that included children. In this case people initially gave their time and energy to participate in the fellowship and education of these events. This participation was later followed by the committing of personal financial resources to support the event by purchasing a projection system and screen.

Third, in practices with children, inconsistency appears to be the norm for congregational life. The three congregations studied have pockets of amazing vitality and strength in one area of their practices with children, only to totally miss other seemingly obvious opportunities for vital ministry with children elsewhere in congregational life. At this point, we attribute some of this inconsistency to the difficulty congregations and their leaders have in being intentional about keeping children in the foreground. In the absence of a consistent vision held by the entire congregation that prioritizes and advocates for children in all aspects of the congregation's life and ministry, practices in one area of ministry may be haphazard or not be linked to practices in other areas. For example, liturgical practices that exclude children may compete, unnoticed, with educational practices intended to empower children's participation in worship. When practices with children are not subject to theological reflection, as is often the case with adults, such reflection may only emerge unintentionally and then infused with meaning after the fact. This is in part the nature of a practice and is not necessarily negative as it can be part of the transformative quality of practices. And yet, this accidental manner in which many practices with children are established in congregations can lead to unintegrated, haphazard ministries with children.

Finally, we notice that amidst the shared faith heritage and meanings implicit in many Christian practices, practices with children have a strongly contextual character. That is, each congregational context shapes and reshapes particular practices in relation to its own identity and culture, such that the same practice may look different and mean something quite different in two congregations. For example, the practice of providing children with "activity books" in worship may occur in one congregation as a practice primarily concerned with noise control, while the identical practice in another congregation is an intentional pedagogical technique to increase engagement of children in worship.

These implications are merely preliminary observations. We will continue to explore and analyze the practices of Shepherd of the Hills, Bethel, and First Presbyterian Church, anticipating many new questions and issues to be raised from our study of these three congregations and their practices with children.

References

Ammerman, N. T., Carroll, J. W., Dudley, C. S. & McKinney, W. (1998). *Studying congregations: A new handbook*. Nashville: Abingdon.

Bass, D. C. (1997). *Practicing our faith*. San Francisco: Jossey-Bass.

Berryman, J. (1991). *Godly play: An imaginative approach to religious education*. Minneapolis: Augsburg.

Berryman, J. (1995). *Teaching godly play: The Sunday morning handbook*. Nashville: Abingdon.

Bourdieu, P. (1977). *Outline of a theory of practice*. (R. Nince, Trans.). Cambridge Studies in Social and Cultural Anthropology. Cambridge: Cambridge University Press.

Chopp, R. S. (1995). *Saving work: Feminist practices of theological education*. Louisville: Westminster John Knox.

Eiesland, N. (2000). *A particular place: Urban restructuring and religious ecology in a southern exurb*. New Brunswick, NJ: Rutgers University Press.

Foster, C. R., and Brelsford, T. (1996). *We are the church together: Cultural diversity in congregational life*. Valley Forge, PA: Trinity.

Hopewell, J. F. (1987). *Congregation: Stories and structures*. Philadelphia: Fortress.

Little, S. (1983). *To set one's heart: Belief and teaching in the church*. Atlanta: John Knox.

Manley, J. (1985). *Part of the family* (book and tape). Sunnyvale, CA: Jim Manley Music.

Mercer, J. A. (2002, November). *Practicing liturgy as a practice of justice with children*. Paper presented at the Association of Practical Theology Annual Meeting. Toronto, ON.

Ng, D. & Thomas, V. (1981). *Children in the worshiping community*. Atlanta: John Knox.

Prichard, G. W. (1992). *Offering the gospel to children*. Cambridge, MA: Cowley.

Stonehouse, Catherine (2001). Knowing God in childhood: A study of Godly Play and the spirituality of children. *Christian Education Journal, 5NS*, 27–45.

Chapter Seventeen

Nurturing Children's Spirituality in Intergenerational Christian Settings

HOLLY CATTERTON ALLEN[1]

S omething happened to me in the 1990s that forever changed the way I see children and the way I view Christian education. I had been involved with children's ministry since I was eleven years old and had taught Sunday school for decades. Then in 1993, my family became part of a small-groups-based church, and for the first time I was regularly with children in Christian *intergenerational* settings. The children had the opportunity to worship in small intimate settings with their parents and other adults, to hear their parents pray, and to see their parents minister to others in the group. The children themselves began to pray for one another, to minister to each another and even to the adults. These experiences profoundly changed my understanding of children as well as my understanding of Christian education.

Those years began a ten-year journey toward understanding the impact of intergenerational Christian experiences (IGCE) upon children. That journey led to doctoral dissertation research on the topic where I examined IGCE empirically, theoretically, practically, educationally, and theologically. The first section of this chapter defines terms and describes various types of intergenerational ministry. The second section provides biblical/theological premises and learning theory concepts that undergird

---

1. Holly Catterton Allen is an associate professor at John Brown University and the Director of the Children and Family Ministry program in the Biblical Studies Division at JBU. Her Ph.D. in Christian Education is from Talbot School of Theology. She has also studied at Abilene Christian University, received an M.A. from The University of Iowa, and a B.A. from Harding University. Dr. Allen's areas of specialty are children's spirituality and intergenerational issues. She speaks regularly at conferences and churches concerning these issues, and has written about them for several journals and other Christian publications. She also wrote a chapter in *Children of Promise* (by McAlpine and Russell, World Vision, 2003). She has served as an adjunct professor in Hong Kong and for Talbot School of Theology. She is the co-chair of the planning team for the second national Children's Spirituality Conference: Christian Perspectives to be held in June of 2006.

intergenerational experience. The third section offers empirical support for the benefits of IG experiences from my research.

Intergenerational Christian Experiences

Scores of definitions of spirituality, Christian spirituality, spiritual formation, and spiritual development exist. To better understand nurturing children's spirituality in intergenerational settings, certain terms need to be defined.

What Is Spirituality?

Three definitions of spirituality have significantly informed my study of intergenerational ministry. Graven (1999) comments, "Spiritual dimensions of life involve beliefs, an understanding of God, relationship to God, and understanding the relationship of God to the world and creation" (p. 56). Schneiders (1986) adds that, "Christian spirituality . . . is constituted by the substantial gift of the Holy Spirit establishing a life-giving relationship with God in Christ within the believing community" (p. 266). Sheldrake (2000) speaks of Christian spirituality as, "a conscious relationship with God, in Jesus Christ, through the indwelling of the Spirit and in the context of community of believers" (p. 40).

A prevailing motif in these and most other current definitions of spirituality is the idea of relationality. For example, Mead and Nash (1997) comment that "spirituality is properly defined as the creation and cultivation of an intimate relationship with God" (p. 54). The definition of spirituality that captures this basic recurring theme of relationality and provides the operative definition for this chapter is "awareness of relationship with God."

What Is Meant by the Term "Intergenerational"?

White (1988) says that "characteristically intergenerational is meant to involve adults-with-children" (p. 21). Other phrases that connote the same general idea are interage, multi-generational, and cross-generational. White emphasizes that the generations are to be "involved" with each other in mutual activities, in group experiences together, and with several from each of the generations present. Prest's (1993) definition of intergenerational Christian experience is "the socializing of two or more different age groups, interacting in learning, growing, and developing in the faith, through common experiences of fellowship, worship, sharing, and relationships" (p. 15). The term "intergenerational" is not typically used to describe the adult-as-teacher/children-as-learners model of education, nor a one-on-one mentoring relationship.

What Are Intergenerational Settings?

Intergenerational (IG) activities can take many forms in Christian settings. Six promising forms are described below.

1. *Including children in worship.* Many churches include the children for 15–20 minutes (or more) of praise in the Sunday morning worship. Major religious educationists (e.g., Westerhoff, 1976; Fowler, 1991) recommend this approach as well as IG advocates (e.g., White, 1988; Prest, 1993).

2. *Special programs.* Another common IG activity is allowing children to be present at special programs such as baptisms, "baby dedication Sunday," and church-wide congratulatory celebrations for graduating seniors of the church, retiring ministers, and the like.

3. *Intergenerational events.* Some churches plan one or more events a year that are envisioned, planned, created, and performed by an intergenerational group of people. This could be a Thanksgiving program, a short drama for Easter, a Christmas musical, or some other event that requires time, effort, creativity, brainstorming, and work for a group of people of all ages.

4. *Family camps.* Some churches annually rent camp facilities for week-long or weekend family camps. Though typically only a small percentage of church families can participate (due to financial or time constraints), these camps provide excellent opportunities for families to bond spiritually.

5. *IG Sunday Schools or Bible study.* A few churches have experimented with intergenerational Sunday School classes studying a topic such as the fruit of the Spirit or the Beatitudes for four to six weeks.

6. *Intergenerational small groups.* A more comprehensive approach to IG Christian experience is forming weekly (or bi-weekly) intergenerational small groups. This approach is a church-wide undertaking requiring support of not only the leaders but also the whole church.

Activities in Intergenerational Small Groups

The following descriptions of the kinds of things that happen in IG small groups come from my family's experience in the church mentioned earlier as well as from stories from children, their parents, or pastors in my research. When IG small groups meet, typically the adults and children stay together for about half of the time. During this time the children participate with the parents and other adults in the ice-breaker, worship, and prayer. After this the children are dismissed for the children's small group.

Icebreakers. Typically the first thing that happens in a small group is the ice-breaker. A question is asked to which both adults and children respond. One time the icebreaker in our group was "What are you afraid of?" Some of the responses were:

"Gaining too much weight in my pregnancy."

"That I will die young like my dad did."

"That I won't be able to finish my thesis."

"That I won't pass fourth grade."

"That my cancer will return."

"That Ben won't get his parole."

Then it was Jeremy's turn. He was a second grader at the time. He put his head on his arm and began to cry, and said in a small, jerky voice, "I'm afraid to go to sleep because I have nightmares." One of the fathers in the group immediately came over to Jeremy and put his arm around his shoulders. He held him for a minute, and then prayed with him and over him, that God would take away the nightmares. Then one of the older elementary girls in the group came over and said to Jeremy, "You know, Jeremy, I used to have nightmares, but I prayed to God and he took them away." A mother in the group said, "I was reading the Psalms last night and I found a scripture for you, Psalm 4:8, 'I go to bed and sleep in peace. Lord, you keep me safe.'"

This story illustrates the kind of intergenerational ministry that can and does happen even in the "lightweight" part of the evening, the icebreaker. Of course, often the icebreaker is simply light and fun, such as "What did you enjoy most at the Fourth of July fireworks celebration?"

Worship. Worship holds an important place for the children and adults who are part of intergenerational small groups. Sometimes a child chooses the songs and may even lead the music. Occasionally a parent and his/her child choose the songs together. In the groups I have participated in, the praise time might last a few minutes or half an hour, depending on such factors as the leaders' choices, the spirit of the group, response to the week's experiences, or the needs of the evening. Sometimes the praise time turns into a time of lament if some or many in the group are suffering difficult times. Worshiping together in a close and intimate setting reveals inner spiritual lives to both children and adults.

Lord's Supper. The small groups that my family attended observed the Lord's Supper in small, close settings which brought new meaning and depth to what can become a rote ceremony, especially for children. The children in my church partook of the Lord's Supper with the adults. The church found no Biblical prohibition of this practice and it offered an opportunity for children to hear their parents and other adults they knew talk about their feelings and thoughts as they took of the bread and the cup. The group discovered ways to make the observance of communion meaningful for both children and adults. This way of taking the Lord's Supper clarified the spiritual concepts surrounding it. The children began to discern the many facets of Christ's sacrifice. An added benefit was that it became more and more natural to discuss spiritual things within the families.

Prayer. Most of the children interviewed as part of my research mentioned prayer as a significant part of their experience in IG small groups. Many of them referred to the fact that they prayed in their groups. In my own experience in small groups, we did not usually have long periods of prayer while children were present, but we always prayed with and for families that were going through a transition.

When a child graduated from high school, joined the military forces, got a job, or went to college, we prayed for the whole family. When a child entered kindergarten, middle school, junior high, or high school, we prayed with and for that child. We knew the children in our small group, and they knew us. Some children were comfortable praying in the group from the beginning; others waited a few months before they chose to pray. However it usually took about six months before a child was comfortable enough to be prayed for by the whole group.

Other small group activities. The children in the research study mentioned that in their groups they usually ate, sometimes a meal and sometimes only a snack. They also mentioned that they enjoyed simply playing with the other children. Several spoke of group ministry opportunities such a cleaning out an older person's garage or taking food to the sick.

Benefits from Intergenerational Small Groups

Children who regularly participate in IG small groups have special opportunities for spiritual development. In a sense, they gain an extended family that is otherwise unavailable to most children today; they gain spiritual "aunts" and "uncles," "grandparents," and "cousins." They also see other role models for parenting. More importantly they often participate in the spiritual lives of their parents. They learn the spiritual disciplines by watching and doing. They learn to share as they see their parents and others share their lives. They see others minister to one another and they begin to minister. They see their parents and others pray for concerns in their lives and they too begin to pray.

While the children are benefiting immensely from the IG activities, parents and other adults must give up some of their own cherished desires such as tranquil, uninterrupted worship and deep spiritual discussions that last until midnight. However, most relinquish these gladly as they discover the blessings for adults and children who participate in each other's spiritual lives.

Learning Theory and Intergenerational Christian Education

Intergenerational gatherings are not a new invention of contemporary churches. God's directives for the Israelites included many opportunities for families and the community to celebrate together, to worship together, to discuss theological matters. In the religion of Israel, children were not just included, they were drawn in, and absorbed into the whole community. They had a deep sense of belonging (Harkness, 1998, p. 436). Though many examples could be cited, the directives for feasts and celebrations illustrate this point best. These festivals required by God were celebrated annually and included elaborate meals, dancing, instrumental music, singing, and sacrifices. All of Israel participated, from the youngest to the oldest (Ratcliff, n.d.).

These festivals included Passover, the Feast of Weeks, the Feast of Booths, and the Feast of Trumpets.[2] The purpose of these festivals was to remind the Israelites who they were, who God was, and what God had done for his people in ages past. As children and teens danced, sang, ate, listened to the stories, and asked questions, they came to know who they were and who they were to be. And their knowing would carry the sense of the Hebrew word *yada'* which connotes more than intellectual information, but rather knowing by experiencing (Fretheim, 1997, p. 410). In these settings, God clearly expected the older generation to be available to the younger to answer questions and to explain the reasons for their confidence in God (see e.g., Exod 12:27).

It seems today that learning how to be God's people has become less a joining in with community, and more a gathering of age-segregated groups *to study about* being God's people. This insight leads to the important issue of learning theory; the content of learning is interrelated with the process of learning (the what and how of learning).

Situative/Sociocultural Learning Theory

The situative/sociocultural perspective on knowing and learning focuses on the way knowledge is distributed among individuals in a social group, the tools and methods that they use, and the practices in which they participate (Greeno, Collins, & Resnick, 1996). Lev Vygotsky[3] (1926/1997) is the best-known theorist in this category, although Jerome Bruner (Bruner & Haste, 1987) shifted from the cognitive to the social cognitive and sociocultural positions over his career. The situative/sociocultural theory

2. Passover (Exod 12; 23:15; 34:18, 25; Lev 23:5–8; Num 9:1–14; 28:16–25; Deut 16:1–8; Ezek 45:21–24), the Feast of Weeks (Exod 23:16; 34:22; Lev 23:15–21; Num 28:26–31; Deut 16:9–10), the Feast of Booths (Exod 23:16; 34:22; Lev 23:33–36; Num 28:12–39; Deut 16:13–18), and the Feast of Trumpets (Lev 23:23–25; Num 29:1–6).

3. Lev Vygotsky was born in Byelorussia in November 1896 to middle-class Jewish parents. He graduated with a law degree from Moscow University in 1917 and studied history and philosophy at Shanyansky's Popular University just before the Bolshevik revolution. He began teaching at Moscow University's Psychological Institute in 1924 and wrote and taught in the area of psychology, human development, and learning over the next ten years. He died of tuberculosis in 1934 at the age of 37. During those ten years (1924–1934) Vygotsky authored approximately two hundred papers, most of which have only recently been published in English. After Vygotsky's death, his work was suppressed during Stalin's reign. His works began to be published in the 1950s in Russia, but only in 1978 with the publication of his works in English has Vygotsky's thought begun to widely impact educational thought and practice in the West.

places a strong emphasis on the social interaction of the learning environment and assumes that for persons to learn concepts, they must experience them and socially negotiate their meaning in authentic, complex learning environments.

During Vygotsky's era (1920s–1930s), psychologists were divided on the issue of human development and learning into two basic camps—either behaviorist or cognitivist (Collins & Resnick, 1996). Vygotsky initially identified more closely with the behaviorist position but was also in contact with Piaget and those from the cognitivist position. He eventually rejected both theories. Rieber and Carton (1987) explain it best: "Vygotsky argued that [psychological processes] have their source not in biological structures or the learning of the isolated individual but in historically developed socio-cultural experience" (p. 19). Two main concepts are crucial in understanding Vygotsky's theory: the role of signs and the zone of proximal development.

The role of signs. When Vygotsky speaks of the human use of signs, he is speaking of mental tools. These mental tools are sociocultural elements such as language, writing, other symbols (such as gestures), and art. Vygotsky purports that culture is mediated to the individual through these mental tools, particularly language. Just as persons use physical tools to expand their physical capabilities, persons use language and other mental tools to expand their mental capacities.

Interestingly Deut 6:6–9 captures a very similar understanding:

> These commandments that I give you today are to be upon your hearts. Impress them on your children. Talk about them when you sit at home and when you walk along the road, when you lie down and when you get up. Tie them as symbols on your hand and bind them on your foreheads. Write them on the doorframes of your houses and on your gates.

God says talk, write, and tie symbols. These descriptions sound much like Vygotsky's "mental tools" or "signs."

According to Vygotsky, it is through mental tools that children and adults develop the higher mental functions that characterize human life. Such higher mental functions include such abilities as planning, logical memory, and the formation of concepts. "All higher functions originate as actual relations between human individuals" (Vygotsky, 1978, p. 57). Thus humans grow and learn in social settings where they utilize their mental tools interacting with other humans. They speak, write, listen, and read others' ideas. This is how humans develop, according to Vygotsky.

Zone of proximal development. An important concept advanced by Vygotsky that has widely impacted education is the idea of the zone of proximal development (ZPD). Actually Vygotsky describes three zones of developmental activity:

Zone of Actual Development: Where the student *actually* is developmentally

Zone of Potential Development: Where the student *potentially* could be

> Zone of Proximal Development: The amount of assistance required for a student to move from the Zone of Actual Development to the Zone of Potential Development (Estep, 1999, p. 15)

Vygotsky says that most learning takes place in the Zone of Proximal Development (ZPD).

Wertsch and Rogoff (1984) have conceptualized the ZPD as:

> that phase in development in which the child has only partially mastered a task but can participate in its execution with the assistance and supervision of an adult or more capable peer. Thus, the zone of proximal development is a dynamic region of sensitivity in learning the skills of culture, in which children develop through participation in problem solving with more experienced members of the culture. (p. 1)

This concept of ZPD supports Vygotsky's whole sociocultural theory—that learning together in context is the way humans grow and learn.

Sociocultural Theory and Intergenerational Christian Education

The basic concepts underlying this discussion of sociocultural theory are that persons learn to be members of their community as they actively participate in that particular identified social community. Those communities define the types of learning that take place, and content alone does not determine what is learned. Learning is a social matter, made up of all those present as well as the general social milieu.

Christian educators seek to grow persons into mature Christians. The situative/ sociocultural theory describes how churches can enhance this process by bringing people together. In intergenerational Christian education the goal is to grow persons of faith who identify with and participate in faith communities. Situative learning and social constructivist approaches fit what those in intergenerational Christian education have been saying for years—to be a Christian one must participate fully in Christian community. When children experience intergenerational Christian education they learn from each other, younger children, older children, teen and adults the essence of Christian community. All benefit from each other. They essentially "grow each other up" (Erikson, 1963, p. 69).

My Research on Children's Spiritual Experience and Intergenerational Ministry

My doctoral research (2002) consisted of interviewing forty 9- to 11-year-old children in six Evangelical churches, representing two *types* of church settings. The first group belonged to churches where children were intentionally included in intergenerational activities. In particular, these children were a part of an intergenerational small group that met at least twice a month (IG churches). The second group attended churches where children are almost always segregated from adults (non-IG churches). The goal of the research was to use grounded theory research methodology to examine children's spirituality in intergenerational and non-intergenerational church settings.

A main difficulty was constructing questions that tap into the spiritual realm and not merely the cognitive realm. Berryman (1997) emphasizes the necessity of distinguishing the *knowing of the spirit* by contemplation from the *knowing of the body* by the senses and the *knowing of the mind* by reason in order to clarify the primary kind of knowing that makes religious education unique. I wanted to examine this knowing of the spirit, a difficult task and I was not entirely successful. Some of the questions in my interview protocol were as follows:

> Who do you know who knows God?

> What is it about that person that makes you think they know God?

> Do you know God? How does someone get to know God?

> What does it mean to know God?

> What is the difference between someone who knows God and someone who knows about God?

> Can you tell me about a time when you felt surprised or amazed about God? Happy about (or with) God? Sad about God? Have you ever felt angry at God? Scared of God?

> Do you talk to God? What sort of things you talk to God about?

> Do you ever listen to God? Have you ever thought God talked to you?

Knowing God

Table 1 displays the definitions the children gave for the concept "Knowing God." The comments represent a surprisingly balanced understanding of the concept of knowing God. The children seemed to comprehend that knowing God entails relationality, but they also placed a strong emphasis on the outward signs of that inward relationship, such as obedience, church attendance, and godly behaviors. In addition, they recognized that knowing God is a faith issue, that is, that believing in God is part of knowing God. The last category was surprising. Twenty-one statements focused on God himself, saying that knowing God inherently means literally knowing his character—that he is faithful, merciful, loving. Though basically a cognitive question, the simple question, "What does it mean to know God?" elicited profound statements from the children that offer insights into their understanding of this complex, important concept.

Table 1 Definition of Knowing God, All Children (n=40)

| Relationality | Appropriating | | Believing In God | Awareness of God's Character |
	Outward Religious Behavior	Observable Character		
Love him (5)	Go to church (8)	Do what God says (6)	Believe in him (8)	Know about him (4)
Have a relationship with him (4)	Involved at church	Try to be like God (5)	Know he's coming back	Know he is faithful
Pray/talk to him (22)	Sing in cantata	Like to be with those who know God (2)	Have faith	Know his character
Worship him (7)	Read the Bible (6)	Help people/care about feelings (2)	Believe he died on the cross/was raised (2)	Know he's loving (4)
Trust him (4)	Is a Christian (4)	Kind/nice/fun (7)		Know he's merciful
There for you	Go to small group	Generous/loving (2)		Know what he expects
Ask into your heart (8)	Read daily devotional	Don't gossip		Know he cares
Walk with God		Less worry (2)		Keeps his promises
Give life to him (3)		Tender conscience		Is awesome
Have a connection with him		Bring him glory		Understand God
Spend time with him		Aren't afraid		Know he's there
Think about him		Good attitude		Lets us choose good
He's in you		Don't lose temper		Know he is good
		Tell others about God		Gets us out of messes
				Know he means what he says
59 relational statements	22 statements on religious behavior	33 statements on observable character	12 "believing" statements	21 statements of God's character
30 different children	15 different children	17 different children	10 different children	11 different children

275

Prayer

When I began the microanalysis of the data, the first category that emerged was *prayer*. I had not originally planned on its being a major area for data analysis, but what the children said about prayer, more than any other topic, opened their spiritual lives to me. The children mentioned prayer frequently in describing people who know God, in their definitions of knowing God, in their recommendations for getting to know God, and when they described their own relationship with God. The children said they talked to God when they were alone, sick, afraid, angry, in need, sad, hurt, and happy. They said they prayed about their birthday parties, pets, fears, schoolwork, parents, siblings, grandparents, friendships, and jealousies. Because of the pervasiveness of the concept of prayer, it was the first major concept I coded. Eventually I gathered everything the children said concerning prayer, creating a "prayer file" for each child.

The following excerpt is one of the longer prayer files. It is the file of Timothy,[4] 11:

H: Can you describe a time when you felt really happy about God?

T: Well, I've been praying for my great grandmother and she's been staying alive and that's pretty cool.

H: Can you describe a time when you felt sad about God?

T: Well, sometimes I have prayed for somebody to get well and they don't.

H: Can you describe a time when you felt angry at God?

T: Yes. Well, sometimes when I'm done praying for something and I don't get it, like something that I really wanted to happen.

H: Can you describe a time when you felt an overwhelming love for God?

T: Well, a few nights ago I was just laying in my bed and I was just like, "God you are so awesome."

H: What does it mean to know God?

T: Like my friend Brandon, I can tell he knows God because I've been to church with him and he just really gets into it.

H: Gets into what?

T: The worship and prayer.

H: How do you think someone gets to know God?

T: Praying, reading the Bible, listening to Him.

H: What are some things that you do that help you know that you know God?

T: Well, I just pretty much every night I just talk to him a lot. If there's anything I want to say to him I just say it.

4. All children's names are pseudonyms. The churches also were given pseudonyms.

H: What sort of things do you talk to God about?

T: I talk to him about Harry Potter and stuff like that, if he thinks I should stop reading it. So far I think he hasn't really told me anything about it, just kind of drawn me away from it just a little bit. . . . My dad's reading the first one to see if it's okay.

H: What else do you pray about?

T: Well, if I like this girl or something I will pray that I don't go into anything bad or anything like that.

H: What else do you talk to God about?

T: I pretty much pray about my family, if anybody is sick that they will get better.

H: What else?

T: Sometimes I pray that I will get to know him better.

H: Were you ever afraid or alone, and you think God helped you? Would you tell me about that?

T: Yes. At night when I was going to bed when I was younger I would see the tree shadow and I would be scared. I would, like, see shadows on the wall and like be really afraid and ask him to protect me. There was one time where I think a month ago when it was really good weather and the lights went out and I was really scared and I asked him for protection.

H: Has your family ever needed special help and you think God helped? Would you tell me about that?

T: Well my other grandmother, my mom's mom had cancer and we prayed for her and she got better and now she's having cancer again but we don't think she's going to get better this time.

H: How will you deal with it this time if she doesn't get better?

T: Well, I'll just ask God to comfort us. I think she's 74.

Many of the children spoke eloquently concerning prayer, revealing rich, thick descriptions of their prayer lives. Others had less to say; some prayer files consisted of only one or two paragraphs. The incidental comments concerning prayer, as well as those comments given in response to direct questioning, perhaps more than any other set of comments on a particular practice or subject, shed light on the depth and quality of the spiritual lives of these children.

People Who Know God

One of the most fascinating analyses involved looking at the people who, according to the children, know God. Many of the children named their parents, grandparents, and friends. Some named their pastor, their teachers or another adult. The question, "What is it about that person that makes you think they know God?" yielded interesting comments as well. The categories that emerged were somewhat different from those in response to the question, "What does it mean to know God?" Table 2 lists the ways the children described people they know who know God.

Another seminal questions was, "What is the difference between someone who *knows* God and someone who knows *about* God?" The children's responses to this question also revealed the depth of their understanding about God and relationality:

Table 2 Characteristics of People who Know God, Intergenerational (n=20)

Relationality	Appropriating		Parents' Relationship with Child
	Outward Religious Form	Observable Character	
Prays (22)	Goes to church (9)	Acts like it/I can tell (12)	Takes children to church (2)
Is spiritual	Reads the Bible (11)	Obeys God/does what is right (3)	Teaches me about God/not to be angry/how to share/ kindness/how to handle money/how to do better/what is appropriate/to get along (11)
Close to God	Talks about the Bible (4)	Is good/pure (3)	Prays with me at night (2)
Praises/worships (7)	Teaches a Bible class (4)	Makes right decisions	Helps us memorize verses
Loves God (3)	Has a missionary group	Brings people to Christ/tells people about Jesus (5)	Reminds me to do my devotions
Trusts God	Leads Christian music (3)	Faithful/committed (4)	Makes me bring my Bible
Spends time with God	Volunteers at church (5)	Good example	Do Christian stuff together
Journals/has quiet time/devotional (3)	Home group leader	Disciplined	Deals with us children well

| | Appropriating | | |
Relationality	Outward Religious Form	Observable Character	Parents' Relationship with Child
Talks about God all the time/brings God into the conversation (7)	Has a Christian family	Helps people (5)	Tough on us when we do wrong/disciplines us (2)
Accepted Jesus in his heart (2)	About pastor: is the pastor (4) preaches (3)	Not easily angered (2)	Keeps us out of trouble
		Asks what Jesus would do	
		Does what he says he will do	
		Endures/is patient (2)	
		Calm (not stressed) (5)	
		Sweet/happy (2)	
		Generous (4)	
		Nice/kind (7)	
		Loves everybody (2)	
		Tells clean jokes	
		Doesn't steal	
48 statements/ 18 children	46 statements/ 16 children	63 statements/ 18 children	23 statements/ 10 children

Hannah, 11: He knows about him, but he doesn't believe. He says he knows him, but he never talks about him. He will say, "Yes I believe in him" but he doesn't even have a connection with him.

Luke, 9: Someone who knows about God knows he died on the cross and what he did—and someone who knows God worships him.

Junia, 10: Someone who knows God knows him and worships him and a person who knows about him isn't always praying to Him.

Caleb, 11: Usually a person who just knows about God doesn't exactly act like him a lot—like he'll get mad and things, make fun of people sometimes. They would be a lot different if they believed in God.

James, 10: Well, my dad doesn't really know God but he knows about him and my mom knows God and knows about him too. To know about God isn't everything . . . people that know God pray to him and talk to him, read the Bible because they want to.

Stephen, 11: A person who knows God wants to do what's right and that is follow God. The person who knows about God, Satan himself knows about God, but just because they know about God doesn't mean they want to do what is right or what is good.

Esther, 9: They have Jesus in their head, but they don't have Jesus in their heart.

These children reflected fairly sophisticated distinctions between people who know God and people who simply know about God, and they articulated that difference quite eloquently.

Reciprocal Relationality

The operational definition for reciprocal relationality is "any clear indication of relating back and forth between God and child, such as conversation or emotional response from God felt by child." It also includes response to the questions: "In what ways do you listen to God? In what ways does God talk to us? Have you ever thought God talked to you?"

Priscilla, 11: [Response to story]: When my sister and me argue, I start thinking that my parents only love my sister. She's younger, the baby. And God tells me they love me too, don't think bad thoughts. And my animals comfort me too. And God is never mad at me.

Lydia, 11:

> H: Do you think you know God?

> L: I know God [spoken confidently]

> H: How do you know you know God?

> L: Because he's told me that I'm his child.

> H: When did he tell you that?

> L: When I was praying he told me.

Abigail, 10:

> H: Have you ever thought God talked to you?

> A: He showed me a sign once because I was being really bad that day because I was being really mean because I was angry but I don't know why and you know how they always have a dove for a sign? Well there's this dove at the library and then we were getting in the car and then this car backed up right on top of him and I was thinking

that was a sign, but I don't know. It killed him, he was smushed. It was like God was telling me that He died for me and I shouldn't be acting like that.

Peter, 11:

H: How do you feel about God most of the time?

P: That he's a good guy. He doesn't like it when I do bad things. He gets sad.

Andrew, 10:

H: How do you feel about God most of the time?

A: Well, I feel like that he's really watching over me. That he loves and cares for me. That I am his son and that he'll never do anything bad that would hurt me. [Context: During the interview process, this child described being in foster care, and how God had provided for him to be adopted.]

Leah, 9:

H: How do you feel about God most of the time?

L: Good, because he's always there to take care of you, there to help you up when you're down, cry with you when you're sad.

Tabitha, 10:

H: How do you know God?

T: He's my dad. He's the one that I can come to for forgiveness and for mercy and for love and comfort. [Context: During the interview, the child described the pain of her father's recent infidelity and her feelings of distance from her own father.]

These comments are representative of the children in the study who seemed very comfortable with the idea that God talks to them, and even spoke the idea before prompted.

Feelings about God

In an attempt to tap more affective aspects of spirituality, I asked several "feeling" questions: Can you tell me about a time when you felt surprised or amazed about God? Happy about God? Sad about God? Scared about God? Angry at God?

The question, "Have you ever felt angry toward God/Jesus?" seemed to tap deeply into the essence of the children's spirituality, that is, their relationship with God. Altogether 23 children said they had been angry with God. Though some could not think of a specific time, most affirmed this idea. Their responses varied widely in scope and subject matter. A sampling of their responses follows:

James, 10:

> H: Can you tell me about a time when you have been angry at God?
>
> J: When I was little, when my parents got divorced I wasn't able to see both of them all the time.
>
> H: You were angry at God?
>
> J: Yes.
>
> H: You remember being . . .
>
> J: Frustrated, like it was his fault that he didn't keep them together.

Noah, 11:

> H: Can you tell me about a time when you have been angry at God?
>
> N: Maybe just a little bit.
>
> H: Do you remember specific examples?
>
> N: The way my sister's been acting drives me crazy and it makes me angry at God to think why did he stick me with her! I think what he's done is kind of raised my tolerance level.

These responses reflect the same relationality that the children exhibited in their comments about their prayer lives. The children seem to connect the ordinary events of their lives with God's care and protection.

Differences between the Two Groups of Children

Eventually I compared the interview data of the two samples of children for similarities and differences. There were both similarities and differences. Children in both settings spoke of prayer frequently, said they knew God, defined knowing God similarly, named about the same number of persons that they think know God, offered similar reasons for why they think those persons know God, and understood the basic difference between someone who knows God and someone who only knows *about* God. Children in both samples offered a wealth of evidence attesting to their close and loving relationships with God.

However there were differences, and most of the differences lay in the particular area this research is examining—an awareness of one's relationship with God.

Prayer. I tallied the number of times the children mentioned prayer (before the questions about prayer) and did a statistical comparison between the two groups of children. The differences were statistically significant, $t(38)=2.37$, $p=.02$. The children who participated in intergenerational small groups mentioned prayer more often than the children who did not participate in intergenerational groups. The analysis of the children's comments concerning prayer apparently revealed the spirituality of the children better than any other analysis.

Differences in other categories. Table 3 displays several other computable differences that emerged from the data analysis. The IG children in this sample referred to prayer significantly more often than did the children from non-intergenerational settings. In defining the concept of knowing God, IG children gave substantially more relational descriptions of that concept than non-intergenerational children.

Another comparison that also yielded a slightly heavier emphasis on relationality by the IG sample was the question concerning the difference between someone who knows God and someone who knows *about* God. In addition, more IG children in the sample shared instances of reciprocal relationality than did non-intergenerational children in this sample.

In general, though both groups of children gave eloquent testimony to their relationships with God, the IG children in this sample were more aware of their relationship with God, that is, they spoke more often and more reciprocally of that relationship than did the children in the non-intergenerational sample. Certainly, this sample is too small to draw definitive conclusions about the benefits of intergenerational small group experience, but the results suggest that when children and adults worship, pray, learn and serve together their spiritual lives are enriched.

Table 3 Comparison of IG and Non-IG Children, by Concept

Concept	How concept measured	IG Children (*n*=20)	Non-IG Children (*n*=20)
Anger toward God	Number of children who described the concept in relational terms	14	8
Knowing God	Number of children who defined the concept relationally	17 (35 comments)	13 (24 comments)
Reciprocal relationality	Number of children who offered un-prompted comments exhibiting concept	12	8
Knowing God vs. Knowing about God	Number of children who described differences in relational terms	14 (33 comments)	12 (26 comments)

Conclusion

Christian educators spend much time, effort, and energy in finding ways to facilitate growth in Christ, maturity and perfection. They often desire to enhance this process. They want to know how best to nurture spiritual development in children—and adults.

It is my hope that this research will be replicated in other settings, in other states, in other countries, and with other populations. I hope that in churches leaders will begin to actively and intentionally seek ways to bring the generations together on a regular basis so that children will learn from each other, from younger children, from older children, teens, and adults. Adults will learn from teens and children as well. All can benefit from one other and everyone will "grow each other up" in Christ.

References

Allen, H. (2002). A qualitative study exploring the similarities and differences of the spirituality of children in intergenerational and non-intergenerational Christian contexts. *Dissertation Abstracts International, 163*(04A), 1291.

Berryman, J. (1997). Spirituality, religious education, and the dormouse. *International Journal of Children's spirituality, 2,* 9–23.

Bruner, J. S., & Haste, H. (Eds.). (1987). *Making sense: The child's construction of the world.* New York: Methuen.

Erikson, E. H. (1963). *Childhood and society* (2nd ed.). New York: Norton.

Estep, J. R., Jr. (1999, October). *Spiritual formation as social: Toward a Vygotskyan developmental perspective.* Paper presented at North American Professors of Christian Education Annual Conference, San Diego, CA.

Fowler, J. W. (1991). *Weaving the new creation: Stages of faith and the public church.* New York: HarperCollins.

Fretheim, T. E. (1997). *Yada'.* In W. A. VanGemeren (Ed.), *New international dictionary of Old Testament theology and exegesis* (Vol. 2, pp. 409–414). Grand Rapids: Zondervan.

Greeno, J. G., Collins, A. M., & Resnick, L. B. (1996). Cognition and learning. In D. C. Berliner & R. C. Calfee (Eds.), *Handbook of educational psychology* (pp. 15–46). New York: Macmillan.

Graven, S. N. (1999). Things that matter in the lives of children: Looking at children's spiritual development from a developmentalist perspective. In S. K. Morgenthaler (Ed.), *Exploring children's spiritual formation: Foundational issues* (pp. 39–68). River Forest, IL: Pillars.

Harkness, A. G. (1998). Intergenerational education for an intergenerational church? *Religious Education, 93,* 431–447.

Mead, L. B., & Nash, R. N. (1997). *An eight-track church in a CD world: The modern church in a postmodern world.* Macon, GA: Smyth & Helwys.

Prest, E. (1993). *From one generation to another.* Capetown: Training for Leadership.

Ratcliff, B. (n.d.). *Celebrating our Jewish roots.* Retrieved July 22, 2004, from http://don.ratcliff.net/brenda/roots.htm.

Rieber, R. W., & Carton, A. S. (Ed.). (1987). *The collected works of L. S. Vygotsky* (Vol. 1). New York: Plenum.

Sheldrake, P. (2000). What is spirituality? In K. J. Collins (Ed.), *Exploring Christian spirituality* (pp. 21–42). Grand Rapids: Baker.

Schneiders, S. (1986). Theology and spirituality: Strangers, rivals, and partners. *Horizon, 13,* 253–274.

Vygotsky, L. S. (1997; 1926). *Educational psychology* (R. Silverman, Trans.). Boca Raton, FL: St. Lucie.

Vygotsky, L. S. (1978). *Mind in society: The development of higher psychological process* (M. Cole, V. John-Steiner, S. Scribner, & E. Souberman, Eds.). Cambridge: Harvard University Press. (Original works written in the 1920s and 1930s, published in 1930, 1935, 1956, 1960, and 1966)

Wertsch, J., & Rogoff, B. (1984). Editors' notes. In B. Rogoff & J. Wertsch (Eds.), *Children's learning in the "zone of proximal development": New directions for child development* (pp. 1–6). San Francisco: Jossey-Bass.

Westerhoff, J. H., III. (1976). *Will our children have faith?* New York: Seabury.

White, J. W. (1988). *Intergenerational religious education.* Birmingham, AL: Religious Education Press.

Chapter Eighteen

A Narrative of Children's Spirituality: African American and Latino Theological Perspectives

KAREN CROZIER AND ELIZABETH CONDE-FRAZIER[1]

There is a growing body of literature on children's spirituality. Myers (1997) provides readers with the linguistic tools and sophistication to articulate the spiritual reality of young children. As a professor of child development, Myers challenges developmental paradigms that tend to limit and/or dismiss the spiritual experience of the child. She proposes a paradigm that allows parents, educators, and religious leaders to be companions with children in children's construction of transcendence that is sensitive to diversity and multicultural experiences. In a similar vein, Stonehouse (1998) provides readers with an interdisciplinary approach that includes psychosocial development, moral development, cognitive development, biblical theological analysis, the interplay between early childhood education and religion, as well as psychology and religion. Like Myers, Stonehouse points to how spiritual formation can and should occur in childhood, and how adults in the lives of children need to rethink the role of spirituality in the early years.

---

1. Karen Crozier is a doctoral student at Claremont School of Theology in the Theology and Personality program in the Religious Education option. She received her B.A. in psychology from UCLA, and her M.A. in Early Childhood Education from California State University, Fresno. She has published two other articles, both of them on public education.

Elizabeth Conde-Frazier is Associate Professor of Religious Education at the Claremont School of Theology and adjunct professor at the Latin American Bible Institute. She received a B.A. degree from Brooklyn College of the City University of New York, an M.Div. from Eastern Baptist Theological Seminary and a Ph.D in theology and religious education from Boston College. Her publications include the recent book *Hispanic Bible Institutes: Communities Doing Theology*, the co-authored book *A Many Colored Kingdom: Multicultural Dynamics for Spiritual Formation*, an edited book titled *Multicultural Models of Religious Education*, a chapter in the book *Christian Scholarship for What?* and several journal articles on the spirituality of the scholar, multiculturalism, theology, and education.

While Myers and Stonehouse discuss children's spiritual development or formation, Houskamp, Fisher, and Stuber (2004) present a provocative discussion on how children's spirituality can be used in clinical and research settings. In addition, they provide historical and contemporary research that has been conducted with children experiencing traumatic illness and violence that demonstrates the role spirituality plays in the lives of these children (also see chapter 22).

Research on children's spirituality from African American perspectives focuses on the resilient manner in which the Black Church, community, and family draw upon spiritual resources in order to be sustained in a sometimes hostile, racist America. Haight's (2002) longitudinal, developmental-ethnographic study of a Black Baptist church in Salt Lake City, Utah poignantly captures the role the Black church plays in the spiritual and social development of African American children. Moreover, Haight offers a progressive research strategy that allows for the diverse developmental experience of African Americans to be interpreted from the context of the community being studied instead of from the theoretical minds, paradigms and cultures of the professional researcher who is usually white (2002, p. 33). In no uncertain terms, Haight presents African American children's spirituality in the context of race, racism, and oppression as a rich sociocultural phenomenon that is to be understood on its own terms. While there are other studies that focus on the role the Black Church plays in the spiritual and social development and empowerment of African American children (Brashears & Roberts, 2001; Jackson, 1989; Mitchell, 1986; Newman, 1994; Poole, 1990; Roberts, 1980; Smith, 1985; Tyms, 1979–1980), Haight's work is by far the most extensive and reflective of African American children's spiritual experience (see chapter 7).

The more specific role of the Black community and family in the spiritual development of African American children is documented in the contributions of Riggs (2001), Hill (1999), and Hudley, Haight, and Miller (2003). Riggs does a historical, social, cultural, and theological analysis of Mary Church Terrell and the Black Women's Club Movement in the 19th century. She persuasively argues that Terrell—as a member of the Black Women's Club Movement—positioned African American children as the hope of the race, and thereby invested in African American children's spiritual, social, and educational development. In the exposition of Terrell's life, Riggs demonstrates how the theological and spiritual perspectives concerning children informed her response to the injustices experienced by African American children and families. Unlike Riggs, Hill (1999) conducted a contemporary analysis of the strengths of African American families in nurturing the spiritual development of African American children. Hudley, Haight and Miller (2003) provide an oral history of Hudley's life from 1920 to the present, and reveal the role her African American family and community played in her psychological, social, and spiritual formation and maturity.

As researchers and clinicians in counseling, Boyd-Franklin (2003), Smith (1997), and Wimberly (2000) analyze the spiritual depth and experience of African

American families in therapy in ways that account for the havoc race and racism wreaks on the mental and spiritual health of African American families and children. These African American therapists are privy to the role that spirituality plays in the life of African American families and children, and consequently have been emphasizing the need for mental health professionals to affirm the positive influence of spirituality. Predating Houskamp, Fisher and Stuber (2004), Boyd-Franklin (2003), Smith (1997), and Wimberly (2000) were all well aware of the implications of children's spirituality on clinical practice. Unfortunately, none of these African American scholars are cited in the Houskamp article.

There exists little research concerning the spiritual life of the Latino child. The research that has been done comes from the behavioral sciences as it relates to a general understanding of cross cultural counseling (Cervantes & Ramirez, 1992). Within the behavioral sciences, the spirituality of the Latino community is seen as an important medium of healing (Leon-Portilla, 1980; Vaughan, 1986). The only serious work in the area of Christian education in the Latino community, as it relates to the spirituality of children, is done by Emilio Marrero (2000), a Latino pastor in Yuma, Arizona.

This brief review of the literature reveals no study on African American and Latino children's spirituality from an in-depth theological perspective in which the child's experience and story are given center stage. Although Sophia Cavalletti (1979/1983) and Robert Coles (1990) give rich descriptions of children's religious/ spiritual experiences, their social location and research focus are different. Neither Cavaletti nor Coles emphasize ethnic minority cultures in the United States, although Coles' work does briefly explore the spirituality of several African American children and the spirituality of Latino migrant children (see also PBS Home Video, 1995). They explore children's spirituality that includes, yet transcends, Christian perspectives, but they do not give sustained attention to racial/cultural distinctions in their dialogues with the children. Hence, as authors of this chapter we are helping to create a body of literature on children's spirituality from Christian perspectives, as insiders of the African American and Latino communities, with the hope to inform, engage, and inspire researchers, professors, clergy, lay leaders, and parents.

With these goals in mind, first, we provide a background of the study, including the research method and terminology. Second, the first author's research findings on an African American child's spirituality are presented. A discussion of the strengths and limitations of the study will come at the end of this second section. After the examination of children's spirituality from an African American theological perspective, the second author presents similar issues from her Latina social location. She speaks to the research method from that context. Finally, we conclude with a discussion on the implications of this study for further research and Christian education.

Background Influences (Crozier)

As a child of 5 or 6, I was in my mother's bedroom one night when it was raining, lightning and thundering, and the lights had gone out. As my mother and I were lying on the bed, I said to my mother that I wished I had died as a baby or had never been born because then I knew I would be going to heaven. I do not remember my mother's response, but I do remember the seriousness of my statement. I was afraid that I would not make it to that place where I believed God abides. I did not know how I would be able to continue to live and please God in a way that would allow me into heaven. For some reason, I had made up my mind that babies had easier access into the heavenly realm than did adults. Consequently, if I had never been born, I would not have to deal with the possibility of living in hell without God.

Although I have not thoroughly analyzed this episode in my life, I now have a somewhat better understanding of this experience. Within African American Evangelical Christianity, hell is a very real place. As a child in a Baptist church, my pastor went through great efforts to save people from eternal damnation. He would often say, "I would rather scare you into heaven than to lullaby you to hell." I believe I internalized the reality of hell, even though I was unsure of how to make it to heaven.

As a former early childhood educator I have experienced that children perceive and connect to God in a very different manner from my own experience. I recall a conversation that I had with one of my second-grade students about Jesus. My student was adamant that Jesus was still on the cross. I told him that I believed Jesus rose from the dead and is no longer on the cross. But that did not convince him. When I asked why he thought Jesus was still on the cross, he replied that he saw him on the cross at his church. I responded, "Oh, I see." I did not try to convince my student otherwise because that symbol in his church was very significant to him. I did not want to impart my beliefs that were disconnected from my student's experience, so I remained silent. What good would a cognitive response do in response to a highly affective affirmation?

Even though I had made a rational decision not to respond to my student's conviction, emotionally I felt as if his disagreement with me was based on a literal, concrete observation of Jesus. Thus, on some level I understood his disagreement to be based upon what he had tangibly observed and experienced. Then, on another level I wondered about the church's responsibility in using symbolic representations of the divine that do not necessarily come from children. Did the icon of Jesus on the cross become a static representation to my student or was it something different? Could it have been both static and dynamic at the same time? What other symbols would be present if children were allowed to display their understanding of Jesus in the sanctuary? What contribution could children make to Christianity's understanding of Jesus and God?

These two stories represent African American children's understanding and experience of God. It is an understanding that my former student and I were able to articulate in separate ways at particular points in time. Although these two stories and experiences may not be unique to African American children's spirituality on the surface, it would have been interesting if a researcher had probed further into my understanding of death and immortality, heaven and hell, and good and bad to see if even more prevalent cultural distinctions exist. Then, for my student, what new insight would he have contributed concerning the theology of the cross and his social location if his position was thoroughly explored?

Unfortunately, I do not have access to my former student, and I have limited recall of my own experience that occurred over twenty-five years ago. Although these experiences have influenced my interest in child spirituality, I consider the current study to be a starting point in exploring the spirituality of African American children. Using narrative inquiry, exploration through experience, and story, the spirituality of a three year eight month-old African American female will be presented.

According to Clandinin and Connelly (2000),

> Narrative inquiry is a way of understanding experience. It is a collaboration between researcher and participants, over time, in a place or series of places, and in social interaction with milieus. An inquirer enters this matrix in the midst and progresses in this same spirit, concluding the inquiry still in the midst of living and telling, reliving and retelling, the stories of the experiences that make up people's lives, both individual and social. (p. 20)

In this vein, narrative inquiry allows for the researcher to be an active participant in the research process. My experiences and stories are allowed to enter into the research process in ways that are liberating and affirming for me as an African American, educated female from a working class Christian family. I do not have to assume a neutral, "objective" position in the process as if I am not affected by what I am observing, experiencing and hearing from the participant involved in the study. Nor is who I am or what I bring to the research process rendered invisible; I am able to reflect on my own experience and story in my social location without apology.

When I entered into the matrix of the African American child and her family that included two 60-minute sessions with the child and two sessions with her parents (one 90-minute session with both parents and one 30-minute session with just her mother), I entered with many experiences and a personal story to be retold and relived. Throughout this narrative, my experience and story as a researcher who is a person of faith are presented as well as that of the child.

Before I describe the spiritual life of this young child, I will define how I understand the term spirituality.[2] Spirituality has to do with acknowledging that there

___

2. At the time of the study I had a less mature understanding of spirituality. Although my understanding has developed, I will not introduce my new perception because it would skew the research

is a power, force and being that exists outside of myself and is greater than me. I call this power, force and being "God." While God's existence is not contingent upon my acknowledgment of God, the existence of my spiritual life is contingent upon this acknowledgment.

With this rather broad, ambiguous working definition of spirituality, I sought to understand an African American child's spirituality by interviewing her parents, and observing and interacting with the child at home. My original research design included interviewing and observing the child at church and her daycare center. In addition, I had hoped to have conversations with her pastor and daycare teacher. However, limited time and resources prohibited me from fully implementing this original research goal.

The Spirituality of Sylvia[3]

At the age of three, I believe that Sylvia has a spiritual life. It possibly began at birth. Sylvia's mother Natalie shared how she knew that she needed to get herself "together" when she was pregnant with her first child, Sylvia. Before Sylvia's birth, Natalie felt mentally and emotionally inadequate so she turned to God in order to find strength to nurture and provide for her daughter. Sylvia was Natalie's first blood relative because Natalie is adopted, and Natalie wanted Sylvia to have the best. In providing for her daughter, she became empowered to also take care of herself. Sylvia's birth was a turning point in the life of Natalie and, consequently, Sylvia was able to enter into a spiritually nurturing environment.

Parenting plays a significant role in Sylvia's spiritual formation. Sylvia's father, Walter, noted how he and Natalie met in social services and both of them had a background of working with kids. When they met, Natalie was a schoolteacher and Walter worked with children who were emotionally, physically and sexually abused. This background influenced their desire to be spiritually and emotionally prepared to provide for their child when so many of the children with whom they worked were without stable, spiritual home environments.

Both of Sylvia's parents believe that God can provide for Sylvia what neither of them are able to give. They want their daughter to focus on God and not them because they are mere humans. More specifically, Natalie stated,

> I have a journey and she (Sylvia) has a journey. I am comfortable with her finding her way in the Lord. I want her to recognize that she is part of mommy and daddy, but God is at work with who she is because she is more precious to God than she is to us. Wherever she wants to go, God can take her.

---

data. It should be noted that this definition does not represent Elizabeth's understanding of the term.

3. All names given are pseudonyms.

Humility and trust in a sovereign God, as exhibited by Natalie, are reflective of parenting practices in many African American Christian homes. Knowing their human limitations as well as the often racist, hostile environment of the United States, parents entrust their children to a God who is "able to make a way out of no way" and who is more than able to provide what they cannot.

Spiritual Gifts

What God is doing in the life of Sylvia is being manifested through Sylvia's spiritual gifts as identified by her parents. Her father stated that she has the ability to forgive and repent. Her mother stated that she has the gift of intercessory prayer and the ability to discern people's spirits. Walter shared an experience when Sylvia was just one year old related to the gift of discernment: "One time Sylvia had stared down a minister and it made the minister feel uncomfortable because the minister felt as if Sylvia was reading her." Natalie described another context when Sylvia's ability to discern people's spirits was apparent. Natalie stated that sometimes she would be thinking something and Sylvia would ask, "What are you thinking?" Natalie interprets this behavior as Sylvia's sensitivity to others and her ability to discern. On yet another occasion, Natalie shared how Sylvia stated, "I love you," when she (Natalie) was going through a difficult time. She asked her daughter, "Who told you to say that?" and Sylvia replied, "God."

Conversations with God—prayers—are an integral part of African American spirituality. For African Americans, God speaks today in a myriad of ways including through Scriptures, other people, and sometimes even in an audible voice. Sylvia's sensitivity to God's voice is being nurtured by her mother. Moreover, her mother's experience of the divine through her daughter points to how African American children are respected as ministers of God's grace. Another example of Sylvia as minister is when her parents noted how she prayed for her father when he was sick.

The Role of Prayer

Sylvia and I prayed at the beginning and end of our times together. On both occasions I asked Sylvia if she would like to pray and she said "yes." I asked her who she would prefer to pray. At the beginning she said, "You pray," but at the end we both prayed. In our closing prayer I said, "Bow your eyes and close . . ." While I was laughing at what I had said, Sylvia had interjected with, "Bow your head and close your eyes." I said, "You are right." After the laughter and correction, I began to pray. After I finished praying, she prayed as well.

The mistake was not intentional, but it yielded insight. Sylvia knew a particular position and posture of prayer that many people use before a prayer is rendered to God. She knew it so well that she was able to correct me when I did not say it properly.

This may speak to the role the formal saying has in her life at the beginning of prayer, and may have little to do with her understanding of the different postures and positions of prayer. Perhaps it reflects a bit of our shared ethnic heritage, albeit with a statement that may not be unique to that heritage.

A somewhat different posture and position occurred on another occasion, suggesting that the rote comment was not seen as absolute by Sylvia. In the beginning, Sylvia chose not to pray with her mother and me. She refused our invitation to pray, possibly because I was spending time interviewing her mother first and she was looking forward to our time together afterward. However, after I had spent time with her, she agreed to pray with us. We grabbed hands while her mother and I sat on the floor and she sat on a stool. She prayed first a prayer of thanksgiving. She said, "Thank you Lord for mommy and daddy. Lift 'em up Lord. Amen." Then, I prayed. After we had said "amen," Sylvia said, "Don't break up yet! Don't break up yet!" I looked up at her and asked why, and she said, "Because no one prayed for you." Does prayer for Sylvia mean that everyone involved in the prayer must be prayed for? Interestingly, she did not see separate, individual prayer as an option at the time. We had to stay in the position we were in so that I could be prayed for. Was there power in the connection that Sylvia wanted to maintain as I was prayed for? How would Sylvia have responded if we had not remained in the prayer circle?

Due to the urgency and authority of her statement, we did not break up the circle. Yet, I was moved by the moment. In my prayer I had prayed for her and her family. To know that she was attentive to the prayer and would not let us break up until I received prayer reflected the role of God in her life. I was ministered to because she appeared to value my presence and personhood. She demonstrated a concern for me when it was not required. She expressed love in a way that was able to penetrate deep within me. I knew God was present in and through her.

Did she become empowered to pray for me when no one else did? After she brought it to our attention that no one had prayed for me, her mother suggested that she would pray and she did. She said, "Bless Karen, Lord. Lift her up. Thank you for Karen. Amen." At the end of the prayer, I thanked her. Her mother gave Sylvia an intimate, heart-felt hug and said, "I love you."

Thanksgiving and petition are a part of Sylvia's prayer language. Although she uses "Lord" in her prayers and sometimes "God," she was not able to or chose not to articulate in words who she was praying to or why she was praying. I tried to understand more about this from her, but she became silent when I asked her who she prays to and why she prays. It might have helped to have her draw a picture or for me to name specific individuals to whom she could have been praying.

How does she understand the behavior and practice of prayer? What purpose is it serving in her life? While I sense the presence of God in her life in prayer, does she? In her prayers that I heard, the term "Lord" was used more than "God," and "Jesus" was never addressed. However, both Jesus and God were mentioned at other times, as will be explored in the next section of this chapter.

The Position and Presence of Jesus and the Power of Jesus and God

"God took the keys away from the devil. Mia was scared when God took away the keys from the devil." This is what Sylvia said when I asked her to share what she saw at church yesterday. This interview took place the day after Easter and I wanted to use this moment to ascertain what Sylvia had grasped from her church experience.

The fact that Sylvia was able to respond to the question suggests that she understood something about a church. Churches have played a prominent role in the spiritual formation of both Sylvia and her parents. Natalie was part of an African Methodist Episcopal (AME) church when she was an undergraduate in New York. When she came to California, she and her husband Walter both gave their lives to Christ at an AME church in Los Angeles in 1994. Walter is a licensed minister in the AME church as well as an ordained minister in the Apostolic church.

In African American Christianity, the church is often the first and primary home. The church is where many African Americans are able to experience the parenthood of God with their sisters and brothers, free from the constant assault of racism and marginalization. This familial connection is particularly important when relocation or another form of change occurs for an individual and/or family.

In their church home on Easter Sunday, Sylvia and her parents saw a play. Sylvia had the opportunity to watch the play because Sylvia's mother believes that it is better for her child to worship with adults so that she can have role models. Natalie stated, "Sometimes Sylvia writes and colors in books, but usually she will sit in worship and that is important to me that she learns that skill. The pastor has not said anything that I do not feel comfortable with."

When I heard this from Sylvia's mother, I began to reflect on the debate that occurs in many churches concerning children and worship. Many children's ministries and churches separate children from adults during worship in an attempt to address more appropriately the needs of children in worship and faith development. However, the opposing argument is that it separates children from both their biological and corporate faith families. I have struggled with the positive and negative aspects of separate children's church and ministry. However, as I listened to Natalie, I sensed that she was intentional about the experience she desired for her child and family and she appeared to have realistic expectations of what worship with adults entailed for Sylvia. Natalie was not expecting Sylvia to sit through a two-hour worship experience like an adult because she allowed her to do other things like write and color. Sylvia writes and colors while worshipping God. Whatever children do in worship with adults, they must be allowed to be children and not encouraged to be something they are not.

Many may wonder if Sylvia's worship experience is appropriate, because it is not designed for her developmental level, and one wonders if she is really paying attention because she is coloring and writing at times. Natalie reported a comment by Sylvia on the way home from church: "I'm so glad that Jesus got the keys." Natalie said, with great enthusiasm, "Wow! She got it." I, too, was impressed with Sylvia's response. What does she know about the keys? Was there some kind of reaction from the church during the play, when Jesus got the keys, to make her celebrate that fact? What resonated with Sylvia about the keys?

I was eager to explore this with Sylvia once I had finished interviewing her mother. However, I had to delay my excitement because her mother continued to share about Sylvia's responses in daily life to what she is grasping from her church experience. One day when Sylvia was walking with her mother to work, she said, "Mom, Jesus died on the cross, but he's alive again. He rose again." In Sylvia's comment are found four key theological terms in the Christian tradition: Jesus, death, cross and resurrection. Unlike my former student who believed that Jesus is still on the cross, Sylvia has an understanding that Jesus is no longer on the cross. Once again, I was eager to see what this meant to her. Unlike the case of my former student, I was in a situation to learn more about her statement and in what way her understanding of Jesus dying on the cross and rising again has influenced her spirituality.

Anticipating the opportunity to delve deeper into her two theological statements, I restated what her mother told me and then asked a question: "What do you mean that Jesus died on the cross and he is alive again?" Sylvia responded, "Jesus died on the cross and he came back." While she answered the question with what she understood, in a manner consistent with what she had shared with her mother, I could not find any deeper insight into her understanding. The follow up probe, "How did he come back?" only produced an "I don't know" from Sylvia. While this was disappointing, it suggests that she is not hindered by her lack of cognitive understanding from making strong declaratory statements about his death and resurrection. Does this suggest that what Sylvia is unable to express cognitively is something deeply affective in nature? Apparently, she is content with the dissonance between what she cannot explain cognitively and with what she claims to be real. This may produce disequilibrium over time, and require her to form new understandings, in keeping with Piagetian theory. Yet sociocultural theory emphasizes that cognitive advancement will occur because of the prominent role of her family and environmental context, including the church.

Even though Sylvia did not know how Jesus came back again, I asked if she could draw a picture of Jesus dying on the cross and rising again. She agreed to do so. This was intriguing because our last meeting together, she stated that she did not know how to draw Jesus or God. Now, it appeared as if she would be able to illustrate Jesus based on the conversation we were having. She picked the color white to begin her drawing, then changed her mind because white is difficult to see. As she began to draw a picture, she commented, "I am drawing a picture of Jesus." After she had worked awhile on her picture, I asked her, "What is Jesus doing?" She replied, "This is me. This is not Jesus. Jesus is back here." When she turned to the back of the paper she then realized that she had drawn a turtle on the back of the paper and thus she concluded, "That is a turtle. I don't know how to draw Jesus."

At this time, Sylvia knows that she does not know how to draw Jesus or God. For a brief moment, I thought I was going to get a concrete, visual of her understanding of Jesus. In the end when she stated that the picture was of her instead of Jesus, I am now wondering if she sees herself as Jesus. Could she understand herself to be an image of Jesus in some shape, form or fashion? Or is she suggesting that an understanding of self leads to an understanding of Jesus? Does she believe that one day she will die, and rise again? Or was she sidetracked momentarily by the drawing process, only to return to her earlier conclusion that God could not be drawn? This conclusion might indicate that her understanding of God may be like that of the adult who resists an anthropomorphic representation of God. Could it be that children being asked to draw God coerces them to be anthropomorphic?

I realize I am speculating about how to interpret Sylvia's indication that she was going to draw Jesus, but ending up with a picture of herself while confessing once again her inability to draw a picture of Jesus. Although she does not know how to draw Jesus, she may believe that there are people who are able to draw a picture of Jesus. Perhaps she is projecting on adults a far greater ability than what they in fact posses.

When Sylvia and I were drawing together, she asked her mother "How did Jesus come back again?" Her mother said Karen wants to know what you think and I agreed. "What do you think, Sylvia?" I asked, and again she replied, "I don't know." Her inquiry after we had moved past that part of the conversation suggests that she was reflecting further on my earlier question about how Jesus came back to life. The two adults in the room refrained from giving her an answer. I wonder, if we had provided her with our understanding of the experience, how she would have interpreted it and made it her own. Would our understanding of how Jesus came back to life again have made sense to her?

At the time of the interview, I assumed that offering my comments on the issue would influence her response and I wanted to avoid that. I now realize that I underestimated Sylvia. I did not give her a chance to grapple with new information. I did not use an opportunity to explore more deeply the death and resurrection of Jesus. My understanding and that of her mother could have been a springboard to something more for all of us.

Sylvia's understanding of Jesus not being on the cross appears to have great significance, and is not a mere repetition of what she has been told. When I showed her a picture of a Black Christ that has Jesus' life depicted in small captions from the crib to ministry to the crucifixion and finally to the resurrection with a larger picture of

Jesus in the middle, Sylvia pointed to the man on the cross and said, "This is where Jesus was." However, when she looked at the picture of the resurrected Christ, she said, "This is Jesus." From this observation, Sylvia understands that Jesus was once on the cross but is there no longer. Jesus is alive and well to Sylvia.

With Jesus being alive and well, Sylvia explained her connection to Jesus when she walks, eats and rides. Jesus is present to Sylvia in these daily routines and activities of her life. This seems to be a reflection of her parents' spirituality. Sylvia's mother noted, "Spirituality is not separated from my life existence. It is why I exist and it is my foundation." Sylvia's father has a similar grounding and understanding of spirituality when he stated, "It is similar to Natalie's. It is everyday life and more how I relate to God and others. It is acknowledging that we are something outside of this physical body."

Although Jesus walks closely with Sylvia and her family, there are some areas of Sylvia's life to which Jesus does not have access. When I asked Sylvia about other places where Jesus is near, I mentioned the restroom. This was an arbitrary reference because I was trying to get at other places that she sensed the presence of Jesus, as I was moving towards a possible understanding of God's omnipresence. When she stated that Jesus is not with her in the restroom, I asked her where Jesus was when she uses the restroom. She replied, "Jesus stays out here with daddy when I go to the restroom." Her mother laughed and joined in the conversation when she heard this and said, "We have told her that the restroom is private and no one is to be in there with her." This explanation was provocative for two reasons. First, I was wondering if she saw Jesus as being a mere man like her father, and thus limited in space, or if he was seen as more than merely a human. Second, I thought of how Christians have a theology of Jesus as Lord of all of life, but also have places where Jesus is not allowed to enter, such as personal finances, recreation, or racist attitudes. Regardless, Jesus is nevertheless near and real in Sylvia's life.

It is unclear if Sylvia sees Jesus and God as being one and the same. At the beginning of this section, I quoted a statement she made after seeing a church play on Easter Sunday: "God took the keys away from the devil. Mia was scared when God took away the keys from the devil." Then, with her family returning from church, Sylvia said, "I'm glad Jesus took away the keys from the devil." At the time of interview, I did not fully comprehend these statements. Perhaps my Trinitarian theology interfered with how I processed and understood Sylvia's statements. Although I see Jesus and God as one and the same, Sylvia may not. I missed an opportunity to explore how a young child might provide insight on the humanity and divinity of Jesus.

What was gleaned from her statement is that she was not afraid, unlike her cousin Mia who was afraid. Although I do not know why her cousin Mia was frightened, I do know that Sylvia was not. Could this lack of fear be because God and Jesus are considered to be good and more powerful than anyone or anything, so there is nothing to fear? Does Sylvia see God and Jesus as being kind yet powerful? Is the devil also not to be feared? In God and Jesus taking away the keys from the devil, does Sylvia rest assured in knowing that God and Jesus are in control over things that look and are bad and evil? These questions and others are intriguing and could provide further insight into Sylvia's spirituality, although they were not obtained during my interviews.

Limitations of the Study

Narrative inquiry was the research method used to assess the spirituality of a young, African American child. The use of this method proved to be rewarding yet extremely challenging. I enjoyed establishing a relationship with a young child in a way that allowed her words, her experience and her story to be told, by her and with her. I was constantly challenged to interpret the story in ways that would accurately reflect Sylvia's experience and not something that I wanted to impose upon her experience. To ensure this accuracy, Sylvia's parents read and critiqued drafts of this research inquiry. Furthermore, my colleagues and one of my professors played an active role in helping me to reflect on how I was processing the data. While I realize that Sylvia did not necessarily critique drafts of this research inquiry, I am challenged to create a way to include children's critical analysis of the data gathered about them. Ratcliff (2001) shares how he checked reliability issues with nine- to eleven-year-old students in his study, but not for a child who is as young as three. Possibly, I could have drawn a picture of how I understood Sylvia's responses to my questions and discussed it with her. If this was done, I wonder what else could have been revealed concerning Sylvia's spirituality.

Narrative inquiry requires sufficient time to observe, interview and gather relevant data including—but not limited to—memoirs, historical documents and literature. In this study, I used open-ended interviews with Sylvia's parents that provided me with insight on how better to elicit a story from her. Although I struggled with commenting on what I knew based upon two 60-minute sessions with Sylvia and two sessions with her parents, I was able to see themes emerge from the interviews, observations, and transcriptions.

There are many ways of interpreting data in qualitative research (Fairbanks, 1996; Graue & Walsh, 1998). As a non-positivist research approach, qualitative research in general and narrative inquiry in particular do not focus on making proof claims, but rather on providing rich description and explanations that enable the readers to reflect on their own stories and/or social locations (Fairbanks, p. 321). This suggests that while there may be wrong ways of interpreting data, there are many appropriate ways to interpret and tell the story.

Child psychiatrist Robert Coles (1990) notes,

> So often our notions of what a child is able to understand are based on the capacity the child has displayed in a structured situation. If the child fails to respond to a researcher's predetermined line of questioning, the researcher is

likely to comment on a "developmental" inadequacy. If another child responds well, he or she is considered developmentally advanced. (p. 23)

Coles' analysis of research on children speaks to the many ways the experiences of children have been framed within a myopic adult's framework and theoretical paradigm. In my study, I was conscious of this possibility. Thus, I sought to create and convey what I came to understand about Sylvia, instead of having Sylvia fit into a predetermined framework of what constitutes children's spirituality.

Coles' comment also reminds me of the difficulty I had in accessing several aspects of Sylvia's spirituality. She stated that she was not able to draw a picture of God or Jesus. She did not know how Jesus came back to life again. She did not respond to the question of to whom she prays and why she prays. However, at the age of 3, she has an understanding that Jesus is no longer on the cross, in contrast with the seven-year-old student mentioned earlier. It was tempting to compare her comments with my former student, but because narrative inquiry seeks to ground the participant in their social location, developmental comparisons are likely to be unwarranted. In other words, I would need to know more about my former student's understanding of the significance of Jesus on the cross, as well as know more about the significance of Jesus coming back to life again for Sylvia. Perhaps their respective experiences and stories would speak to different aspects of the Christian tradition instead of being merely more or less developed understandings.

Finally, in this study, only one child participated directly. Thus generalization about children's spirituality, or more specifically African American children's spirituality, was not the focus. Rather, this study provides a detailed contextual analysis and description. The narrative has revealed aspects of Sylvia's parents' spiritual journey and theology, and this information has been used to better understand the child participant in the study. Furthermore, it has provided a more grounded understanding of the child in family and in faith community instead of an isolated view of the child. Myers (1997) comments that adults are companions with children. As an African American adult and researcher, I am one of many companions—including the African American church and family—attempting to understand and nurture the spiritual lives of African American children.

The Latino Child's Spirituality (Conde-Frazier)

Narrative inquiry is better suited to work in the Latino context particularly when it comes to issues of spirituality. This is because the sites of significant self expression of Latinos can be found in folk wisdom, including various art forms and stories (Pineda, 1996). *Testimonios* are public faith stories. They are stories that constitute a meaning-making ritual of people seeking and sharing together a process of understanding God's mystery and grace in their lives. Thus narrative is the best means for determining the authentic spirituality of the people, especially children.

Children in the Latino community are exposed to narrative very early in life as a primary vehicle for making meaning of daily life events. It is also a means of creating and maintaining relational bonds with parents and extended family. An important dimension of spirituality is a nurturing relationship with God. The child who attends church learns to relate to God through the faith stories or *testimonios* of the community and later through the Bible stories.

Latino spirituality has been described from the perspective of the behavioral sciences. The Latino child's spirituality will first be considered within the framework of psychotherapy with Latino families. Subsequently, a Christian understanding of the child's spirituality is summarized. By exploring both frameworks, a broader perspective is possible, and the categories each contribute to a fuller understanding making the analysis richer. Finally, I include the work of Emilio Marrero (2000) who uses the Reggio Emilia approach (Boyd Cadwell, 1997; Gandini, 1997) as a way of nurturing the spiritual lives of Latino children. I will consider his understandings in the context of the work of Christian educator Frank Rogers. The stories used as illustrations are from my practice as a Christian educator in the Latino church. I have recorded them throughout the years for my teaching.

From a behavioral science perspective, expressions of spirituality can be found in each person's life story. In that story, expressions of spirituality are reflected in a belief in the balance and respect for all living things and openness to diversity which fosters an attitude of mutual respect and acceptance of all persons (Cervantes & Ramirez, 1992).

Cervantes and Ramirez (1992) point out that respect sanctions "an inclination toward wholeness, harmony and balance in one's relationships with self, family, community and the physical and social environment" (p. 106). Respect manifests itself by the spiritual lives of children in the central role that their relationships with family and its extended members play in their lives. God is present to the child in the many ways that family bonds and the rules that encourage commitment toward one another exist as a way of building a strong communal base. This provides a focus on children's conversations and pictures about God that are more openly connected in their understanding with family and nature.

Spirituality is also linked to the religious language and rituals of that child's religious community. Spirituality may also be exhibited through informal family practices that do not entail a consistent connection to a parish or religious group although the family may be Christian.[4]

---

4. When one migrates to a new location, finding a parish or church that connects with one's spiritual and cultural needs may be challenging. For this reason, one may not always belong to a faith community but may still continue to live out a Christian lifestyle and to practice Christian rituals at home.

Looking at spirituality through the lens of a communal culture, points to different aspects of spirituality that give it a distinct texture. The communal culture provides a broader understanding of the aspects of a child's life that awaken and nurture spirituality. In culturally philosophical definitions as well as theological definitions of the Latino community, spirituality has to do with relationship. Spirituality encompasses the ways people interact with God, others and creation.

Therefore, as religious educators and researchers of children's spirituality in the Latino context, there must be an appreciation for how familial symbols, patterns of relationships, beliefs and existential postures of the family of origin and church family nurture the child's emerging spiritual consciousness or—when these experiences are destructive—distort or thwart the child's spirituality. These perspectives are helpful in the interpretation of narrative as they can enhance the narrative.

The connections between significant family members in the child's life, and the growing image of God in the child's consciousness, is elaborated by Ana-Maria Rizzuto (1979). Rizzuto reveals how, at each level of maturity, a child's concept of God is closely related to the care and relationship of a main caretaker. When the relationship is positive, the child's image of God is likely to be positive and the child's ability to trust and relate to God thrives. When the relationship is abusive or neglectful, the image of God reflects that unhealthy relationship and the child's capacity or desire to trust God is hindered (see chapter 13).

The work of Cervantes and Ramirez (1992) as well as Rizzuto (1979) indicate that spirituality is more than religious rituals or doctrines. Spirituality is innate in all of life and in the acts of embracing life. When there is reverence for nature, and the simple routines of family life—such as preparing and eating meals or being dependable and providing care and love—we show children the face of God. The child learns to trust through everyday nurturing relationships. Trust will bring a child beyond the traditional images and names of God. The child explores fresh views of God, thus potentially enriching even the adult's awareness of the divine. This possibility does not exclude naming God for the child and using the Christian story to give shape to the image of God that emerges for the child. It simply allows both the adult and the child to listen for God's own way of speaking to the child. The adult becomes a guide, mentor and companion on the spiritual journey.

Joselito's Spiritual Explorations

Joselito was four years old and often visited the home of his Catholic grandparents where they had an altar upon which they placed a rosary, a small statue of the Virgin Mary and flowers. Joselito would watch his grandmother pray the rosary as she held each bead of the rosary and when she finished she would genuflect in front of the altar. He asked his *abuelita* (grandmother) about each item on the altar and she answered by telling a story in which the significance of each symbol was explained as she let him touch and explore each sacred item. Every time he visited he would ask the same question and his *abuelita* would repeat the ritual; but her stories about answered prayers would change, providing him with a variety of faith stories related to prayer and the symbols on the altar.

At home, his parents were Pentecostal and they too had an altar but the symbols were somewhat different. There was a Bible, anointing oil and a devotional book placed on a very pretty hand-crocheted table covering. When his father came home from work Joselito would watch him as he knelt down to pray and then read his Bible and devotional book. As he read, Joselito would sit on his father's lap and his father would tell him a Bible story. Joselito wondered about the bottle with the oil in it, so one day his father opened it and dabbed his finger in the oil, anointed Joselito's forehead making the sign of the cross, and asked God to bless him. Joselito was delighted to experience this ritual.

One day he was playing while his mother prepared dinner. He sat at the table humming a song or *corito* that they sang at church. He put two place mats together, placed a Bible on them, a picture he had colored in Sunday School, his mother's necklace made of colored beads, some dandelions from his front yard, and the new cap his uncle gave him the night before. His mother approached and asked what he was doing and he told her that he was showing God how much he loved him. "God answered my prayer and brought me this new cap and I am putting all the pretty things here that I know he likes. The picture is my story of God and how I love him." He pointed to the trees and birds and flowers he had drawn and said, "You see these are the things God gives us and I want him to know that I share them with him too because they are so pretty and I like them too. When Abuelita and Papá and you and Tio [uncle] Mike and all the people who visit us come to this house, they share pretty things and this is one way of showing love. When you cook I want to share some food with God too because we always share food with the people we love. I have to bring God a present because when we visit someone we always bring a present. I am not sure what present he would like." His mother went back to her food preparation. Finally Joselito brought in a small truck and placed it on the altar. "Mamá, this is going to be God's present!"

While they had dinner, the altar remained at the table. Joselito then told everyone his story of how God answered his prayer for a pretty new cap and how he was saying I love you to God. He then sang a corito to God.

For the next years the altar remained but soon changed location to Joselito's room. Joselito continued to bring new things to the altar to say I love you to God. Everyone who visited the house would hear a story of the newest prayer God had answered for Joselito. Telling his story of answered prayer was an integral part of his expression of faith and love for God. These were the expressions of his spirituality.

The altar is a very common expression of faith and connection with God in the Latino home. Each altar is personalized, representing the faith story of the person or family who sets it up. Joselito has access to the altar whenever he wants and can continue to use it to express himself to God. He can manipulate the symbols and confer meaning to them. He can tell his own faith stories to those who come to his altar. It changes as his own journey with God changes. It is the sacred space that he has for his own spirituality. The adults in his life also have altars, and he continues to enjoy listening to their stories while he is glad to have his own sacred space for the telling of his stories and making meaning of his relationship with God. Both the stories and the symbols allow him to find the language for the expression of his spirituality.

The Reggio Emilia Approach

It is with the understanding of this familial relational bond that Emilio Marrero (2000), a Latino pastor and Christian educator, uses a community model of education to nurture the spiritual lives of children at the child care center that he directs. The Reggio Emilia approach is an early childhood educational development program. It is not a Christian education method. Marrero has adapted it and has thus added theological dimensions in order to use it as a way of nurturing the Christian spirituality of the Latino child.

The approach reflects a Piagetian constructivist influence. There are several fundamental principles which define this pedagogical approach. It sees the child as protagonist, collaborator and communicator. It understands that the environment is a third teacher, the teacher and parents are partners, nurturers and guides. Emilia's approach is not so much a methodology or technique as it is a spirit of doing education. As such, it has a different approach to the attitudes about child creativity and what constitutes effective teaching strategies (Marrero, 2000, p. 27). It views the child as being powerful, capable of revealing ideas and reflections, and an active agent in the learning process. The child is an integral member of the learning community. Thus, he is viewed as a constructor of knowledge, in this case knowledge about God. Theologically this is possible when the child is viewed as created in the image of God, which means he can reason and be creative. The child is loved by God and is the model of those who belong to the kingdom of God. God therefore reveals Godself to the child.

Art becomes the language for the child's expression of reflections. In addition to verbal or written reflections, collages, clay and other arts are used as a language of expression and tools to foster exploration and reasoning. The teacher's role becomes one of collaborator, working together with child and parents. The purpose of the approach is to uncover what the child knows and thinks, and to foster the emergence of projects based on the child's reflections and interests. This makes for a fluid, generative, dynamic curriculum.

The question to be asked in relation to the subject of spirituality is: How is the child's interest in God awakened? The Reggio Emilia approach depends on the communal and environmental surrounding of the child as the source of the child's interests. In the case of a Latina child, the religious life of the community (family, church and neighbors) serves as the stimulus.

Another dimension opens the child to the grace of God, the natural environment surrounding the child. Within the Reggio Emilia approach the environment is viewed as the third teacher (Boyd Cadwell, 1997). Children interact with their environment with awe and wonder. In Marrero's appropriation of the Reggio Emilia approach, wonder brings the child to question and to deepen her awareness of the spirit of God as we help her identify the elements of God already present. This can be done, for example, by looking at flowers, fish swimming in a pond or clouds in the sky rolling by. As children wonder and question, their eyes open to the reality of God. The question many times is: How can pre-operational children be actively engaged in constructing an understanding of God? The more common view of children at this stage is as involuntary participants in organic growth. Piaget (1967) states that the intuitive thought of a child is based on immediate impressions that are rooted in the senses. The Reggio Emilia approach is conversation with the child to help the child use her senses to explore and to help the adult appreciate the child's insights. It gives direction to conversation with the child.

These conversations come from the child's and not the adult's impressions. Hence, Marrero's adaptation of the Reggio Emilia model does not focus on an expedient delivery of information but is patient, allowing time, opportunity and the Holy Spirit to bring forth truth for the child. The focus is on the process of God revealing to the child and not on a product of a directed teaching process or curriculum. Berryman's (1995) approach to play also allows space for such wonder and conversation. It is education that builds on experience and understanding over time. This is much more in keeping with the Latino approach to knowledge construction and education.

Francisco's Spiritual Experiences

Francisco, age six, has parents who do not take him to church. However, the neighbor next door had a garden with vegetable plants, flowers and a white wooden cross in the midst of her garden. Francisco often heard his neighbor, Marta, speak to God about the plants and how she was growing her vegetables for the neighbor who had many children, and her flowers for Ana, the elderly woman who lived two houses away. She would throw kisses up at God as she spoke to God. This was her act of worship to God after kneeling and praying in the garden. Francisco asked Marta if he could help her in the garden because he too wanted to bring something good to the neighbors. She motioned to him to enter and taught him about how each plant grew. When she was ready to kneel and pray, she told him he need not to do this if he did not want to but that it was her way of getting strength from God to love her neighbors everyday. Francisco asked how this happened if he could not see God. She said to him that just as one cannot see the wind and yet can feel it, God could not be seen but could be felt in the heart. Francisco heard the neighbor's short prayer and watched her throw a kiss to God.

A few weeks later he accompanied her to Ana's house with some freshly cut flowers in a vase. Ana was quite moved. Francisco kissed Ana on the cheek as he gave her the flowers. They stayed and visited for a while with Ana. Later he told Marta, "You throw the kisses to the air where you think God is and I gave a kiss to Ana because, when she cried as I gave her the flowers, I saw God in her eyes and tears, so I kissed her."

Francisco had been reflecting on his neighbor's expressions of spirituality and had been searching for that which was congruent with his own understandings. His spirituality had been awakened by Marta's practice of growing flowers and vegetables for the neighbors. Her spirituality through her love to others awakened his own, but her expressions of love to God did not connect with him. He searched for his own until he found the face of God.

With Francisco it is clear that even when a child is not attending church, there are religious conversations taking place and symbols are everywhere, since the sacred and the secular are not as firmly bounded and separated as in western culture. The church helps to make sense of these religious artifacts and conversations. It is God, through the Holy Spirit, who brings clarity. The story shows that God was awakening Francisco's spirit to God's Spirit. As a spiritual guide, Ana could be more intentional in helping him reflect about his understandings. Where and how would Christian educators enter his journey? What role would they take? How would they participate in the work that God was already starting? These are the issues Marrero seeks to work with in a Latino community replete with religious symbols but without intentional direction.

Children's Spirits Enlivened by the Holy Spirit

Religious educator Frank Rogers (1994) also sees the child as an active agent. He claims that the Holy Spirit awakens the spirit in children, making them equally capable of participating with the community of faith in God's redeeming acts. His focus on the spiritual development of the child is not the child's religious articulation but the true awakening of the child's spirit by God.

Rogers (1994) speaks of three movements of the Spirit. The first is where the Spirit initiates an awakening of spirits by making people aware of God's smiling at them. To see God, to be aware of God, is to become an agent of God that helps others also see God. As one enters into the activity of the Spirit he or she finds the self in touch with the spirit. This is the second movement. The third stems from it. The Spirit of God moves outward into the brokenness of the world to bring wholeness and reconciliation, to bring in the reign of God. At this point, the Spirit helps the individual to see the face of God in the faces of those who suffer, and within the spirit one hears a whisper of the Spirit of God who seeks to lift up and to make humanity fully alive.

Rogers (1994) insists that children participate in the very same Spirit as adults so that they are capable of the same yearnings that impassion adults and see glimpses of the Sprit that enlivens adults. As examples he uses some of the conversations that Coles (1990) has with children.

Paulita's Spirituality of Caring for and Encouraging the Homeless

In my own work with children I have found a tremendous capacity in children to not only show compassion but to act upon it in their own way. One such child, Paulita, was seven years old when she heard of the church's food ministry with a homeless shelter in the area. Curious, she began asking her parents questions about what would take place at the shelter. She learned that the church would be holding conversations with those dining in order to provide for other needs as well. As each question was answered she would ask another until finally she began to gain an understanding of homelessness. She went to her room and sat silently for quite some time. She later told her mother that she was very sad and angry at the same time because "it must be very, very hard to be homeless." The next Sunday Paulita signed up to be a server at the shelter. Her mother cooked but Paulita went with the deacons and deaconesses to help serve. Her job was to pour the milk from the dispenser. Once she felt confident about her task and her surroundings, she was sensitive and friendly with those who came. She became popular with them.

When the committee was recruiting new members, Paulita was one of the committee members making a presentation. She said, "When you do not have a house to live in you feel very sad and you want to hide. If somebody just puts food on your plate you want to look down. So, I make jokes and people laugh and look at me and so I look at their eyes and smile too. When I see their happy eyes I know God is happy too." Paulita had seen God in the faces of the homeless. She had become part of God's redemptive activity in the world because she was capable of feeling compassion. Her spirit was alive to God.

Conclusions

Narrative inquiry has the potential to unfold the contexts of not only children's spiritualities/theologies, but adults as well. Consequently, as intergenerational exchange and journeying together occurs in the faith community, this has implications for how generic developmental models can be challenged and the reality of diverse lived experiences can be affirmed for their strengths instead of emphasizing their "deficits." Both child and adult are teachers and learners as they assist one another in their own respective faith journeys. Moreover, in this context, one assumption of Cavalletti (1983, p. 9) that "God cannot be fully caught by the logic structures of any age or stage anyway" can be embodied, and both child and adult can be affirmed where they are, regardless of chronological age. Nevertheless, Cavalletti's assumption is not shared by all. Hence, when are adults interfering with the work of the Spirit by imposing the understandings and framework of their own questions and when are they needed as guides?

This question is important in the narrative inquiry approach, which is so helpful in facilitating the gathering of children's narratives, which form part of communal narratives of faith. In the interpretive stage, how does the researcher separate her own interpretive frameworks from those that the child is shaping? What language can one use to give credence to the experiences of children in this interpretive work?

Narrative inquiry can help one listen to the language that comes naturally to children in their spiritual journeys by simply allowing the narrative to stand on its own without needing to ask questions that say more about one's own doctrinal understandings than they do about the child's emerging understanding of God. What Sylvia shows is that there is more than just religion in her life. One might argue that she is simply imitating what her parents and other significant caretakers in her life are doing. However, Edward Robinson in *The Original Vision* (1983) indicates that church may provide the child with a congenial atmosphere and experience, but the child is capable of discovering something more than the textures of a religious setting. A child's spirit can be awakened by the spirit of God. This awakening begins a way of being aware of God and God's activity through the senses; the mystery of God becomes part of the child's life. Sylvia does not have the need to answer all of Karen's questions but is possibly satisfied with the knowledge about Jesus that she has at this point. Mystery, or not knowing everything, appears to be fine with her. It should be so with everyone.

At times, the child's own sense of God may differ from the images of God painted by sermons, Sunday School or the symbols in the songs. Although these sermons, Sunday School experiences, and symbols are not presented by the child and therefore may be irrelevant, the child is able to receive in her own spirit God's revelation in a language she can understand. Marrero's work adapted from the Emilia approach provides more helpful framework for working with the Spirit in the journey with the child, and includes the adult as one who guides the journey by facilitating wonder and conversation, as well as affirming different languages that are not verbal and written. This allows for greater avenues of the child's spiritual expressions.

It is the evidence of the capacity of children to understand God, mediated by God's grace, that convinces both of us that Sylvia—when given the opportunity to share her reflections about God with an adult—may be speaking with language learned at church or at home but she is nonetheless speaking of her authentic experience with God. The love of Sylvia's parents is part of God's grace that nurtures her sense of trust and ability to understand concretely God's love for her. Paulita and Francisco also find ways to express that love to those around them and the experience continues to cycle into their reflections and deeper comprehension and encounter with God.

Writing about these issues from the context and experiences of the African American and Latino communities has also revealed the spiritual/theological world of these communities and how these are connected to the familial and communal lives of persons. In these contexts, people are opened to God's infinite ways of revealing Godself. This informs the listener's interpretive frameworks as one listens to the narratives, but it also informs approaches to Christian education.

References

Berryman, J. W. (1995). *Godly play: An imaginative approach to religious education.* Minneapolis: Augsburg.

Boyd Cadwell, L. (1997). *Bringing Reggio Emilia home: An innovative approach to early childhood education.* New York: Teachers College Press.

Boyd-Franklin, N. (2003). *Black families in therapy: Understanding the African American experience* (2nd ed.). New York: Guilford.

Brashears, F., & Roberts, M. (2001). The Black church as a resource for change. In S. L. M. Logan (Ed.), *The Black family: Strengths, self-help, and positive change* (pp. 181–192). Boulder, CO: Westview.

Cavalletti, S. (1983). *The religious potential of the child: The description of an experience with children from ages three to six.* (P. M. Coulter & J. M. Coulter Trans.). Ramsey, NJ: Paulist. (Orig. publ. 1979)

Cervantes, J. M., & Ramirez, O. (1992). Spirituality and family dynamics in psychotherapy. In L. A. Vargas & J. D. Koss-Chioino (Eds.), *Working with culture: Psychotherapeutic interventions with ethnic minority children and adolescents* (pp. 103–128). San Francisco: Jossey-Bass.

Clandinin, D. J., & Connelly, F. M. (2000). *Narrative inquiry: Experience and story in qualitative research.* San Francisco: Jossey-Bass.

Coles, R. (1990). *The spiritual life of children.* Boston: Houghton Mifflin. Fairbanks, C. M. (1996, Summer). Telling stories: Reading and writing research narratives. *Journal of Curriculum and Supervision, 11,* 320–340.

Gandini, L. (1997). Foundations of the Reggio Emilia approach. In J. Hendrick (Ed.), *First steps toward teaching the Reggio way* (pp. 14–23). New Jersey: Prentice Hall.

Graue, M. E., & Walsh, D. J. (1998). *Studying children in context: Theories, methods, and ethics.* Thousand Oaks, CA: Sage.

Haight, W. L. (2002). *African-American children at church: A sociological perspective.* New York: Cambridge University Press.

Hay, D. and Nye, R. (1998). *The spirit of the child.* London: HarperCollins.

Hill, S. A. (1999). *African American children: Socialization and development in families.* Thousand Oaks, CA: Sage.

Houskamp, B. M., Fisher, L. A., & Stuber, M. L. (2004). Spirituality in children and adolescents: Research findings and implications for clinicians and researchers. *Child and Adolescent Psychiatric Clinics of North America, 13*(1), 221–230.

Hudley, E. V. P., Haight, W., & Miller, P. J. (2003). *"Raise up a child": Human development in an African-American family.* Chicago: Lyceum Books.

Jackson, F. M. (1989). Educational experiences of Black children: The case of the Black church. In J. Allen & J. Preissle (Eds.), *Qualitative research in education: Teaching and learning qualitative traditions* (pp. 36–43). Athens, GA: The Georgia Center for Continuing Education.

Leon-Portilla, M. (1980). *Native Mesoamerican spirituality.* New York: Paulist.

Marrero, E. (2000). *The competent reflector: A Reggio Emilia inspired religious education model.* Unpublished doctoral project, Claremont School of Theology, Claremont, California.

Mitchell, E. P. (1986). Oral tradition: The legacy of faith for the Black church. *Religious Education, 18* (1), 93–113.

Myers, B. K. (1997). *Young children and spirituality.* New York: Routledge.

Newman, S. D. (1994). *With heart and hand: The Black church working to save Black children.* Valley Forge, PA: Judson.

PBS Home Video (Producer). (1995). *Listening to children: A moral journey with Robert Coles* [Videotape]. Alexandria, VA: PBS Video.

Piaget, J. (1967). *Six psychological studies.* New York: Vintage.

Pineda, A. M. (1996). The oral tradition of a people. In F. Scgovia & A. M. Isasi-Díaz (Eds.), *Hispanic/Latina Theology: Challenge and Promise* (pp. 104–116). Minneapolis: Fortress.

Poole, T. (1990). Black families and the Black church: A sociohistorical perspective. In H. E. Cheatham & J. B. Stewart (Eds.), *Black families: Interdisciplinary perspectives* (pp. 33–48). New Brunswick, NJ: Transaction Publishers.

Ratcliff, D. (2001). Rituals in a school hallway: Evidence of a latent spirituality of children. *Christian Education Journal, 5NS*(2), 9–26.

Riggs, M. (2001). African American children, "The hope of the race": Mary Church Terrell, the social gospel, and the work of the Black women's club movement. In M. J. Bunge (Ed.), *The child in Christian thought* (pp. 365–385). Grand Rapids: Eerdmans.

Rizzuto, A.-M. (1979). *The birth of the living God: A psychoanalytical study.* Chicago: University of Chicago Press.

Roberts, J. D. (1980). *Roots of a Black future: Family and church.* Philadelphia: Westminster.

Robinson, E. (1983). *The original vision: A study of the religious experience of childhood.* New York: Seabury.

Rogers, F. (Presenter). (1994). *And I saw God's face: The spiritual life of children* [Video cassette]. Pacific Grove, CA.: Pacific Southwest Conference on World Christian Mission.

Smith, A., Jr. (1997). *Navigating the deep river: Spirituality in African American families.* Cleveland, OH: United Church Press.

Smith, W. C. (1985). *The church in the life of the Black family.* Valley Forge, PA: Judson Press.

Tyms, J. D. (1979–1980). The Black church as an ally in the education of Black Children. *Journal of Religious Thought, 82,* 73–87.

Vaughan, F. (1986). *The inward arc: Healing and wholeness in psychotherapy and spirituality.* Boston: Shambhala.

Wimberly, E. (2000). *Relational refugees: Alienation and reincorporation in African American churches and communities.* Nashville, TN: Abingdon.

PART IV

Encouraging Children's Spirituality in the School and Other Contexts

Chapter Nineteen

Narrative and the Moral Education
of the Christian Child

VICTORIA M. FORD AND ESTHER WONG[1]

In this two-part chapter, the narrative is examined as a potential tool in assisting the moral education of children. Victoria Ford introduces the chapter by describing the narrative process and how it may be applied to moral education. While Ford highlights the potential contribution of schools in this respect, a corollary vision is cast by Esther Wong related to how the home and church can provide moral education through effective communication of the Christian story.-ed.

1. Victoria M. Ford holds a BA in Anthropology, with a minor in Peace Studies, from McMaster University (2001). She also holds a Masters in Religious Education (MRE) from McMaster Divinity College (2003). Victoria's graduate studies focused on the roles narratives play (or could play) in the education of children. She learned of the value of narratives as an educational tool, and designed a methodology for narrative education based in a Christian context. In 2002, Victoria ran a "Children's Ministry Consultation," at McMaster Divinity College, and in 2003 Victoria presented a paper titled "Narrative Education and the Spiritual and Moral Development of Children" at a Baptist Women of Ontario and Quebec, Toronto Association, conference. Her masters thesis, "Telling Tales: The Role of Narratives in the Education of Children," was published by McMaster University Press in 2003. She continues to research the role of narratives in education and working on the further development and possible implementation of her methodology of narrative education in both the Christian and public educational spheres. Victoria lives in Dundas, Ontario, Canada, with her husband and is expecting their first child in November 2004.

Esther Wong holds a BS from Michigan State University and has taught Bible classes for children, youths, and adults for over 20 years. She was the associate director at Fuller Seminary's Doctor of Ministry program where she developed educational strategies to equip pastors and church leaders to respond effectively to contemporary ministry challenges in the US and abroad. Prior to her work at Fuller, Esther was a project manager for World Vision and was involved in the development of communication strategies and in the coordination of program coalitions. Esther is currently working on program initiatives to implement Christian Education for the 21st Century in churches and homes. She is also associated with Lifespring Ministry where the focus of her work is on educating and mobilizing the community of faith to respond to urban ministry challenges in Aurora, Illinois. Esther lives in Naperville, Illinois with her husband and three children where she also chairs the curriculum committee of the Parent Diversity Advisory Council in her school district.

Part One: Narrative Education: A Tool for the Moral Education of Children (Victoria M. Ford)

What is education? This is an age-old question. Answered briefly, to educate is to "give intellectual, moral, and social instruction to (a pupil, a child), [especially] as a formal and prolonged process" (Barber, 1998, p. 445). While intellectual and social instruction are generally understood functions of education, the notion of "moral instruction" remains ambiguous and demands clarification. Essentially, the concept of "morality" is concerned with the examination of "good and bad" and "right and wrong" human tendencies and actions. Moral instruction, therefore, is "the study of what is considered right [or proper] conduct," in contrast to wrong [or improper] conduct (Angeles, 1992, p. 194).

Education can be both formal and informal. Formal education is the domain of the traditional classroom, with students seated at desks passively awaiting the transmission of knowledge from an instructor. Informal education, on the other hand, is the domain of the world, that is, education that occurs in all other non-classroom contexts. When a child observes the parents within the confines of the home, he or she is actively engaged in learning in an informal environment. Education, in either context, can be a life-long endeavor. Despite the significance of informal education, this paper will be speaking of formal education when it speaks of the "education of a child."

In formal education, effective teaching is an important factor in the learning process and can contribute to a positive learning experience. Ann L. Brown writes that instructors should employ "procedures that enable children to experience a sense of mastery, that lets them see that they have some control over learning situations, and [provide a] systematic analysis [that] can lead to successful performance" (Brown et al, 1998, p. 306). In other words, teachers should utilize educational methods that provide the students with the potential to interact with the information, their instructors, and each other. Students should play a more active role in the learning process. When a teacher chooses to actively engage students in the learning process, such educators can enrich the child's capability for reasoning, provide them with a sense of embodied learning, and establish an empowered voice within each child. The question then remains, what type of educational framework will allow for such a learning experience? The answer is narrative education.

Narrative education—applied within a Christian context—can assist in the moral development of the child. The chapter begins with an overview of narrative education, including four crucial elements of narrative education. Christian biblical examples of narrative education will be considered, along with a vision for moral education in the home, church, and school at the conclusion of the chapter.

Narrative Education: A Brief Overview

Human beings love to tell stories. A story can capture the mind and captivate the imagination. A well-told story can have a powerful impact on an individual, and can invite the listener "into a transformative realm in which old ways of living may be opened up to new possibilities" (Shaw, 1999, p. 5). A story can be a powerful educational tool for both change and growth.

In the context of formal education, stories may be employed in a methodology known as narrative education. According to Michael Connelly and Jean Clandenin, "narrative is the study of how human beings make meaning of experience by endlessly telling and retelling stories about themselves that both refigure the past and create purpose in the future" (Connelly and Clandenin, 1998, p. 24). Through this narrative process, people can "engage in a process of self-creation and meaning making that is an important condition of learning" (Shaw, 1999, p. 4).

Narrative education is different from other forms of formal education because of the emphasis on voice, embodied learning, and reason as educational tools. In narrative education students are engaged in the mutual exchange of stories, both transmitting and receiving stories with others in a group. Once a story has been shared, each person has an opportunity to share his or her personal experiences, understandings, and interpretations of the story. The result is a group that can be dramatically transformed by the oral sharing of the experiences of its members in response to a shared story or narrative.

Narrative Education: A Methodology

Methodology is "the branch of knowledge that deals with method and its application in a particular field" (Barber, 1998, p. 912). The methodology for narrative education is based in research and theory, and represents the manner in which narratives can be applied to a formal educational setting. The process of narrative education is composed of many different, yet interrelated, aspects. By examining the different aspects in detail, one can comprehend better how these independent parts make up the whole. There are four crucial elements necessary for the methodology of narrative education: planning the experience, the experience proper, speaking the experience, and the transformation of personal understanding.[2]

The planned experience. The first element in narrative education is the planning of the learning event. This is any experience or event prearranged by the instructor and which all students will share. When an instructor is preparing an experience, he or she must ensure that the experience chosen: (a) is age-appropriate; (b) is suited for

---

2. Please note that when writing this chapter, a methodology of narrative education is still in its infancy. As a result, the four elements of narrative education defined in this chapter, as well as other details prescribed in this chapter, may not be found elsewhere.

the overall learning expectations of the school grade being taught (i.e. conducive to the curriculum); (c) allows children to apply their current knowledge; and, (d) provides the teacher with some control over the experience proper, while also allowing the children to feel that they share control over their learning situation.

The *planned experience* is selected by the teacher and situated within "typical" classroom life. By typical I am implying that the planned experience should not disrupt the overall flow of the class, but instead be a normal function of the learning process. When an instructor chooses to apply narrative education, it will change the dynamic of a traditional classroom,[3] but this change should not be entirely disruptive to overall classroom behavior. Children will no longer be sitting passively in their desks listening to their teacher. Instead, through narrative education they will be able to move about the classroom with relative ease, and there will be various experiential stations in the classroom suited to the different scholastic disciplines. For the mathematics and sciences the experiences selected will differ from those presented in language and culture.

The experience of the learning event. The experience proper is the second necessary element of narrative education. Students will participate as a collective whole in the initial experience. That is, they will take part in it simultaneously. While all participants share the experience, the interpretation of it may differ *among* the participants. For example, an earlier personal experience may affect the understanding or interpretation of the communal experience. As such, while the planned experience is common to all, the experience of the learning event may differ for each person.

Speaking the experience. The third necessary element is talking about the experience. After the group has experienced the learning event, they regroup to share individual interpretations or understandings of the event. At this point those who participated in the experience verbalize their interpretation of it. It is imperative to note that at this stage a narrative of the experience is being told, a story recounting the events as understood by the narrator. Each member of the group will have an opportunity to be the narrator and to contribute to the overall understanding of the shared experience.

Once the students have regrouped, the instructor selects one individual to begin the narrative process. The instructor should vary the first narrator for each planned experience. This allows every student the opportunity to present a personal narrative of their understanding unaltered, or perhaps transformed by hearing others (see the next stage), at different points throughout the overall learning process. The chosen student will then express his or her understanding of the experience. When *speaking the experience* the students are encouraged to retell the experience based on their personal understanding of it. If a child has had a previous personal

---

3. The work in this portion of the chapter is based primarily on Canadian research, however, Canadian public education shares much in common with North American and European models of education.

experience that he or she feels is similar to the shared experience, the child may incorporate this into the personal story, as long as the child explains why the two experiences are believed to be similar.

During this stage, the instructor may ask some clarifying questions of the student *speaking the experience,* to promote reasoning within the children. According to Connelly and Clandinin, "in trying to understand the personal, one needs to ask questions not only about the past, or the present, or the future, but about all three. For any one teacher, therefore, clues to the personal are obtained from one's history, from how one thinks and feels, and from how one acts" (Connelly and Clandenin, 1998, pp. 24–25). When asking clarifying questions, instructors and other students must be certain that they do not challenge the feelings and interpretations being shared by the narrator, and that they do not ask questions in a leading manner, causing the narrator to reevaluate what is being said at the time.

During this stage, all members of the group are invited to verbalize their interpretation of the experience; all are encouraged to voice their understanding. This act empowers each student. The students are required to find their voice and to state what they understand in an accurate and clear manner. If the experience was upsetting for a student, the instructor should attempt to comfort him or her and should encourage compassionate responses from fellow classmates. Moreover, the instructor should stress that all interpretations of the experience are valid and valuable. This strengthens the overall learning process, because the various interpretations and understandings are treated with respect.

Transformation of Personal Understanding. Finally, there is the result of narrative education: the transformation of the child's understanding. It is here that the understandings of those involved with the narrative education experience may be changed in a significant manner. Information garnered from actively listening to shared interpretations of the common experience will enable students to confirm, build upon, or dismiss entirely their previous understandings of an experience in which they participated or about which they heard.

The process of *transformation* is incorporated within speaking the experience. As soon as the first student narrates a personal understanding of the experience, that understanding will become communal. While listening to the narrator, fellow classmates have the opportunity to do more than simply hear the story being shared—they may also incorporate the narrator's interpretations and understandings into their own cognitive framework. Because of this, other students' interpretations and understandings may be transformed because of any newly acquired data, or may remain unaltered. This transformation will be different for each child because each has a unique past and present.

Further, this process enables the students to readily apply their reasoning capabilities. At this stage, students will need to discern which information to keep and which to discard as a result of their classmates' interpretations of the experience. That is, each child will need to work through not only one's own understanding of the planned experience, but also the interpretations offered through the stories of the peers in order that the personal understanding and knowledge be transformed. This stage incorporates previous knowledge and experiences, and applies them to the current situation. At this stage, children will also begin to work out other scenarios where the information might be relevant.

Narrative education and embodied learning. The overall result of narrative education is *embodied learning.* Legs, arms, hands, feet and the senses will be forever changed because of the learning process. The various events experienced and shared will have used the different senses and appendages of the body. As the learning process is based upon experiences, the students will learn that all parts of the body are valuable and necessary for the role of active learning. For example, if the planned experience is based on the sense of taste, the child will learn how his or her tongue, mouth, lips and teeth function based on various tastes (i.e. sweet versus sour).

Instructors that practice narrative education will quickly learn that while the planned experience is common to all students, speaking of the experience involves a unique interpretation for each child. As such, the third and fourth elements of the methodology will be repeated until every member of the class has voiced her or his story.

Through the process of narrative education, not only are the students' previous understandings altered—by their personal experience and by the narratives of others—they are also applying reason in its fullest sense. Students are encouraged to analyze what has happened and draw conclusions as a result. In reasoning, the students embody the experience as their instructors and fellow students encourage them to use their voices that were empowered during the learning event.

Moral Development through Narrative Education: A Biblical Example

It is a very difficult task to teach someone right from wrong. This is because the concepts of right and wrong are often abstract, and reflect the cultures within which they are taught. Narrative education is an important tool for the moral development of children, which is the main goal of religious education in general. This is because "storytelling organically unites substantive and structural content and can bring a holistic way of learning into the religious educational setting [and] can bring together experiential, intuitive, imaginative knowing and rational, analytic knowing in ways that engage the whole being of the learner" (Shaw, 1999, p. 114).

Jesus used narratives for precisely this reason when instructing His followers. In Matt 13:34, "Jesus told the crowds all these things in parables; without a parable he told them nothing" (New Revised Standard Version). It was through His narratives that Jesus was able to reach His followers, because narratives allowed for the sharing of experiences. In short, when examined from a methodological standpoint, Jesus' acts of teaching fulfill the various aspects of narrative education. These meaningful transmissions of moral laws are seen most clearly in the parables of the Gospel accounts.

An example of one of Jesus' teaching parables is seen in Luke 10:30–37, "The Parable of the Good Samaritan." In this parable, Jesus uses a story to illicit the emotions of His listeners. The story discusses how a traveler fell into the hands of robbers, was beaten, stripped of his clothes and possessions, and left for dead in the road. Jesus explains how various people treated this traveler who was in need. A priest, a highly respected and revered individual, left this traveler to suffer. A Levite, a Jew who followed the Law closely, also left the traveler for dead. But the Samaritan (someone whom Jesus' followers would normally dismiss since they were not Jewish and therefore were considered void of faith) helped this traveler to get well.

By hearing this story Jesus' followers begin to see what it means to be a neighbor—to reach out to someone in need. The parable lists people with whom Jesus' followers could identify (i.e. traveler, priest, Levite, and Samaritan), and places them in a situation that would be readily understandable. Furthermore, through His oral transmission of this story, Jesus allows for His followers to interpret the meaning of the story, based both on their current knowledge and past experiences. This parable teaches an important lesson in a meaningful manner for various listeners.

Moral Development through Biblical Narrative

The Parable of the Good Samaritan was chosen to exemplify the role of narratives in moral education because I believe it holds important implications for the moral development of children. In their moral development, children need to learn the appropriate (morally correct) ways of treating others. This does not mean others who are necessarily "like" them, but instead refers to all human beings. This is a complex moral lesson. Often, children find it difficult to associate with people or things that are different from them. However, in this parable, Jesus instructs His followers to treat everyone with a kind heart, because everyone is a neighbor.

Children are able to identify with the concept of neighbor, for they are likely to have someone living in the house or apartment next to theirs. Because the concept of neighbor is not foreign to children, they are able to begin to associate with the parable and the moral truths it contains. It is this initial association, followed by the sharing of the experience, that allows children to learn "right" and "wrong" ways to treat others. The concepts of right and wrong in relation to the treatment of others become more concrete and readily applicable for the children as they share in the experience of Jesus' story of the Good Samaritan. Further, through sharing this story, children will have the opportunity to interpret it from their own vantage point. Through the application of the methodology proposed in this paper, the children will also be provided with the opportunity to hear the interpretations of others. In the end, the understanding of what it means to be a good neighbor, and potential actions one may take when he or she finds another in need, may be transformed as a result of applying narrative education in a Christian context.

Through narrative education, the Bible comes alive for children. They are able to empathize with individuals important in the history of their faith. As a result of this educational methodology, children will also have the opportunity to grow in their personal understandings of who God is, and how He functions in their own lives as well as in the lives of their religious ancestors. This helps promote the development of faith in children, as children come to understand who God is personally. Finally, through narrative education, children will come to understand Christian theology. For "theology tells us primarily about the nature of God and the nature of [human beings] and about the relations between them" (Miller, 1956, p. 5). This understanding develops from the children's experience of relationships amongst themselves, and with their instructor. These relationships are an integral component of faith education in children, for relationships provide "the language by which we communicate the truth of God at work in history" as well as in the lives of humanity today (Miller, 1956, p. 11).

While the Church is important in the educational process of children, the family unit is an integral component of the overall intellectual development of a child. "The levels of [moral] development about which the Christian parent and teacher are concerned have to do with the child's growing awareness of the presence of God in the world and in individual lives" (Cully, 1979, p. 11). That is, Christian parents and educators seek to instill "a sense of love and trust that is without fear, and an empathy with the needs of others that makes possible acts of generosity and self-giving" (Cully, 1979, p. 11). As such, by applying the methodology of narrative education (in whole or in part) in the home, as well as in formal educational settings, further assists the faith development of a child.

The methodology for narrative education is a practical educational tool in that it can function within various educational situations. Whenever applied, narrative education equips children with reason, embodied learning, and an empowered voice. In the church, narratives bring the Christian scriptures to life, bringing meaning to the otherwise distant lessons of the Triune God.

The Need for Narrative Education

When applied in the church, home, or school, the methodology for narrative education assists in the embodiment of understanding of right and wrong. Moreover, this methodology promotes the embodiment of empathy, the capacity to reason empathetically, and the skills to articulate one's story in an empowered voice. Narrative education is a theoretically sound and practically applicable approach to education and therefore should be examined carefully by educational practitioners. The concept of narrative education need not simply be a theory, but instead a practical educational methodology.

Part Two: The Christian Story and Moral Education in Church, Home, and School (Esther Wong)

The importance of the church, home and school in the task of Christian education can be traced back to early American history. In his text *Protestant Strategies in Education*, Robert Lynn (1964) notes that prior to 1833 the responsibility of Protestant church education rested on the church, home, and school, in that order.

> Prior to disestablishment [of the colonial state-church system, 1833], church education rested upon a triangular institutional base: congregation, home, and school. It was the responsibility of the congregation to provide catechetical instruction and of parents to teach their children both the Scriptures and the catechism, and of the school (such as they were) to assist in this enterprise as well as instruct the young in their letters and heritage. Such interlocking cooperation seemed to be a natural working arrangement, an ideal intended though not always realized. (Lynn, 1964, p. 14)

By the end of the Civil War, the triangle arrangement was dissolved and the "dual system" of education—public school and Sunday School—was adopted. In time, as Protestant church education became marginalized in relation to American public education, the triangle arrangement of education was eventually reversed. The public school, not the church, became the "central, pivotal institution" and "a major 'social source' of understanding education, whether in school, church, or elsewhere" (Lynn, 1964, pp. 64–65). Over time, the home was eclipsed by these two other sources of education.

Lynn contends that "understanding the presentness of the past as it is expressed in the 'typical Protestant parallelism of public school and Sunday School'" should guide the development of a vision for Christian education strategies (Lynn, 1964, p.12). The professionalizing of both the public school and church was associated with a shift away from the home for spiritual education. Perhaps parents feel less capable of encouraging their children's faith, even though dozens of research studies clearly indicate that parental influence generally overshadows all other influences in this respect (Hyde, 1990).

The Importance of Parental Christian Education

The task of Christian education, then, must begin with parents, yet the church can provide valuable assistance in this respect. The church has the responsibility to teach the Bible and bring theology and theological reflection from the pulpit into all church ministries, including ministries that specifically encourage and support parental faith formation of their children. Churches can also assist parents by affirming the historical doctrine and creeds that are bedrocks of Christian education. With a strong biblical foundation and philosophy taught and lived in the life of the church, parents can be equipped to teach their children how to view the world and live life from a Christian perspective. As pastors see their role as the theologians of their churches, teaching the Word of God becomes central for their ministry to the Christian family. Scripture and theology must be reflected in all ministries of the church, including Sunday School and Bible classes, fellowship and small groups, missions work and support, and social ministries. Strong theological and biblical teaching in the church will help prepare parents to teach these in the home.

It is imperative, therefore, that churches see and accept the divine teaching role they have for the people of God. This means setting high standards—both doctrinally and pedagogically—for ministers, administrators, teachers, and lay leaders. Churches must be committed to educating and equipping parents to accept the challenge of cultivating in their children a "thoroughly Christian understanding of knowledge" (Green, 2002, p. 76). This requires that parents and children be lifelong students of the Word of God so that they will think and live within biblical values and perspectives.

The relationship between parents and children is conducive to discipleship. "Christianity," says Frank Gaebeline,

> is a religion of independence growing out of continued dependence upon God . . . The aim of believing parents should be to develop in their children a progressive freedom from parental control, based on an increasing submission to God, which will make them independent Christian personalities. (Gaebelein, 1951, pp. 249–250)

He continues,

> If childhood religious receptivity is not cultivated at home, it is sure to be filled later and then usually with error and half truth but to experiment intelligently, he must be thoroughly grounded in what others have thought and done. The idea that education, whether in home or school, must remain in a perpetual attitude of suspended judgment about the eternal verities is simply unrealistic. (Gaebelein, 1951, p. 252)

Theological and Philosophical Foundations of Christian Education

Sound theological and philosophical foundations must be present for education in any context—church, home, or school—to be effective. Brad Green (2002) analyzes Christian higher education in these respects and proposes a "twofold organizational scheme" which can be applied to education in the church, home, or school. Green's first aspect is called "the history of redemption" and deals with the doctrines of creation, fall, redemption, and lordship of Christ. The second aspect deals with the central themes of Scripture, knowledge and truth, faith seeking understanding, communication, the importance of the past, and the centrality of a *telos*. Green discusses each of these "core Christian realities" and central themes as they relate to the Christian understanding of education. He argues, "any vision of a truly Christian higher education will contain no *less* than these commitments" (Green, 2002, p. 62). The same can be said for the education of children, regardless of age.

Communicating the Christian Story

In the Scriptures, it is clear that the historic Christian faith is rooted in a story—the story of God's relationship with his people. John Bolt calls the narrative character of the Christian faith "our spiritual autobiography" (Bolt, 1993, p. 185). The individuals and events of the past should be highlighted, for they establish identity and context and shape children's perspective of the future. The story of God and his people continues to unfold in the lives of his people today. The Christian story becomes alive in children's minds and hearts by telling and retelling both the personal story of faith and the collective stories of God's activities to one's children (see chapter one). Children are inundated by alternative and often contradictory stories through the mass media and other sources, and thus the church and parents must be certain the Christian story is heard and owned by their youngsters.

To communicate the Christian story effectively and meaningfully to children, parents need to view the Christian story not as merely a set of facts to be transmitted, but schema-setting accounts that can be discussed thoughtfully and explored for personal applications. Children need to see the biblical narrative within an all-encompassing view of reality, to encourage discovery of the ways they too can participate in God's redemptive mission for the world. Parents and churches must teach biblical narrative in a manner that engages and inspires youngsters to become lifelong learners, a requirement for genuine discipleship.

Unfortunately, parents do not always teach their children to think for themselves and internalize matters related to belief and ultimate truths, thus their faith may be vulnerable in the face of cultural and educational challenges. However, if critical thinking is part of the faith education at home and church, they are more likely to withstand such challenges. Critical thinking can be encouraged by asking children engaging questions, and encouraging them to discuss ideas deeply, and thereby evaluate contemporary thought and culture. Parents and teachers can help children develop skills of discernment in all areas of life by encouraging them to seek and arrive at God's truth in their own way.

The Moral Imagination

In his book, *The Call of Stories: Teaching and the Moral Imagination*, Robert Coles provides valuable examples of how stories have the power to transform lives. He writes, "a compelling narrative, offering a storyteller's moral imagination vigorously at work, can enable any of us to learn by example, to take to heart what is, really, a gift of grace" (Coles, 1989, p. 191). It is precisely because stories reflect human experience that narrative is powerful and persuasive. As Bolt indicates, "The key to moral growth for Christians, then, is the capacity for our imaginations to be transformed by the image of Christ, by the metaphors, stories, and images of the Christian faith" (Bolt, 1993, p. 168).

Narratives of the Christian faith, told in a compelling manner and lived by the people of God, past and present, can lead children to authentic Christian living. Christian education centered only on the mind is inadequate; the goal is to live in a distinctively Christian manner. Christian educators, and parents as teachers of their children, need to be sensitive to how the moral character of children is facilitated not only through moral reasoning, but also through the moral imagination. Parents need to engage their own moral imaginations with the stories and images of Christ and the Christian faith before they can engage their child's imagination. The more a child's moral imagination is shaped by the stories of Christianity, the greater will be their capacity for spiritual and moral formation.

Moral Education in the Christian School, Home, and Church

The importance of the Christian story presented with the moral imagination has been emphasized thus far for parents teaching their children, as well as in church education both directly (in the Christian education program) and indirectly (through parent education programs). Narrative education—including biblical narratives—is likewise an important component in moral education in the school, as Victoria Ford has ably demonstrated in section one of this chapter.

Complementing the role of narrative is Nicholas Wolterstorff's (2002) "shaping tendencies" strategy, which may have application in the home and church as well as the school setting. A Christian philosopher, Wolterstorff asserts that a child's "action *requires* knowledge" of the right thing to do, but "knowledge does not just flow automatically into action" (pp. 85–86). Thus the goal of moral education is not just to think in a Christian manner, but also to live as a Christian.

> The main point to notice here is that just initiating students into the Christian mind—especially when that is understood as a mind good for all citizens for all seasons—is not likely to have much effect on their actions unless the initiation incorporates reasons for acting in certain quite specific ways and unless it makes appropriate use of discipline and modeling. If the schooling of our children focuses just on mind formation, then we must expect that when they emerge from school and take up their adult lives, they will *talk* the Christian mind and *live* the mind of the world. (Wolterstorff, 2002, pp. 81–82)

While not guaranteeing certain actions from children, "tendency goals" can be instilled using three strategies—discipline, modeling, and giving reasons—for morally desired actions (2002, pp. 86–89). Similarly, Catherine Stonehouse (1998, pp. 115–117) advocates inductive discipline, role-playing, and moral instruction as a means of encouraging moral development.

Discipline or inductive discipline involves making children aware of the consequences to their actions to other people, and the assumption of responsibility for their own actions. Imposing consequences is to "lead them to expect consequences of their actions that they find pleasant or unpleasant" (Wolterstorff, 2002, p. 119). Stonehouse (1998) adds that children should be given responsibilities commensurate with their maturity level, gaining new responsibilities as they grow in competence. "When, within the family, children are given responsibilities, they experience new roles, exercise choice, discover the consequences of their actions for themselves as well as for others, and have the opportunity to mature morally . . . Too often parents [and perhaps teachers] short-circuited the learning potential of events by intervening so that the child does not have to bear the consequences that naturally flow from choices" (pp. 115–116).

The second strategy for moral development is modeling or role-taking. Imitating teachers and adults is a powerful influence upon children's behavior. Wolterstorff comments, "A child can be induced to set higher or lower standards of performance by putting him or her in the presence of a model who sets higher or lower standards" (2002, p. 87). What causes the child to take on that role? Stonehouse explains, "When children feel attached to another, they want the other person to be pleased with them. Therefore to try to discover what the other person wants, they watch, listen, and imitate" (1998, p. 113). Thus it is through love and a sense of belonging that parents and teachers influence the behavior of children. "By loving children, we help them feel loved and valued, making it possible for them to love themselves and others, to develop attachments, and to learn from those they love. Positive moral influence begins in a relationship of mutual love and belonging, which draws the child into imitation and role-taking" (p. 114). Wolterstorff notes that "People tend to take as models those persons for whom they feel affection or esteem" (2002, p. 120).

A third strategy for encouraging moral advancement is giving reasons or moral instruction. Providing reasons for actions helps influence children's tendencies to act in certain ways, as well as helping them internalize moral actions (Wolterstorff, 2002, pp. 121–122). But in communicating reasons for actions, the child's level of development must be considered so that concepts are presented in a manner that they can understand. As noted earlier, stories from the Bible or from life may help engage the child in discussions of moral conflicts, and stimulating questions can challenge inadequate moral reasoning (Stonehouse, p. 119). Providing reasons can "serve to bridge the gap between thought and practice," comments Wolterstorff (2002, p. 89).

Conclusion

Clearly responsibility and consequences, imitation and role-taking, as well as developmentally appropriate reasoning are implicit or explicit in many of the best stories, as well as useful tools in influencing the moral behavior and thinking of children. Biblical narratives regularly include these components as well. Ultimately the goal of Christian education, at home, church, or school, is that children will "learn the story of God and his people, identify with it, and develop the habits and character that are consistent with the mission of God's people in his world" (Bolt, 1993, p. 194).

References

Angeles, P. A. (1992). *The Harper Collins dictionary of philosophy* (2nd ed.). New York: HarperCollins Publishers.

Barber, K. (Ed.). (1998). *The Canadian Oxford dictionary*. Toronto: Oxford University Press.

Bolt, J. (1993). *The Christian story and the Christian school*. Grand Rapids: Christian Schools International.

Brown, A. L. (1998). The cognitive revolution in learning. In F. Schultz (Ed.), *Sources: Notable selections in education* (2nd ed., pp. 295-326). Guilford, CT: Dushkin/McGraw-Hill.

Coles, R. (1989). *The call of stories: Teaching and the moral imagination*. Boston: Houghton Mifflin.

Connelly, M. E., & Clandinin, D. J (1988). *Teachers as curriculum planners: Narratives of experience*. New York: Teachers College Press.

Cully, I. V. (1979). *Christian child development*. San Francisco: Harper & Row.

Dewey, J. (1997). *Experience and education*. New York: Touchstone.

Durkheim, E. (1961). *Moral education: A study in the theory and application of the sociology of education* (E. K. Wilson & H. Schnurer, Trans., E. K. Wilson, Ed.). New York: Free Press.

Gaebelein, F. E. (1951). *Christian education in a democracy*. New York: Oxford University Press.

Green, B. (2002). Theological and philosophical foundations. In D. S. Dockery & G. A. Thornbuy (Eds.), *Shaping a Christian worldview* (pp. 62–91). Nashville: Broadman & Holman.

Hyde, K. E. (1990). *Religion in childhood and adolescence*. Birmingham, AL: Religious Education Press.

Lynn, R. W. (1964). *Protestant strategies in education*. New York: Association Press.

Miller, R. C. (1956). *Education for Christian living*. Englewood Cliffs, NJ: Prentice Hall.

Montessori, M. (1964). *The Montessori method*. New York: Schocken.

Piaget, J. (1948). *The moral judgment of the child* (M. Cabain, Trans.). Glencoe, IL: Free Press.

Rousseau, J. (1993). *Émile*. (B. Foxley, Trans.). London: Everyman.

Shaw, S. M. (1999). *Storytelling in religious education*. Birmingham, AL: Religious Education Press.

Stonehouse, C. (1998). *Joining children on the spiritual journey*. Grand Rapids: Baker.

Wolterstorff, N. (2002). *Educating for life: Reflections on Christian teaching and learning* (G. G. Stronks, & C. W. Joldersma, Eds.). Grand Rapids: Baker.

Chapter Twenty

The Ecology and Social Dynamics
of Childhood Spirituality

JAMES RILEY ESTEP, JR AND
LILLIAN BRECKENRIDGE[1]

The spiritual formation of children should be a concern for all Christian educators, pastors, parents, or relatives of younger children. Our academic interest in children's spirituality began from reading Robert Coles' *The Spiritual Life of Children* (1990) and continued over the next decade in preparation for teaching classes on children's ministry and spiritual formation. As one surveys the literature produced by the Christian education community on the subject of human development as it relates to Christian education in general and more directly to childhood spiritual formation, one dimension seems to have been given relatively little attention: the context in which children develop. This involves their personal ecology and the social dynamics that shape them and their spirituality.

Has developmental theory made an impact on the Christian education community? Has it shaped theories of Christian education and more specifically the work in the spiritual formation in children? Gabriel Moran (1983) commented that, "The modern history of religious education can be read as a struggle around the idea of

1. James Riley Estep, Jr. is Professor of Christian Education at Lincoln Christian Seminary. He earned a bachelor's degree at Cincinnati Bible College, then an MA in Near East Studies, an MA in New Testament Studies (1988), and an M.Div. in Apologetics (1989) from Cincinnati Bible Seminary. He completed his D.Min. in Christian Education from the Southern Baptist Theological Seminary and his Ph.D. in Educational Studies from Trinity Evangelical Divinity School. Dr. Estep was the co-editor and contributor to two books: *C.E.: The Heritage of Christian Education* and *Management Essentials for Christian Ministry*, as well as publishing several chapters and articles.

Lillian Breckenridge possesses a Ph.D. in Religious Education from Southwestern Baptist Theological Seminary, an M.A.L.S. degree in sociology from the University of Valparaiso, and an M.R.E. in Religious Education from Southwestern Baptist Theological Seminary. She coauthored *What Color is Your God? Multicultural Education in the Church* with James Breckenridge. She has contributed several topics to *Magill's Encyclopedia of Social Science: Psychology* as well as writing a number of entrees in *Baker Dictionary of Christian Education*.

developmentalism" (p. 21), noting the early attempts at developmental approaches to Christian education by Bushnell and Coe. Similarly, Osmer (1990) comments that "the recent discussion of faith development has been sparked by advances in developmental psychology," citing the influence of "life cycle and the structural development" theories of Erikson and Piaget respectively (p. 249). Susanne Johnson (1989) perhaps said it best when stating that the "foundational theory and practice in Christian education today are development theories rooted in psychodynamic thought (Freud, Jung, Erikson) and in structural-developmental theory (Piaget, Kohlberg, Fowler)" (p. 106).[2] A notable exception to this trend was Neal's (1995) emphasis upon using Vygotsky's theory in Christian education.

Hence, it seems apparent that the Christian education community maintains that developmental perspectives provide valuable lenses through which a theory of spiritual formation can be better conceptualized, understood and articulated. Ted Ward (1995) regards areas of human development—physical, intellectual, emotional, social and moral—as a "spiritual ecology," although he does not regard spirituality itself to be necessarily a developmental process. He comments that "a developmental perspective invites the educator to see each human life as a unique person emerging through common aspects that can be observed, measured, and evaluated, yet in essence a human soul, a soul with spiritual reality at [the] core" (p. 16).

This chapter will address the contextual factors of spiritual formation in childhood. Two developmental theorists will provide insights into the process of human development from a contextual perspective, and their implications for understanding childhood spiritual formation will be assessed. Dr. Breckenridge will focus on the theory of Urie Bronfenbrenner and the ecology of the person, while Dr. Estep will give attention to the theory of Lev Vygotsky and the social dynamics in learning and development. These contextual perspectives on human development will provide unique insight into the formative process of spirituality in childhood.

An Ecological Perspective and Spiritual Direction in Childhood (Lillian Breckenridge)

An ecological perspective is one of the more recent approaches to human development. Urie Bronfenbrenner introduced the perspective as an approach to children's development in his 1979 work, "The Ecology of Human Development." In 2000, Bronfenbrenner added biological influences to his theory and described it as a bioecological theory. However, ecological contexts still dominate his approach.

An ecological perspective is traditional in its highlighting the importance of both the individual and the environment. Its uniqueness is its conception of the

---

2. Technically speaking, Fowler could be included in either the psychodynamic group or the structural-developmental theory group, as he draws upon both for his theory of faith development.

environment as a set of *embedded structures,* or as identified by Bronfenbrenner, a series of environmental systems, with smaller systems embedded within the larger systems. These systems represent varying levels of interactions from face-to-face to global interaction. All such interactions impact human and, consequently, spiritual development. The influence of the environment is not limited to the perception of a single setting such as the home or church but includes the *interconnections* or relations between environmental settings, such as the church-school influence or the church-ethnic culture influence. A child's perception of a biological father's care will have an effect on the perception of God's care. However, little attention has been given to influences such as the *interaction* between the child's ability to learn to read in school or the sense of academic competency and what is learned about God through the church's educational agencies.

Strengths of the theory include the focus on the various dimensions of environmental systems, the emphasis on the interconnections between systems, and the inclusion of sociohistorical influences on development. Criticisms of the theory have been the minor attention given to biological foundations of development (even with the recent addition of biological influences) and a similar lack of attention to cognitive processes.

Childhood and Spiritual Formation

Childhood is often viewed as a unique period of life that prepares the youngster for adult life. Research of childhood has tended to be structured primarily around the physical-cognitive-socioemotional dimensions. Piaget's stage theory of children revolutionized the church's approach to curriculum development but less was offered in the spiritual dimension. Kohlberg's theory was thought-provoking and many Christians were attracted to the idea of progressive stages in the way understandings of morality were structured (Stonehouse, 1998). In spite of the popularity of the theory, concern has been raised about the disconnect between moral reasoning and behavior as well as the gender differences in moral thinking (Clouse, 1993). Fowler's theory of faith development also met with a generally warm reception, with its roots in both structural developmentalism and—like Erikson—psychodynamic thought, although the stages are not specific to Christian faith (Stonehouse, 1998). Yet spirituality seemed at best a latent concept, if not missing altogether in these theories. The concept of spiritual formation with its legacy in church history seems more amenable to describing the spirituality of children.

Spiritual formation became a frequently used term in evangelical ministry settings during the 1990s but one of the least understood concepts when it comes to actual application. This comes as no surprise to those who have struggled with constructing an operational definition for spirituality as a starting point. The problem is compounded when the term is used in stated objectives or a mission statement prior to a clear definition. There is then the tendency to define it in terms of its *goodness of fit* with the previously determined purpose or desired outcome.

There are often unrecognized difficulties in contemporary attempts to apply the concept of spiritual formation to Christian ministry settings. These difficulties include:

- spiritual formation implies that it is the responsibility of some people to *form* spirituality in others.

- spiritual formation is often cast into a linear model, suggesting that if certain experiences or activities are planned, then specific desired spiritual outcomes will be achieved.

- spiritual formation as an objective assumes its measurability since the goals and objectives are often viewed as inadequate if they are not measurable.

- spiritual formation is commonly perceived as a progressive process in which higher level stages can be clearly identified.

The purpose of this section of the chapter is to consider Bronfenbrenner's (1979) ecological approach as a model for understanding the development and direction of children's spirituality. I do not intend to promote a comprehensive Christian model in its final form. Rather, the objective is to provide the basic parameters for an ecological model that can be considered as an alternative to current approaches for spiritual formation.

Primary Components of an Ecological Model

Systems perspective. In an ecological model, settings are analyzed as *systemic* rather than linear. Systems thinking represents a fundamental change from focusing on the content of knowledge and instruction to a consideration of pattern, process and communication as the essential components for explanation and description (Bronfenbrenner, 1979). The systems concept, which began in the late 1940s and 1950s, was originally applied in the areas of mathematics, physics and engineering. However, the overarching principles have been used to describe and connect many varied types of systems. Systems thinking has become especially helpful in the field of family therapy.

In a systems approach, it is believed that entities are best understood in terms of relationships with other entities. This is in contrast to the view that everything can be reduced to a simple entity and studied in isolation, one entity at a time. This latter view is the foundation of Newtonian physics and the assumption for much of the research in psychology.

Larger-system perspective. Bronfenbrenner's (1979) view of development gave increased attention to the wider social context in which individuals and families exist. Most families and individuals are a part of a larger system that includes schools, churches, health-care systems and a work setting. Within family therapy, literature and research has focused on certain systems that manifest particular presenting problems. Bronfenbrenner, however, insists that all systems within the larger-system perspective have a role in normative development for individuals. If he is correct, and I believe he is, this would give a more inclusive understanding of spiritual formation. However, this does not mean that all systems will impact spiritual formation equally. To apply this concept, it would be necessary to determine the *systems of import* involved in influencing the development and direction of a child's spirituality.

Five levels of environmental systems. The ecological perspective is structured around five environmental levels, varying in the degree to which there is input as a result of direct interactions with people, in contrast with the input from the broader culture (Bronfenbrenner, 1979). The most immediate setting is the *microsystem,* the environmental level in which the child lives. This level has the earliest influence on the child and includes interactions with settings such as the family, the school, peers, the neighborhood play areas and the church. The next level, the *mesosystem,* involves connections between contexts, such as family experiences and school experiences or school experiences and church experiences. The next broader level, the *exosystem,* is a level in which the child is not actively involved but one that influences the immediate setting. An example would be the parent's work setting, which has an influence on the child at home. The fourth level, the *macrosystem,* includes the influence of the larger culture with its behavior patterns, beliefs, and the common traditions of a particular group of people. The fifth and the outermost level, the *chronosystem,* includes sociohistorical conditions, and the events and transitions experienced over the life course.

Basic Ecological Assumptions

The interconnections between settings influence development. Bronfenbrenner (1979) argues that the connections between settings are as influential on the child's development as the activities within a given setting. The ecological perspective of development suggests that an environmental setting could even influence an individual's development without the individual being present in that setting. Thus, development is a result of biological influences, environmental influences, and the influence of the relationship between environmental systems.

Perceived reality of an environment should be the reference point rather than objective reality. Although perception is deemed influential in theoretical perspectives of development, it is often de-emphasized in an application of the theory. In spiritual formation, the child's perceived reality must be given priority, as spiritual experience often involves perceptual shifts (Hay & Nye, 1998) and all religious knowledge is mediated by the child (see the second part of this chapter).

Influences within and between environmental levels are the basis for understanding development rather than levels of individual development. The ecological perspective is structured around five environmental systems, successively embedded as one moves from the single setting to ever larger levels of context. This contrasts with the idea of levels or stages related to individual spiritual development. The theoretical framework will center on environmental levels of influence on the child's development rather than levels of spiritual formation in the developing child.

Applying the Ecological Model for Childhood Spiritual Formation

A Working Definition for Children's Spirituality. Numerous attempts to define the nature of spirituality can be found which emphasize the transcendent, the relational, the creative, the mystical and the reflective (see chapters 1, 2, 6, and 11 of this book). Spirituality is difficult to define since there is often a lack of shared consensus on its meaning even in homogeneous religious groups. The working definition suggested here is: *Spirituality is one's concern for the ultimate meaning and purpose of life* (adapted from Best, 2000, p. 106). Necessary elements within this definition include personal identity, relationships with others, and a relationship with God or a higher meaning in life. Spirituality involves the total essence of an individual. It refers to a direction in life rather than a state of being. Spirituality represents that part of the individual that is non-negotiable under pressure and permeates every aspect of the individual just as the carbonation in a cold drink is dispersed throughout the liquid. It is the result of a personal and authentic relationship with God and with others. Although often associated with spirituality, moral development differs in that it is limited to the acquisition and application of principles that influence ethical judgment and behavior in a manner that contributes to the well being of others.

Spiritual formation should be viewed as different from an imposed doctrinal and/or moral framework. It is not about being told that one should conform to specified values and beliefs. Instead, spiritual formation is the awareness and recognition of one's own responsibility and ability to make choices. The *essence of spirituality* should be self-determined and self-imposed. At the same time, this is not to deny that the individual may choose to conform to a set of values or certain standards for spiritual practice.

Spiritual formation as human development. If spiritual formation is viewed as permeating every aspect of the individual, it should be understood in a way that is consistent with general principles of human development. However, at the same time, there is a basic difference. One's spirituality is greater than the sum of the other areas of development. Elements of the spiritual dimension are fundamental to human experience. It is all of one's humanity and more. The cognitive component added to the physical component plus the socioemotional component does not equal an individual's spirituality. Thus it eludes measurement whereas cognitive and physical development—because of their identifiable boundaries—are often described in terms of stage characteristics or *markers* of change and progress. Gregory Bateson (1979), an important contributor to the early development of the ecosystemic approach to epistemology, suggests that it is important to draw a distinction between what one can and cannot know, what can and cannot be accepted as proof of the existence of something. Numerous propositions suggest alternative ways of measuring elements of spirituality, and some clearly are more verifiable than others. The question, however, is whether the variable that is being measured is a true indication of spirituality.

Spiritual formation as a process. How should spiritual formation as a process be perceived in the framework of ecological theory? Bronfenbrenner (1979) maintained that development never takes place in a vacuum but it is always expressed through behavior in a particular environmental context. The same is suggested for spiritual formation. Bronfenbrenner defined the process of human development in the following way: "Human development is the process through which the growing person acquires a more extended, differentiated, and valid conception of the ecological environment, and becomes motivated and able to engage in activities that reveal the properties of, sustain, or restructure the environment at levels of similar or greater complexity in form and content" (Bronfenbrenner, 1979, p. 29). As a foundational consideration, this description of development provides a framework for spiritual formation. As a sum bigger than all aspects of human development, the spirituality of the individual develops as the individual lives out the life span within various contexts and across a specified time line.

Joan Borysenko (1996) provides us an example of a model for the *individual life cycle in context*. She identifies the following descriptors for different age levels during childhood. During the first two years, there is the development of empathy and emotional attunement to others. During early childhood, a growing understanding of interdependence is experienced. During middle childhood, moral development occurs, including *heart logic* and *mind logic*, and preadolescents experience the beginnings of authenticity. Within each of these time periods, certain bio-psycho-spiritual accomplishments can be expected, such as the emergence of empathy, relationality, interdependent perception and intuition during early childhood (Borysenko, 1996). In some respects this model may be similar to a potential model of children's spirituality formation constructed within Bronfenbrenner's framework.

Propositions of an Ecological Model for Childhood Spiritual Formation

Proposition 1: Influences from environmental systems. Spiritual formation is, at least in part, a result of influences from all environmental systems in which the child participates. Of primary interest is the influence of relationships within each context and the influence of relationships between contexts. The home, first, and the church, second, have traditionally been considered primary agents for spiritual formation. However, the relationships between church and school, home and school, home and work, and any of the other environmental systems have usually been overlooked in terms of their possible influence on spirituality. All five environmental systems that impact human development become sources for spiritual formation.

Proposition 2: Life as context. The context for spiritual formation is the life-course itself. Spiritual formation occurs as a result of living and adapting to the various environmental systems throughout the life span. The most important aspects of human experience are relational and it would be impossible to consider the existence of spirituality without placing it within a personal context. Therefore, individual spiritual formation takes place in the context of significant emotional relationships. Adult and peer support for children, and their adapting and interacting as spiritual beings, are embraced as the beginning point. Religious content, spiritual disciplines, and spiritual experiences will all be a part of the organism's interaction but no one of these is considered equivalent to spiritual formation.

Proposition 3: Adaptation versus linear change. Stage theories of development suggest a discontinuous approach in which there is a qualitative change in the individual relative to each stage (Erikson in social development, Piaget in cognitive development, Fowler in faith development and Kohlberg in moral development). Spirituality, however, is different from such approaches in that the component being considered is most accurately viewed as permeating the organism in a holistic manner, and, thus changes cannot be compartmentalized. Holistic organismic change fits well with the concept of *adaptation*. As the individual moves through different periods of the life cycle and experiences the influences of a variety of contexts and the tasks of a given developmental period, various types of adaptation as a spiritual organism are necessary. This results in change but these are systemic rather than stage-oriented changes. Parents, teachers, and additional *significant others* function as part of a support system for this adaptation throughout the child's life journey.

Proposition 4: Development-in-context versus development-out-of-context. A traditional program of Christian education or spiritual formation is often designed for the child in an immediate, concrete setting and focuses on the child's behavior in that setting. In such cases, a program of spiritual formation might be perceived as a series of teaching sessions in a church classroom in which each child is assumed to be on a continuum at a specific level relative to spiritual maturity. This is representative of a linear model that suggests if certain elements are present, specific results can be expected. According to Bronfenbrenner (1979), this is development-out-of-context. Following his model, spiritual formation should be seen as development-in-context, as taking place in multiple systems of interactions, rather than single isolated settings, such as the home, church, or Christian school.

Proposition 5: Increasing complexity. Spirituality is experienced as a part of one's developing identity, a process that is currently viewed as being dynamic rather than a static achievement. There is continual change but no arrival at an ultimate destination. The increased complexity of life situations stimulates ongoing development of identity. As the individual interacts with environmental systems, there is a mutual influence; the influence of the context upon the individual and the influence of the individual upon context. Spiritual formation is experienced in terms of the ability to adapt spiritually to increasingly complex life experiences as one ages.

Proposition 6: Spiritual formation as maturity. Although used throughout this paper, the term *development* is problematic in that people tend to assume linear and hierarchical connotations. For some, maturity is understood as having an end point such as being *mature* or *completely developed*. Of course, this presents the problem previously mentioned that there is a lack of consensus as to what constitutes a mature Christian. From an ecological systems approach, the linear model with progressive stages is misguided. Maturity is most accurately viewed as being maximally spiritually adapted, consistent with one's developmental status in the overall life cycle.

The concept of differentiation, an important element in a systemic approach to the family life cycle, is often equated with maturity. It is described as the fabric of one's existence, one's integrity. In its practical application, it refers to the ability to be both self-directed and self-supporting while staying connected to others. Some descriptions used for differentiation in a systemic approach could be adapted for the possibility of *spiritual differentiation* (Gurman & Kniskern, 1991). Spiritual maturity as differentiation would mean a state of self-knowledge and self-definition that does not rely on the approval of others. It would mean being self-directed and able to choose and pursue one's course through life. It is the capacity to take a stand, to be clear about one's own personal values and goals, and to take maximum responsibility for one's own destiny rather than blaming others. It is apparent that this description applies to a direction in life rather than a state of being.

Viewing spiritual maturity in this sense emphasizes the complexity of spirituality. In a non-Christian system, these characteristics would be dependent upon the individual's ability to establish a sense of identity through a balance of mutuality and individual identity; a healthy combination of individuation and connectedness. In spiritual formation, the source for differentiation would be the individual's relationship with God (connectedness) and empowerment from the Holy Spirit (individuation). In its practical application, spiritual differentiation would be represented by the mutuality/ connectedness from an internal ideology and the external church community. Children could only be expected to participate in a fully differentiated manner according to the degree of autonomy, sense of self, and realization of self-identity that has developed relative to their status in the normal life cycle.

In sum, Spirituality from an ecological perspective involves the mutual accommodation between an active, growing child and the changing properties of the immediate setting in which the developing child lives, as this process is affected by relations between those settings and by the larger contexts in the which the settings are embedded (Bronfenbrenner, 1979, p. 21). Moving through time, the individual changes as a result of influencing factors from a number of environmental systems. This involves all areas of development, including spiritual formation. Some influences will have a tremendous life-shaping impact; others will be more subtle and less recognized.

Thus, spiritual formation occurs as one lives life in all of life's contexts rather than merely during a series of isolated lessons or directed experiences. This does not mean that the content of religious education is irrelevant. It will be a part of the environmental context and thus influence the response of the developing organism (child) to various life situations. But the content will not be the initial starting point, the center of focus, or the end that is assessed. And thus, in response to the classic question of whether to begin with child or content (or, as commonly concluded, the interaction of the two), another alternative is possible: begin with context. The focus is child-in-context.

Spirituality resides in one's identity. Spiritual formation occurs in the process of living life. The spirituality of the child is the innermost person, the basis for answering the question, "Who am I?" It is a part of one's core identity, that which makes up the inner person. It is not a set of prayers or a memorized dogma, although such will certainly influence the individual's response to life.

If Bronfenbrenner's "ecology of human development" aid in understanding the development and direction of children's spirituality, it could be used as a framework for the selection of curriculum and methodology. This section of the chapter has presented an *approach*, an understanding of "background beliefs, orientations and commitments that give rise to one pattern rather than another" (Best, 2000, p. 57). Methods follow as the ways to realize the approach.

It is not the intent of the writer to be preoccupied with preserving the ecological purity of a theoretical framework for spiritual formation. However, the ecological perspective is believed to have important implications for those who assume the task of identifying such a framework. The subsequent task will be to provide a set of operational principles to provide guidance for methodology and curriculum. The awareness of the ecological interconnectedness of human systems with one another can constitute a fundamental shift that views spiritual formation as embracing the totality of human existence.

The Social Dynamics of Childhood Spiritual Formation (James Riley Estep, Jr.)

Vygotsky's theory became popular among Western educators in the late Twentieth Century. His works, which were repressed by Stalin, were given wide accessibility and discussed in depth near the end of the "Cold War" era. His impact on educational theory was almost immediate, as he became a leading figure in textbooks on human learning and development. His theory of learning and development is clearly distinct from developmental theories that rest on stage-centered structuralism, such as Piaget and Kohlberg.

Components of Vygotsky's Theory

First, the human mind is dependent on the social-cultural context in which the individual lives. Vygotsky's theory is frequently called "socio-historical," "socio-cultural," or part of "social reconstructionism" due to the weight given to the social, historical, and cultural influence on the individual (Moscovici, 1998). According to Frawley (1997), Vygotsky's theory advanced the idea that "society precedes the individual and provides the conditions that allow individual thinking to emerge" (p. 89), and hence the individual's thought is in fact dependent on the context, unlike the emphasis on genetic or biological determinants in structuralism.

Second, the socio-cultural context is transferred (or mediated) to the individual through mental tools. Vygotsky's doctoral dissertation, *Values in Art*, stressed how artistic expression conveyed values to the viewer, wherein they become participants within the artistic work as individuals process the values being conveyed by the artist. Mental tools are not limited to works of art, but include language (vocabulary and grammatical structures), symbols, writing, and concepts. These mental tools are similar to physical tools used to amplify physical abilities (e.g. a hammer, screwdriver, or saw). The mental tools increase human mental capabilities.

Third, learning precedes and facilitates cognitive development. A distinctive mark of Vygotsky's theory regards that children do not learn according to a preexisting developmental level, but that learning actually advances their cognitive development. "Vygotsky saw learning not as development but as a process that results in development" (Hausfather, 1996, p. 3). As such, learning-development is a unified concept in Vygotsky's theory of cognitive development. *Learning and development are equated and are not to be separated.* The process of learning-development is one of appropriation, processing the socio-cultural context in which one lives.

Fourth, real learning is contingent on intentional instruction. Veer and Valsimer (1991) summarize this uniqueness, stating, "Child development cannot be seen in isolation from the teaching process, however, since the relation between these two processes is highly complex and is certainly not to be compared to the relation between an object and its shadow" (p. 330). Teaching is not done in response to the developmental level of the students, which operates independent of the instruction; rather, teaching facilitates learning that in turn advances the process of cognitive development.

Fifth, the product of cognitive development is higher thought or metaconsciousness. Lower thoughts are those genetically instilled or instinctive; whereas higher thoughts are those acquired through the appropriation of one's socio-cultural context (Grigorenko, 1998; Subbotsky, 1996). The dynamic between higher and lower thought, forms a spiral effect wherein the higher thoughts begin to become the instinctive lower thoughts and hence the higher thoughts become even higher. R. Murray Thomas (1985, pp. 313–314) endeavors to convey Vygotsky's concept of higher thought by providing three levels of thinking in Vygotsky's theory of cognition:

Level 1: "Thinking in Unorganized Congeries or Heaps" (e.g. trial-and-error).

Level 2: "Thinking in Complexities" (e.g. associative categories, collections, chains).

Level 3: "Thinking in Concepts" (e.g. synthesis and analysis).

All of these general statements characterizing Vygotsky's approach to cognitive development find full expression in his Zone of Proximal Development.

Vygotsky's Zone of Proximal Development

Vygotsky maintained that development occurs in a variety of "zones," not stages, to denote a non-linear description of development. *Proximal* is limited by behaviors that are in development or that will develop soon (see Figure 1). He identified three zones of development.

- *Zone of Actual Development*: Where the student currently functions, without assistance

- *Zone of Potential Development*: Where the student *potentially* could function

- *Zone of Proximal Development*: The amount of assistance required for a student to move from the Zone of Actual Development and the Zone of Potential Development

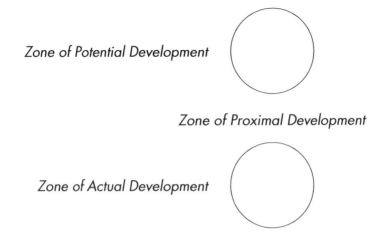

Zone of Potential Development

Zone of Proximal Development

Zone of Actual Development

Figure 1. Vygotsky's Zones

Vygotsky (1978) explained the ZPD as "the distance between the [child's] actual developmental level as determined by independent problem solving and the level of potential development as determined through problem solving under adult guidance or in collaboration with more capable peers" (p. 87). As stated previously, Vygotsky was convinced that development was dependent on learning/instruction. Vygotsky stated:

> *From this point of view, learning is not development; however, properly organized learning results in mental development and sets in motion a variety of developmental processes that would be impossible apart from learning.* Thus, learning is a necessary and universal aspect of the process of developing culturally organized, specifically human, psychological functions.
>
> To summarize, the most essential feature of our hypothesis is the notion that developmental processes do not coincide with learning processes. *Rather, the developmental process lags behind the learning process; this sequence then results in zones of proximal development.* . . . Our hypothesis establishes the unity but not the identity of learning processes and internal developmental processes. . . . A second essential feature of our hypothesis is the notion that, though learning is directly related to the course of child development, the two are never accomplished in equal measure or in parallel [since development is dependent on learning]. (pp. 90–91, emphasis added)

The zone of proximal development is interactive with the society and environmental context, and is always in a state of transformation, hence development is neither linear nor unidirectional. Gallimore and Tharp (cited in Moll 1990, 185–187) identify four stages to the ZPD that further explain Vygotsky's concept of development:

- Where performance is assisted by more capable others
- Where performance is assisted by the self

- Where the performance is developed, automatized, and fossilized

- Where deautomatization of performance leads to recursion through the zone of proximal development

For Vygotsky, *school*, or alternative settings of formal instruction, was the most efficacious social context fostering development. Teachers were facilitators of the learning-development process. Hence, development does not occur, according to Vygotsky, in a classroom of peers, but only in the presence of a more knowledgeable other, an instructor.

A Vygotskyan Approach to Spiritual Formation

Vygotsky represents a departure from the typical structural developmentalism to which most Christian educators are accustomed. Just as developmentalism has influenced the general conceptualization of spiritual formation, Vygotsky's approach reformulates the understanding of spiritual formation. If structuralist developmental theory was removed from the conceptualization of spiritual formation, the Zone of Proximal Development, and the entire Vygotskyan approach to cognitive development, could provide an alternative conceptualization of spiritual formation. Vygotsky, like most other developmentalists, did not directly address spiritual formation or spirituality; however, his schema for development can influence the Christian educator's understanding of spiritual formation with three important implications (for an earlier yet expanded consideration of these, see Estep, 1999, 2000, 2002).

*The community of faith is an **essential and primary** element for spiritual formation.* Spiritual formation is dependent on conducive relationships that help advance faith. Vygotsky's developmentalism more readily lends itself to understanding spiritual formation as a social dynamic. Neal (1995) notes that the Christian faith has a relational dynamic, and hence "we cannot understand the developing human person apart from the relationships that help shape that development" (pp. 124) noting that faith grows in macro to micro contexts: Christianity is a macro-context, while the home, church, classroom are micro-contexts of spiritual formation. In the absence of such communities and contexts, spiritual formation is deterred. Childhood faith is a dependent faith, dependent not only on individuals as care-givers and spiritual role models, but on the community of faith as a preservative of the corporate tradition of spirituality it embraces and embodies.

Spirituality and spiritual formation begins in the context of Christian community, outside the individual. Spiritual formation is not simply an internal process, but begins with the process of acquiring the spiritual tradition of the community of faith in which the individual engages. While spirituality is often perceived as an individual or personal quality, it also has a social or cooperate dimension. In short, it is a real *community* of faith. The spiritual traditions and practices of a given congregation pre-exist the child or adult entering the community of faith and in turn impacts the spiritual formation of the individual within it. Children begin their spiritual lives by acquiring the spiritual practices of the faith contexts (home and congregation). In this case, faith becomes a collective as well as individual phenomenon *beginning* within the Christian community. As such, children are also given the impression that faith is more than just their independent personal experiences, but that it is communal and meant to be shared collectively.

Spiritual formation is facilitated by a multitude of contextual factors, and hence its ecology is holistic. Spiritual formation is the result of a coalescing of factors within the individual. Spiritual formation is seen as being more than any single developmental theory can address, since it is the result of multiple factors. The concepts of spiritual formation and Christian education are in effect *singular* from this perspective, rather than education being understood as a parallel process or antecedent to development. Hence, spiritual formation in the child is not simply to be seen as an age-related, staged and sequenced phenomenon, but as an individual journey taken in the company of others that may or may not be strictly tied to age. Indeed, the use of the term *development* becomes somewhat questionable. The process involved is more *formative* than uniform (the latter might be implied by use of the term *development*).

*Spiritual formation is **not** a linear or unidirectional process.* Vygotsky's use of "zones" of development, rather than linear stages of advancement, adds a new approach to the understanding of spiritual formation. For example, Fowler's (1981) stage theory of faith development presents a perspective of faith development that uses a pattern similar to traditional developmentalism: linear, stage-by-stage development. In contrast, the notion of "zones" rather than "stair-step" stages introduces an entirely new perspective on the subject of spiritual formation. Also, such a perspective would lend itself to explaining how development can also recede, since change need not be unidirectional. Hence, spiritual formation cannot only become halted or stagnant, but can even retreat and weaken. [It should be noted that the psychodynamic influence upon Fowler's theory, which includes the concept of regression, also indicates the possibility of reversals in faith development—see Fowler, 1981, p. 289.]

Spiritual formation occurs when faith is mediated between the community and individuals. Vygotsky spoke of mediation through words, symbols, and images as a means of leading the developmental process. Bible, liturgy, rituals, iconography . . . all of these mediate the message of faith, as well as provide the child with an affective and psychomotor/behavioral experience of faith. For example, Berryman (1992) discusses the symbolism of the cross in childhood, noting the development of its significance in the child's faith. Fowler (1981, p. 123) made limited use of Vygotsky to explain the Intuitive-Projective Faith stage, wherein a child can begin using language as a means of expressing faith or experiences. Hence, spiritual formation occurs when one's faith is mediated through words, symbols, and images of faith are shared. The words and symbols associated with the Christian faith have a formative impact on spirituality because they enable the individual to appropriate the faith of the community. The symbolism of ritual, icons, architecture, and liturgy all contribute to the spiritual formation of the individual (Ng & Thomas, 1981). Also, the concept of mentoring is emphasized by Vygotsky for education, a practice that has become very popular in some Christian circles.

One recent work emphasizing the influence of the sacraments as part of Christian initiation in childhood is Elizabeth Francis Caldwell's (1996) *Come Unto Me*. However, Barbara Kimes Myers (1997) makes use of Vygotsky's Zone of Proximal Development in combination with ritual theory to explain how participation in ritual, such as the sacraments of the Church, are conducive to spiritual formation by mediating the convictions of the community of faith symbols that transcend words. In her work, she identifies four factors conducive to spiritual formation in children: hospitable space, recognition of experience, adult presence, and expectation of transcendence. Figure 2 (below) is an adaptation of her use of Vygotsky and ritual theory in this matter (p. 79).

Core Conditions	Vygotsky's Theory	Ritual Process Theory
Hospitable Space	Zone of Proximal Development	Invocation of sacred space
Recognition of Experience	Connection to what the child can not yet do on his own	Liminality
Adult Presence	Mentor, coach, teacher, etc. as more knowledgeable other	Ritual leader
Expectation of Transcendence	Expectation of transcendence (?)	Expectation of transcendence

Figure 2: Myers' Core Conditions and Vygotsky's Theory

For Vygotsky, mediation means that values can be conveyed through mental tools. Certain signs or symbols aided in mental processing, become mental tools.

In so far as language (vocabulary and grammar) reflect mental concepts, the acquisition of a spiritual vocabulary (i.e. Christian language acquisition) is essential for spiritual formation. Berrymann (1992) writes "Beware the loss of religious language!" (p. 49), noting its importance in participating in the Christian community and life. He also discusses the idea of inviting children into the world of religious language (p. 22). Vygotsky's background in language acquisition, and his cognitive theory that reflects that background may better address the necessity of religious language as a reflection of theological constructs and the formation of theological concepts within the mind, aiding the spiritual formation of the child.

*More-mature-others and deliberate instruction are **essential** for spiritual formation.* Vygotsky maintained that cognitive development does not occur on its own. It requires a socio-cultural impetus, which for him was education, specifically schooling or other intentional instruction. While all developmental theories value formal education, Vygotsky's concept of development requires it. Parents, older siblings, teachers, pastors, and church volunteers, all have an impact on the spiritual formation of the child. The teaching ministry of the church, and deliberate Christian instruction that occurs within the home or other faith-contexts, has an explicit impact on spiritual formation, since learning is the driving force behind the developmental process.

Spiritual maturity is a life-long process, whereby the natural or carnal mind (lower thought) of the individual is converted into spiritual mind (higher thought) (see 2 Cor 2:1ff). Spiritual formation has no terminal stage in the present life. Just as Vygotsky conceived an increasing spiral of ever increasing higher orders of thinking as the developmental process progressed, it would be possible to conceive of spiritual formation as a process of making the instinctive reaction of an individual (lower thought) become the spiritual, Christ-minded reaction (higher thought), and hence eventually the higher thoughts become the natural ones. Children begin this process by beginning to integrate the concepts of faith into their daily lives. [In some respects this resembles the faith spirals of Fowler's (1982, p. 275) theory, which is more reflective of the psychodynamic influences upon his theory than the structural-developmental influences.]

What does Vygotsky's approach to cognitive development provide for the Christian educator? *First*, a new developmental perspective is offered from which to view childhood spiritual formation. As noted earlier, this perspective is quite different from the traditional developmentalism associated with educators in the West. However, it adds a needed corporate dimension that has been generally underestimated. Spirituality is a part of childhood, and children are individuals-in-community. *Second*, his theory provides an emphasis on the importance of teaching-learning as a single endeavor, elevates the role of the more mature members of the faith tradition, and education in general is seen as a necessary means to spiritual formation. Education is not simply a response to the developmental process, but a component of that process. Teaching is for spiritual formation. *Finally*, this approach to spiritual formation secures for children a pronounced ecclesiastical status as growing and participating members of the faith community. They indeed need ministry, but also *do* ministry. Spiritual formation in childhood is a process fostered by, in, and through the community of faith.

Conclusion

Spiritual formation is both social and individual, each balancing out the other. Faith communities—home, congregation, and school—are the contexts wherein the Christian faith is conveyed (mediated) to the child through relationships, symbolism (ritual and liturgy), and intentional instruction. They form a comprehensive ecology in which human development occurs and spirituality is formed. Children as individuals-in-community are active participants within the faith community as they appropriate for themselves pre-existing spiritual traditions, including theology, worship, and practices of the congregation. This is accomplished by being in the presence and in relationship with more mature Christians (mentors) to guide, direct, and instruct the individual. This culminates, with the Spirit's activity, in a renewing of the mind (Rom 12:2) as the Christian's mind is transformed into the mind of Christ, and eventually becoming a mentor to other individuals who are less mature in the faith. Hence the process of spiritual formation is one of acquisition of the spiritual tradition of the faith community, participation in that tradition, internalizing the values of that tradition, and then adding to and advancing one's personal spiritual tradition.

References

Bateson, G. (1979). *Mind and nature.* New York: Dutton.

Berryman, J. W. (1992). Faith development and the language of faith. In D. E. Ratcliff (Ed.), *Handbook on children's religious education* (pp. 21–55). Birmingham, AL: Religious Education Press.

Best, R. (Ed.). (2000). *Education for spiritual, moral, social and cultural development.* London: Continuum.

Borysenko, J. (1996). *A woman's book of life: The biology, psychology and spirituality of the feminine life cycle.* New York: Riverhead.

Bronfenbrenner, U. (1979). *The ecology of human development.* Cambridge: Harvard University Press.

Caldwell, E. F. (1996). *Come unto me: Rethinking the sacraments for children.* Cleveland, OH: United Church Press.

Clouse, B. (1993). *Teaching for moral growth.* Wheaton, IL: BridgePoint.

Coles, R. (1990), *The spiritual life of children.* Boston: Houghton Mifflin.

Estep, J. R., Jr. (2002). Spiritual formation as social: Toward a Vygotskyan developmental perspective, *Religious Education 97*, 141–164.

Estep, J. R., Jr. (2000, October). *Religious instruction as social activity: Toward a Vygotskyan perspective on Christian learning.* Paper presented at North American Professors of Christian Education annual conference, Toronto, Ontario.

Fowler, J. W. (1981). *Stages of faith.* San Francisco: Harper and Row.

Frawley, W. (1997). *Vygotsky and cognitive science.* Cambridge: Harvard University Press.

Grigorenko, E. L. (1998). Mastering tools of the mind in school: Trying out Vygotsky's ideas in classrooms. In R. J. Sternberg (Ed.), *Intelligence, instruction, and assessment: Theory into practice* (pp. 201–231). New Haven, CN: Yale University.

Gurman, A. S. & Kniskern, D. P. (Eds.) (1991). *Handbook of family therapy, Volume II.* Bristol, PA: Brunner/Mazel.

Hausfather, S. J. (1996). Vygotsky and schooling: Creating a social context for learning. *Action in Teacher Education, 18*(2), 1–10.

Hay, D., & Nye, R. (1998). *The spirit of the child.* London: Fount/Harper Collins.

Johnson, S. (1989). *Christian spiritual formation in the church and classroom.* Nashville: Abingdon.

Mmoscovici, S. (1998). The history and actuality of social representations. In U. Flick (Ed.), *The psychology of the social* (pp. 209–247). Cambridge: Cambridge University Press.

Moll, L. (Ed.). (1990). *Vygotsky and education.* Cambridge: Cambridge University Press.

Moran, G. (1983). *Religious education development.* Minneapolis: Winston Press.

Myers, B. K. (1997). *Young children and spirituality.* New York: Routledge.

Neal, C. J. (1995). The power of Vygotsky. In J. C. Wilhoit & J. M. Dettoni (Eds.), *Nurture that is Christian* (pp. 123–137). Wheaton, IL: BridgePoint.

Ng, D., & Thomas, V. (1981). *Children in the worshipping community.* Atlanta: John Knox Press.

Osmer, R. R. (1990). Faith development. In I. V. Cully & K. B. Cully (Eds.), *Harper's encyclopedia of religious education* (pp. 247–253). New York: Harper and Row.

Stonehouse, C. (1998). *Joining children on the spiritual journey.* Grand Rapids: Baker.

Subbotsky, E. (1996). Vygotsky's distinction between lower and higher mental functions and recent studies on infant cognitive development. *Journal of Russian and Eastern European Psychology, 34*(2), 61–66.

Thomas, R. M. (1985). *Comparing theories of child development* (2nd ed.) Belmont, CA: Wadsworth.

van der Veer, R., & Valsiner, J. (1991). *Understanding Vygotsky: A quest for synthesis.* Cambridge, MA: Blackwell.

Vygotsky, L. (1978). *Mind in society.* Cambridge, MA: Harvard University Press.

Ward, T. (1995). Foreword. In J. C. Wilhoit & J. M. Dettoni (Eds.), *Nurture that is Christian* (pp. 7–17). Wheaton, IL: BridgePoint.

Chapter Twenty-One

Using Developmentally Appropriate Practice in Faith-Based Early Childhood Settings

JOYCE RUPPELL[1]

"Not now! When you're older"

"That's for grownups, not children."

"Don't touch that! You might break it!"

These kinds of remarks are all too often spoken to young children in Christian communities. In a world of adults, young children frequently confront situations that make them feel incapable, insecure and sometimes unwanted. Similar comments were made by Jesus' followers when a group of children interrupted their discussion. But Jesus became indignant and said: "Let the children alone, and do not hinder them from coming to me, for the kingdom of heaven belongs to such as these" (Matt 19:14, Revised Standard Version). Jesus commanded His followers not to turn away children who came to Him. He indicated clearly that children hold an important place in His kingdom.

It is true that in the first five years of life children have different understandings, skills, and responsibilities than adults. However, children are equipped with an amazing array of capacities that make thoughtful, loving ministry to them a necessity. How much do children understand about the religious concepts incorporated into faith-based weekly or Sunday programs?

Fortunately young children's capacities are becoming better understood through recent advances in brain research. For example, the brain clearly is affected by

---

1. Joyce C. Ruppell has an M.Ed in Early Childhood Education from Rhode Island College. She has served as a director and teacher in faith based early childhood programs throughout the state of Rhode Island since 1978. She currently holds the position of Project Coordinator for the Keys to Quality Project which provides support, training and technical assistance to school districts in Rhode Island. Joyce is a member of the Ecumenical Childcare Network and the National Association for the Education of Young Children.

environmental conditions. The quality of the surroundings and kinds of stimulation in the environment are vital to enhancing the appropriate development of children. In addition, the way that parents, families, and teachers respond to young children directly affects their brain's development.

Children who are attracted to Jesus are never told they have to wait until they fully understand theological concepts before they can come to Him. He did not preach to them or reprimand them, but instead "laid hands on them" (Matt 19:15) and told adults to "turn and become like children" (Matt 18:3). In calling children to Him, Jesus tells His disciples: "Whoever humbles himself like this child, he is the greatest in the kingdom of heaven" (Matt 18:4). But this esteem-building characteristic of "greatness" bears a warning and great responsibility for adults who are concerned about the spiritual development of young children. As a young child I was very afraid of God when I asked Him into my heart at age four. A minister had come to my church and preached a sermon about hell. I was so frightened when he finished that I ran to the altar as if I was the world's greatest sinner. I remember well the great fuss everyone made over me because I made this decision. I know I was relieved at the time but it did not remove the guilt I felt well into my adult years.

When adults provide inaccurate ideas about God to children, it can turn a child's mind off to spiritual matters and deprive the youngster of life's most important discoveries—how much God loves him and how important he is to God. Young children often believe anything that an adult says. What a tremendous responsibility this places on parents, teachers, and church leaders alike to ensure that a child's experiences are interpreted for her in spiritually healthy ways.

In many faith-based programs inappropriate practices abound. Young children are given the leftover basement rooms no one else wants and supplied with donated materials. In addition they are subjected to curricula that includes abstract and irrelevant concepts. They often contain activities that require rote memorization. Some curricula are characterized by adult-made products that present no real challenge, engagement or enlightenment for children.

Schedules for classes or sessions are rigid and based on adults' needs or some adult's arbitrary concept about what children should be doing rather than on the children's real needs. Group times are imposed on children, forcing a large group to listen or watch an activity without providing an opportunity for the children to engage in learning.

Finally, adults participating in faith-based programs frequently expect too much or too little of children. This problem is caused by adult ignorance of how they can build warm, nurturing, and secure relationships from which young children can build sound spiritual concepts and principles.

Parker Palmer, author of *The Courage to Teach* (1997), outlined what he termed "the shadow side" (p. 18) of the church's approach to children. Here are some of his indicators:

- Too many parents who are willing to drop off their kids at church and have someone "do religion to them" (p.18).

- Too many Christian education leaders coerce people into becoming teachers.

- Too much canned curriculum attempts to make up for adults' insecurity from not knowing their faith from the inside out.

As a result, too many children are missing the one element that they most need—a relationship with caring adults who can lead them to contemplate God's intended plan for their lives. How often are Christian education practices keeping children away from Jesus? The developmental needs of children must be met if adults are to be supportive of their spiritual development and not become a hindrance.

There is much that can and should be done to ensure that children's minds and spirits are being nurtured, challenged and fully engaged in educational programs. A high-quality, faith-based program that is sensitive to the development of spiritual aspects of young children will involve staff training in the needs and abilities of children according to developmental characteristics. Religion is communicated differently at different stages of the development (Rizzuto, 1979). Each time there is change, or a child passes a developmental milestone, her thinking about God and faith grows and adjusts. Thus, knowledge about child development and learning styles is vital if Christian educators are to plan appropriate instruction for young children.

For example, young children need rich sensory experiences in order to learn. One way this need is met is through providing experiences with adults who model behaviors of warmth, sensitivity, and caring, so that the nature of God is clearly demonstrated. Children need adults who are dependable and consistent to help foster the development of trust, which is an essential aspect of spiritual development (Ratcliff, 1992).

What can concerned adults do beyond that? Addressing faith and supporting young children's spiritual development are not easy because young children think about and try to make sense of these issues within their own understandings of the world. "Children try to understand not only what is happening to them but why; and in doing that, they call upon the religious life they have experienced, the spiritual values they have received, as well as other sources of potential explanation," Coles (1990, p. 38) writes in his landmark book, *The Spiritual Life of Children*. Preschool children are concrete in their thinking. They tend to think of God in literal terms and cannot separate Him from parents or authority figures.

At the beginning of each year in the faith based preschool program with which I am affiliated, I take the children on a tour of the church building, stopping to visit the pastor in his study is a highlight. One year when we arrived back in the classroom a little boy asked: "When can we go back and see God again?" Often in preschoolers' drawings, God wears pants and a shirt, He eats with a fork, and even has a wife!

Apart from the humor in these incidents, it is important to note that children have a natural interest in God that should be nurtured. Mark 10:15 states not only that adults are to become like little children to enter the kingdom of heaven, but also so they can *assist* children in entering the kingdom. Just as the foundations of all learning are formed in the early years, so too are the foundations of adult faith.

One religious group intent on liturgical reform devised a way to shock themselves into realizing that children are key members of the community and needed by adults to understand God. They constructed a giant pew and took turns having everyone in the congregation sit in it. When sitting in this pew, an adult feels like a three-year-old, pointing out that no one is more marginalized than a three-year-old. If teachers and other adults can identify with three-year-olds, then they are able to learn from anyone, including very young children. When adults imagine themselves as children, perhaps they see things through their eyes and will be better prepared to address their needs in all aspects of development.

Implications for Developmentally Appropriate Practices in Christian Education

Until the Twentieth Century little attention was given to how children grow and develop. In the past 75 years, however, research has provided a great deal of information about childhood. This relatively new body of knowledge reinforces the idea that childhood is a distinct stage of life with its own characteristics, can be applied to a way of teaching called developmentally appropriate practice. In high-quality early childhood settings, the principles of developmentally appropriate practices are used to assist teachers in making decisions about children based on what educators know about:

- How young children develop and learn
- The individual children in their group
- The social and cultural context in which those children live and learn

This approach emerged in the field of early childhood education during the second half of the twentieth century, and will continue to be reshaped and elaborated in the Twenty-First Century.

Developmentally appropriate practice has been refined and redefined most notably in *Developmentally Appropriate Practice* by Sue Bredekamp (1998). Published by The National Association for the Education of Young Children, it represents the early childhood profession's consensus on what constitutes appropriate education in early childhood programs.

The fundamental principles of developmentally appropriate practice include:

- Appreciating the critical role of teachers in supporting children's development and learning

- Considering groups of children as communities of learners in which relationships among adults and children support development and learning

- Acknowledging the importance of meaningful curriculum

- Using assessment practices that are authentic and meaningful for children and families; fostering significant involvement by families

- Giving adequate support and resources to ensure high-quality developmentally appropriate practices for children

Developmentally appropriate practices lead educators to acknowledge that what is acceptable for one age group is inappropriate for another because it does not match the latter's developmental level. Trying to drill a child on memorizing the Ten Commandments is like trying to force feed him a meal of broccoli! In the remainder of this chapter, I will describe how Christian education programs can apply these basic principles of developmentally appropriate practice in their settings.

Prepare Teachers to Support Children's Development and Learning

I believe it is essential for Christian educators to create better experiences and guide children in a more intentional and explicit manner so that spiritual growth will be fostered. Teachers who acquire training in developmentally appropriate practices will act more appropriately in guiding and nurturing children, ages birth to eight, in matters of faith. With this training as a foundation, leaders and teachers will then be able to make better decisions about how they set up programs, the kind of curricula they select, and ways to foster relationships with families. Finally, through training in developmentally appropriate practice, Christian educational leaders will gain an understanding of how children's spiritual development can be influenced by both appropriate and inappropriate practices.

Arrange for Children to Develop in Communities of Learners

A community of learners is a social system in which all participants consider and contribute to one another's well-being and learning. In such environments, each child is valued in ways that support growth in all areas of development. But how can an environment be created that enables young children to encounter and gain an understanding of God?

Cultivate in children the basic belief that they are safe in the world. Without this essential aspect children will not ever develop the capacity to trust in a loving, guiding divinity. This idea is described in Erickson's very first stage, trust *vs.* basic mistrust. (Erikson, 1963). Erikson says that it is critical that a child's environment be dependable, secure and loving. The ability to trust, which develops during this stage, is essential for a growing faith in God, Erikson believed (pp. 250–251). When the child feels that her environment is a good place to be, teachers can accomplish their teaching ministry effectively.

One way to ensure that this happens is to provide children with a sense of security and safety by having staff, schedules, space, and materials that are consistent and predictable. Children need a place at church and school where the following messages are clear to them:

- They are trusted

- Their decisions are meaningful

- They are valuable

- Help is available

- Questions are good

- People have different ideas and that is okay

- Feelings are important

- Talking and discussion helps you understand

- Listening helps everyone learn

Teach children to care. The best methods and most carefully planned programs are useless unless we teach children to take good care of themselves and of each other. Each time a person listens while others are talking, respect for them is demonstrated.

Teach children they have gifts to give. An example of a successful program that utilized this principle is God's Garden, where churches and schools attempt to make spiritual values relevant by planting crops that they tend throughout the summer. In the fall they donate the harvest to a local food bank. Life lessons about nurturing and caring for others can be discussed much more meaningfully in a program that follows this type of activity. Jobs for children to do in the classroom or around the church communicate to them a sense of belonging: "They need me; I have a special job here." It can help children feel capable and confident, and provide them with a better understanding of the need to serve God.

Set up an appropriate environment for learning. Since children learn from the environment through all their senses, it is critical that educators create environments that will expand their awareness and experiences. Learning environments need to be healthy and safe. Children's creativity, self-esteem, and empathy will blossom in safe environments.

But caring environments also need to be places where children feel comfortable and secure. To accomplish this goal several guidelines should be followed.

1. *Provide a trustworthy place where promises are kept.* This is reflected by statements such as, "I will make sure you get the red truck when Sandra is finished with it," "I will look for the missing puzzle pieces before I leave today," and "I'll take good care of you while your mom is gone." Children need to feel love and care and see it in action. Only after children have seen love and care manifested in the teacher's actions will they begin to form a foundation for understanding the stories the teacher will share. This will build the teacher's credibility whether they are sharing Bible stories or good children's literature.

2. *Place children's artwork on the walls of the classroom and other areas of the church to communicate a feeling of belonging.* This communicates, "This is my room." It says to children that they are appreciated. In setting up the space, ask "What could I do to make this room more inviting?" "Is this classroom saying that this is a place that cares about children?" "Is the message being conveyed that this is a place where children want to come to sit, to learn, to stay, and talk?" Having a colorful, appealing room with materials and displays at children's eye level helps capture their interest and invites them into learning.

3. *Arrange classrooms and other child spaces in ways that show "we care what we do in this place."* Having equipment and materials prepared and ready for children to play with and manipulate as soon as they enter, communicates a welcome feeling. They may come to believe, "Somebody has been thinking about me and is glad I am here."

Teach children in ways that enhance development and learning. In developmentally appropriate teaching approaches, children often choose and plan their own activities. In such settings teachers can:

1. *Pose problems, ask questions, and make comments and suggestions* in order to extend the range of children's interests. The teacher acts as companion and guide in the learning process.

2. *Phrase directions to stimulate children's thinking and problem solving* regarding what must be done to accomplish activities and projects and extend the child's thinking.

3. *Plan for every young child to succeed.* "I want to do it myself!" is the common cry of children who need the sense of satisfaction that comes from achieving a goal. Children do not need adults who do everything for them; they need adults who plan ways in which children can find success. Each new accomplishment will, in turn, stimulate children to further effort and their learning will increase.

4. *Plan activities that feature a sensorimotor style for learning so that all the aspects of learning about God can be experienced, not just explained.*

In thinking about concrete ways to enhance children's learning, bear in mind that young children learn what they want to learn, and they can only want to learn what involves them fully. Thus, learning activities should most often be in the form of play, and the choices they make in play will indicate the level of their understanding. Young children are not yet able to play with words and ideas, so they must play with materials and real objects. They need to use all of their five senses—seeing, touching, tasting, hearing, and smelling—in order to learn efficiently and effectively.

Moreover, children build on what they already know. If the experiences they have in a faith-based program relate to their own lives, the experiences will be remembered and will carry over into children's everyday activities. Many of the families that are served in faith based programs lack an understanding of typical faith practices such as prayer. Frequently parents will express that they are giving thanks for meals because it is what their child learned at preschool.

One activity that occurs in many early childhood classrooms is the gathering time, circle, or story time. During this time it is important for children to know that they can share their thoughts and that they will be heard when they express their ideas, questions, and feelings.

Construct a Developmentally Appropriate Curriculum

A developmentally appropriate curriculum provides for all areas of a young child's development—physical, emotional, social, linguistic, aesthetic, cognitive, moral-spiritual—and it builds upon what children already know and are able to do. The curriculum content also should have intellectual integrity. In some respects Sunday School materials today do not demand enough of children; in other ways, they demand too much of the wrong thing.

Children want breadth and depth. Adults need to respect their "natural theological brilliance," according to Rev. Suzanne Guthrie (personal communication), Chaplain of the convention on Christian Formation for the Episcopal Church. The human experience of children should form the basic content of their spiritual development. When my son was four-years-old, he was struggling with trying to understand how Bible stories fit into his world when he asked: "Did the dinosaurs come before the 'God people' or after?"

Here are some suggested ways to make Christian education more concrete and meaningful for young children.

Help young children connect Bible stories with their own experiences. Support young children's thought processes and expressions of faith by providing opportunities to tell and retell biblical truths in a variety of creative ways (see chapter 19). For example:

1. *When a child works to portray an incident in a Bible story, the teacher should ask questions to stimulate the child to rethink the story,* such as "What happened just before the scene you are making?" and "Which person in this scene is a good example to follow?"

2. *As a child draws, paints, or models a scene the teacher should connect this experience to the Bible story.* One might ask, "What are you doing in this picture that is the same as what David did in our story?" or "How would it help the person in your picture if s/he remembered the Bible verse we heard?" These kinds of creative experiences can help a child to demonstrate in a concrete way an abstract concept such as loving, forgiving, or serving.

3. *Help children to think in terms of specific actions that may apply to what they have learned.* For example, as a result of learning the verse "Children obey your parents" (Eph 6:1, New International Version), children may draw a picture of a child doing a chore such as taking out the trash. At the same time, important literacy skills may be encouraged as children illustrate a story with a series of pictures that can be placed in proper sequence.

Give children many opportunities to manipulate their environment. For example, the nativity is displayed all year in our program. The children never seem to tire of setting up the scene over and over again. They need to touch, taste, and experience props used to tell the stories and to make them come alive. Having a set of garments children can use that look and feel like the clothing worn by people in the Bible can help children take on the role of characters they have heard about in the planned lessons.

Use what interests them to stimulate conversation about spiritual concepts. For example, young children are interested in nature; they have a natural curiosity about the world. Teachers who nurture that curiosity are nurturing their souls. A common theme to expand upon nature is the story of creation. In the program with which I am involved, the Genesis account is broadened by adding stories such as *The Carrot Seed, All the Colors of the Earth,* and *Owl Moon.* Children love animals and stories about animals. We include stories such as *The Kissing Hand, The Deep Blue Sea* and *Owl Babies* (an annotated bibliography I developed of these and other recommended resources is available—see www.childspirituality.org to access the bibliography). Children especially enjoy discussing how God displays His sense of humor in His creation of animals like the giraffe or the furry, egg-laying mammal known as the platypus. By pointing out some of the foibles in nature and in the general human condition, one can make God and a relationship with Him seem livelier and more interesting, especially to young children.

Make the content of your curriculum meaningful and relevant and easily applied to their lives as well as intellectually stimulating. In my recent study of a typical theme—taking a trip with one's family—the story of Abraham played a prominent part, and adults became learners along with the children. First, everyone dressed as Abraham's family, then pretended to pack travel bags, tents, and household utensils. Everyone traveled the length and breadth of the church, even through adult Bible class, finally arriving in the land that God had promised (the children's classroom). The tent was erected and a snack was supplied. This is the same method that Jesus used, which involves connecting a truth—in this story, God's faithfulness to Abraham—with the listener's experience. For more on story enactment, see Ratcliff (1988).

Children also enjoy hearing about other children from the Bible. Examples include Moses in the bulrushes, Samuel in the temple, Jesus as a baby and as a child, and the boy who helped Jesus feed a multitude by sharing his lunch.

Offer activities that are challenging, and that are just a little beyond where children currently are in their development (see the "Zone of Proximal Development" in chapter 20). Use stories that encourage character building, such as *The Little Match Girl* and *Brundibar*. Children can talk about how the main character(s) might feel or how the children would feel in similar situations. Stop the story at crucial points and invite the children to suggest how they might solve a character's problem.

The use of stories and books provides many opportunities for enriching the curriculum with Bible thoughts. With books like *When Autumn Comes* and *Whisper from the Woods*, point out the words that relate to God's creation and His plan for the earth, such as "God planned for the trees to lose their leaves to help prepare them for winter." Teachers can use *Alexander and the Terrible, Horrible, No Good Very Bad Day* to remind children to obey their parents, and that no matter what happens God still loves and cares for them (again, see my online annotated bibliography mentioned earlier).

Provide a place for children to practice the skills being emphasized in the curriculum. Important skills such as learning to share and being generous are good examples. *The Selfish Giant* by Oscar Wilde is a timeless story that can be read to enable children to see the benefits of sharing and caring. Stories can correspond to the needs of the children and their current struggles. A good story can speak to their fears as well as help them work on critical life issues. Stories can also provide an excellent springboard for discussions about God.

Make the program environment a place for active exploration and interaction. Include props in a home life area, such as care for "babies," or taking care of pets and plants. These items help children learn to notice and be reassured by the design of life and the world and the intelligence at work in that design. Similarly, when children work in the block area it can provide them with opportunities for cooperation and sharing. They learn to respect the rights and ideas of others while also problem solving and making decisions. In the story of Abraham, my program used blocks to build a Ziggurat. The structure was related to the aspect of idol worship that so concerned Abraham. A clay model of an idol constructed by the children was placed at the very top of the Ziggurat. When that large tower was knocked down and the idol was smashed, everyone left the space quickly, as there was a deep social and emotional response as well as cognitive understanding. The three- and four-year-olds appeared to comprehend that God is the only one who deserves human love and worship (compare this with some of the suggestions offered by Torrence & Torrence, 1988).

Another way to use the block area is to build a wall that separates the children from each other, then break the wall down together and discuss how they felt when they could not see one another and how it felt to be together again. Parallels can be drawn to compare this separation to the feelings when one is separated from God.

Assess Children's Learning and Development During Curriculum Development

Assessment measures how well teachers' activities and approaches are helping children to learn and progress. It should be ongoing and purposeful, and teachers should use the results to make curricular adjustments and to inform families of their children's progress (Starks & Ratcliff, 1988). Assessment may consist of observation and/or collections of representative work done by children, and of demonstrated performance during authentic, rather than contrived activities. Assessment is not meant to "grade" young children; instead it should be used to improve teaching. How else can one know if "they've gotten it?" The following paragraphs offer some suggestions related to assessment.

Teachers should keep personal records of the progress of each child in their classes. Teachers should take time to observe and be aware of each child's development in relation to the goals of the program. This assessment may include the following:

1. *Self Concept*: To what extent does the child become involved in the activities that are prepared, and what might this reflect about the self concept?

2. *Attitudes towards others*: What skills is s/he exhibiting to encourage participation in a group setting?

3. *Attitudes towards church*: How does s/he respond to worship experiences in a corporate setting?

4. *Attitudes towards Bible, prayer, Jesus, God*: What statements have been made that reflect the child's current understanding about these concepts?

Ask children questions that demonstrate how well children understood a story. The Christian Character Foundation Curriculum (Holt & Vanderweide, 1982), lists six different kinds of questions designed to help children with recall, comprehension, application, analysis, synthesis, and evaluation (also see Bloom, Englehart, Frost, Hill, & Krathwohl, 1956). A question that reflects at least some of these levels might be developed for stories told. Here are a few suggestions, using the first three levels as applied to the woman who shared her food with the prophet Elijah, and possible responses by children:

1. *Recall:* "What was wrong with the woman in the story?" She was very poor and had only enough food to feed herself and her little son for one more meal.

2. *Comprehension:* "What did Elijah want the woman to do?" He wanted to share the last bit of her oil and flour with him.

3. *Application:* "How would you feel about sharing the last of your food with someone who was a stranger?" It might be hard to do.

Examine children's drawings and what children say about them to determine what they remember about the concepts that are taught. Drawings reflective of Bible stories can be collected and saved each week in a special location. Some programs provide a large box such as a pizza box for children to decorate and then use to store and preserve their work. At some point one can let children be engaged in their own assessment of what they have learned by sorting their drawings and selecting the ones that were most meaningful to them throughout the year.

Make a book illustrating a story or parable. To assess their comprehension of The Ten Commandments, have each child draw a picture of one the commandments. Combine these drawings together into a book that can be added to the classroom library.

Good assessment—and teaching—requires that teachers take the time to listen to children and record what they hear and observe. One Sunday I was watching Mandy at the easel, anxious that she not get distracted and wander around the room with her paint brush extended. She painted a house, added windows, and even added what looked to be people at the windows. Then she took her brush and painted long abrupt slashes of red, covering and mixing with the browns of the house. The red got thicker and the strokes more intense. After the red, there came wide swathes of black, until the other colors only peeked from the edges and the figures were gone. Upon my inquiry she told me for the first time about the fire that had destroyed her home. It was the first glimpse I had of what might be prompting her outbursts and distracting behaviors.

Because I took the time to observe, I could talk about the story behind her painting. This observation supports the importance of not only taking time to assess children through observation, but constructing or refining curriculum. Educators need to allow children the freedom to make their own verbal and artistic responses to lessons and stories, instead of requiring everyone to do the same curriculum or artwork prepared by the teacher or make the same memorized responses.

Foster Reciprocal Relationships with Families

Reciprocal relationships among the church ministry leaders, teachers, and families require mutual respect, cooperation, shared responsibility, and frequent two-way communication. Parents are the most important people in the lives of young children.

Therefore, developmentally appropriate practice must include partnering with families to provide the kind of quality care and education parents have a right to expect from a faith-based setting.

As the primary influence on young children, families have the capacity to strengthen their children's learning in every area. The ways in which Christian educators work with families to help children move from the known world of their homes to the unknown world of an early childhood setting can be an important component of a child's faith foundation. Children can learn spiritual concepts through what they experience with their parents. Children need to see a faith lived in order to make it their own. Another compelling reason for working with parents is that children's own faith closely mirrors what they think their parents believe. In her book, *Family, the Forming Center,* Marjorie Thompson (1996) states persuasively that families of committed faith are the initial and the most natural context for the positive Christian spiritual formation of children.

Start by considering these key assumptions as a basis for establishing such a relationship:

- Children grow and develop best when parents and those who care for them within the Christian community communicate with one another on a routine basis.

- Parents and educators are most effective when they respect one another's views.

- Parents and educators have a responsibility to build upon children's learning experiences that occur in the home, church, and community.

- Educators have the responsibility to learn about children's lives outside the classroom in order to develop meaningful learning environments.

- Parents have the responsibility to share information with educators about their children's home lives that can support their classroom learning.

One of the practical means for building these kinds of relationships is for teachers to make home visits. This informal visit can be used as a time to ask questions about the family and home, or a time for families to describe their favorite activities together. Teachers and caregivers may ask questions like: "What do you hope for your child?" and "How can we best share a relationship with your child?" Most parents respond positively to concerned friendly individuals who reflect God's love for their children. This can be a time to share with parents how to use the Bible story leaflets that may be sent home on Sundays, as well as important policies parents need to know regarding the program or church.

A teacher should approach parents not as someone who has all the answers, but as a friend who wants to involve them in teaching and helping their child. In this way the teacher truly becomes the servant, one who follows Jesus' example of care and concern. As one makes personal contacts with families, keep in mind the goal of establishing a friendship and ministering spiritually to them. The teacher's ministry to the home should emphasize helping families to become more Christ centered, and thus home ministry should be just as vital as planning Bible lessons (see chapter 19). Faith-based programs can provide families with ideas of how to make spiritual development a more natural part of family life.

Make periodic home visits, observing these guidelines:

- *Have a stated reason for calling,* such as to deliver a gift to a sick child, esxplain new policies, or making this a general practice.

- *Call and make an appointment to ensure the time is convenient.*

- *Make the visit with a friend, a spouse, or another teacher*

- *Keep the visit brief (15–20 minutes)*

- *Talk about the child's positive behavior*

- *Pray for the family before and after each visit*

Encourage every family to observe at least one session of the program. By seeing the activities, parents can gain knowledge of the program's goals and help them to understand their children better. For a child's birthday, ask a parent to come in to tell the child's life story, sing a song, or show baby pictures. Any time there are differences in practices it is important to work out with parents what words are acceptable to use in class. For example, people believe different things about how holidays should be celebrated. Some children are encouraged to believe in Santa Claus. Some churches celebrate advent with an advent wreath. Teachers can ask parents to share in class what the observance of special holidays means to their families. After parents have observed a class or session, solicit and discuss their responses and answer any questions they may have.

Commit Resources to High-quality Christian Education for Young Children

What children learn about God during early childhood may well set the pattern for their thinking and decision making for the rest of their lives. Every faith-based organization that is serving children should expend adequate resources on helping children from infancy to develop their relationship with God. Children should receive the best that is reasonably possible, not what is left over.

The question of whether one's faith will involve children should be at the top of the church's mission priorities to ensure the future of the church (Westerhoff, 1976), but more importantly if people want to see faith that will last and be significant in people's adult lives. Adults are responsible for setting the stage for what children will internalize. Whatever methods chosen must engage their hearts, minds, and spirits.

By using a developmentally appropriate framework in children's ministries, one can capitalize upon the critical knowledge of child development and be better able to excel in the role of Christian educator.

> We will tell the next generation the praise-worthy deeds of the Lord, His power, and the wonders He has done . . . so the next generation would know them, even the children yet to be born, and they in turn would tell their children. Then they would put their trust in God and would not forget His deeds but would keep His commands. (Psalm 78:4, 6–7, New International Version)

The author has made available an annotated bibliography of faith-based resources, which can be accessed at: www.childspirituality.org.

References

Berends, P. (1991). *Gently lead: How to teach your children about God while finding out about yourself.* New York: Harper.

Berryman, J. (1985). *Children's spirituality and religious language. British Journal of Religious Education, 7*(3), 126.

Bloom, B. S., Engelhart, M.D., Frost, E. J., Hill, W. H., & Krethwohl, D. R. (1956). *Taxonomy of educational objectives. Handbook I: Cognitive domain.* New York: David McKay.

Bohlin, K., & Ryan, K.(1998). *Building character in schools: Practical and moral instruction to life.* Hoboken, NJ: Jossey-Bass

Bredekamp, S., & Copple, C. (1997). *Developmentally appropriate practice in early childhood programs* (Rev. ed.). Washington, DC: National Association for the Education of Young Children.

Catalfo, P. (1993, March). Helping children think about God, *Parenting,* 90–93.

Coles, R. (1990). *The spiritual life of children.* Boston: Houghton Mifflin.

Dewey, J. (1934*). A common faith.* New Haven, CT: Yale University Press.

Dodge, D. T., Colker, L. J., Heroman, C. (2002). *Creative curriculum* (4th ed). Washington, DC: Teaching Strategies, Inc.

Erickson, E. (1963). *Childhood and society* (Rev. ed.). New York: Norton.

Fowler, J. (1981*). Stages of faith: The psychology of human development and the quest for meaning.* San Francisco: Harper.

Holt, P., & Vanderweide, R. (1982). *Christian character foundation curriculum.* Old Tappan, NJ: Fleming Revell.

Lebar, L. E. (1989). *Education that is Christian.* Colorado Springs, CO: Chariot Victor.

Macaulay, S. (1984) *For the children's sake.* Wheaton, IL: Crossway.

Myers, B. K. (1993, January). Faith foundations of all our children. *Young Children, 48*(2), 49–55.

Palmer, P. (1997). *The courage to teach.* Hoboken, NJ: Jossey-Bass.

Ratcliff, D. (1988). Stories, enactment, and play. In D. Ratcliff (Ed.), *Handbook of preschool religious education* (pp. 247–269). Birmingham, AL: Religious Education Press.

Ratcliff, D. (1992). Baby faith: Infants, toddlers, and religion. *Religious Education, 87*(1), 117–120.

Rizzuto, A.-M. (1979). *The birth of the living God.* Chicago: University of Chicago Press.

Shelly, J. A. (1982). *The spiritual needs of children*. Downers Grove, IL: InterVarsity Press.

Skidmore, D. (2003, May). Will our faith have children? *Risen*. Providence, RI: Episcopal Dioceses of Rhode Island.

Shore, R. (1997). *Rethinking the brain*. New York: Families and Work Institute.

Starks, D., & Ratcliff, D. (1988). Planning, evaluation, and research. In D. Ratcliff (Ed.), *Handbook of preschool religious education* (pp. 270–287). Birmingham, AL: Religious Education Press.

Stewart, S. M., & Berryman, J. (1989). *Young children and worship*. Louisville: Westminster John Knox.

Thompson, M. J. (1996). *Family the forming center: A vision of the role of family in spiritual formation*. Nashville: Upper Room Books.

Torrence, E. P., & Torrence, J. P. (1988). Creativity and teaching concepts of God. In D. Ratcliff (Ed.), *Handbook of preschool religious education* (pp. 224–246). Birmingham, AL: Religious Education Press.

Westerhoff, J. H., III. (1976). *Will our children have faith?* San Francisco: HarperSanFrancisco.

Chapter Twenty-Two

Spiritual Influences in Helping Children to Cope with Life Stressors

SARA PENDLETON, ETHAN BENORE, KATHERINE JONAS, WENDY NORWOOD, AND CAROL HERRMANN[1]

Sarah had always longed to be a dancer, a beautiful ballerina. Her dream was to flit across the stage in a beautiful pink tutu and pointed pink satin ballerina shoes. The crowd would roar with applause as she took her bow and performed one last graceful leap as she left the stage.

Her dream would have to wait. Suddenly, her life changed from thoughts of dancing, crafts, and snack time in pre-school to the reality of doctors,

1. Sara Pendleton received her M.D. degree from the University of Michigan and is currently Assistant Professor of Pediatrics at Wayne State Medical School and the Children's Hospital of Michigan. She also completed the Robert Wood Johnson Clinical Scholars Program training at the University of Michigan. The recipient of numerous honors and awards in medicine, she has served as a consultant and speaker for the National Institute for Healthcare Research, the International Center for the Integration of Health and Spirituality, and speaks on Spirituality in Medicine for the Templeton Foundation. She serves on several regional and university boards as well. Her current research includes both qualitative and quantitative research on religion and spirituality in pediatric medicine. She has developed a religious-spiritual coping model for children with chronic illness.

Ethan Benore recently received his Ph.D. in Clinical Psychology from Bowling Green State University. He is currently completing a post-doctoral fellowship in Pediatric Psychology at the Cleveland Clinic. Ethan co-authored articles and chapters on bereavement and religious/spiritual coping in adults, pursued empirical research on sanctification theory and religious coping in children, and conducted several studies in the psychology of religion with a research team located at Bowling Green State University.

Wendy Norwood graduated magna cum laude from the University of Tennessee at Chattanooga with her Bachelor of Science degree in Psychology. She then went on to obtain her Master of Arts degree in Professional Counseling from Psychological Studies Institute in Chattanooga, Tennessee.

Katherine A. Jonas holds a M.A. in Professional Counseling from Psychological Studies Institute, received an M.A.T. from Columbia International University, and a B.A. from King College. She is counselor at The Guidance Center in Murfreesboro, Tennessee.

Carol Herrmann received her Ph.D. from Northwestern University, an M.A. from Wheaton College, an M.S. in education from Northern Illinois University, and a B.S. in education. She has conducted several research studies of missionaries and their children, served as a missionary seminary professor in the Philippines for nearly a quarter of a century, and was the Missionary Scholar in Residence and Resident Scholar at the Billy Graham Center in Wheaton. She is currently an independent researcher.

needles, hospitals, and pain. Her parents talked in hushed voices and seemed so very sad. They seemed to hold her closer, she thought. "Dear Jesus, make me all better so I can dance," she prayed demanding His healing and expecting Him to do it immediately.

The months dragged on and on. While she frequently considered her faith, Jesus' love for her, and the support of her family and friends, she sometimes thought, "Why do I have to go to the hospital and get poked and take medicine that makes me feel so sick?" In these moments of feeling lousy, helpless and overwhelmed, sometimes she got angry. She was mad at the nurses, at the doctors, at the people who came to the hospital to pray with her, at her mom and dad, and sometimes she even got angry at God. Although she was not aware of it, her thoughts sometimes mirrored her parents.' "Why did You let me have cancer? Why can't You make me better? Are You really there? What did I do wrong? Am I being punished for something I did?" She did not feel that way for very long. Those who surrounded her with love chased those scary feelings away, prayed with her, and reminded her of Jesus, her Savior and friend. Then she could sleep.

"The prayer people" is what she called the people that came to pray with her and her mom, dad, little sister, and baby brother. The prayer people came to see her whenever she was in the hospital. They often came to her home. They prayed for hours, sometimes. The prayer made her feel better, usually. At least, it made her mom and dad less sad. The prayer people brought her gifts and sometimes dinners and treats. She knew them well; she knew they were fighting against this awful cancer with her. She could feel the love they had for her. It was like the love of Jesus that she knew so well in her heart.

She saw the angels that protected her bed, which had become her home and her entire world since she was too weak to walk. Sometimes, she saw Jesus, too. She knew they were all watching over her. She sensed their love. The cancer had grotesquely extended her tummy and was starting to steal the nutrients from the rest of her body. She often prayed when she was awake, which was not very often now because the pain medicine made her mercifully sleepy. In this time of trial, she was greatly comforted when she saw Jesus. She knew it would not be long until she would be with Him and escape the pain and uncertainty and horror she experienced. She prayed, "Please take care of my mom and dad and sister and brother and the prayer people—especially if I am not here any more." She also never gave up hope and never stopped praying, "Please make me better, so I can dance."

The story of Little Sarah, although a unique experience, is an example of the common means children use to cope with the tragedies and tribulations of life. This chapter will survey the basic concepts and previous research on religious coping in the lives of children. Three research studies conducted by the authors of the chapter also are summarized: a study on religious coping styles of children, the religious coping strategies of youngsters, and the religious resilience of children of missionaries. The chapter concludes with potential applications of the research.

Theory and Research on Religious Coping

As a critical review of the literature on religious coping in youth has recently been published (Mahoney, Pendleton, & Ihrke, 2004), an exhaustive review will not be repeated here. Suffice to say that there are currently few studies focusing directly on religious coping in children and adolescents. These studies investigate a variety of stressors such as chronic medical conditions (e.g., asthma, cancer, cystic fibrosis, spina bifida) (Tebbi et al., 1987; Johnson, 1988; Spilka, Zwartjes & Zwartjes 1991; Friedman et al., 1997; Pendleton, Cavalli, Pargament, & Nasr, 2002), medical procedures (e.g., hospitalization, needle stick) (Silber & Reilly, 1985; Ebmeier, Lough, Huth, & Autio, 1991), ethnic-related stressors (Dubow, Pargament, Boxer, & Tarakeshwar, 2000), academic or school problems (McMichael & Plunkett, 2001), depression (Pearce, Little, & Perez, 2003) conduct problems (Pearce, Jones, Schwab-Stone, & Ruchkin, 2003), and everyday events (Britt, 1993). Studies have also documented relationships among various measures of religiousness/spirituality and increased health protective behaviors as well as decreased health risk behaviors (Wallace & Forman, 1998; Donahue & Benson, 1995; Regnerus, 2003; Wills, Yaeger, & Sandy,2003) which may be mediated through religious coping. These studies support the frequent use of religious coping strategies among youth.

Coping and Religious Coping

Coping involves the use of cognitions and behaviors by children to mediate stressful aspects of their ever-changing world. Lazarus and Folkman (1984) depict coping as a two-step process. The first step is *appraisal* whereby a person evaluates a stressful situation. Appraisal includes both assessing the stressfulness of the situation (primary appraisal) and assessing the coping resources available to deal with the stressor (second appraisal). If the situation is appraised as stressful enough, it is followed by the second step which involves a coping *process* which is a response to reduce the effect of the stressor. The outcome of this two-step coping sequence is entitled the effectiveness of religious coping.

While Lazarus and Folkman (1984), as well as others, (e.g., Silver & Wortman, 1980; Tix & Frazier, 1998) describe *coping* as an individual's response to a stressful event, other researchers studying children (Compas, 1987; Compas, Connor-Smith, Saltzman, Thomsen, & Wadsworth, 2001) and religion (Pargament, 1997) highlight the importance of a goal-orientation in coping. To them, *coping* includes a set of behaviors that individuals engage in when facing distress while pursuing identified goals. These goals may be multifaceted and include reduction of distress (Lazarus & Folkman, 1984; Compas et. al., 2001), a search for significance (Pargament, 1997), making meaning out of the situation (Park & Folkman, 1997), or pursuing developmental milestones (Compas et. al., 2001). As an example, Robert Coles (1990) makes a powerful statement about children using their religiousness/spirituality to make meaning of a stressful event:

> Children try to understand not only what is happening to them, but why; and in doing that, they call upon the religious life they have experienced, the spiritual values they have received, as well as other sources of potential explanation. (p. 100)

Pargament defines *religious coping* as a search for significance in times of stress in ways related to the sacred (Pargament, 1997).

Based on the above literature, *children's religious coping* can be defined as cognitions and behaviors that: 1) occur in response to a stressful event, 2) draw upon religious/spiritual resources or include the sacred dimension of life, and 3) pursue a personal or developmental goal. Restated, *children's religious coping* includes spiritually-based cognitions and behaviors an individual engages in to reduce the impact of a stressful situation and progress toward personal or developmental goals (Benore, 2003).

The story of Little Sarah highlights three coping constructs, providing a personal testimony of religious coping in children.

Religious Coping Apprasials

Primary appraisal is an assessment of the *threat of the stressor* to the individual's identity and needs. Little Sarah revealed her primary appraisal of the cancer stressors, exemplified by her statement: "Why do I have to go to the hospital and get poked and take medicine that makes me feel so sick?" An example of *secondary appraisals* occurred when she considered her religious/ spiritual resources in the face of suffering: *"While she frequently considered her faith, Jesus' love for her and the support of her family and friends . . .".*

Religious Coping Processes

Although, several authors have evaluated the complexity of religiousness/ spirituality and coping (e.g., Koenig, 1998 & 2001; Koenig, McCullough, & Larson, 2001; Levin, 2001; Tix & Frazier, 1998), two examples of religious coping are provided to elucidate the underlying constructs because they complement the research described in this chapter.

The first theoretical construct is *Religious Coping Styles*. It categorizes religious *coping processes* as three religious *coping styles* measured by Pargament's Religious Problem Solving Scale (Pargament et al., 1988). The three *religious coping styles* center on one's relationship to God. They are 1) *self-directing* (rely on self instead of God), 2) *deferring* (rely on God completely), and 3) *collaborative* (work together with God). Each of these styles of religious coping differentiates the amount of control a person perceives when problem-solving a difficult situation. The research in this chapter by Norwood and Jonas is based on this construct.

The second theoretical construct, *Religious Coping Strategies,* is a newer more elaborate model. Pargament (et al., 2000) developed a scale called the *RCOPE* based on coping strategies to capture five key religious functions: 1) meaning, 2) control, 3) comfort/spirituality, 4) intimacy/spirituality, and 5) life transformation. Factor analysis of the initial 100 specific religious coping items revealed 17 different adult religious coping strategies. These 17 strategies were divided into two subscales: *Positive Religious Coping Scales* and *Negative Religious Coping Scales*. The research in this chapter by Pendleton, Benore, and colleagues stems, in part, from this construct.

While complete discussion of these models is beyond the scope of this chapter, Little Sarah's experiences will highlight some of the key ideas. The specific coping strategies are indicated by parenthesis. For example, Little Sarah also demonstrates some of the coping strategies entitled *religious reappraisals,* in which a stressor is re-defined as a positive opportunity for religious/spiritual growth or, conversely, in a negative manner as a punishment from God, work of the devil, or questioning of God's power to affect the situation. She demonstrates such religious reappraisals and a negative religious coping strategy when she states, "Why did You let me have cancer? Why can't You make me better? (*Reappraisals of God's Powers*) Are You really there? (*Spiritual Discontent*) What did I do wrong? Am I being punished for something I did?" (*Punishing Reappraisals*). In addition, she demonstrates a positive religious cop-ing strategy when she forms a spiritual connection with Jesus for comfort and actively surrenders her life to God's hands (*Religious Surrender*).

Religious Coping Effectiveness

Empirical study of religious coping strategies has demonstrated both the predictive power of religious coping and the differential effects of coping strategies. Not all reli-gious coping strategies are beneficial. The outcome of religious coping depends upon the type of strategy used and the nature of the stressor involved. One may easily accept that trying to reframe a stressful event as a positive experience created by a benevolent and omniscient God (*Benevolent Religious Reappraisal*) would reduce one's distress and facilitate adaptive coping (e.g., "God is trying to teach me something or make me stronger"). However, viewing a stressful situation as a punishment from a wrathful

God brought upon by a selfish or sinful act (*Punishing God Reappraisal*), or as the handiwork of Satan (*Demonic Reappraisal*), may result in increased helplessness, hopelessness, and less ability to cope. In other words, religious coping strategies may be summarized as either positive or negative, based on the demonstrated association with coping outcomes (Pargament, et al., 2000).

In a review article, Harrison, Koenig, Hays, Eme-Akwari, & Pargament (2001) reported that positive religious coping was generally related to less depression, enhanced quality of life, higher self-esteem, greater life satisfaction, and positive global ratings of health. Negative religious coping was generally associated with increased depression, diminished quality of life, increased anxiety and traumatic stress, and poorer global ratings of health. Some researchers have noted that, although negative religious coping is less prevalent, it has demonstrated stronger predictive value than positive religious coping (e.g., Pargament et al., 1998).

Similar to secular coping research in children, researchers are finding that the malleability and nature of the stressor may also affect whether a coping strategy has positive or negative effects on outcomes (Compas et al., 2001). For example, although *Pleading for Direct Intercession* is often associated with negative outcomes, it may be adaptive in the face of an immutable stressor such as serious illness or imminent death. Therefore, in any evaluation of religious coping, researchers and clinicians must be open to the possibility that some strategies may either be helpful or harmful, depending upon the circumstances. They should also explore the fit among religious coping strategies and the nature and malleability of the stressor involved.

For Little Sarah, both her parents and the "prayer people" recognized certain coping strategies as having negative effects exemplified by their actions: "Those who surrounded her with love chased those scary feelings away and reminded her of Jesus, her Savior and friend." Her consistency in prayer in the face of serious illness, an uncontrollable stressor, exemplified an adaptive use of the generally negative religious coping strategy, *Pleading for Direct Intercession*, when she prayed, "Please make me better, so I can dance."

Influences on Religious Coping in Children

Children are not just "little adults." When assessing religious coping in children a few additional influences need to be examined. Before exploring these further, consider three underlying constructs that shape religious coping in children: *religious/spiritual development, social influences,* and *supernatural influences.*

Ways Religious/Spiritual Development Can Affect Religious Coping

The age and developmental level at which Little Sarah confronted cancer affected the religious coping strategies available to her and how she used them. The following brief overview of religious/spiritual developmental theories outlines key developmental issues to consider that can affect religious/spiritual coping in children.

The development of children's faith remains an enigmatic feature of children's religious/spiritual life, with relatively little attention being devoted to children in the area of psychology of religion (c.f. Wulff, 1997). Several renowned researchers have investigated and established theories to explain faith and religiousness/spirituality in children (Goldman, 1964; Elkind, 1978, 1997; Fowler, 1981, 1991; Oser, 1991; Hay & Nye, 1998). These theories generally overlap with other models of development such as Piaget's cognitive development theory (Piaget, 1970) and Kolhberg's (1984) stages of moral development. This chapter provides only a cursory overview of three religious/ spiritual developmental theories, as they may mediate developmental differences in children's religious coping. For more detail on Nye's work, see chapter 6 of this text (for details on other theories, see Hyde, 1990; Bucher & Reich, 1991; Oser & Scarlett, 1991; Rosengren, Johnson, & Harris, 2000).

Fowler: Development of faith. Fowler (1981, 1991) understood faith development as the evolution of a child's conceptualization of the spiritual realm. According to this theory, children progress through six hierarchical stages of faith, three of which are applicable to child development. Beginning in infancy, children begin to lay the foundation for their faith development by working on developing trust, in a stage called *undifferentiated faith.* At the preschool level (around age 3), children engage in *intuitive/projective faith*, guided by youthful imagination and unbounded by logical thinking. By middle childhood (around age 7), children enter the *mythical-literal faith* stage where their faith takes a more literal characteristic, guided by acceptance of symbols and stories present in one's faith culture. Toward late childhood and adolescence (around age 12 or older), many children begin to question the nature of their established beliefs and incorporate them into their current values and self-identity in a stage called *synthetic-conventional faith.* This progression of development is in line with Piaget's (1970) movement from concrete to formal operations in cognitive development.

Oser: Development of religious judgment. In contrast to Fowler's focus on faith, Oser (1991) focused his study of religious/spiritual development on children's *religious judgment.* Oser defines *religious judgment* as "reasoning that relates reality as experienced to something beyond reality and that serves to provide meaning and direction beyond learned content (p. 6)." He explores responses to seven polar dimensions of religiosity including freedom versus dependence, transcendence versus immanence, hope versus absurdity, transparency versus opacity, faith (trust) versus fear (mistrust), the holy versus the profane, and eternity versus ephemerity (pp. 7, 8). Oser's stages are delineated by the changing perceptions of locus of control over children's lives, as influenced by the child's level of cognitive processing and moral framework. In Stage 1, children view God as powerfully active and effective, while the child merely reacts to God. In Stage 2, God is still seen as external and all-powerful, yet the child can influence God's actions with good deeds and religious/spiritual rituals. In Stage 3, God (if acknowledged as existing) is understood as a transcendent figure in a separate, hidden realm, while the child holds immanent autonomy and responsibility for what happens. In Stage 4, God and the child exist in relation to one other. The child sees himself as "free and responsible, but freedom now is tied to the God who gives and sustains freedom" (p. 12). Oser's Stage 5, "orientation to religious intersubjectivity and autonomy, universal and unconditional religiosity" (p. 10), is found only in adults.

Development of spiritual actions. Although not a specific theory of development, Woolley's (2000) study of wishing and prayers provides an example of the development of personal spiritual activities in children, based on levels of cognitive development. Woolley (2000) described wishing and prayers of children as the development of "thought-causal attributions." Specifically, most 3-year-olds can differentiate between the mental and physical worlds; however many continue to believe that mental thoughts can control the physical world. For young children, wishing has a magical power (c.f. Wulff, 1997). For example, when asked if a wished-for item would appear in a closed box, 71 percent of three- to four-year-olds agreed compared with 31 percent of five- to six-year-olds. As children grow older, belief in this self-propelled magic apparently fades. During the middle elementary years, children's understanding of their own minds includes recognition of the limitations of their mental power, although the power of magical/supernatural intercessors (e.g., God, spirits) persists. By adolescence, prayer is better represented as an internal dialogue between the teenager and God, a mutual "meeting of the minds" to work through difficult situations. This progression of the content and form of prayer through childhood (from selfish, magical wishes to realistic conversations with the Divine) is supported by other researchers as well (Nelsen, Potvin, & Shields, 1977; Hyde, 1990; Worten & Dollinger, 1986).

These theories begin to explain how growing children understand spiritual concepts, engage in spiritual activities, and how their spiritual development intertwines with other aspects of development. As Coles (1990) points out, "the entire range of children's mental life can and does connect with their religious and spiritual thinking" (p. 108). As children's minds and worlds develop and vary over time, so do their concepts of religiousness/spirituality, relation to the Divine in their world, and styles of engagement in religious/spiritual activities. Still, research suggests that there is some form of progression which helps us to understand the trajectory children take in their development. This is important to children's religious coping because developmental differences may significantly influence a number of coping factors, such as appraisals, coping processes, and coping effectiveness.

Ways Social Influences Can Affect Religious Coping

Also important to understanding children's religious coping are the social settings and resources which encourage and/or discourage children's development of religiousness/spirituality, affect the building of religious/spiritual resilience, and serve as positive and/or negative coping resources to children in times of stress. These social influences include the child's community (the faith community, in particular) and the child's family (with special focus on parents). Several religious coping constructs will be examined to highlight social influences on religious coping under the social contexts of the child's community and the child's family.

The Child's Community

Religious coping appraisals. It is important to consider general community and faith community dynamics, as they likely influence the ways a child draws upon religious/spiritual resources during times of stress. Community institutions such as day care centers, schools, worship centers, and the child's faith community may influence religiousness/spirituality through social learning and social support, which are very important in dealing with illness and other life stressors. These social resources can shape the child's religious coping resources.

The religious community can be likened to a second family. In Kendrick and Koenig's review (2000) of coping with cancer—examining religion as a resource for families—they found that although children's most immediate source of support was their own families, having a religious community can offer "back-up" not only to children directly, but also to the parents and siblings. This may bolster hope, help keep spirits and energies higher, and potentially stave off marital or inter-family crises that could result from the additional stress of having a seriously ill child (Kendrick & Koenig, 2000). The story of Little Sarah suggests how important a child's community can be. It was the endorsement of community-based belief in Jesus as Savior which helped her to challenge her hopelessness, anger, and emotional distance from God, and stave off family crisis.

Religious coping processes. Pargament (et al., 2000) identified multiple religious coping strategies that are strongly affected by social influences. Five coping strategies found among adults are also likely to affect children's religious coping. These strategies are *Seeking Support from Clergy or Church Members* (searching for comfort and reassurance through the love and care of congregation members and clergy), *Religious Helping* (attempting to provide spiritual support and comfort to others), *Religious Focus* (engaging in religious activities to shift the focus from the stressor), *Marking Religious Boundaries* (clearly demarcating acceptable from unacceptable religious behavior and remaining within religious boundaries), and *Interpersonal Religious Discontent* (expressing confusion and dissatisfaction with the relationship of clergy or church members to the individual in the stressful situation).

In her actions when she got angry, Little Sarah demonstrated both strategies focusing on discontent: "She was mad at the nurses, at the doctors, at the people that came to the hospital to pray with her, at her mom and dad, (*Interpersonal Discontent*) and sometimes she even got angry at God (*Spiritual Discontent*)." In response to this, the faith community helped her accomplish *Religious Focus* exemplified in the statement: "Those who surrounded her with love chased those scary feelings away, prayed with her, and reminded her of Jesus, her Savior and friend." Little Sarah demonstrated *Religious Helping* with her prayer even in her suffering, "Please take care of my mom and dad and sister and brother and the prayer people—especially if I am not here any more."

Religious coping effectiveness. While in adults, *Seeking Support from Clergy or Members*, *Religious Helping*, *Religious Focus*, and *Marking Religious Boundaries* are generally associated with positive outcomes and *Interpersonal Religious Discontent* is associated with negative outcomes, empirical evidence has yet to determine if all of these strategies are employed in childhood and, if so, the effectiveness of each of these strategies at each developmental level.

The Child's Family

Religious coping appraisals. The role of the family as a source of support in the face of life stressors should not be overlooked. How the family interacts as a system and the make-up of the family system may impact development of trust and more advanced levels of a child's religiousness/spirituality.

Parenting attitudes and methods within the family system may also impact the development of the child's image of God and spirituality, and thus the use of primary religious coping appraisals. Following an extensive review of the research on this topic, Hyde (1990) concludes:

The image of God is thus seen to develop in early childhood from children's perceptions of their parents—what they are and what they ideally should be. Punitive or loving images of God are closely related to parental attitudes.

How a child sees God and faith, as well as family normative modeling, can affect the ways a child formulates primary religious coping appraisals. For example, the child may appraise the context in terms of *desecration* (perceiving a sacred aspect of life as violated) (Pargament, Magyar, Benore, & Mahoney, 2004), *sacred loss* (loss of an aspect of life that was previously viewed as sacred) (Pargament, et al., 2005), or *demonization of the perpetrator* (attributing supernatural demonic forces as responsible for actions of human perpetrators of negative events) (Mahoney, et al., 2002).

The religious/spiritual influences within the family system can impact development of a child's religiousness/spirituality and religious coping resources. The religious/

spiritual beliefs and practices of each member of the family system also impact the child's development of religiousness/spirituality. Discrepancies in religious/spiritual beliefs between family members, intensity of beliefs, and frequency and importance of practices can all impact the development of the child's religiousness/spirituality. In extremes cases, religiously-based beliefs and practices can be harmful to children such as religion-motivated medical neglect (Asser & Swan, 1998).

Modeling of religious/spiritual beliefs and practices within the family system also varies considerably and can impact the development of the child's religiousness/ spirituality and development of religious coping resources. For example, in Spilka, Zwartjes, and Zwartjes's (1991) cancer research, effects on siblings may also be quite serious. With so much attention focused on the ill child, siblings may become the "forgotten family members" (Spilka & Hartman, 2000). They may feel isolated or develop fears of medical treatment, death, and the like. Faith practices may help maintain some unity and normalcy in the lives of the siblings. This may reduce the negative effects of isolation and also provide them a source of support and explanation to help allay their fears. Thus, the entire family system copes with cancer as well as other stressful events. The ways in which each individual within the family system, as well as the family system as a whole, copes can add to or detract from the child's available religious coping resources.

It is important to look at the individual's definition of "family," which may include relatives and non-relatives outside the nuclear family unit (Nierenberg & Sheldon, 2001). One study that looked at 585 grandparents in Iowa found that those who were more religious were correspondingly more involved in the lives of their grandchildren, providing support ranging from caring for a sick grandchild to discussing the grandchild's personal problems. One hypothesized explanation for the results is that pro-family messages are intrinsic to many religious teachings. A second hypothesized explanation is that religious communities provide a social arena that fosters family interaction (King, Speck, & Thomas, 1999).

A family rich in religious/spiritual resources may serve as a powerful resource for the child's religious coping. For Little Sarah, family religious resources provided assistance with overcoming negative religious coping strategies and support for positive religious coping strategies. They demonstrated the development of trust and encouraged Little Sarah's faith development, even in the face of life-threatening illness.

Religious coping processes. Mahoney, Pendleton, and Ihrke (2004) identify four types of family-based religious coping constructs. The first is *Conjoint Religious Coping Activities,* which are overt religious coping activities that the family unit participates in together. For example, Little Sarah and her family often prayed together and attended worship services together to face stressors. Second, *Spiritual Forgiveness* indicates reliance on spiritual influences to facilitate interpersonal forgiveness (McCullough, Pargament, & Thoresen, 2000; Rye & Pargament, 2002). The remaining two constructs emphasize God as an additional person operating in the interpersonal relationship facing stressors. In *Spiritual Mediation*, God is seen as a neutral advocate promoting resolution of interpersonal difficulties. However, in *Spiritual Triangulation*, God is seen as aligning with one side against the other. Further empirical research is needed to determine the impact of these family-based religious coping constructs.

Religious coping effectiveness. Religious coping within the family system can involve either the individual use of religious coping strategies or the family-based religious coping constructs as listed above. A 2001 study of parental use of religious coping in families of children with autism found that parents who sought comfort and understanding using religious/spiritual resources reported fewer stress reactions associated with their child's condition. In contrast, other religious coping behaviors, such as blaming God for their child's condition, were associated with poorer adjustment reflected in increased depression and anxiety (Tarakeshwar & Pargament, 2001). In a study evaluating caregivers of children with HIV, those who reported higher levels of religiousness/spirituality suffered less negative effects (e.g., depression), yet also reported poorer family cohesion and life satisfaction (Armstrong, 1999). These studies show that parental use of specific religious coping strategies can be correlated with either positive or negative outcomes. These parental outcomes could also affect the child in the family context.

In assessing the family-based constructs, *Conjoint Religious Coping Activities* seems more efficacious when there is a close fit in religious/spiritual beliefs among family members (Regnerus, 2003). *Spiritual Forgiveness* seems to be predominantly efficacious (McCullough, et al., 2000; Rye & Pargament, 2002;). *Spiritual Mediation* is often adaptive; whereas *Spiritual Triangulation* is often maladaptive (Yanni, 2003). Clearly, more research is needed to understand better the effectiveness of these constructs in the family system.

Ways Supernatural Influences Can Affect Religious Coping

Most Christians acknowledge that religious/spiritual development is a process accomplished by the Holy Spirit's work (John 14:15–31 NIV). Most Christian denominations believe that the Holy Spirit acts as a Counselor to guide faith development. Faith itself is a gift from God; and many argue that faith in God cannot exist without the influence of God. For many Christians, faith is thought to grow because of many possible influences, such as participation in the sacraments (e.g., Baptism and the Lord's Supper), reading the Bible, and prayer. Many also recognize that there is an unseen battle. "For our struggle is not against flesh and blood, but against the rulers, against the authorities, against the powers of this dark world and against the spiritual forces of evil in the heavenly realms" (Eph 6:12, NIV). It follows, then, that these supernatural forces—both positive and negative—may also affect the *appraisals/*

coping resources, coping processes, and *coping effectiveness* of children in ways beyond knowing in the natural world.

Religious Coping Styles in Children (Norwood and Jonas)

We—the researchers of this study—evaluated the presence of religious coping styles in a sample of 55 children (24 females, 31 males) ages 8 to 11 years, attending two separate Christian schools, using an age-appropriate modified version of the Religious Problem-Solving Scale (Pargament et al., 1988). Children were presented with 18 religious coping items and asked how true each statement described them. In this study, children reported using all three styles to some extent. No age or gender differences were noted in the relative frequency of use of coping styles.

As a group, children reported that both a *deferring coping style* (i.e., perceiving God as in complete control and doing nothing independently) and *collaborative coping style* (i.e., forming an alliance with God) were significantly more consistent to how they approach stressors than a *self-directing coping style* (i.e., coping independently without relying on God). There was no difference in the extent to which they made responses to the *deferring* or *collaborative coping style.* The more children described themselves as *self-directive* copers, the less likely they were to rely on *deferring* or *collaborative styles of coping.* In contrast, children who embraced a *deferring coping style* were more likely to embrace a *collaborative coping style.* These two findings are consistent with research on religious problem-solving styles in adults (Pargament et al., 1988). The association between the *collaborative* and *deferring* styles of coping and increased prevalence of both suggest that children rely on dependent styles of coping. The results suggest children are more likely to rely on God during times of stress rather than avoid God's help and cope autonomously. This is consistent with the cognitive, psychosocial, and spiritual development theories described earlier (Piaget, 1970; Fowler, 1981; Oser, 1991).

However, these results must be interpreted with caution, as the three scales had relatively weak internal reliability (Cronbach alphas < .66). For example, a child who reported strong collaborative coping on one item was not strongly likely to report similar scores on another item intended to measure collaborative coping. Further research is needed to determine if the adult scales are reliable or valid with children or if separate children's scales should be developed.

This initial exploratory study raises several research questions. How do childrens' uses of religious coping styles relate to their general developmental characteristics? Do children cope with all stressors in the same way or would children use different coping strategies for different events? Can children use more than one coping style with a specific stressor?

Religious Coping Strategies in Children (Pendleton, Benore, and Colleagues)

In contrast to a general style of coping, we—the researchers of this second study—evaluated children's efforts to cope with stressful medical events by drawing upon their religious/spiritual resources to engage in specific coping strategies. In the initial study, Pendleton et al. (2002) interviewed children (ages 5–12) with cystic fibrosis and their parents to assess in what ways children drew from their faith to cope with their illness. Children in this study represented a variety of religious denominations. They reported on three main issues: 1) what they do to get better when feeling sick, 2) their thoughts about God, faith, and prayer in health and healing, and 3) the roles of religion in the doctor-patient relationship. In addition, children drew a picture of themselves and God to represent how they viewed religious coping.

As the qualitative data were coded, eleven sets of religious coping strategies emerged. These strategies were *Declarative* (the child announces something to happen and God is thought to automatically do it), *Petitionary* (child appeals to God to intercede), *Collaborative* (child and God both take responsibility for dealing with the stressor), *Divine Support* (God is viewed as assisting, benefiting, protecting, and comforting the child), *Divine Intervention* (God intercedes without direction or appeal from child), *Divine is Irrelevant* (child does not rely on God at all), *Benevolent Religious/Spiritual Reframing, Negative Religious/ Spiritual Reframing, Spiritual Social Support, Discontent with God or Congregation*, and *Ritual Response* (use of ritual in an effort to cope with the stressor). Interestingly, some of the strategies identified (e.g., *Divine is Irrelevant*) were not similar to adult religious coping strategies—highlighting the uniqueness of the child's experience (cf. Pargament et al., 2000). Also unique to children, most reported that coping strategies were helpful to their physical, mental, religious/spiritual, and social adjustment. This suggests that children view religious coping as a source of resilience during difficult times.

Based on this initial evaluation, a quantitative measure of children's religious coping was generated. Ezop (2002) developed scale items based upon the qualitative reports of children's religious coping and items from the RCOPE used to assess religious coping in adults (Pargament, et al., 2000). The result was the Children's Religious Coping Scale (CRC Scale), a 29-item, self-report instrument measuring the specific religiously/spiritually-based strategies that children might use to cope with an identified stressor. This scale was initially validated in a sample of 62 asthmatic children aged 8–15 years. As detailed above, strategies were categorized into positive religious coping strategies (20 items, e.g., "When my asthma bothers me, I try to see how God might be making me a better person") and negative religious coping strategies (9 items, e.g., "When my asthma bothers me, I wonder if God is mad at me"), based on reported associations with outcomes in the adult literature and preliminary qualitative work.

Several significant findings were drawn from this initial validation study. First, children reported frequent use of positive religious coping, and infrequent use of negative religious coping when facing asthma as a stressor. This is consistent with the Pendleton, et al. (2002) qualitative data. In other words, even when prompted to report negative religious coping strategies, children still demonstrate a strong preference for positive coping strategies. Second, children's religious coping appeared independent of other demographic variables, such as age and gender. Third, children's religious coping was related to child and parent religiosity measures, and to secular coping strategies, supporting the theoretical relationship between these variables. In other words, the more one's family practices religion, and the more a child copes, the more frequently that child will turn to religious coping strategies during times of stress.

Two final results support the predictive power of children's religious coping. First, positive and negative religious coping strategies predicted children's adjustment after accounting for demographic and non-religious coping variables. This suggests that religious coping plays a special role in children's lives that cannot be explained away in secular terms (cf., Pargament, et al., 2000). Also, negative religious coping predicted poorer adjustment in several areas of functioning. This is consistent with research in adults; however, it differs from the Pendleton et al. (2002) study, reporting that children view religious coping strategies as beneficial. Interestingly, in the Ezop study, positive religious coping was also associated with poorer adjustment. This suggests that, in a cross-sectional design assessing adjustment measures independent from coping strategies, children's religious coping may be mobilized by the level of perceived stress—greater perceived stress translates into poorer self-reported adjustment and greater use of coping strategies (aimed at reducing distress).

In a third study, Benore (2003) reevaluated the Children's Religious Coping Scale in a sample of children hospitalized for asthma. Again in this study, both positive and negative religious coping strategies predicted poorer adjustment during hospitalization (see Ezop, 2002), although a closer examination of the results revealed important differences. Children who engaged in positive religious coping were more likely to report anxiety about their asthma functioning and medical treatments during the hospital stay. In contrast, children who engaged in negative religious coping were more likely to report poorer quality of life on a variety of dimensions, poorer self-competence, and poorer emotional functioning during the hospital stay. Positive and negative religious coping differentially predicted outcomes one-month following discharge from hospitalization. Specifically, positive religious coping predicted greater spiritual growth one month following discharge. Negative religious coping predicted poorer quality of life and greater anxiety one month following discharge.

The correlation between high rates of religious coping and poor adjustment *during an acute stressor* reflect a mobilization of religious coping in children. Specifically, when children are facing a significant stressor they turn towards religious resources to cope with the event—the greater the perceived threat, the greater they will engage in religious coping. This is similar to the Ezop (2002) study, however here the presence of an acute stressor was experimentally controlled. However, an adequate (and currently undetermined) time frame following the stress must occur for the differential prediction of coping strategies to clearly emerge. In other words, positive religious coping may predict improved quality of life after hospitalization, as hypothesized, but it may take time for children to demonstrate these benefits. These results highlight the importance of evaluating the distinctive aspects of children's spiritually-based coping strategies in coping research. The results also provide preliminary support of a measure for religious coping in children.

Religious/Spiritual Resilience in Missionary Children (Herrmann)

A third, often overlooked component in children's coping and religious/ spiritual lives is a model of resilience. *Resilience* is a *process* of effectively coping with a stressful situation (Luthar, Cicchetti, & Becker, 2000a, 2000b; Woodgate, 1999a, 1999b; Roosa, 2000; Wallander & Varni, 1992). According to a critical review by Luthar et al. (2000a), *resilience* is "a dynamic process encompassing positive [adjustment] within the context of significant adversity"

(p. 543). In other words, in the midst of a stressful situation, the resilient child achieves better adjustment than others in a similar situation. This is, theoretically, the result of various protective factors that characterize resilient children. Protective factors are variables consistently related to better psychosocial adjustment over time that "buffer" the impact of stressful circumstances (Amer, 1999). Protective factors may include personal characteristics (e.g., temperament), environmental factors (e.g., family environment, social resources), and, important to this discussion, coping strategies (Lemanek & Hood, 1999; Wallander & Robinson, 1999). We define *religious/spiritual resilience* as the religious/spiritual resources and behaviors that children routinely integrate into their daily lives that form a buffer against various life stressors. Given what is currently known about religious coping, it is hypothesized that children who integrate religiousness/spirituality into their daily lives may respond better to significant life stressors. Herrmann's (1977, 1979) research on children of missionaries provides a salient example of the development and effectiveness of religious/spiritual resilience.

Missionary Children's Stresses

For nearly a century and a half, missionary families have known the rigor of living between countries, often with "no permanent address" labeled across luggage and belongings. Their experiences are often a contrast between settling in a mountainous tribal area or rain forest village with very primitive living conditions to establishing a home in the mega-complex of large urban cities like Tokyo, Metro Manila, or Singapore.

Children of missionaries are minor dependents known as missionary kids or "MKs" and also are known as third culture kids, TCKs (Useem, 1993). They are in the process of developing their own lifestyle in the interstices between two different societies. These interstices include the passport country of their parents and the host country designated as the parents' field of ministry. As a unique population, MKs face a number of demands and stressors, such as underdeveloped living conditions, transitioning into a minority culture, work related separations for prolonged periods, and political unrest in the host country.

In addition, children must adjust to returning to their passport country. As a child re-entering one's passport country in the twenty-first century he/she is con-fronted with a variety of cultural, social, and emotional changes. For example, an MK could move from primitive living conditions in a nomadic culture to a fast-paced, technologically advanced world of DVDs, internet, and cell phones. In the midst of these life stressors, the religious behaviors learned and practiced as part of a mission-ary family may prove to be efficient coping resources buffering the impact of multiple life stressors during these formative years, thus creating resilient children.

Herrmann's (1977) work built upon previous research of missionary children conducted in the 1970s. She administered questionnaires to 257 seniors attending a missionary school located in Asia that provides an education for children of Western and Asian missionaries living in Southeast Asia (Herrmann, 1997). Students repre-senting nine nationalities, from over sixty Western and Asian missions, participated in the research between 1997 and 2000. She assessed students' retrospective evalua-tion of their experiences growing up as missionary children.

Child behaviors. MKs engaged in a variety of religious/spiritual behaviors which solidified their search for significance in this world and their relationship with the Divine. For example, children often took part in daily devotions and regu-lar religious/spiritual practices. They also were frequently provided opportunities to assist with the work of the mission, such as traveling by ponies to outpoints in mountainous regions, musical or sport activities in town squares. During mission conferences, special activities were planned specifically for the children in the mis-sionary community, such as evening vespers around a campfire, Bible studies, and youth groups. Powell's (1984) conclusion that MKs who took part in their parent's ministry felt a sense of belonging and purpose is reflected in this sample as well. One child reported "I will always remember it as a time of closeness with God and with my father". Another reported that, through group youth activities, "We realized we were spiritually-active beings, not merely the recipients of spiritual teaching". Thus regular engagement in religious/spiritual activities may foster religious/spiri-tual development and a potential for resiliency.

Parental influence. MKs also reported that a great deal of their religious/ spiritual strength derived from the lessons taught and behaviors modeled by their parents and teachers. Routine morning prayers/devotions of the parents encouraged children to routinely seek God's help throughout the day. The context of parental prayer was also influential. One child reported, "Hearing my mother pray specifically for God to move in a certain way—sometimes against all odds—and seeing it come to fruition, I learned that it's OK to ask God for specifics". A second MK reported, "The greatest thing my parents ever did for my spiritual growth and maturity was to pray for me". In addition to a relationship with God, the relationship parents had with the community and with their child also shaped MKs developing religiousness/spirituality, as the following quote describes:

> What impacted me most as an MK was my parents' undying love for people and their seemingly bottomless energy for ministering with [nationals] on their level of living and understanding. My parents are adapters, givers, and creative teachers who sincerely love the Lord. Watching those traits in action throughout my life made me want to be the same way.

When MKs felt valued by their parents and integrated into their parents' mission, they demonstrated a positive attitude toward their situation, their role as MKs, and their parents' work. However, when MKs felt their parents placed their work first, and spent a minimum amount of time or were minimally involved with them, they experienced and expressed negative attitudes with reference to growing up in a missionary environment. This provides an indirect association between parental factors and religious/ spiritual resilience of children.

Children's developing religious/spiritual worldview. Both the child's and parents' religious/spiritual behaviors shape the religious/spiritual worldview (i.e., cognitions) of MKs. This is important to religious coping and resilience because children may draw upon this worldview when forming initial appraisals of stressful events. Reading the following quotes, one may imagine how a particular religious/spiritual worldview may buffer the impact of a stressful event.

- One attitude I noticed in my parent(s) concerning their call to be missionaries: The Lord did not make them go against their will; He just made them willing to go.

- It impressed me deeply that God was a real person who wanted to hear our emotions and our deep longings.

- [commenting on a teacher's personal devotion] . . . this taught me that walking with God had to be a daily choice.

- . . . Wherever we go, and in whatever situations we may find ourselves, if we are in the will of God, He is with us. He will never leave us nor forsake us.

- Faith . . . becomes something between "just" me and God and not something that "they" made me do.

From the above examples, it is easy to imagine that children who view God as ever-present, benevolent, and view themselves as personally responsible for maintaining a strong relationship with God and strong religious/spiritual life, may in the process develop a buffer against the impact of stressful events. It is a religious/spiritual worldview similar to this that, along with child and family religious/spiritual behaviors, may foster the style of coping and use of specific coping strategies which are most beneficial to children.

In Little Sarah's story, she describes engaging in frequent visits with "the prayer people," a group of individuals in religious vocation. These people of religious vocation provided continual support and religious/spiritual guidance, strengthening her to withstand the pain of her cancer and the stress of her death. Perhaps there is much more to be learned from the actions of these "prayer people" and their families that could further elaborate what is known about religious coping and religious/spiritual resilience.

Application of Religious Coping in Children

Despite the lack of scientific data, children are accessing their religiousness/ spirituality to cope with life stressors, and adults are encouraging children to do so. At this time, we the authors cannot provide specific recommendations to enhance the effectiveness of religious coping in children; nor can we provide a manual listing step-by-step instructions for children to religiously cope with life stressors. However, we can provide a general guide of what to attend to in children, and identify where clinical intervention might occur. Utilizing the three coping factors addressed throughout the chapter, here are some ways one could begin to apply this theoretical construct in helping children cope with stressors.

Primary appraisals. When approaching a child facing stressors, understanding the worldview—and the degree to which religiousness and spirituality influence this worldview that the child brings to appraise the stressor—can aid in meeting the child at the point where he or she is. Some key religious/spiritual elements of this worldview include identifying the child's perception of God and the child's religious/spiritual attributions of the stressor. Assessing one's own worldview will better equip a person to identify similarities and differences between the child's worldview and one's own perspectives. This can aid in empathically envisioning the world from the view of the child. Application of this sensitivity to worldview—and the degree that religiousness/ spirituality influences this worldview—can help one see how the child appraises stressors.

Resources for coping. When approaching a child, it is also helpful to assess *religious/spiritual coping resources.* These religious/spiritual coping resources can include their religious/spiritual beliefs and activities, religious/spiritual persons in their lives, relevant religious institutions, their religious community, and religious/spiritual texts that are important (e.g. Bibles). Understanding how the developmental level, social influences, and supernatural resources affect the religious/spiritual resources of the child, the child's family, community, and culture, will greatly affect how one assists the child in utilizing religious/ spiritual resources in coping.

Religious coping processes. As research in children's religious coping progresses, determining which *coping processes* occur and how they change in response to developmental, social, and spiritual influences will be better known. Being open to these theoretical concepts and enhancing one's own understanding of the "end result" of adult religious coping will improve one's ability to identify religious coping processes in individual children.

Religious coping effectiveness. Although determining which coping strategies are adaptive and maladaptive in children is in preliminary stages of being formally tested, being sensitized to which strategies are adaptive and maladaptive in adults may help frame how one assesses a child's use. It is also important to assess the child's view of what is adaptive. Often identifying and reinforcing strategies perceived as adaptive, and identifying and addressing the "red flag" strategies (e.g., those perceived as maladaptive), can assist the child in coping with stressors.

> The story of Little Sarah is a story of tragedy and hope. Interwoven through this story is a young girl's developing religiousness/spirituality. Sarah encounters a spiritual struggle with a terrifying stressor, threatening her life goals and dreams. Her faith is shaken as she tries to assign meaning to her situation, given her youthful understanding of God. Her faith is shaken but not broken. Sarah finds comfort and support in a community of believers—the "prayer people." They tend to her religious/spiritual needs while engaging in some seemingly secular activities, such as meals. Sarah also develops a closeness with Jesus and His angels, fighting alongside herself and the prayer people to defend her from pain and sickness. Finally, Sarah develops an inner peace allowing her to emotionally face her untimely death. Her story is not the only one of its kind. Many children are confronted by terrifying situations and make use of their own (and others') religious/spiritual resources. And it is up to everyone involved—the researchers, clinicians, and "prayer people"—to discover, model, and teach children a life of faith which sustains them through tragedy.

References

Amer, K. S. (1999). A conceptual framework for studying child adaptation to Type 1 diabetes. *Issues in Comprehensive Pediatric Nursing, 22,* 13–25.

Armstrong, T. D. (1999). The impact of spirituality on the coping process in families dealing with pediatric HIV or pediatric nephrotic syndrome. *Dissertation Abstracts International: Section B: The Sciences & Engineering, Vol. 59* (12-B), P6482.

Asser, S. M., & Swan, R. (1998). Child fatalities from religion-motivated medical neglect. *Pediatrics, 101,* 625–629.

Benore, E. (2003). *Religious coping and pediatric asthma.* Unpublished doctoral dissertation, Bowling Green State University.

Britt. G. C. (1993). *Children's coping with everyday stressful situations: The role played by religion.* Unpublished doctoral dissertation, Virginia Commonwealth University.

Bucher, A., & Reich, K. (1991). Annotated bibliography on religious development. In W. Damon (Series Ed.) & F. K. Oser & W. G. Scarlett (Vol. Eds.), *New directions for child development: Vol. 52. Religious development in childhood and adolescence* (pp. 107–120). San Francisco: Jossey-Bass.

Coles, R. (1990). *The spiritual life of children.* Boston, MA: Houghton Mifflin.

Compas, B. E. (1987). Coping with stress during childhood and adolescence. *Psychological Bulletin, 101,* 393–403.

Compas, B. E., Connor-Smith, J. K., Saltzman, H., Thomsen, A. H. & Wadsworth, M. E. (2001). Coping with stress during childhood and adolescence: Problems, progress, and potential in theory and research. *Psychological Bulletin, 127,* 87–127.

Donahue, M. J., & Benson, P. L. (1995). Religion and the well-being of adolescents. *Journal of Social Issues, 51,* 145–160.

Dubow, E. F., Pargament, K. I., Boxer, P., & Tarakeshwar, N. (2000). Initial investigation of Jewish early adolescents' ethnic identity, stress, and coping. *Journal of Early Adolescence, 20,* 418–441.

Ebmeier, C., Lough, M. A., Huth, M. M., & Autio, L. (1991). Hospitalized school-age children express ideas, feelings, and behaviors toward God. *Journal of Pediatric Nursing, 6,* 337–349.

Elkind, D. (1978). *The child's reality: Three developmental themes.* Hillsdale, NJ: Erlbaum.

Elkind, D. (1997). The origins of religion in the child. In B. Spilka & D. McIntosh (Eds.), *The psychology of religion: Theoretical approaches* (pp. 97–104). Boulder, CO: Westview Press.

Ezop, S. (2002). *Religious and spiritual coping in children with chronic illness.* Unpublished doctoral dissertation, Bowling Green State University.

Fowler, J. W. (1981). *Stages of faith: The psychology of human development and the quest for meaning.* San Francisco: Harper & Row.

Fowler, J. W. (1991) Stages of Faith Consciousnes. In W. Damon (Series Ed.) and W. G. Scarlett & F. K. Oser (Vol. Eds.) *New directions for child development: Vol. 52. Religious Development in Childhood and Adolescence* (pp. 27–46). San Francisco: Jossey-Bass.

Friedman, T., Slayton, W. B., Allen, L. S., Pollock, B. H., Dumont-Driscoll, M., Mehta, P., Graham-Pole, J. (1997). Use of alternative therapies for children with cancer, *Pediatrics, 100,* E1.

Goldman, R. G. (1964). *Religious thinking from childhood to adolescence.* London: Routledge & Kegan Paul.

Hay, D. & Nye, R. (1998). *The spirit of the child.* London: Fount/HarperCollins.

Harrison, M. O., Koenig, H. G., Hays, J. C., Eme-Akwari, A. G., & Pargament, K. I. (2001). The epidemiology of religious coping: A review of recent literature. *International Review of Psychiatry, 13,* 86–93.

Herrmann, C. B. (1977). *Foundational factors of trust and autonomy influencing the identity formation of the multicultural lifestyled MK.* Ph.D. dissertation, Northwestern University, Evanston, IL.

Herrmann, C. B. (1979, October). *MKs and their parents: The place of the family in building trust and autonomy.* Wheaton, IL: Emissary: Evangelical Missions Information Service.

Hyde, K. (1990). *Religion in childhood and adolescence: A comprehensive review of the research.* Birmingham, AL: Religious Education Press. Johnson, A. F. (1988). Challenged adolescents with spina bifida. In P. W. Power, A. E. Dell Orto, & M. B. Gibbons (Eds.), *Family interventions throughout chronic illness and disability* (pp. 164–183). New York: Springer.

Kendrick S. B. & Koenig H. G. (2000). Coping with cancer: Religion as a resource for families. In L. Baider, C. L. Cooper & A. K. De-Nour (Eds.), *Cancer and the family* (2nd ed., p. 464). New York: Wiley.

King, M., Speck, P., & Thomas, A. (1999). The effect of spiritual beliefs on outcome from illness. *Social Science and Medicine, 48,* 1291–1299.

Koenig, H. G. (1998). *Handbook of religion and mental health.* San Diego: Academic Press.

Koenig, H. G. (2001). *The healing power of faith: How belief and prayer can help you triumph over disease.* New York: Simon & Schuster.

Koenig, H. G., McCullough, M. E., & Larson, D. B. (2001). *Handbook of religion and health.* New York: Oxford University Press.

Kohlberg, L. (1984) Essays on moral development. San Francisco: Harper & Row.

Lazarus, R. S., & Folkman, S. (1984). *Stress appraisal and coping.* New York: Springer.

Lemanek, K. L., & Hood, C. (1999). Asthma. In R. T. Brown (Ed.), *Cognitive aspects of chronic illness in children* (pp. 78–104). New York: Guilford.

Levin, J. S. (2001). *God, faith, and health: Exploring the spirituality-healing connection.* New York: Wiley.

Luthar, S. S., Cicchetti, D., & Becker, B. (2000a). Research on resilience: Response to commentaries. *Child Development, 71,* 573–575.

Luthar, S. S., Cicchetti, D., & Becker, B. (2000b). The construct of resilience: A critical evaluation and guidelines for future work. *Child Development, 3,* 543–562.

Mahoney, A. M., Pargament, K. I., Ano, G., Lynn, Q., Magyar, G., McCarthy, S., et al. (2002). *The devil made them do it? Demonization and the 9/11 attacks.* Paper presented at the Annual Meeting of the American Psychological Association.

Mahoney, A., Pendleton, S., and Ihrke, H. (2004). Stress, coping, and spiritual development. In E. Roehlkepartain, P. E. King, L. M. Wagener, & P. L. Benson (Eds.). *The handbook of spiritual development in childhood and adolescence.* Thousand Oaks, CA: Sage.

McCullough, M., Pargament, K. and Thorensen C. (2000). *Forgiveness: Theory, research, and practice.* New York: Guilford.

McMichael, B. J., & Plunkett, S. W. (2001). *Stressors, religious coping, and adolescent family life satisfaction.* Poster presented at the 8th Annual Child Health Psychology Conference, Gainesville, Florida.

Nelsen, H., Potvin, R. & Shields, J. (1977). *The religions of children.* Boys Town Center for the Study of Youth Development. Catholic University of America, Washington D.C. Office of research, policy and program development. Department of Education. United States, Catholic Conference.

Nierenberg, B. & Sheldon, A. (2001). Psychospirituality and pediatric rehabilitation—children and religious experience. *Journal of Rehabilitation, 67*(1), 15–19.

Oser, F. K. (1991). The development of religious judgment. In W. Damon (Series Ed.) & F. K. Oser & G. Scarlett (Vol. Eds.), *New directions for child development: Vol. 52. Religious development in childhood and adolescence* (pp. 5–26). San Francisco: Jossey-Bass.

Oser, F. K. & Scarlett, G. (Vol. Eds.) (1991). In W. Damon (Series Ed.) *New directions for child development: Vol. 52. Religious development in childhood and adolescence.* San Francisco: Jossey-Bass.

Pargament, K. I. (1997). *The psychology of religion and coping: Theory, research, and practice.* New York: Guilford.

Pargament, K. I, Kennell, J., Hathaway, W., Grevengoed, N., Newman, J., & Jones, W. (1988). Religion and the problem-solving process: Three styles of coping. *Journal for the Scientific Study of Religion, 27,* 90–104.

Pargament, K. I., Smith, B. W., Koenig, H. G. & Perez, L. (1998). Patterns of positive and negative religious coping with major life stressors. *Journal of the Scientific Study of Religion, 37,* 711–725.

Pargament, K. I., Zinnbauer, B. J., Scott, A. B., Butter, E. M., Zerowin, J., & Stanik, P. (1998). Red flags and religious coping: Identifying some religious warning signs among people in crisis. *Journal of Clinical Psychology, 54,* 77–89.

Pargament, K. I., Koenig, H. G., & Perez, L. M. (2000). The many methods of religious coping: Development and initial validation of the RCOPE. *Journal of Clinical Psychology, 56,* 519–543.

Pargament, K. I., Koenig, H. G., Tarakeshwar, N., Hahn, J. (2001). Religious struggle as a predictor of mortality among medically ill elderly patients. *Archives of Internal Medicine, 161,* 1881–1885.

Pargament, K. I., Magyar, G. M., Benore, E. & Mahoney, A. (2005). *Sacrilege: A study of sacred loss and desecration and their implications for health and well-being in a community sample. Journal for the Scientific Study of Religion, 44*(1), pp. 59-78. https://doi.org/10.1111/j.1468-5906.2005.00265.x

Park, C. L., & Folkman, S. (1997). The role of meaning in the context of stress and coping. *General Review of Psychology, 1,* 115–144.

Pearce M. J., Jones, S. M., Schwab-Stone, M. E., & Ruchkin, V. (2003). The protective effects of religiousness and parent involvement on the development of conduct problems among youth exposed to violence. *Child Development, 74,* 1682–1696.

Pearce, M. J., Little, T.D., Perez, J.E. (2003). Religiousness and depressive symptoms among adolescents. *Journal of Clinical Child and Adolescence, 32,* 267–276.

Pendleton, S., Cavalli, K. S., Pargament, K. I., & Nasr, S. Z. (2002.). Religious/ spiritual coping in childhood cystic fibrosis: a qualitative study. *Pediatrics, 109,* e8.

Piaget, J. (1970). Piaget's Theory. In P. H. Mussen (Ed.), *Carmichael's manual of child psychology* (3rd ed., pp. 703–732). New York: Wiley.

Powell, J. (1984). *Parental influence on MKs.* ICMK Compendium: New Directions in Missions, Implications for MKs. Manila, Philippines.

Regnerus, M. D. (2003). Religion and positive adolescent outcomes: A review of research and theory. *Review of Religious Research, 44,* 394–413.

Roosa, M. W. (2000). Some thoughts about resilience versus positive development, main effects versus interaction, and the value of resilience. *Child Development, 71*, 567–569.

Rosengren, K., Johnson, C. & Harris, P. (Eds.). (2000). *Imagining the impossible: Magical, scientific, and religious thinking in children.* Cambridge: Cambridge University Press.

Rye, M. S. & Pargament, K. I. (2002). Forgiveness and romantic relationships in college: Can it heal the wounded heart? *Journal of Clinical Psychology, 58*, 419–441.

Silber, T. J. & Reilly, M. (1985). Spiritual and religious concerns of the hospitalized adolescent. *Adolescence, 20*, 217–224.

Silver, R. L. & Wortman, C. B. (1980). Coping with undesirable life events. In J. Garber & M. E. P. Seligman (Eds). *Human helplessness: Theory and applications.* (pp. 279–340). New York: Academic.

Spilka, B. Zwartjes, W. J. & Zwartjes, G. M.(1991). The role of religion in coping with childhood cancer. *Pastoral Psychology, 39*, 295–304.

Spilka, B. & Hartman, S. (2000). Religion, cancer, and the family. In L. Baider, C. L. Cooper & A. K. De-Nour (Eds.), *Cancer and the family* (2nd ed., pp. 443–456). John Wiley & Sons, Ltd.

Tarakeshwar, N. and Pargament, K. (2001). Religious Coping in Families of Children with Autism. *Focus on Autism & Other Developmental Disabilities, 16*, 247–260.

Tebbi, C., Mallon, J. C., Richards, M. E., & Bigler, L. R. (1987). Religiosity and locus of control of adolescent cancer patients. *Psychological Reports, 61*, 683–696.

Tix, A. P., & Frazier, P. A. (1998). The use of religious coping during stressful life events: Main effects, moderation, and mediation. *Journal of Consulting and Clinical Psychology, 66*, 411–422.

Useem, R. (1993, January). *Third Culture Kids.* NewsLink—the newspaper of International Services.

Wallace, J. M., & Forman, T. A. (1998). Religion's role in promoting health and reducing risk among American youth. *Health Education and Behavior, 25*, 721–741.

Wallander, J. L., & Robinson, S. L. (1999). Chronic medical illness. In R. T. Ammerman, M. Hersen, & C. G. Last (Eds.), *Handbook of prescriptive treatments for children and adolescents* (2nd ed., pp. 364–379). Boston: Allyn & Bacon.

Wallander, J. L., & Varni, J. W. (1992). Adjustment in children with chronic physical disorders: Programmatic research on a disability-stress-coping model. In A. M. LaGreca, L. J. Siegel, J. L. Wallander, & C. E. Walker (Eds.), *Stress and coping in child health* (pp. 279–300). New York: Guilford.

Wills, T. A., Yaeger, A.M., Sandy, J. M. (2003). Buffering effect of religiosity for adolescent substance use. *Psychology of Addictive Behavior, 17*, 24–31.

Woodgate, R. L. (1999a). A critical review of qualitative research related to children's experiences with cancer: Part II. *Journal of Pediatric Oncology Nursing, 17*, 207–228.

Woodgate, R. L. (1999b). Conceptual understanding of resilience in the adolescent with cancer: Part I. *Journal of Pediatric Oncology Nursing, 16*, 35–43.

Woolley, J. (2000). The development of beliefs about direct mental-physical causality in imagination, magic, and religion. In K. Rosengren, C. Johnson, & P. Harris (Eds.), *Imagining the impossible: Magical, scientific, and religious thinking in children* (pp. 99–129). Cambridge: Cambridge University Press.

Worten, S., & Dollinger, S. (1986). Mothers' intrinsic religious motivation, disciplinary preferences, and children's conceptions of prayer. *Psychological Reports, 58*, 218.

Wulff, D. W. (1997). *Psychology of religion: Classic and contemporary views* (2nd ed.). New York: John Wiley & Sons.

Yanni, G. (2003). *Religious and secular dyadic variables and their relation to parent-child relationships and college students' psychological adjustment.* Unpublished doctoral dissertation, Bowling Green State University.

Acknowledgments

The authors would like to gratefully acknowledge Rachael Andersen-Watts for all her help in preparing this chapter and Kraig Pendleton for his assistance in editing. We especially thank Little Sarah's family for allowing us to share her inspiring story.

Chapter Twenty-Three

Ministering to Unchurched, Urban, At-Risk Children

GARY C. NEWTON[1]

David and Billy, brothers whose ages were 8 and 10 respectively, stepped off the bus with several dozen other children from difficult family backgrounds, most of them from foster homes. Wide-eyed, they scanned the environment to determine if this would be a safe place, or if once again they would be neglected and abused. Their background made them very much "at-risk" and included many years of moving from house to house with their drug-addicted mother, who would sometimes leave them for hours or even days at a time and often forgot to buy food for her hungry children. The children had suffered much abuse throughout their lives, often from the succession of men who lived with their mother.

When they returned home, the boys could not wait to tell their older sister—who had been appointed their legal guardian—about the personal attention they received from their camp counselor, as well as the recreational activities that took place. They proudly displayed the Bibles they had received, and began to sing songs about God and Jesus they had learned. They had discovered the love God had for them and had experienced that love first-hand through this ministry to at-risk children.[2]

---

1. Gary Newton received his PhD in Educational Studies from Trinity Evangelical Divinity School. Presently he serves as Director of the Educational Ministries Program and Professor of Educational Ministries at the Graduate School of Christian Ministries at Huntington College. He has written *Growing Towards Spiritual Maturity* and nineteen book chapters or journal articles. He also volunteers as Director of the Huntington Kids Club, a ministry to unchurched, at-risk children, and is Pastor of Spiritual Formation at a new church planted in downtown Huntington.

An earlier version of this chapter was published in the journal *Lutheran Education* in Spring, 2004, and is reprinted here by permission of that journal.

2. This account is based on a true story although pseudonyms are used. The ministry involved was one of the Royal Family Kids' Camps (3000 W. MacArthur, Suite 412, Santa Ana, CA 92704).

What are the components of effective ministry programs targeted to urban, unchurched, at-risk children? The research to address this question emerged from my own as a pastor and community member ministering to the needs of unchurched children and their families living in my neighborhood. Throughout my ministry I have had a great concern for children outside the influence of the church. Over the past 34 years I have been involved in several different types of programs and ministries to unchurched children within a variety of social contexts. Presently I am directing a ministry to about 85 primarily unchurched, at-risk children in a small-town, urban setting. One assumption of the research is somewhat missiological—one of the best ways to begin an outreach ministry to a people group of another culture is through its children. The question that naturally arises is, "What are the components of an effective ministry to such children that eventually results in their long-term spiritual growth and development and the establishment of stable families, churches, and communities?" Identifying such components of effective ministry to children will help practitioners in this kind of ministry become more purposeful in designing ministries that would promote long-term change in individuals, families, and communities.

Research Design

Leaders were interviewed from fifteen programs that minister to urban, at-risk children ages 8–12 within the United States and Canada. The target programs were identified by key pastors and leaders in cities across North America. These pastors and leaders were asked to name the most effective children's outreach ministries in each city that seem to have produced the most fruit in terms of changed lives, families, and communities.

The main leader from each organization was interviewed by either telephone or questionnaire by students in the Children and Family Ministry class at Huntington College. The questionnaire used in the interviews was developed by the class after significant reading and an orientation on indicators of effectiveness in children's ministry. Four major components of successful ministry with at-risk children were identified from the students' library research, primarily from Strommen and Hardel (2000), Kilbourn (1996), Stonehouse (1998), Joy (2000), Minuchin, Colapinto, and Minuchin (1998), Julia (2002), and Payne, DeVol and Smith (2001). The four components of successful ministry with at-risk children identified in the library research included:

1. Working with parents and families.
2. Developing closer relationships between leaders and children.
3. Motivating children to achieve challenging standards.
4. Assimilating children into local churches.

These four components provided the structure for some of the major questions in the interviews. Data from the interviews were recorded and analyzed. For this chapter, the following three questions will be considered:

1. How do the goals identified by the ministry leaders compare to the four components of effective ministry identified by the library research?

2. What are the most common ministry approaches identified by the ministry leaders?

3. What specific ministry approaches are most related to each of the four components of effective ministry?

The goal of the research was to help professors and practitioners of children's ministries develop more effective strategies to reach at-risk, urban children, their families, and their communities. Both evangelism and discipleship are part of that goal.

Ministry Leaders Interviewed

Leaders from fifteen different types of ministries to at-risk, urban children were interviewed either by phone, in person, or by e-mail. The name and location of the ministries involved in the research, the leaders interviewed, and a brief description of their ministry focus are summarized.

Brothas and Sistas United

Eve Stuglin is the leader for this ministry in Chicago. The purpose of this program is to develop long-term relationships with children, to show them Christ, and to create in them a desire both to use their gifts for God and to graduate from high school. The ministry involves a variety of community-oriented programs including after-school mentoring, family support programs, and emergency assistance programs. The ministry involves eight workers and 50 to 60 children.

Freedom Christian Bible Fellowship

Judy Landis is the leader of this ministry in Philadelphia, Pennsylvania. The stated purpose of this program is to reach the needs of urban communities by bridging the gap between churches and urban communities. The ministry involves a team approach and offers door-to-door visitation, an annual prayer fellowship, networking with community leaders, community celebrations, visiting mission teams, Vacation Bible School camp, and clothing and food distribution. The ministry involves nine workers and 80 children.

Good News Gang

Corri Kinniebrew is the leader for this Saturday morning community outreach and bus ministry in Detroit. The stated purpose for this program is to get children from rough backgrounds off the streets and to teach them to know Christ. The ministry focuses around a large Saturday morning program in which children are picked up in buses and followed up by church volunteers. Children are encouraged to attend church youth programs at other times during the week. The ministry involves 15 workers and 500 children.

In His Arms Ministry (Hawaii Branch)

Rachel Cox directs this program to homeless children in Honokaa Lane, Hawaii. The stated purpose of the ministry is to share Jesus' love with children by meeting their physical and psychological needs for love and acceptance. The focus is on a club program that includes scripture memorization, prayer, Bible stories, worship, activities, snacks, crafts, and attendance incentives. Two leaders are involved, and up to 25 children attend.

In His Arms Ministry (Mississippi Branch)

Kim Burr Turnbull directs this ministry to homeless children in Vicksburg, Mississippi. The stated purpose of this program is to show love to homeless children and to draw them into the body of Christ. The ministry involves a club where Bible study, prayer, scripture memorization, singing, athletics, and crafts are the key activities. This is a large ministry involving an undisclosed number of leaders and 450 children.

Inner City Missions

Frank Vega directs this ministry in urban Philadelphia. Its stated purpose is to respond to the needs of the "unreachables"—prostitutes, the homeless, drug addicts and at-risk children—and to help them become self-sufficient, contributing members of society. The ministry emphasizes a club program involving tutoring and mentoring plus an innovative "Sidewalk Sunday School." This ministry involves nine workers and 100 to 150 children.

Jesus People U.S.A. /Brothers and Sisters United

Cheryl Terwall directs this ministry in Chicago. The stated purpose of this program is to help needy children develop a relationship with God, learn life skills, and build a vision for the future. This ministry includes a variety of community-focused programs including an after-school drop-in center, tutoring, mentoring, special projects, and trips to the theater and Black Hawk games. The ministry involves 36 leaders and 30 children. Although the name of this ministry is similar to another ministry studied, "*Brothas and Sistas United*," the two ministries are not related.

Kidworks

Ava Steaffens directs this ministry in Santa Ana, California. The purpose of this ministry is to provide a safe haven for children in tough neighborhoods to do homework, learn computer skills, and be introduced to the love of Christ. This ministry focuses on a community center with a variety of programs including homework clubs, computer training, school readiness training, parent training, community celebrations, neighborhood clean-ups, youth ministry follow-up, and camps. There are 16 workers and 90 children involved in this ministry.

Mountain View

Fay Niemann and Eileen Starr direct this spring break day camp in Anchorage, Alaska. The purpose of this ministry is to provide a safe, enjoyable, character-building program for unchurched children during spring break. The camp involves a week-long, all-day program in the public school built around energizing character development with recreation, crafts, music, and drama. There are 130 workers and 100 children involved in the program.

Sparroways Kids Ministry

Ruth Heise directs this ministry in Toronto, Ontario, Canada. The purpose of the ministry is to share Christ with children. The ministry centers around a weekly club, mentoring, and summer camp. Eight workers and 25–30 children are involved.

Urban Promise Ministries (Ontario Branch)

Bill Hall directs this ministry also in Toronto. The purpose of the ministry is to help community people to come to know Christ through long-term relationships established through programs involving family support, after-school tutoring, and mentoring. This multidimensional community involves tutoring, mentoring, school system volunteers, Bible studies, family support, street leader training, visitation, and partnerships with local churches. The ministry involves 85 workers and 300 children.

Urban Promise Ministries (New Jersey Branch)

Desiree Guyton directs this ministry in Camden, New Jersey. The purpose of this ministry is to equip children, teens, and young adults with the skills needed for spiritual growth, academic achievement, living, and Christian leadership. This ministry is built around an after-school program offering mentoring, summer camp, job training, and leadership development. Fifty workers and 75 children are involved in this ministry.

World Impact (Los Angeles Branch)

Tim Goddu directs this ministry in Los Angeles. The purpose of the ministry is to evangelize, equip, and empower urban people through church planting. The ministry is built around two Christian schools, clubs, and a church plant. Other components of the ministry include tutoring, mentoring, sports, Bible clubs, entrepreneurial training, leadership training, music, family outreach, and workers who live in the community. One hundred and twenty workers and 200 children are involved in this ministry.

World Impact (New Jersey Branch)

Fred Clark directs this ministry in Newark, New Jersey The purpose of this ministry is to plant churches among the urban poor through church planting, education, and community development. The ministry is built around a Christian grade school and a church plant. Other aspects of the program include tutoring, mentoring, community development, special events, required teacher/parent conferences, home visits, and Bible clubs. There are 56 workers and 130 children involved in this ministry.

World Impact (Fresno, California Branch)

Bob Engel directs this ministry in Fresno, California. The purpose of this ministry is to plant churches led by the indigenous people among the unchurched, urban poor. The ministry is built around clubs, community programs, and a church plant. Other significant components of the program are workers who live in the community, a whole-family focus, camps, and community outreach. There are 38 workers and 75 to 100 children involved in the ministry.

Goals Identified by the Ministries

The goals identified by the various ministries were categorized and rank ordered by the number of times they were identified.

Table 1 Goals Identified by the Interviewed Ministries

Goal	No. of times identified
Evangelism	12
Support in Life Skills	10
Building Relationships	7
Meeting Physical Needs	5
Improving Academics	5
Impacting the Community	4
Establishing an Indigenous Church	4
Spiritual Growth	3
Building Leaders	2

While evangelism was the most prominent goal, it was always linked with other goals relating to the life needs of people in the community. Giving children support in developing life skills was almost as important as evangelism. This seems to indicate that most ministries to at-risk children attempt to integrate traditional evangelistic approaches with a more holistic ministry to the felt needs of children and their families. The other goals identified show the importance of developing a strategy of ministry that meets not only spiritual needs but also physical, mental, emotional, and social needs of at-risk children.

In comparing the goals identified by the ministry leaders with the four components of effective ministry with at-risk children identified from the various readings, some interesting observations arose.

Table 2

The 12 Most Common Ministry Approaches Identified by the Ministry Leader	No. of times identified
1. Structured club program	8
2. After school drop-in center	7
3. Tutoring	6
4. Mentoring	5
5. Providing emergency assistance	5
6. Working with families	4
7. Camping	4
8. Visiting children in their homes	4
9. Community celebrations	4
10. Job training	3
11. Living in the community	3
12. Church planting	3

The most common ministry approaches used to reach at-risk children were the structured club program and the after school drop-in center. Most ministries incorporate either mentoring or tutoring opportunities that focus on developing significant relationships between the children and adult leaders. The various club programs included a wide variety of activities including Bible teaching, stories, drama, recreation, crafts, tutoring, snacks, and music. While club programs were the major events that initially attracted children, most ministries combined other strategies to meet the needs of youngsters. The most effective ministries mobilize a large number of adult or older teen mentors to build significant relationships with the children through tutoring, informal games and activities, visitation, small groups, and camping. Large group club programs and informal after school programs provide the opportunity for adult leaders to develop deeper relationships with the children. The latter two approaches are the most widespread ways of ministering to the needs of at-risk children.

Specific Approaches Related to the Four Components of Effective Ministry

While the general components of effective ministry were identified by the library research, the specifics of how each of these components could be worked out within various contexts was not yet known. In the interviews conducted, each ministry leader was asked to identify and explain the specific approaches and methods they used to apply each of the four components of effective ministry. The various approaches and methods identified under each of the four components represent the most significant findings identified in this research project.

Component 1: Working with Parents and Families

This first goal was the only one identified in the readings that was not described by ministry leaders as a primary goal. A possible reason for this is that several of the ministries worked primarily with homeless children. Another reason could be that ministering to the parents of at-risk children does not happen easily or quickly. While it is often fairly easy to attract at-risk children to an interesting club or activity, getting their parents involved takes much more effort and trust. Since the lack of parental involvement in the lives of children is one of the primary characteristics of at-risk children, changing the parents is one of the greatest challenges. The fact that this goal was not directly identified as a major goal by any of the agencies indicates that this probably is a weak area in most ministries to at-risk children. Working with the parents and families of at-risk children will always be a great challenge because of the dysfunctional nature of many families of the urban poor.

While this was not identified as a major goal by any of the agencies interviewed, almost all of them identified some strategy used to work with the parents and families of their children. The most common strategies were visiting the children in their homes with their parents, contacting parents informally when picking them up or dropping them off, and inviting parents to church. Some ministries offered special programs for parents such as "Mom's day out," parent workshops, family camps and retreats, and neighborhood parents' organizations. Several ministries attempted to reach parents by meeting their needs for employment, food, shelter, clothing, and transportation. Some ministries hosted special events for families at Christmas, Easter, Thanksgiving or high school graduations.

The ministries that were most effective at engaging the parents of their children were those in which the leaders lived in the community. By living closer to the parents, ministry leaders are able to relate to them more on their level and build trust. Several of such ministries actually required some parental involvement for each of the children involved in their programs. While this goal was not specifically identified by any agency as a high priority, it is at the heart of transforming the lives of children and their communities.

Component 2: Developing Closer Relationships between Leaders and Children

This related task was mentioned as a major goal by almost half of the ministry leaders. Building authentic relationships with at-risk children is central to meeting their needs and leading them into a relationship with Jesus Christ and subsequent discipleship.

All of the ministries identified program strategies focusing on developing informal contacts with children both inside and outside ministry events, contacts which included hugs, compliments, sitting together, playing together, working together, and home or community visits. Many used mentoring relationships and small groups with adult or older teen leaders to build relationships with children. Special events such as retreats, sports events, projects, Bible studies, clubs, and tutoring provided opportunities for deeper relationships to develop. The regular weekly club meeting or drop-in center provided a place where children could count on finding a consistent, trusted friend. The most ideal opportunity for building relationships is where the leaders actually live in their children's communities. This seemed to encourage the most natural and effectual relationships.

Component 3: Motivating Children to Achieve Challenging Standards

In the questionnaire used in this study, ministry leaders were asked, "What are some of the expectations you have for your children?" The leaders' responses are summarized below.

Table 3	
Ministry Leaders' Expectations of Children	Number of times identified
1. Proper behavior, respect for self and others, following rules, a good attitude, Christian character	15
2. Academic achievement: completing homework, making progress, doing their best, continuing on to high school or college, learning computer skills	10
3. Salvation or spiritual growth	8
4. Skills relating to living, working, reading, relationships or conflict resolution	6
5. Setting personal goals and working to achieve them	3
6. Lowering the risk level in problem areas: drugs, sex, drinking, gangs and violence	3
7. Attending ministry events	3
8. Breaking dysfunctional family patterns	3
9. Becoming a community change agent for good, being a leader	3

It is significant that all of the ministries identified specific expectations for the children in their ministries. Rather than merely providing a place for children to "hang out," most ministries had clearly identifiable expectations for those attending. Having high expectations for urban, at-risk children seemed to attract rather than discourage children from participation. Beginning ministries tended to have lower expectations for their children than did more established ministries. Ministries that were older, particularly those that had developed schools and tutoring programs, had higher standards of academics, behavior and spiritual growth

All of the ministries identified some specific standards relating to attitude or behavior at ministry activities. More established ministries had higher behavioral expectations. Many ministries encouraged leaders to help their children set and accomplish their own goals. Higher academic achievement was a key goal in many ministries. Helping the children to grow spiritually was a third priority on the list. This indicates that most ministries focus on helping children to meet more concretely felt needs—related to character and academic issues—before challenging them in their deeper spiritual needs.

Other expectations identified related to building practical life skills, lowering involvement in destructive behaviors, breaking dysfunctional family patterns, and having a positive influence in the community. The list of expectations identified by the leaders of ministries to at-risk children represents a balanced, whole-person approach to meeting their needs. Spiritual expectations were integrated with helping children to meet a broad spectrum of social, moral, educational, and practical needs.

The second question from the questionnaire, related to motivating children to achieve challenging standards, was "What are the ways you use to motivate the children to meet those expectations?" The following data summarizes the responses to this question.

Table 4	
The Most Effective Ways to Help Children Accomplish Ministry Expectations	Number of times identified
1. Rewards: encouragement, hugs, accountability, affirmation, certificates or prizes	12
2. Tutoring, mentoring and relationship building	8
3. Bible teaching and training workshops	5
4. Prayer	4
5. Discipline, setting boundaries, and communicating disapproval when expectations are not met	4
6. Modeling expected behavior and showing respect	4
7. Working with parents to reinforce expectations	3

The responses to this question indicate that a wide variety of means are used to encourage children to accomplish goals and expectations. Yet the primary way identified to help children accomplish their expectations was through positive reinforcement through both tangible and intangible rewards. Most ministries used relationships to encourage and affirm the children in positive directions. Tutoring and mentoring relationships were identified by several ministries as effective ways to motivate children to fulfill their goals. Teaching approaches such as prayer, Bible teaching, music, and drama were also identified as effective ways of encouraging the children to accomplish the goals of the various ministries. In these settings mentoring relationships augment and reinforce teaching goals within the large group programs. These informal relationships become important opportunities to reward the children through encouragement, hugs, accountability, affirmation, and challenge. A few ministries also use more tangible rewards such as prizes, certificates, candy, or special privileges to reinforce high expectations. Appropriate boundaries and discipline are also used to help children to follow guidelines and expectations. It is noteworthy that a few ministries realized the importance of working with parents in reinforcing high expectations for their children.

In surveying the various means identified for helping children fulfill their expectations, a positive motivational environment is crucial to effectiveness.

Component 4: Assimilating Children into Local Churches

In relation to this component of ministry, leaders in each of the ministries were asked, "What strategies did you use to get your children involved with local churches?" and "How effective have your strategies been in getting your children to regularly attend church?" The following summarizes responses to the first of these questions.

Table 5	
Methods of Assimilating Children Into Local Churches	Number of times identified
1. Encouragement and invitation	5
2. Encouraging adult leaders to take children to church and gradually introduce them to people at church	5
3. Starting indigenous churches for children and their parents in their communities; living in the community where the ministry is located	5
4. Bringing churches to the community through Bible studies, celebrations, drama, entertainment, and other outreach events	3
5. Providing children transportation to church	2
6. Teaching churches in the urban communities to reach out and assimilate at-risk children and their families	2

Most of the ministries described some way they attempted to encourage their children to attend church. One of the most successful ways was encouraging leaders to take children to church with them or providing transportation for them to get to church. Other more innovative approaches brought church meetings to the community through neighborhood Vacation Bible Schools, community celebrations, sidewalk Sunday schools, or services in the park.

Several ministry leaders stated that their primary goal was not to get children into churches but simply to establish trust. Other leaders expressed a frustration that most churches are not ready or equipped to minister to at-risk children and their families. Several of the ministries attempted to deal with this problem by building their own indigenous churches to minister to at-risk children and their families. A key component of this approach was requiring workers to make long-term commitments to live within the at-risk community where they work, which involves an extraordinary commitment of resources, time, and energy.

While the referenced literature suggested the importance of integrating at-risk children into healthy churches, this did not seem to be a high priority of many of the ministries studied. Integration seems to be one of the greatest challenges that the ministries face.

Effective Aspects of Ministry Programs

Ministry leaders were asked to identify what they thought were the most effective aspects of their programs by answering this question: "In conclusion, what do you think is the most important aspect of your program that makes your ministry to at-risk children so successful?" The following table summarizes the leaders' responses.

Table 6	
The Most Effective Aspects of Ministry Programs	Number of times identified
1. Quality relationships	11
2. Leadership development	5
3. Holistic ministry	3
4. Attractive programs	3
5. Leaders that live in the children's community	3
6. Networking with other community agencies	2
7. Community development	2
8. Involvement of very needy children	2
9. Supporting families	2
10. Education	2
11. Visitation	1
12. Church planting	1
13. Curriculum	1
14. Large events	1
15. Tutoring	1
16. Emergency assistance to families	1

Building relationships with at-risk children is identified as the most effective aspect of most ministries. Children at risk desperately need healthy relationships to compensate for the problems within their homes and communities. Quality relationships must be the foundation of every effective ministry to at-risk children. Leadership development also ranked high as an effective ministry component. Training indigenous leadership among the children and their parents seems to ensure lasting change within at-risk communities. Several ministries noted that it was their attractive program that proved most effective in ministering to the children, and others mentioned that holistic ministry was more effective. Three characteristics of effective programs related to building strong ties within the community, were living in the community, networking with other community agencies, and community development. Other aspects identified as most effective were involving very needy children, supporting families, education, visitation, church planting, curriculum, large events, tutoring, and emergency assistance. While ministries emphasize different approaches, the most effective components of ministry to at-risk children include quality relationships, a community focus, leadership development, a holistic focus, and an attractive program.

Weakest Aspects of Ministry Programs

While the emphasis on positive components of effective ministry was central to this study, weaknesses also need to be noted. The following table summarizes what ministry leaders identified as the weakest areas of their ministries.

Table 7	
Weakest Areas in Ministry Programs	Number of times identified
1. Lack of workers	6
2. Lack of money	2
3. Negative attitudes toward the poor	2
4. Discipline problems	2
5. Difficulty assimilating children into good churches	2
6. Inadequate facilities	1
7. Tracking children's progress	1

It is significant that the weakest area for most ministries to at-risk children is attracting and maintaining good workers. Since quality relationships are at the core of a successful ministry, it is imperative to maintain a low staff-to-child ratio, especially in working with at-risk children. It is difficult to attract and motivate good volunteers[3] and keep staff in positions that are often marked by low salaries and relative obscurity. The need is not a new one. Even Jesus identified a similar problem in Matt 9:37: "The harvest is plentiful, but the workers are few" (New International Version).

---

3. See Ratcliff and Neff (1993) for a detailed outline of guidelines in relation to ministry volunteers.

Other weak areas identified by ministry leaders are a lack of finances, negative attitudes toward the poor, discipline problems, difficulty assimilating children into good churches, inadequate facilities, and tracking children's progress. While some of these problems can be dealt with through added resources, others are inherent in the nature of a ministry to at-risk children and families.

Conclusions

The purpose of this research project was to identify the components of an effective ministry to unchurched, urban, at-risk children. Components identified in prior research were affirmed and elaborated in the specific approaches to ministry identified by the various organizations studied.

This initial study includes only a small sample of ministries focusing on unchurched, at-risk children in urban communities, it is hoped that in the future additional research can be conducted representing an even broader, more diverse sample of ministries. This study paints a clear picture of the strategies that courageous people across this continent are using to reach needy children so often overlooked by the established church.

References

Joy, D. (2000). *Empower your kids to be adults.* Nappannee, IN: Evangel Publishing House.

Julia, C., et al (2002). *Children's ministry that works.* Loveland, CO: Group Publishers.

Kilbourn, P. (Ed.). (1996). *Children in crisis: A new commitment.* Monrovia, CA: World Vision.

Minuchin, P., Colapinto, J., & Minuchin, S. (1998). *Working with families of the poor.* New York: Guilford.

Payne, R., DeVol, P., & Smith, T. D. (2001). *Bridges out of poverty: Strategies for professionals and communities.* Highlands, TX: aha! Process Inc.

Perkins, J. M. (1993). *Beyond charity: The call to Christian community development.* Grand Rapids: Baker.

Ratcliff, D., & Neff, B. J. (1993). *The complete guide to religious education volunteers.* Birmingham, AL: Religious Education Press.

Stonehouse, C. (1998). *Joining children on the spiritual journey.* Grand Rapids: Baker.

Strommen, M. P., and Hardel, R.A. (2000). *Passing on the faith: A radical new model for youth and family ministry.* Winona, MN: Saint Mary's.

Index

Made in the USA
Las Vegas, NV
04 September 2024

94763992R00247